Guardian Angel
GETTE
守護月天

TM

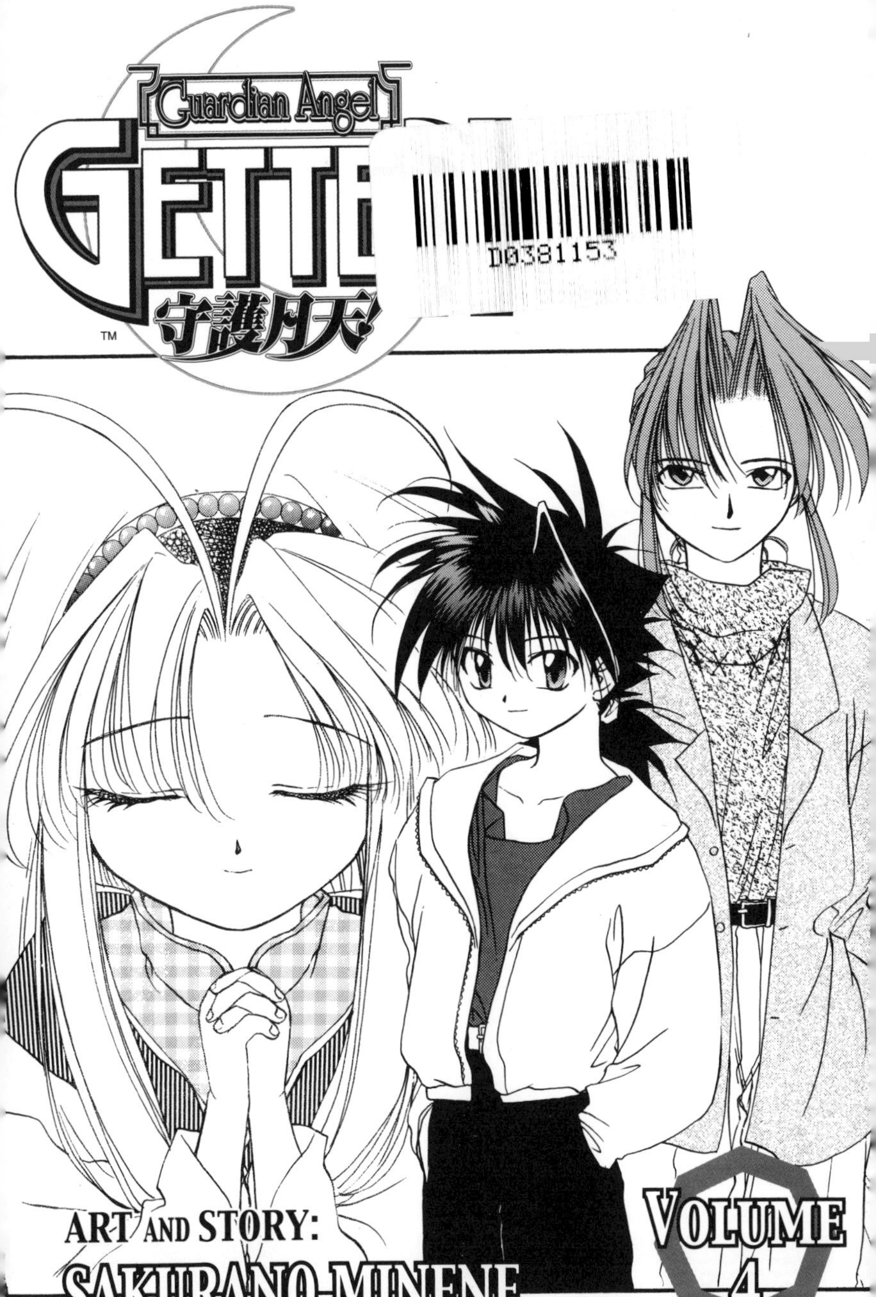

ART AND STORY:
SAKURANO MINENE

VOLUME 4

GUARDIAN ANGEL GETTEN

Volume 4

CHAPTER 19:
A Gift from Shao (Part 2) 5

CHAPTER 20:
Getting the Shitenrin Back! (Part 1)..............................35

CHAPTER 21:
Getting the Shitenrin Back! (Part 2)..............................65

CHAPTER 22:
Tasuke's New Crush (Part 1) 95

CHAPTER 23:
Tasuke's New Crush (Part 2) 125

CHAPTER 24:
Mixed Emotions 155

CHAPTER 19:
A GIFT FROM SHAO (PART 2)

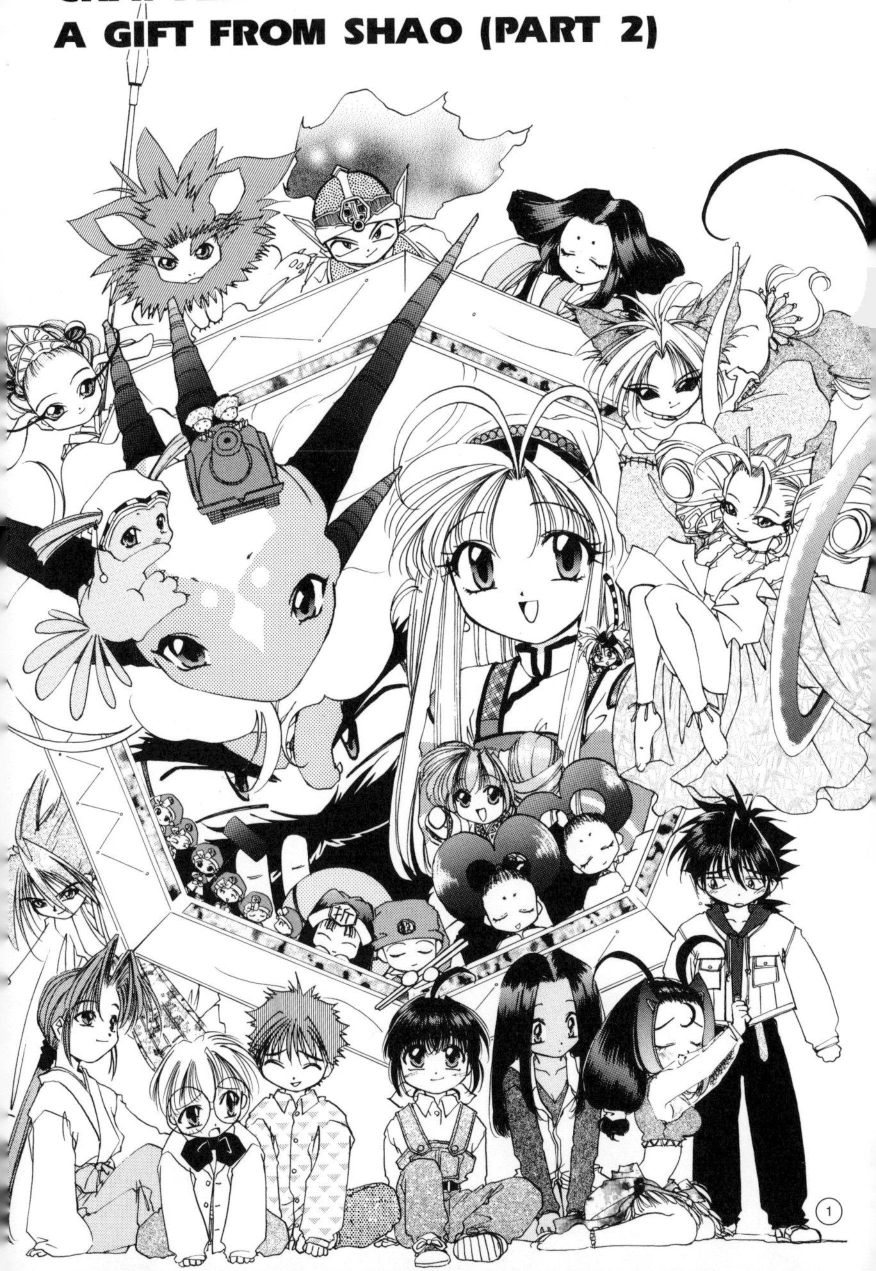

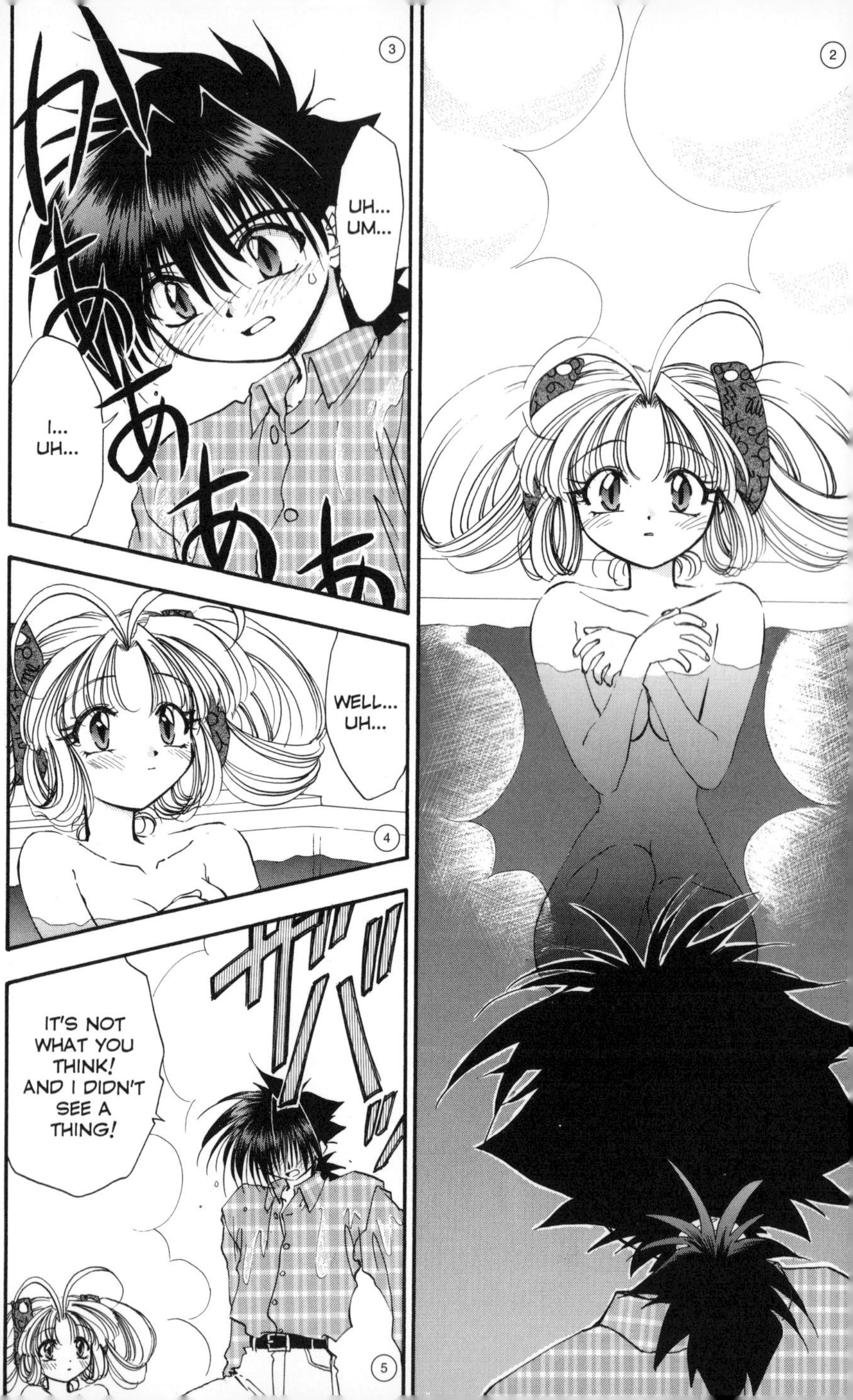
UH... UM...
I... UH...
WELL... UH...
IT'S NOT WHAT YOU THINK! AND I DIDN'T SEE A THING!

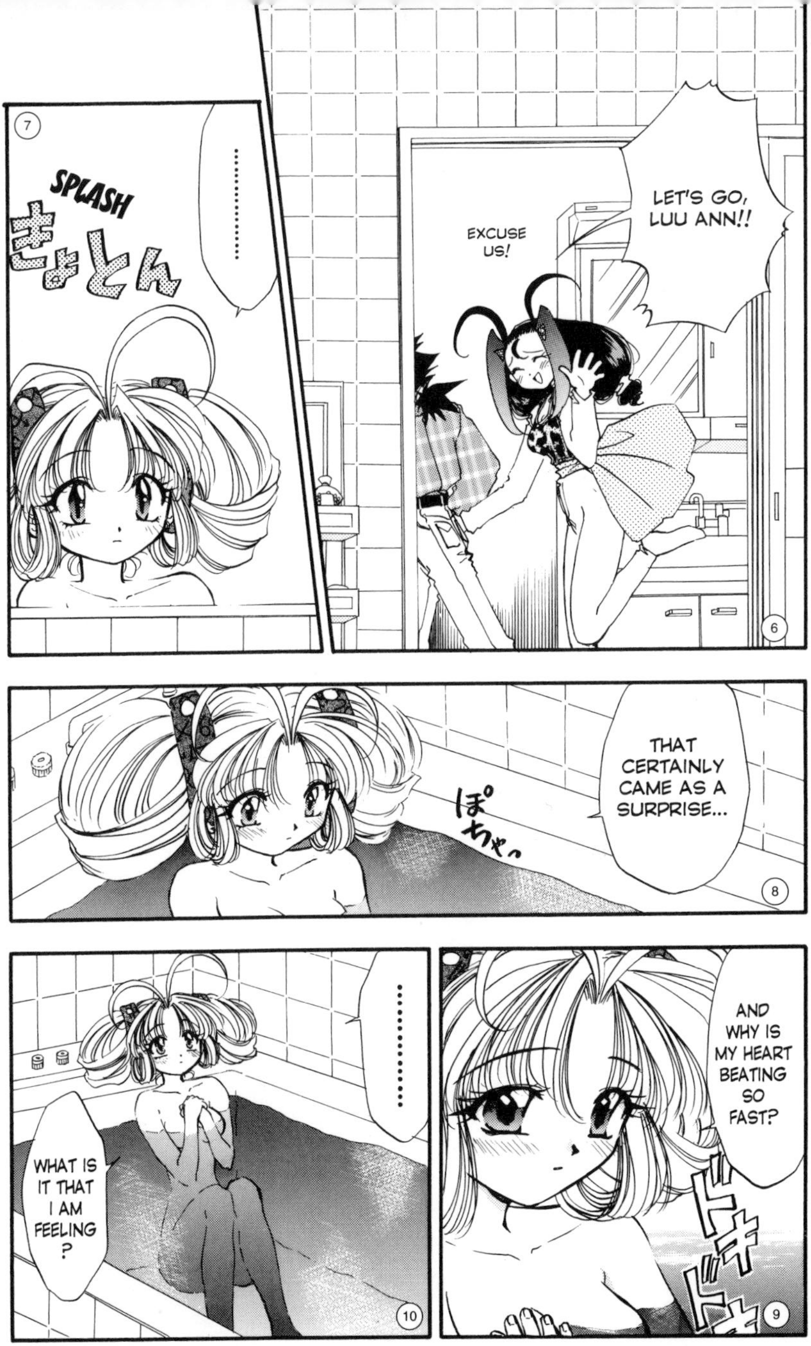
LET'S GO, LUU ANN!!
EXCUSE US!
SPLASH
きょとん
....
THAT CERTAINLY CAME AS A SURPRISE...
ぽちゃっ
AND WHY IS MY HEART BEATING SO FAST?
ドキドキ
....
WHAT IS IT THAT I AM FEELING ?

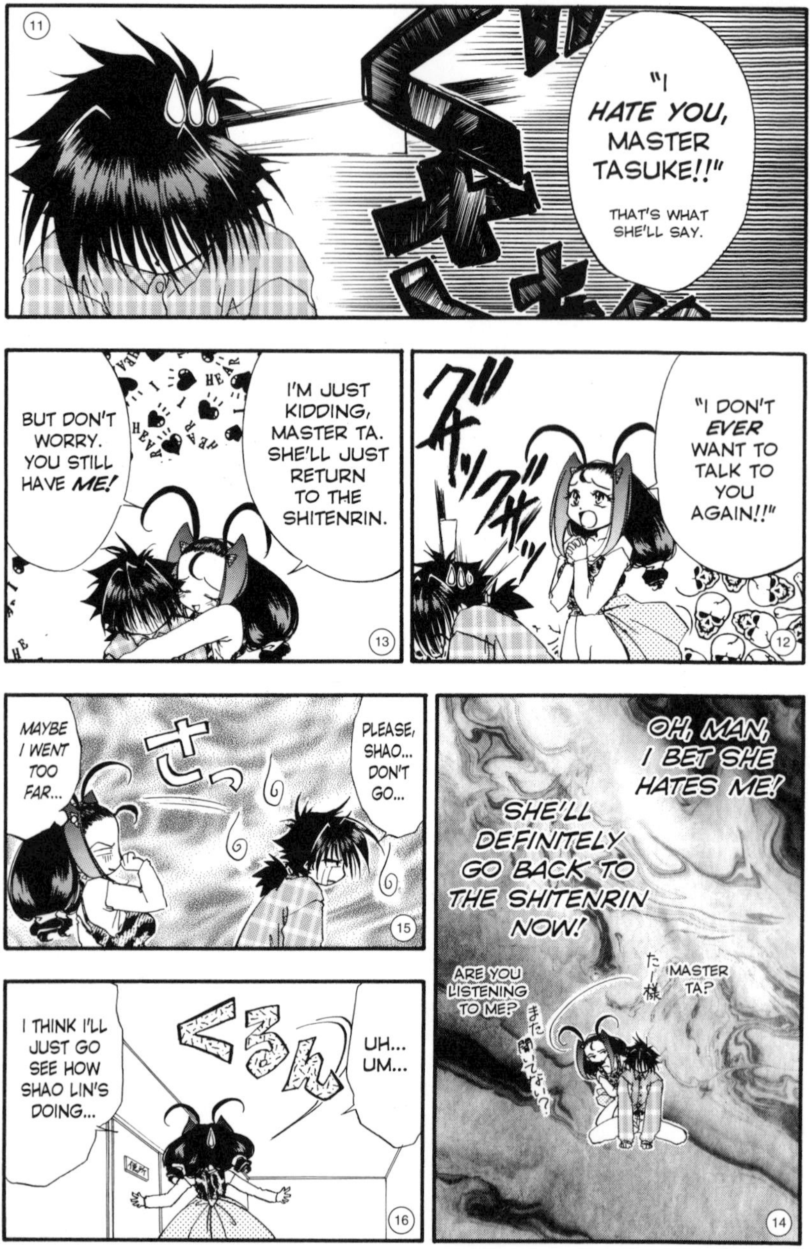
"I HATE YOU, MASTER TASUKE!!"
THAT'S WHAT SHE'LL SAY.
"I DON'T EVER WANT TO TALK TO YOU AGAIN!!"
I'M JUST KIDDING, MASTER TA. SHE'LL JUST RETURN TO THE SHITENRIN.
BUT DON'T WORRY. YOU STILL HAVE ME!
OH, MAN, I BET SHE HATES ME!
SHE'LL DEFINITELY GO BACK TO THE SHITENRIN NOW!
たー様
MASTER TA?
また聞いてなーい?
ARE YOU LISTENING TO ME?
PLEASE, SHAO... DON'T GO...
さっ
MAYBE I WENT TOO FAR...
UH... UM...
くるん
I THINK I'LL JUST GO SEE HOW SHAO LIN'S DOING...

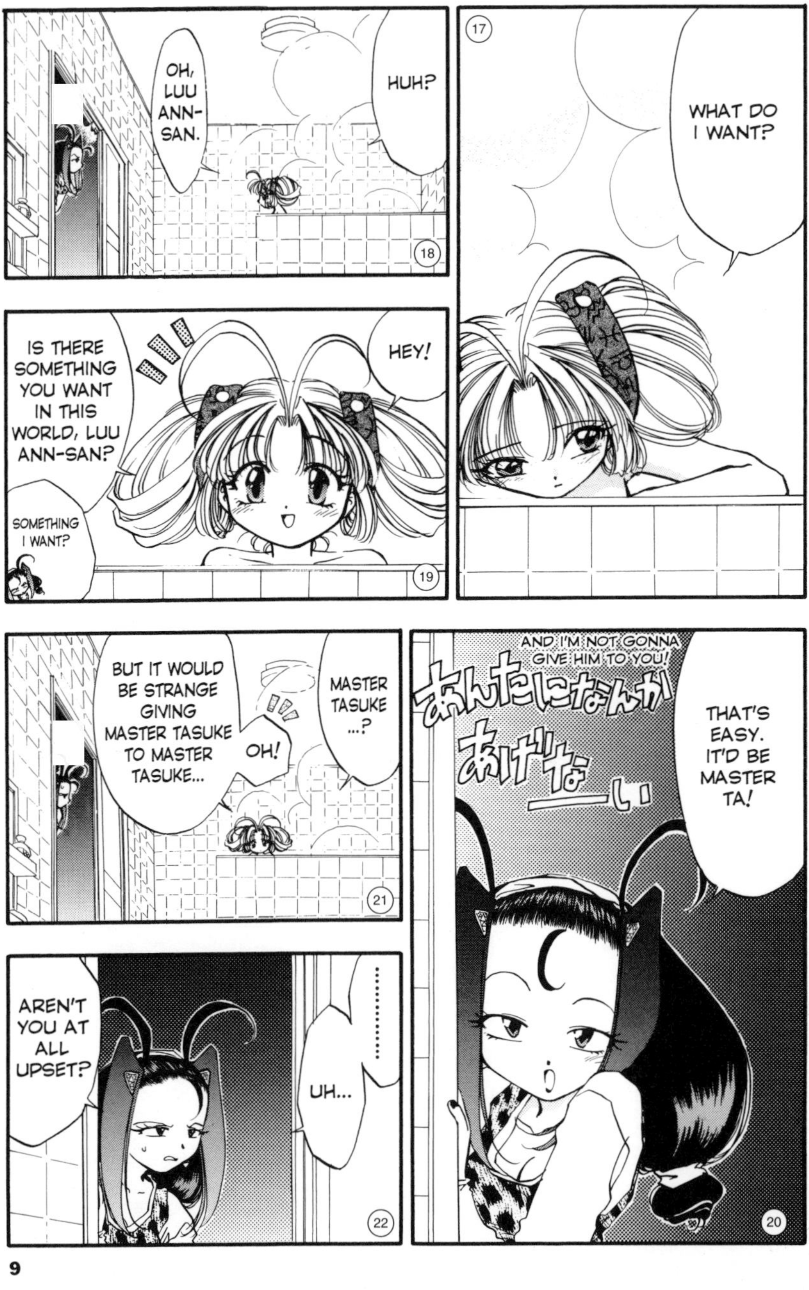
WHAT DO I WANT?
HUH?
OH, LUU ANN-SAN.
HEY!
IS THERE SOMETHING YOU WANT IN THIS WORLD, LUU ANN-SAN?
SOMETHING I WANT?
THAT'S EASY. IT'D BE MASTER TA!
あんたになんかあげなーい
AND I'M NOT GONNA GIVE HIM TO YOU!
MASTER TASUKE ...?
OH!
BUT IT WOULD BE STRANGE GIVING MASTER TASUKE TO MASTER TASUKE...
....
UH...
AREN'T YOU AT ALL UPSET?

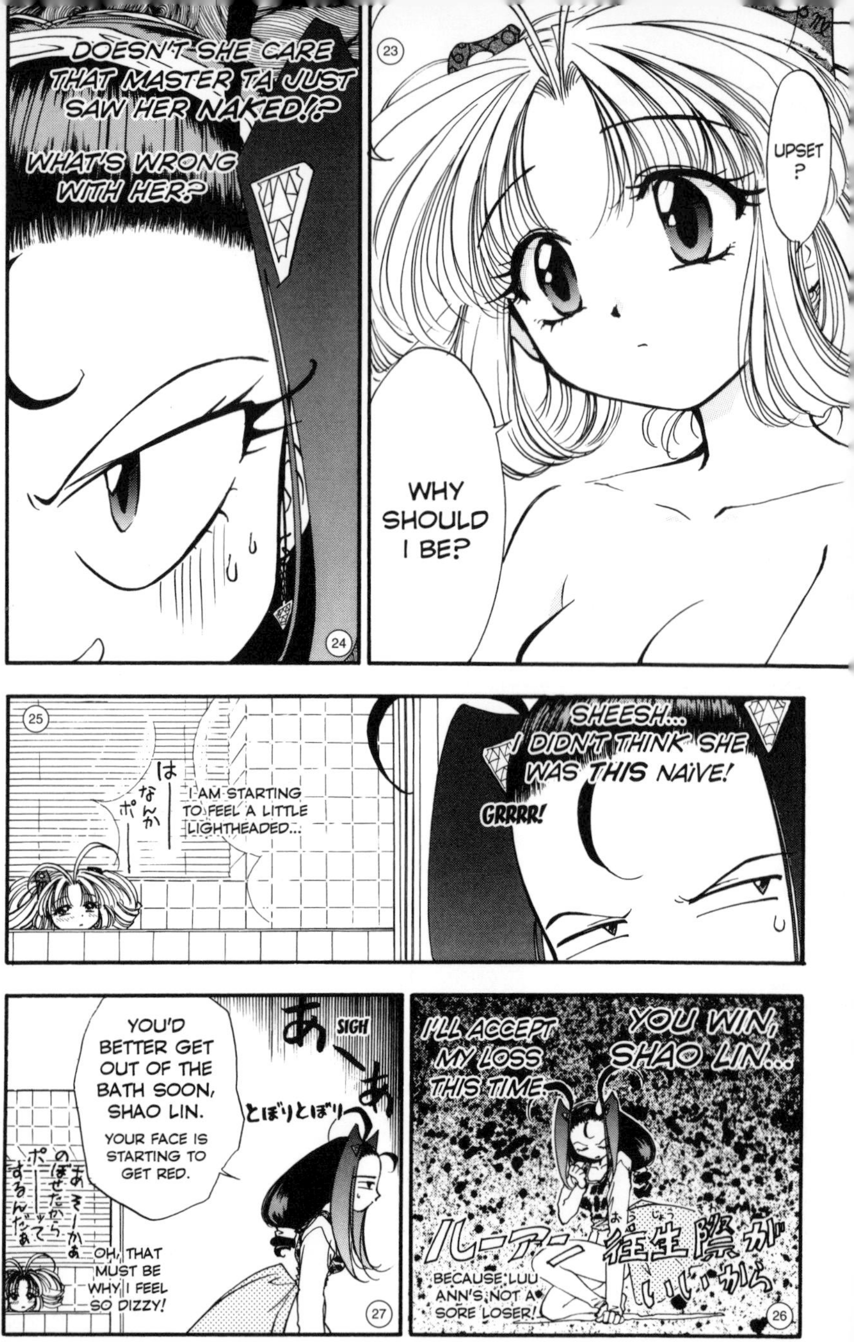
UPSET ?
WHY SHOULD I BE?
DOESN'T SHE CARE THAT MASTER TA JUST SAW HER NAKED!?
WHAT'S WRONG WITH HER?
SHEESH... I DIDN'T THINK SHE WAS THIS NAÏVE!
GRRRR!
はーなんかポー
I AM STARTING TO FEEL A LITTLE LIGHTHEADED...
YOU WIN, SHAO LIN...
I'LL ACCEPT MY LOSS THIS TIME.
ルーアンは往生際がいいから
BECAUSE LUU ANN'S NOT A SORE LOSER!
あーあ
SIGH
とぼりとぼり
YOU'D BETTER GET OUT OF THE BATH SOON, SHAO LIN.
YOUR FACE IS STARTING TO GET RED.
あそーかぁ のぼせたから ポーッてするんだぁ
OH, THAT MUST BE WHY I FEEL SO DIZZY!

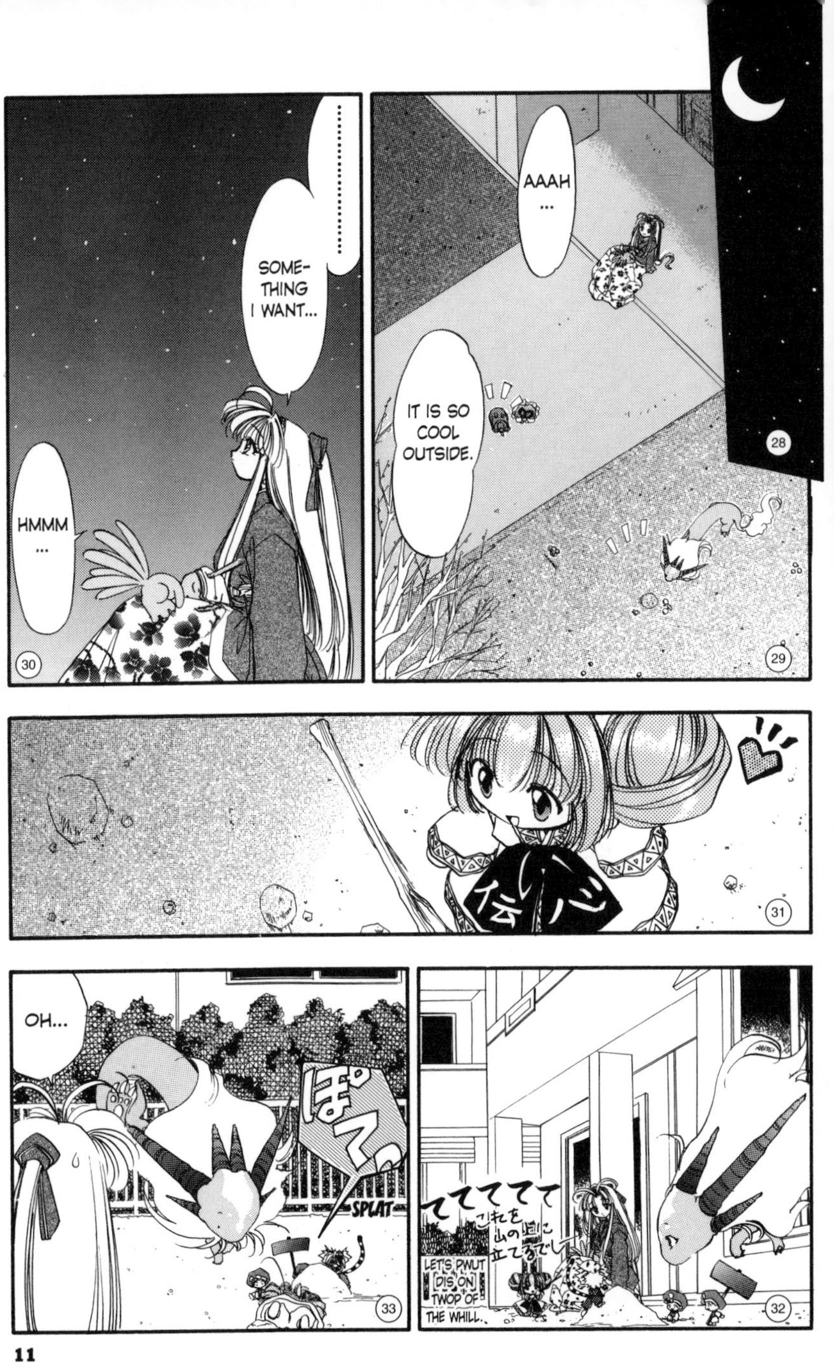
AAAH ...
IT IS SO COOL OUTSIDE.
....
SOME-THING I WANT...
HMMM ...
てててててて
これを山の上に立てるでし
LET'S PWUT DIS ON TWOP OF THE WHILL.
ぽて
SPLAT
OH...

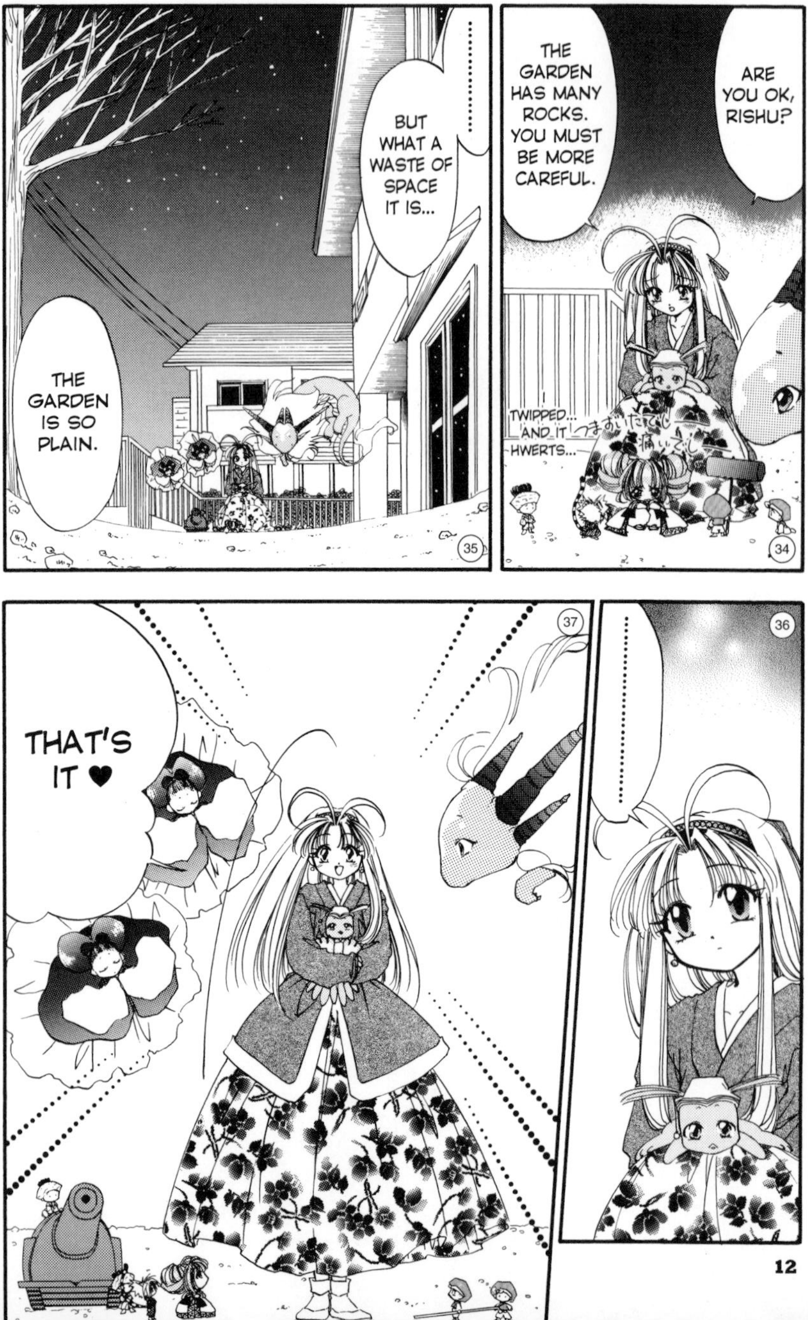
ARE YOU OK, RISHU?
THE GARDEN HAS MANY ROCKS. YOU MUST BE MORE CAREFUL.
I TWIPPED... AND IT HWERTS...
......
BUT WHAT A WASTE OF SPACE IT IS...
THE GARDEN IS SO PLAIN.
......
THAT'S IT ♥

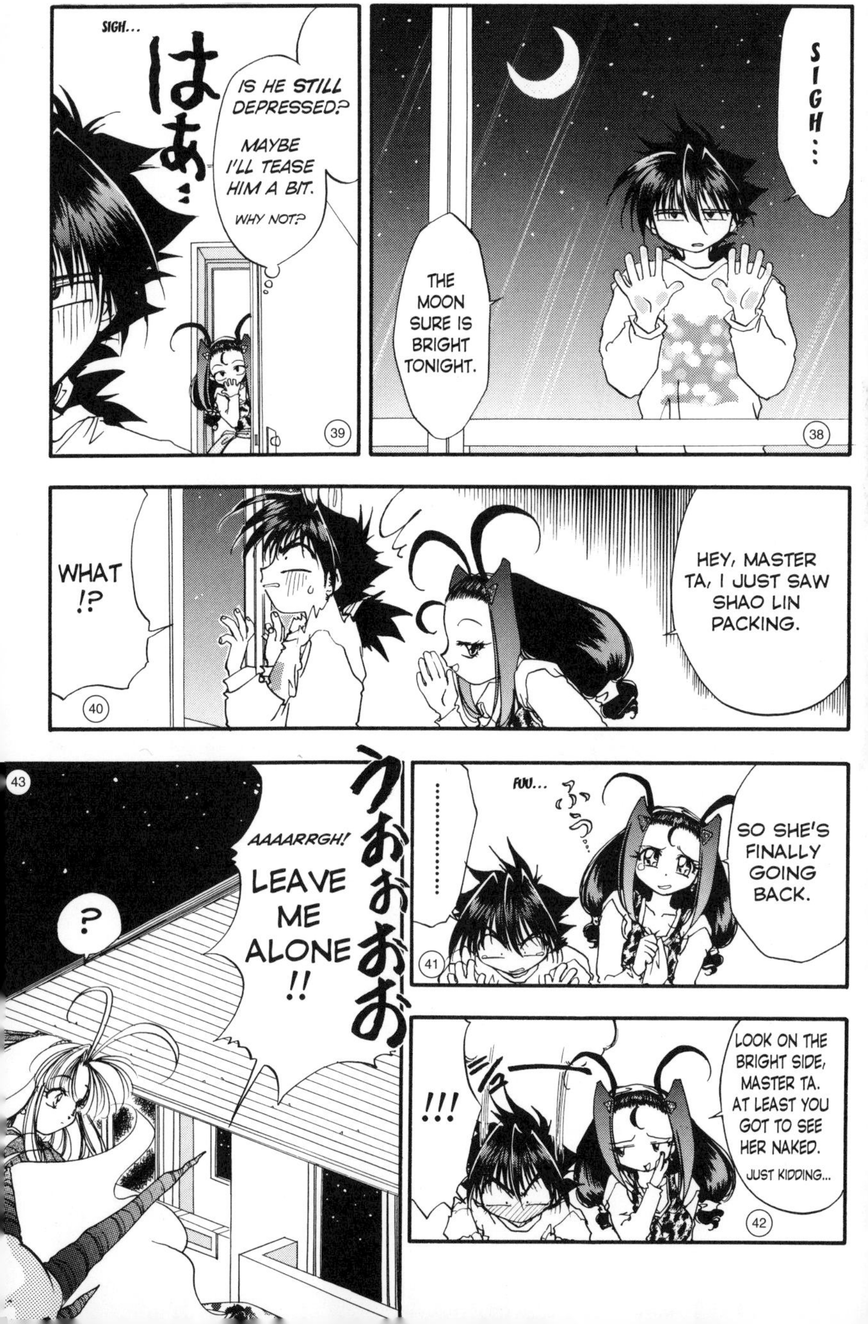
SIGH...
THE MOON SURE IS BRIGHT TONIGHT.
SIGH...
はぁ…
IS HE STILL DEPRESSED?
MAYBE I'LL TEASE HIM A BIT.
WHY NOT?
HEY, MASTER TA, I JUST SAW SHAO LIN PACKING.
WHAT !?
SO SHE'S FINALLY GOING BACK.
FUU...
ふぅ…
....
LOOK ON THE BRIGHT SIDE, MASTER TA. AT LEAST YOU GOT TO SEE HER NAKED.
JUST KIDDING...
!!!
AAAARRGH!
LEAVE ME ALONE !!
うおおおお
?

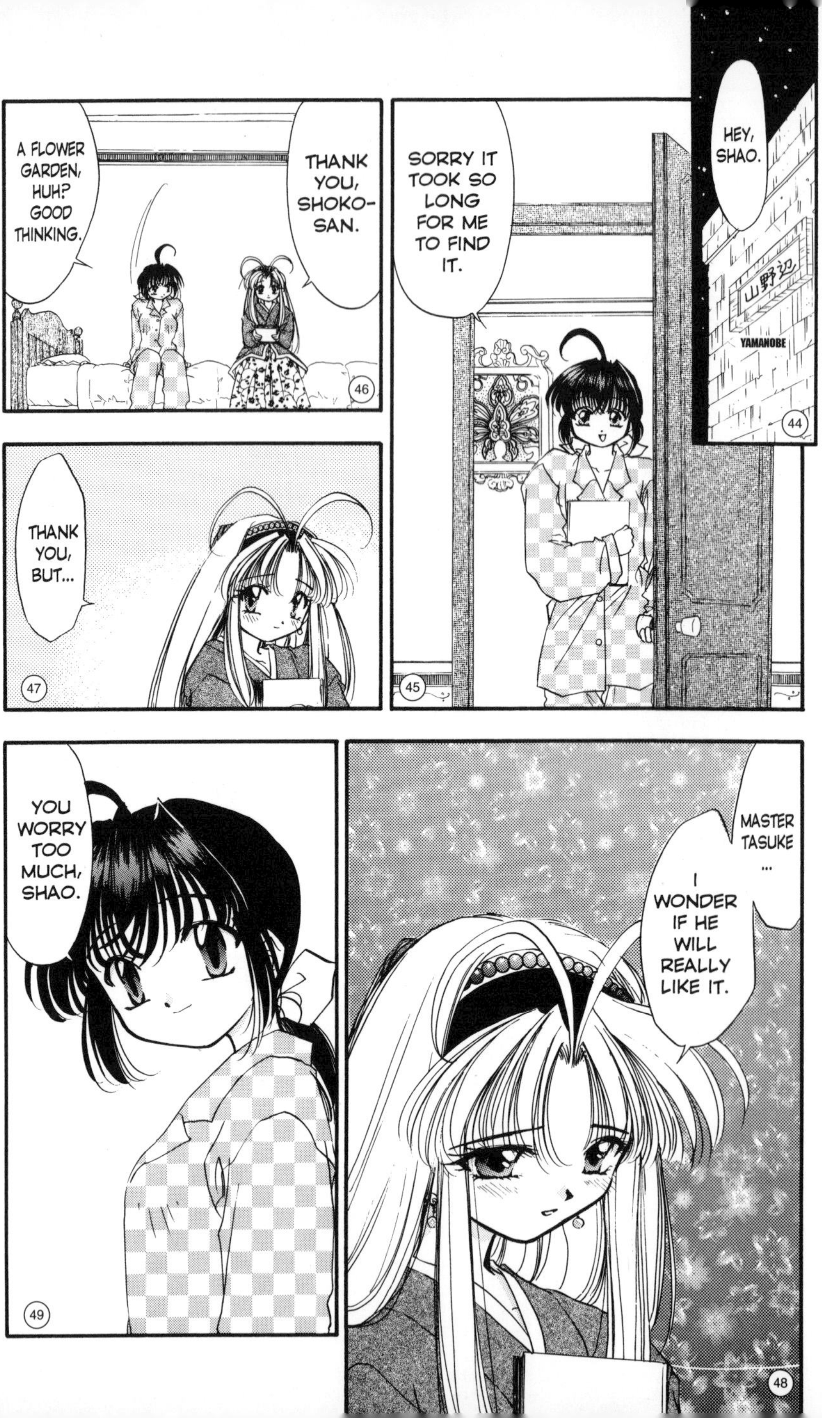
HEY, SHAO.
山野辺
YAMANOBE
SORRY IT TOOK SO LONG FOR ME TO FIND IT.
THANK YOU, SHOKO-SAN.
A FLOWER GARDEN, HUH? GOOD THINKING.
THANK YOU, BUT...
MASTER TASUKE ...
I WONDER IF HE WILL REALLY LIKE IT.
YOU WORRY TOO MUCH, SHAO.

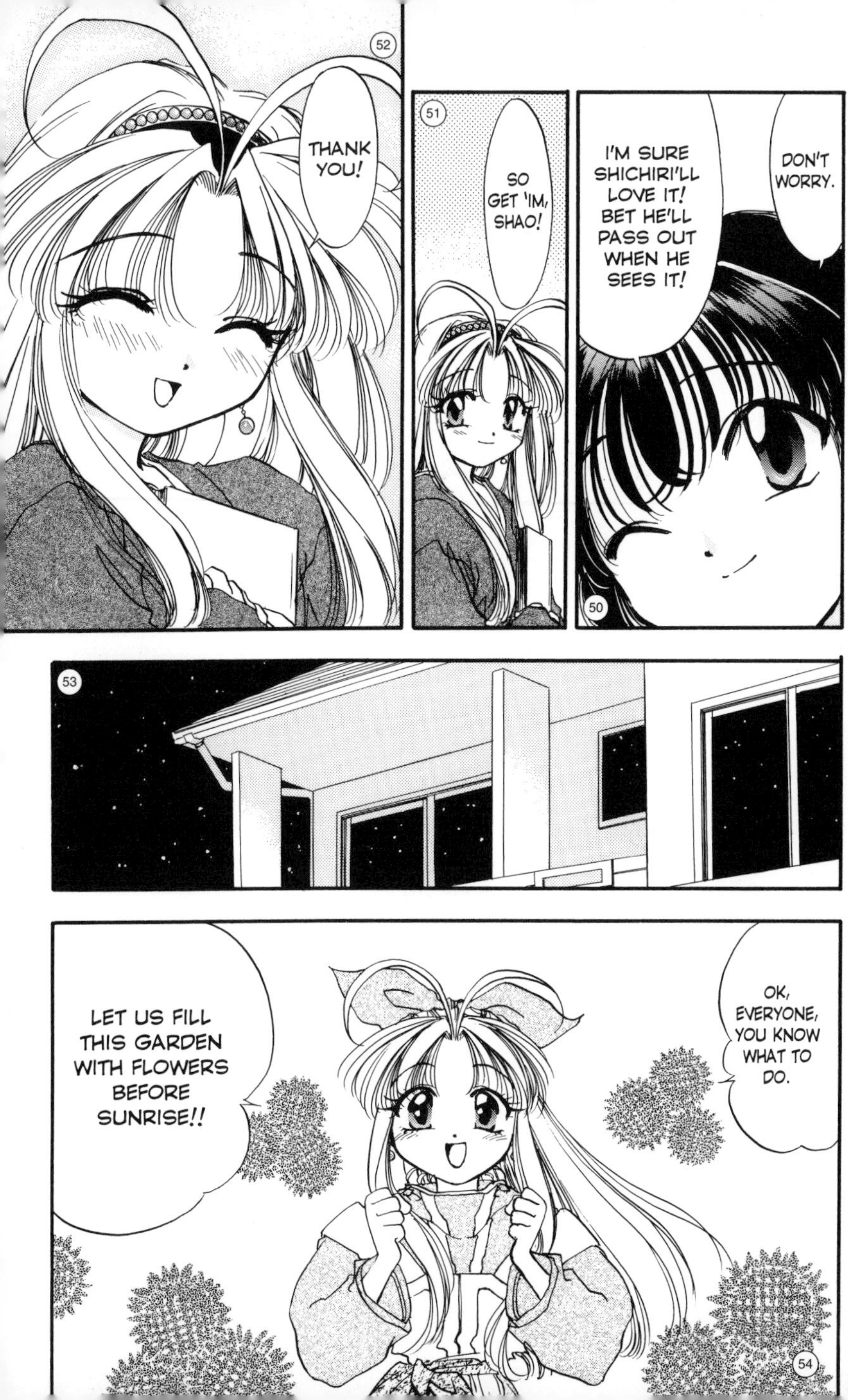
DON'T WORRY.
I'M SURE SHICHIRI'LL LOVE IT! BET HE'LL PASS OUT WHEN HE SEES IT!
SO GET 'IM, SHAO!
THANK YOU!
OK, EVERYONE, YOU KNOW WHAT TO DO.
LET US FILL THIS GARDEN WITH FLOWERS BEFORE SUNRISE!!

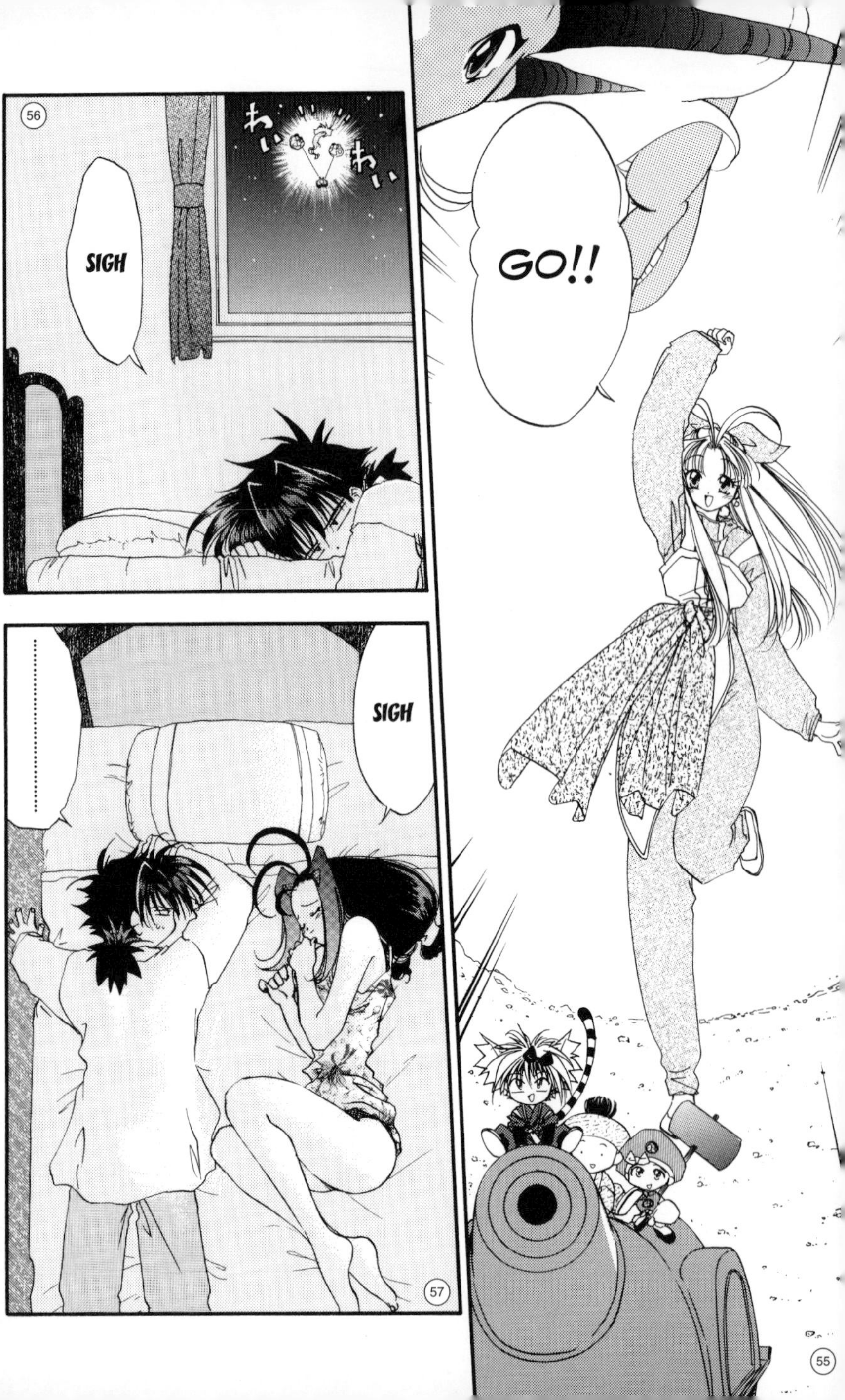
55
GO!!
56
わい
わい
SIGH
57
SIGH
....

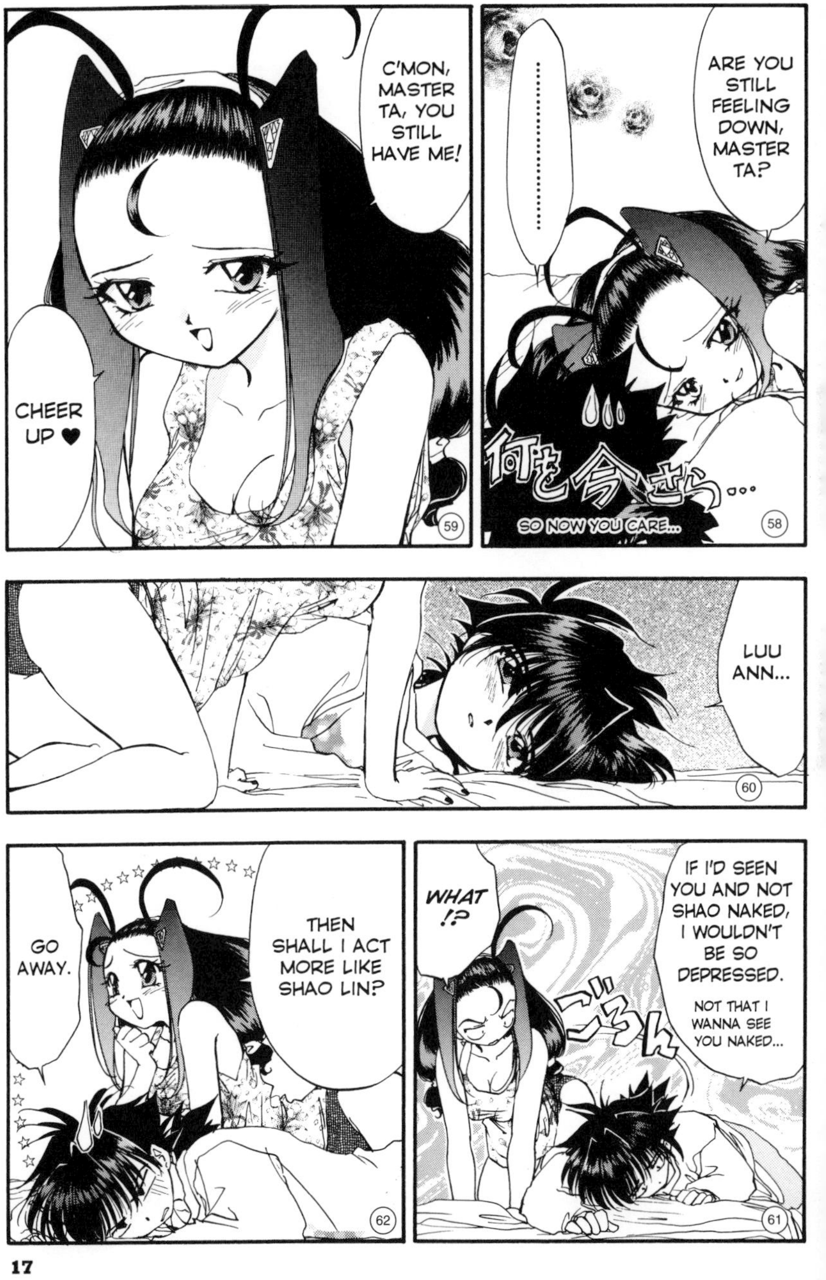
ARE YOU STILL FEELING DOWN, MASTER TA?
......
何を今さら…
SO NOW YOU CARE...
C'MON, MASTER TA, YOU STILL HAVE ME!
CHEER UP ♥
LUU ANN...
IF I'D SEEN YOU AND NOT SHAO NAKED, I WOULDN'T BE SO DEPRESSED.
NOT THAT I WANNA SEE YOU NAKED...
ごろん
WHAT !?
THEN SHALL I ACT MORE LIKE SHAO LIN?
GO AWAY.

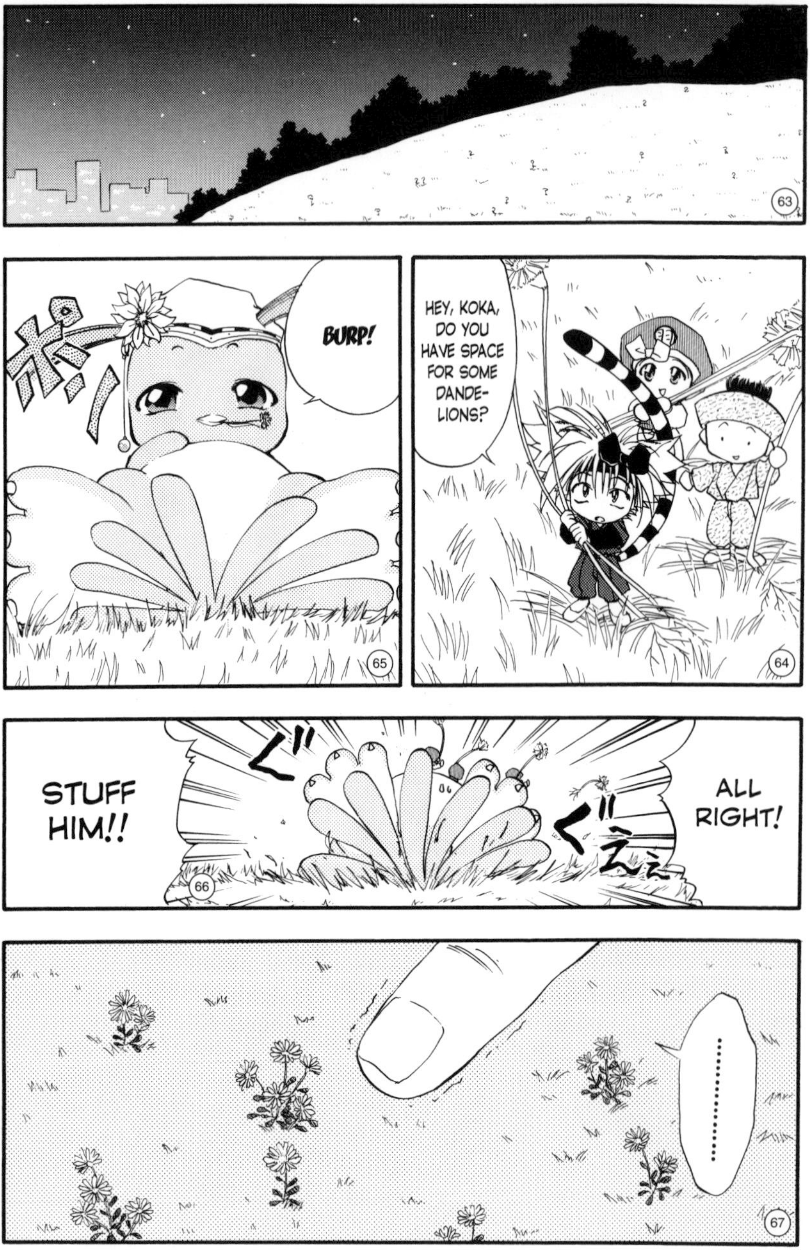
HEY, KOKA, DO YOU HAVE SPACE FOR SOME DANDE-LIONS?
BURP!
ALL RIGHT!
STUFF HIM!!
......

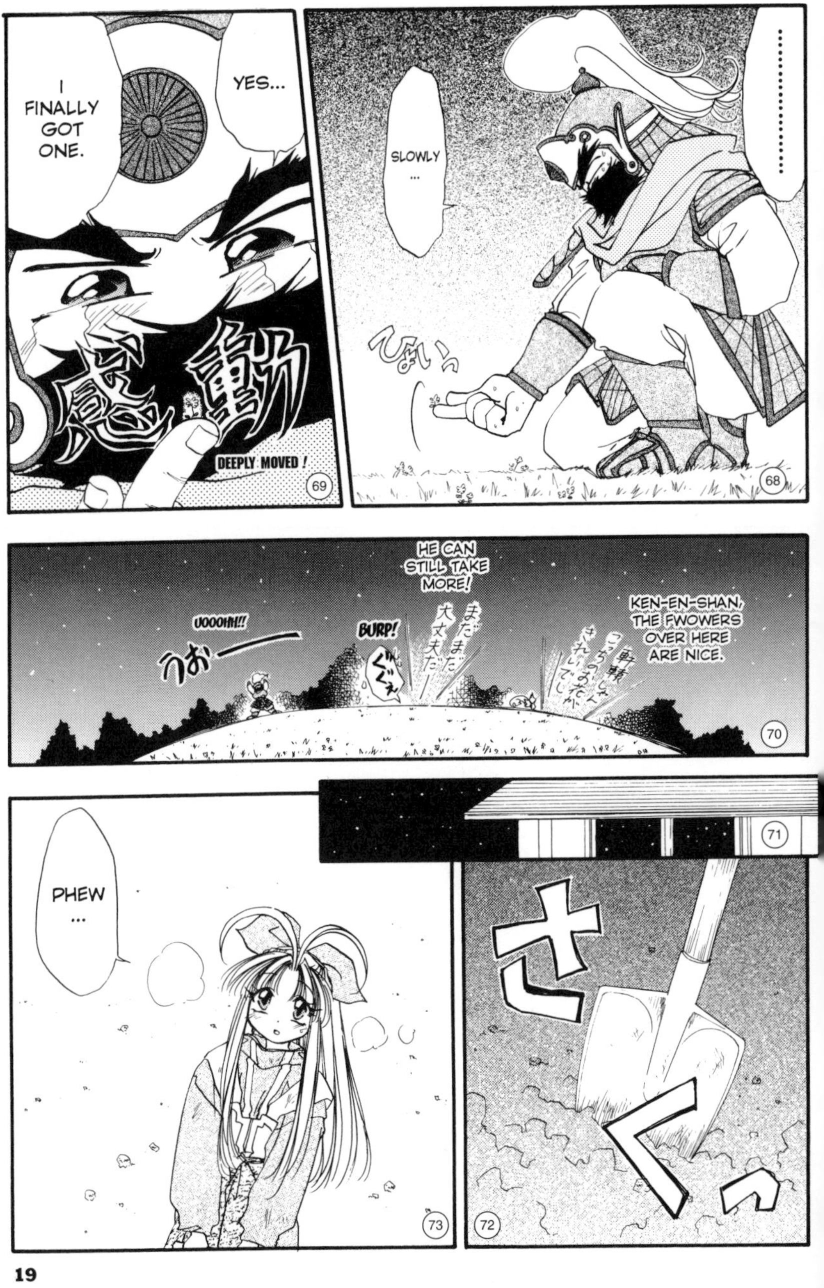

....
SLOWLY ...
YES...
I FINALLY GOT ONE.
DEEPLY MOVED!
KEN-EN-SHAN, THE FWOWERS OVER HERE ARE NICE.
HE CAN STILL TAKE MORE!
まだまだ大丈夫だ
BURP!
UOOOHH!!
PHEW ...

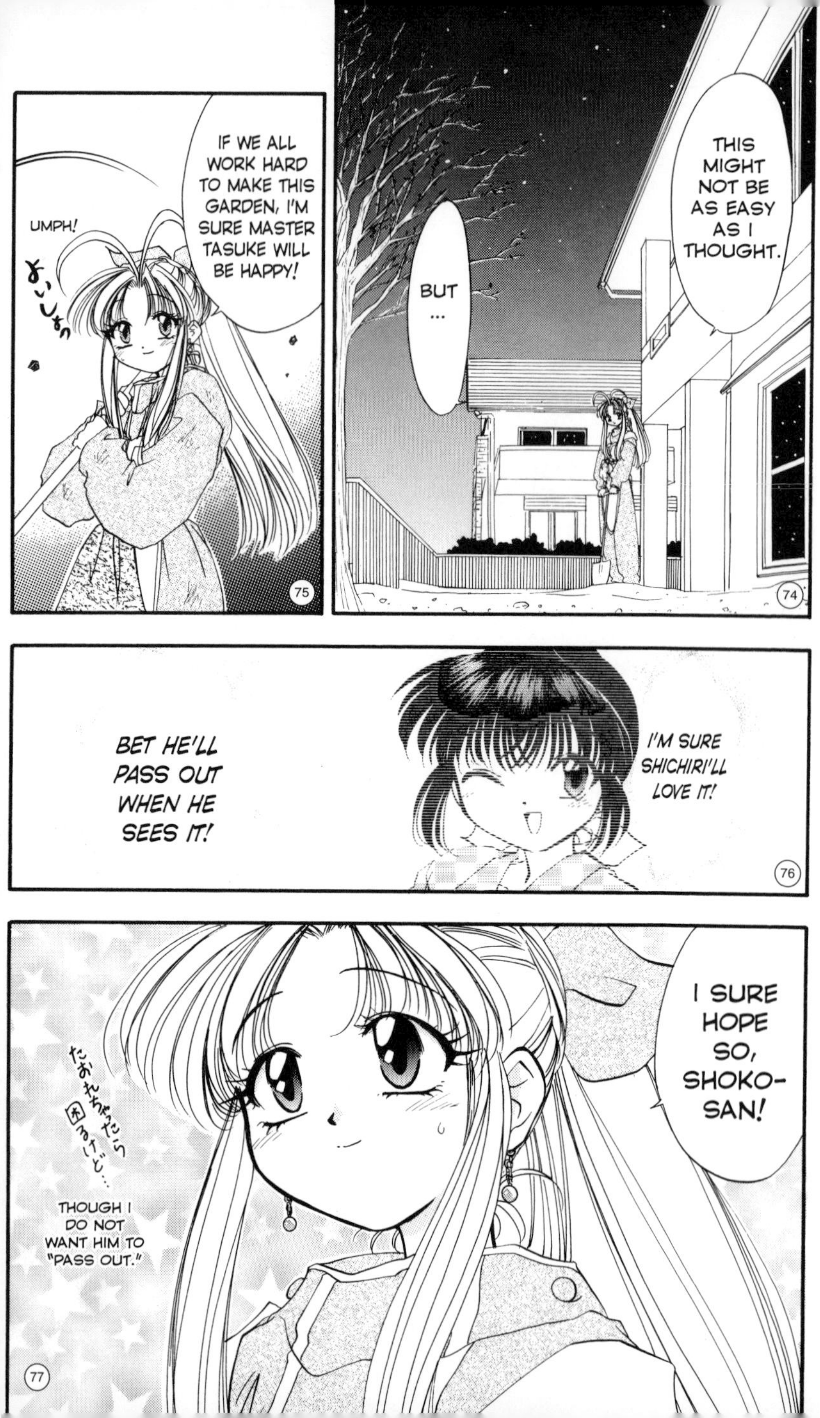
THIS MIGHT NOT BE AS EASY AS I THOUGHT.
BUT ...
IF WE ALL WORK HARD TO MAKE THIS GARDEN, I'M SURE MASTER TASUKE WILL BE HAPPY!
UMPH!
よいしょっ
I'M SURE SHICHIRI'LL LOVE IT!
BET HE'LL PASS OUT WHEN HE SEES IT!
I SURE HOPE SO, SHOKO-SAN!
たおれちゃったら困るけど…
THOUGH I DO NOT WANT HIM TO "PASS OUT."

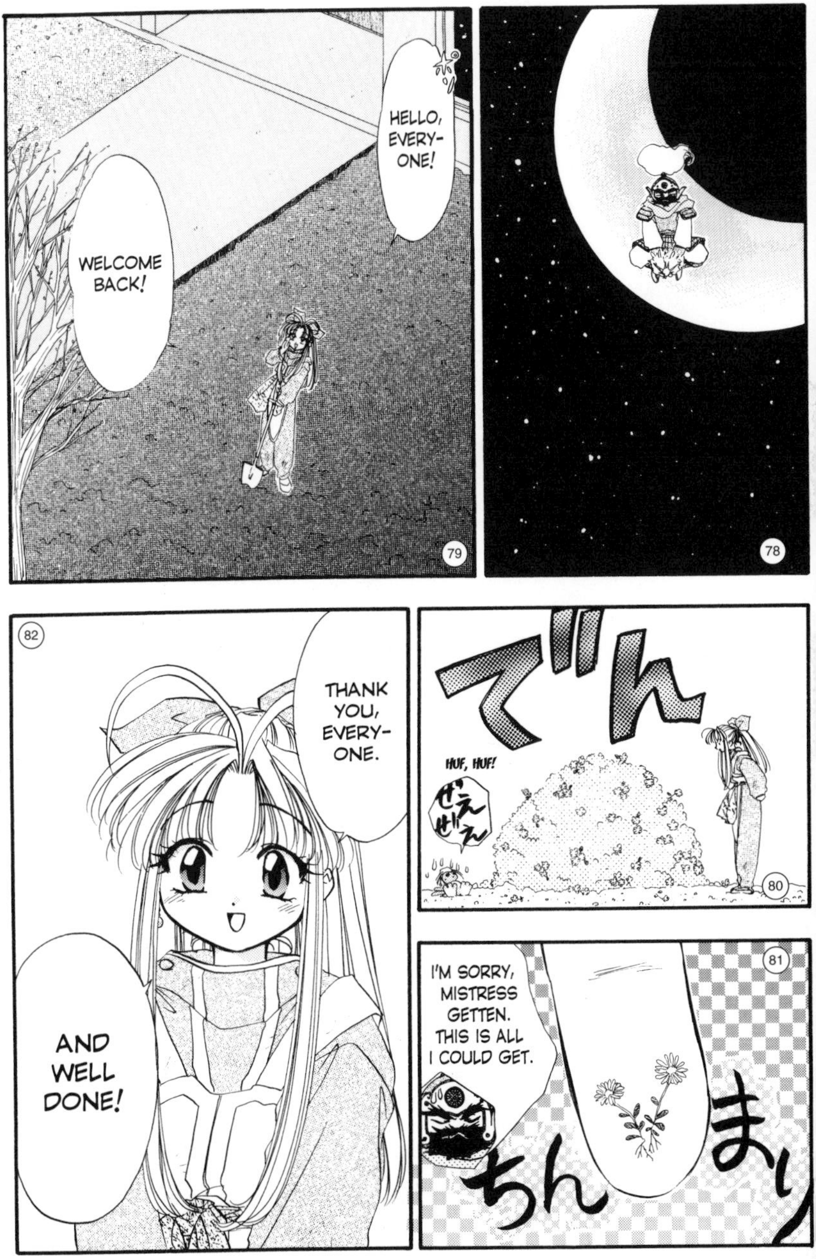
HELLO, EVERY-ONE!
WELCOME BACK!
でん
HUF, HUF!
ぜぇぜぇ
I'M SORRY, MISTRESS GETTEN. THIS IS ALL I COULD GET.
ちんまい
THANK YOU, EVERY-ONE.
AND WELL DONE!

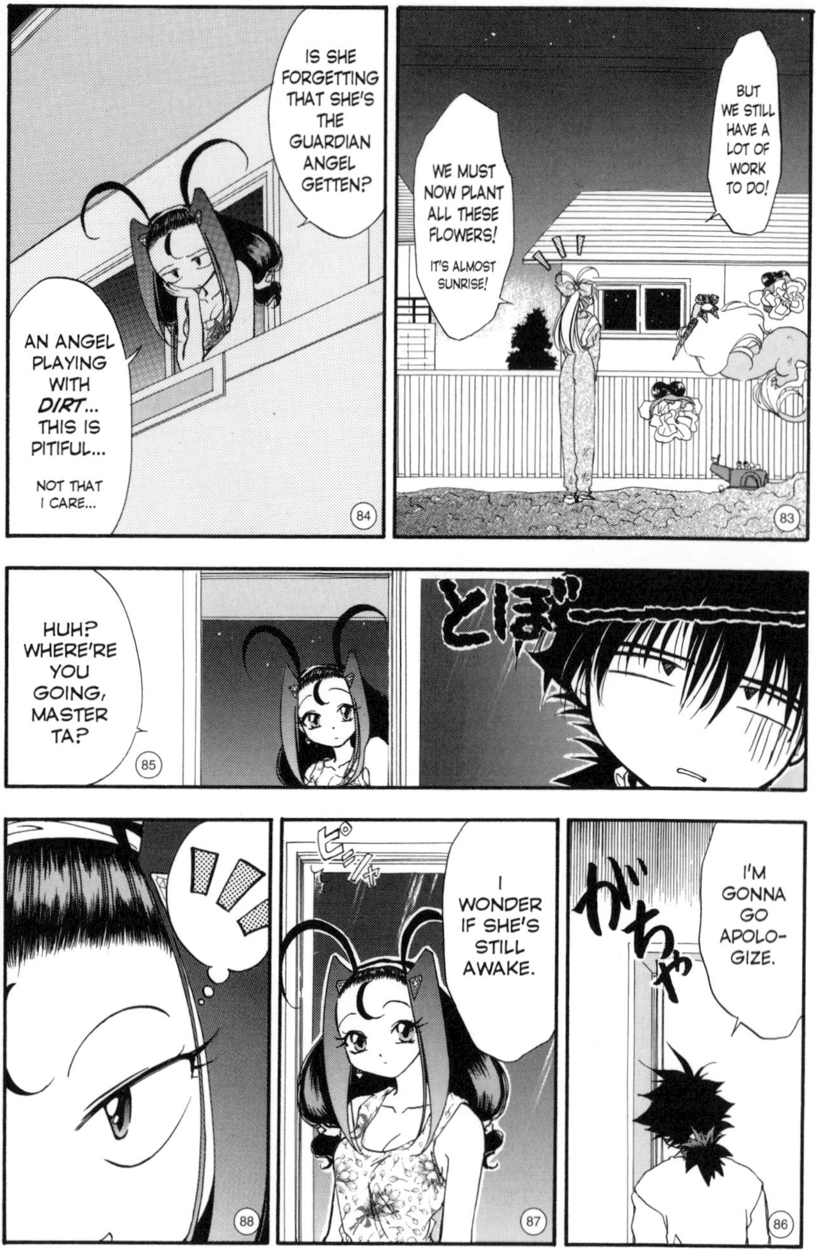
BUT WE STILL HAVE A LOT OF WORK TO DO!
WE MUST NOW PLANT ALL THESE FLOWERS!
IT'S ALMOST SUNRISE!
IS SHE FORGETTING THAT SHE'S THE GUARDIAN ANGEL GETTEN?
AN ANGEL PLAYING WITH DIRT... THIS IS PITIFUL...
NOT THAT I CARE...
とぼー
HUH? WHERE'RE YOU GOING, MASTER TA?
かちゃ
I'M GONNA GO APOLOGIZE.
I WONDER IF SHE'S STILL AWAKE.

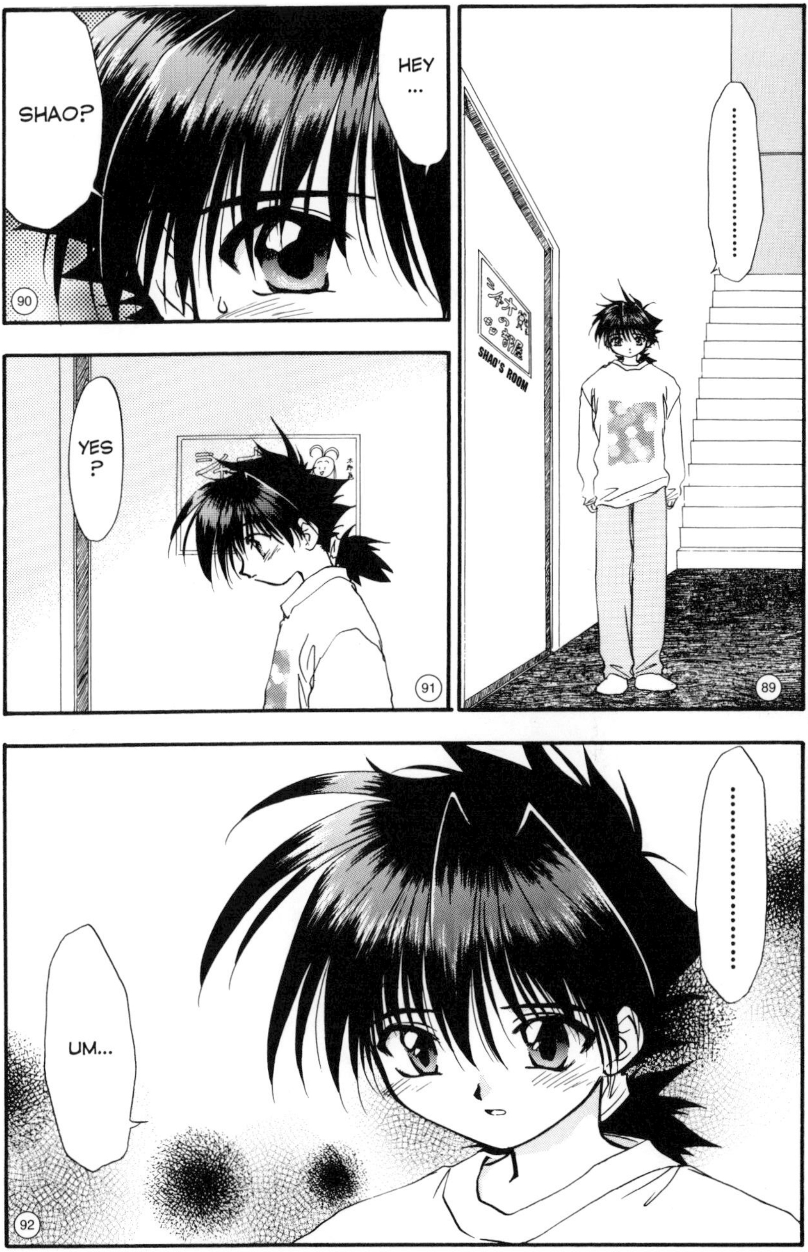

....
SHAO'S ROOM
HEY ...
SHAO?
YES ?
....
UM...

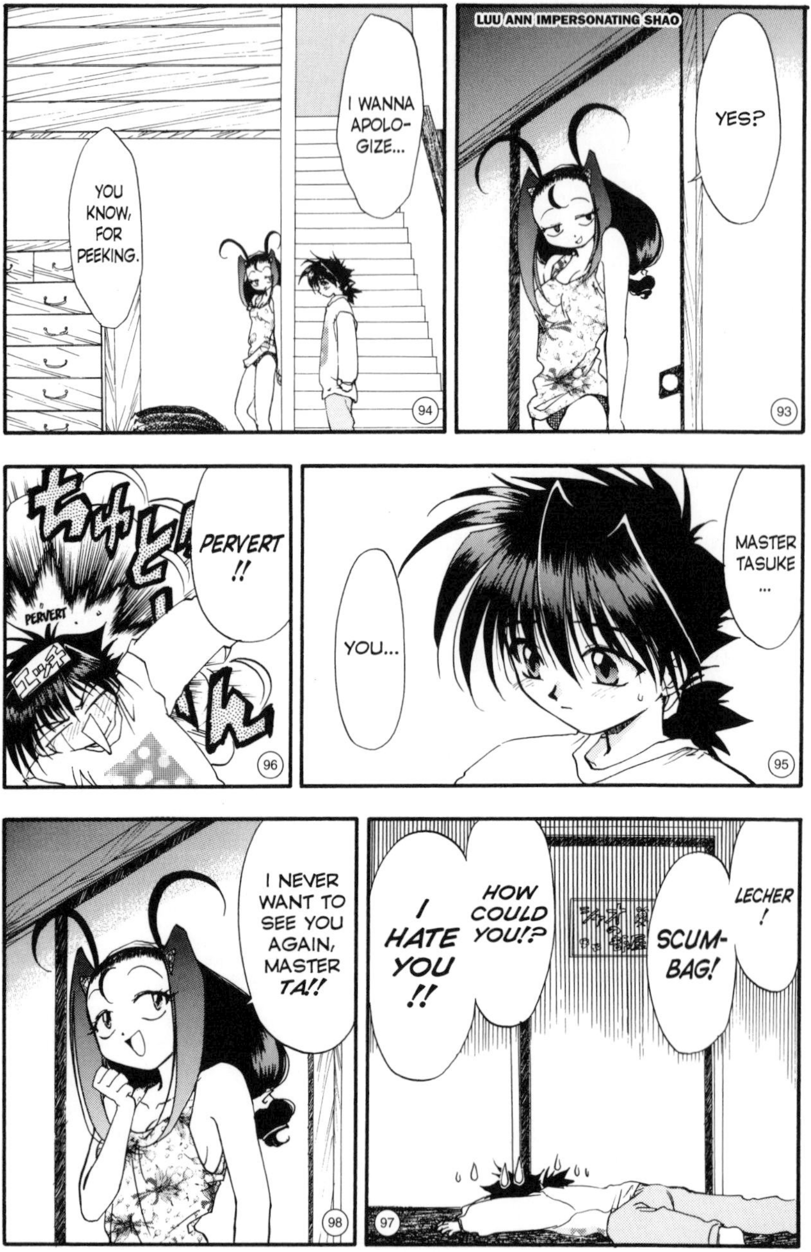
LUU ANN IMPERSONATING SHAO
YES?
I WANNA APOLO-GIZE...
YOU KNOW, FOR PEEKING.
MASTER TASUKE ...
YOU...
PERVERT !!
PERVERT
LECHER !
SCUM-BAG!
HOW COULD YOU!?
I HATE YOU !!
I NEVER WANT TO SEE YOU AGAIN, MASTER TA!!

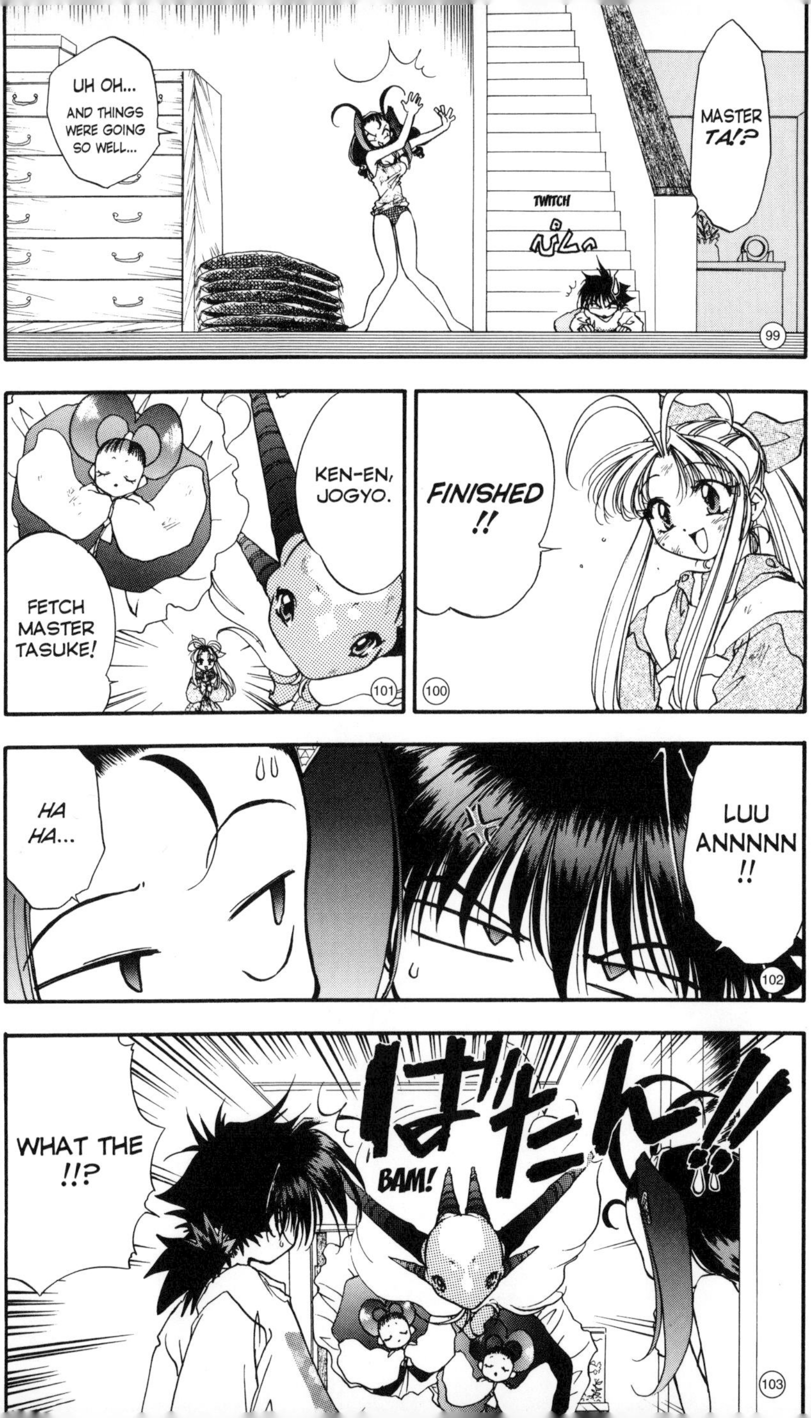
MASTER TA!?
UH OH... AND THINGS WERE GOING SO WELL...
TWITCH
FINISHED!!
KEN-EN, JOGYO.
FETCH MASTER TASUKE!
LUU ANNNNN!!
HA HA...
ばたん!!
BAM!
WHAT THE!!?

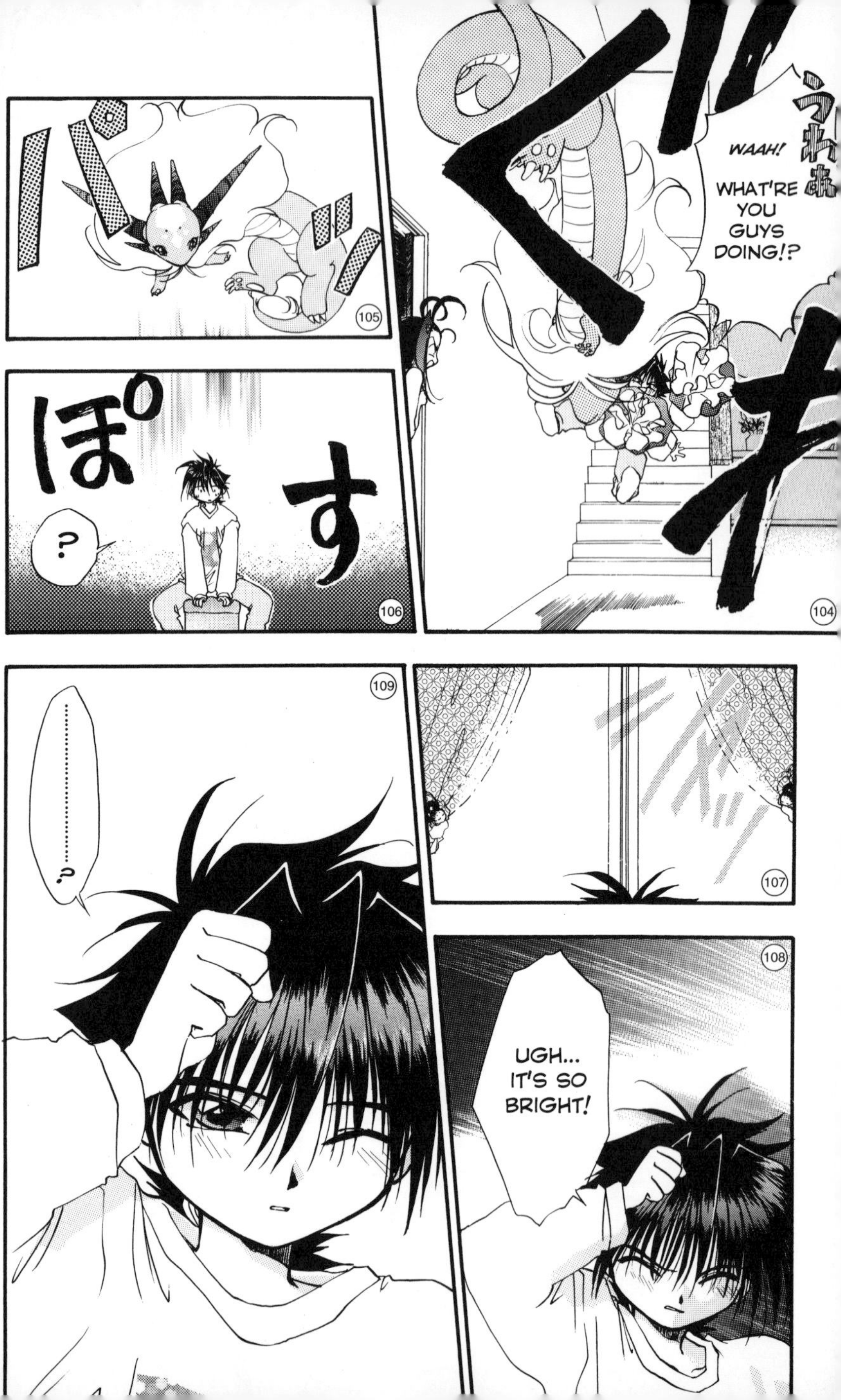
WAAH!
WHAT'RE YOU GUYS DOING!?
ぽす
?
UGH... IT'S SO BRIGHT!
..........?

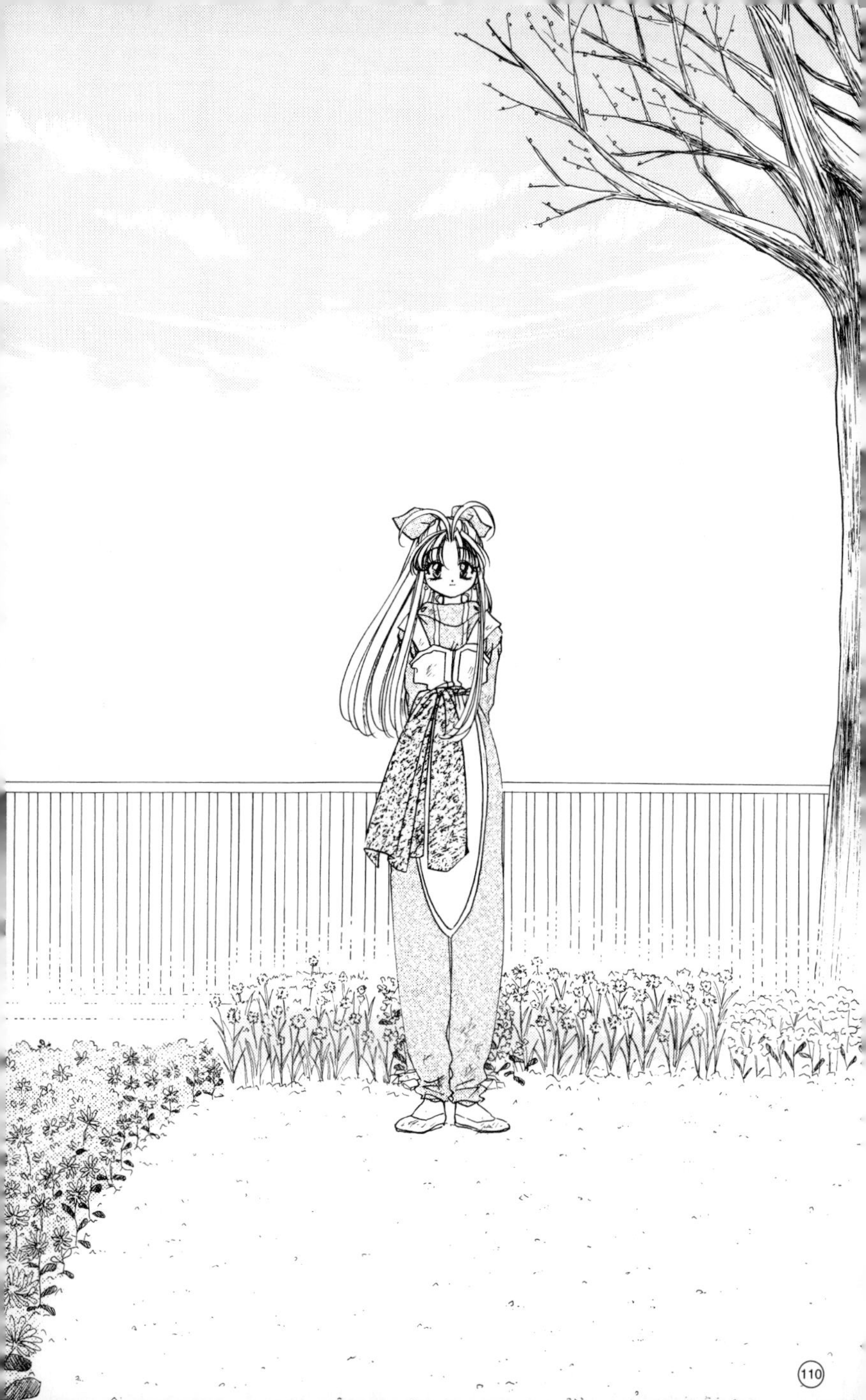

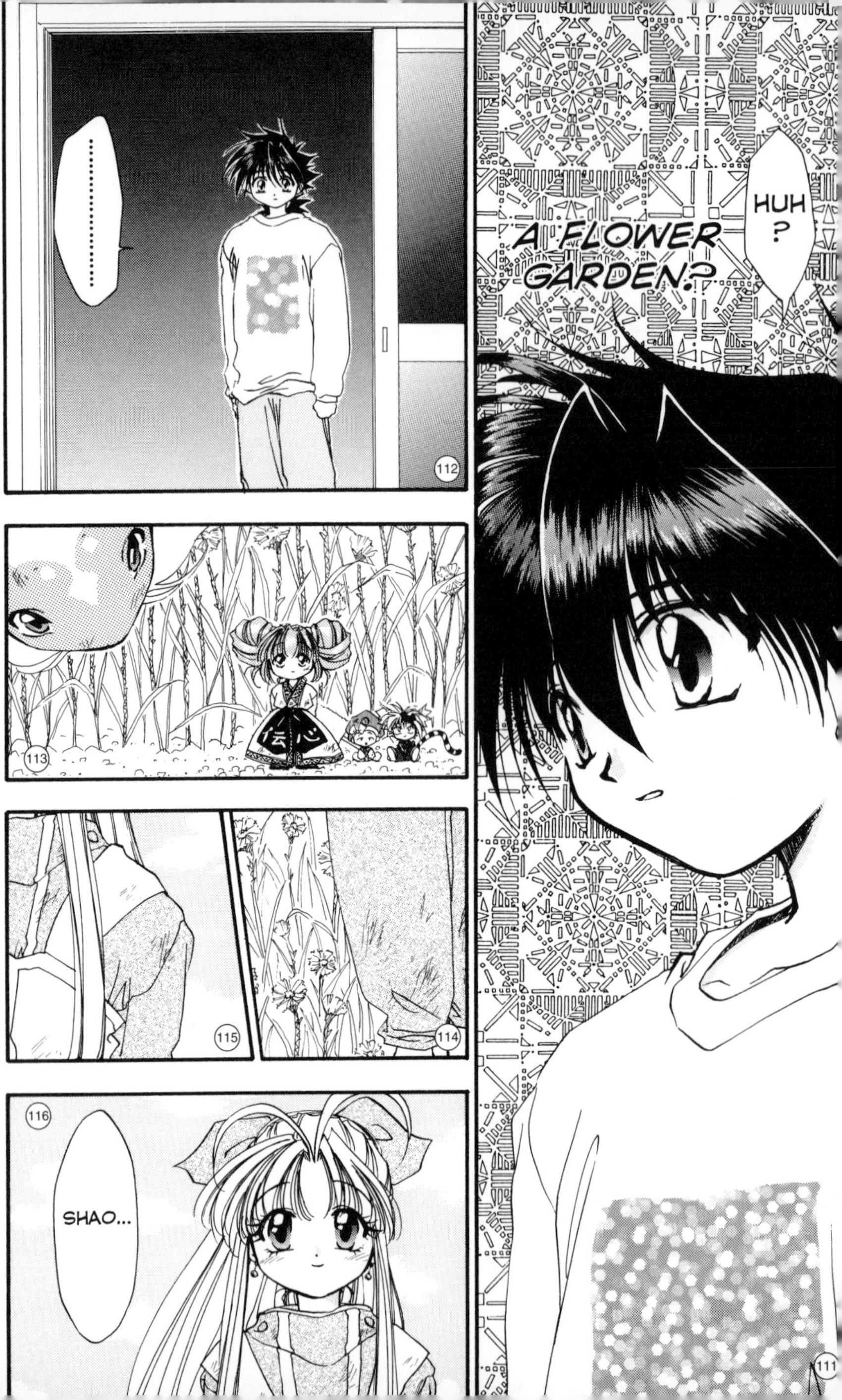
HUH?
A FLOWER GARDEN?
......
SHAO...

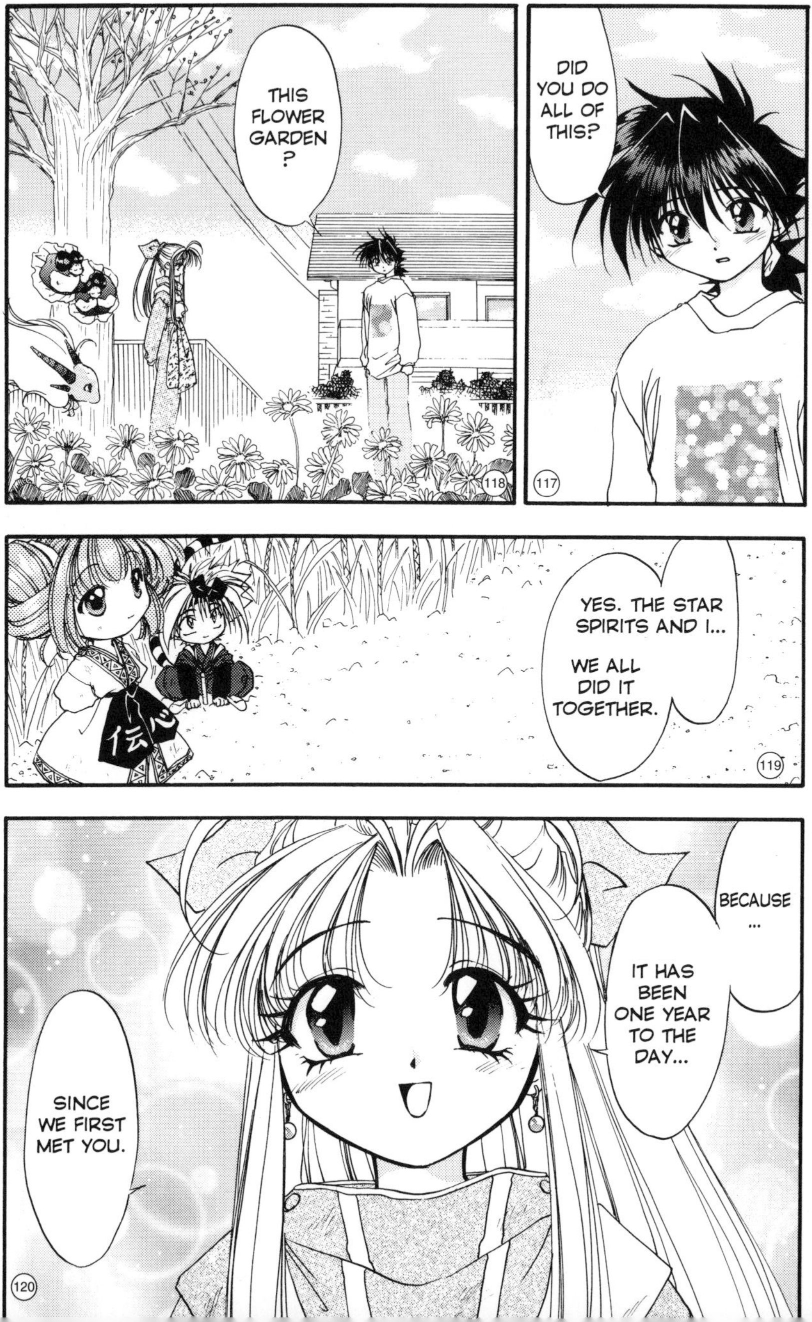
DID YOU DO ALL OF THIS?
THIS FLOWER GARDEN ?
YES. THE STAR SPIRITS AND I...
WE ALL DID IT TOGETHER.
BECAUSE ...
IT HAS BEEN ONE YEAR TO THE DAY...
SINCE WE FIRST MET YOU.

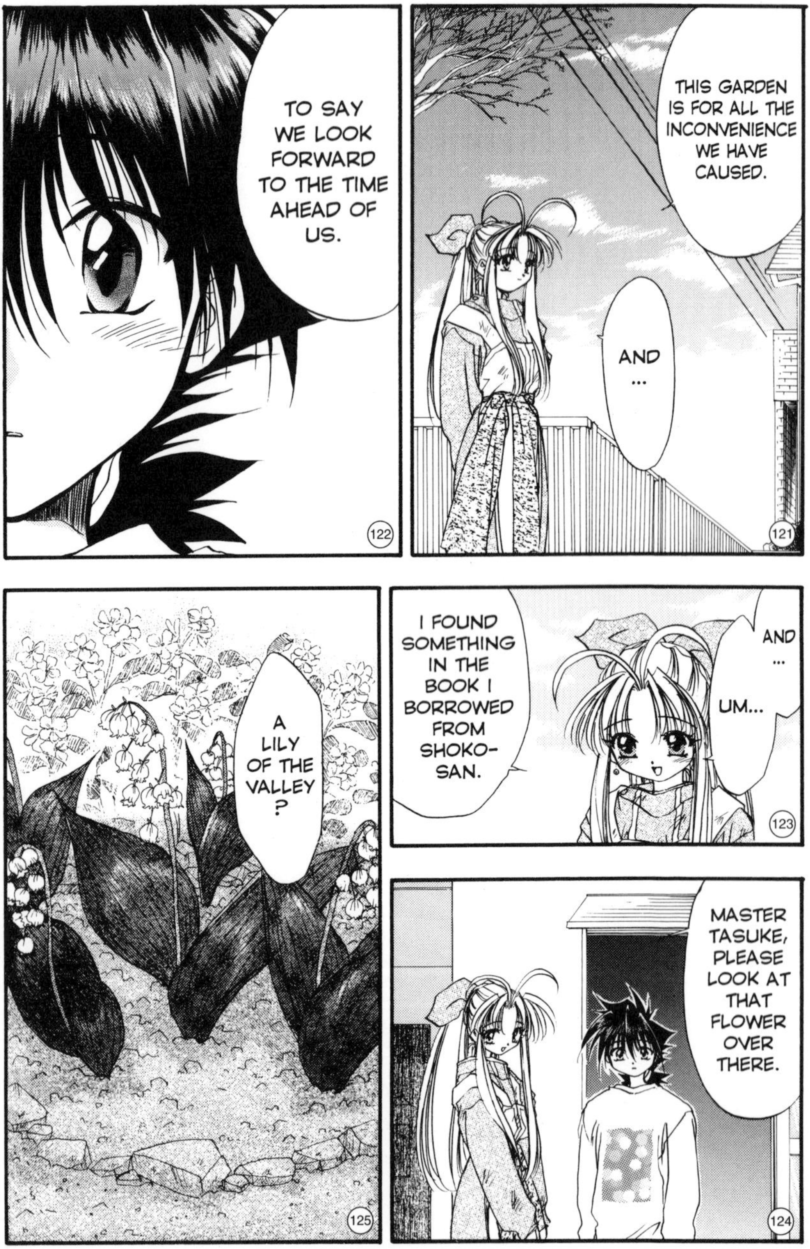
THIS GARDEN IS FOR ALL THE INCONVENIENCE WE HAVE CAUSED.
AND ...
TO SAY WE LOOK FORWARD TO THE TIME AHEAD OF US.
AND ...
UM...
I FOUND SOMETHING IN THE BOOK I BORROWED FROM SHOKO-SAN.
MASTER TASUKE, PLEASE LOOK AT THAT FLOWER OVER THERE.
A LILY OF THE VALLEY ?

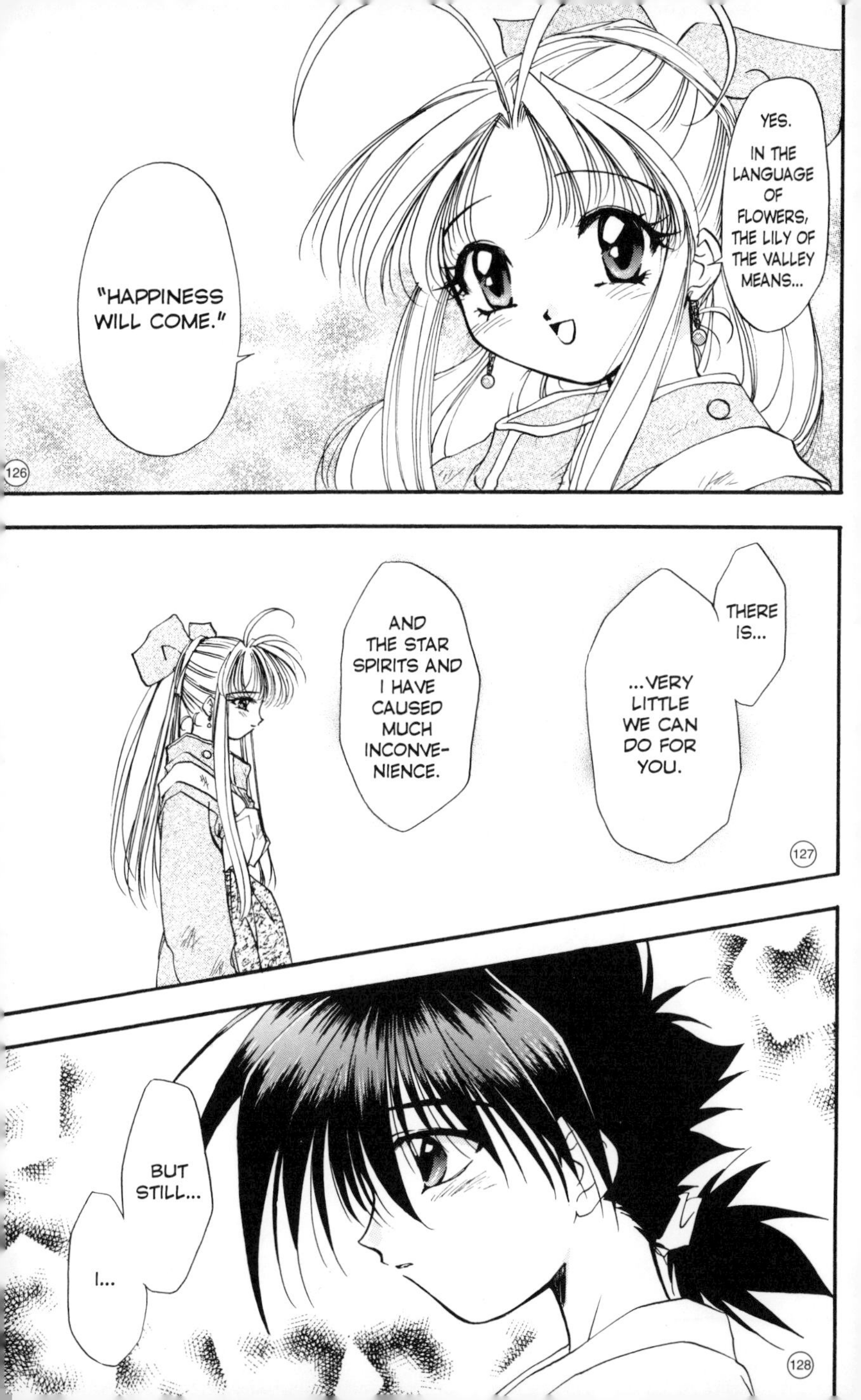
YES.
IN THE LANGUAGE OF FLOWERS, THE LILY OF THE VALLEY MEANS...
"HAPPINESS WILL COME."
THERE IS...
...VERY LITTLE WE CAN DO FOR YOU.
AND THE STAR SPIRITS AND I HAVE CAUSED MUCH INCONVENIENCE.
BUT STILL...
I...

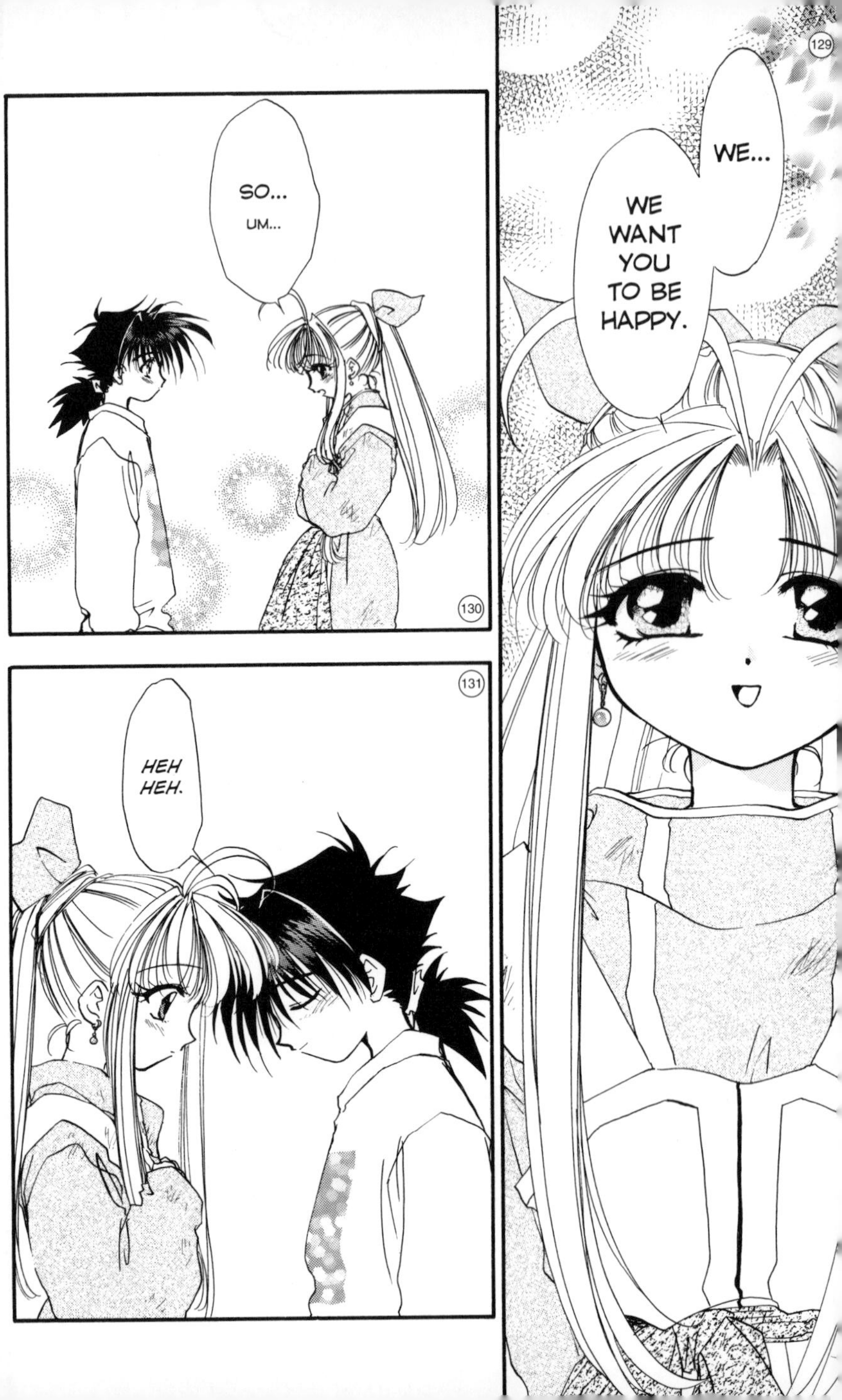
129
WE...
WE WANT YOU TO BE HAPPY.
SO...
UM...
130
131
HEH HEH.

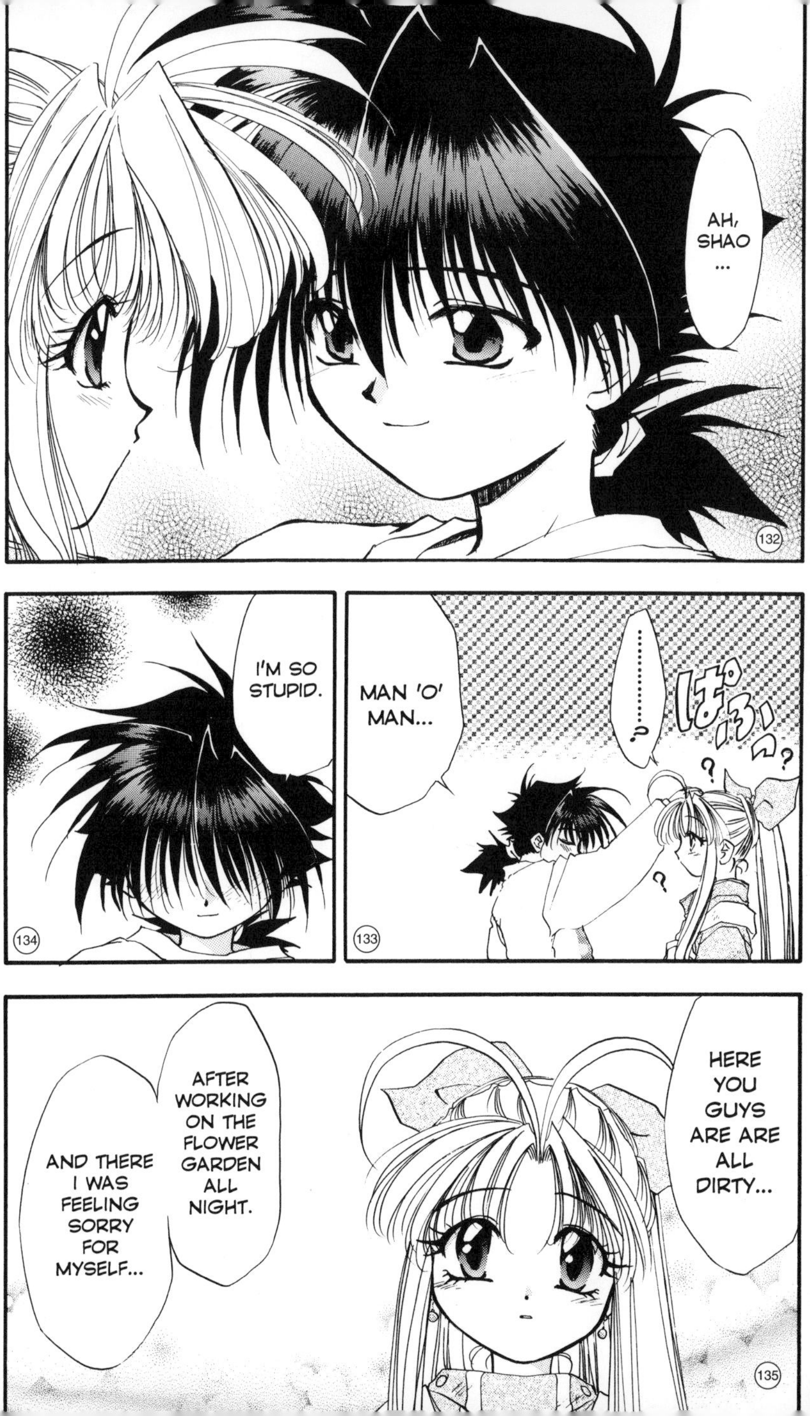
AH, SHAO ...
132
......?
MAN 'O' MAN...
133
I'M SO STUPID.
134
HERE YOU GUYS ARE ARE ALL DIRTY...
AFTER WORKING ON THE FLOWER GARDEN ALL NIGHT.
AND THERE I WAS FEELING SORRY FOR MYSELF...
135

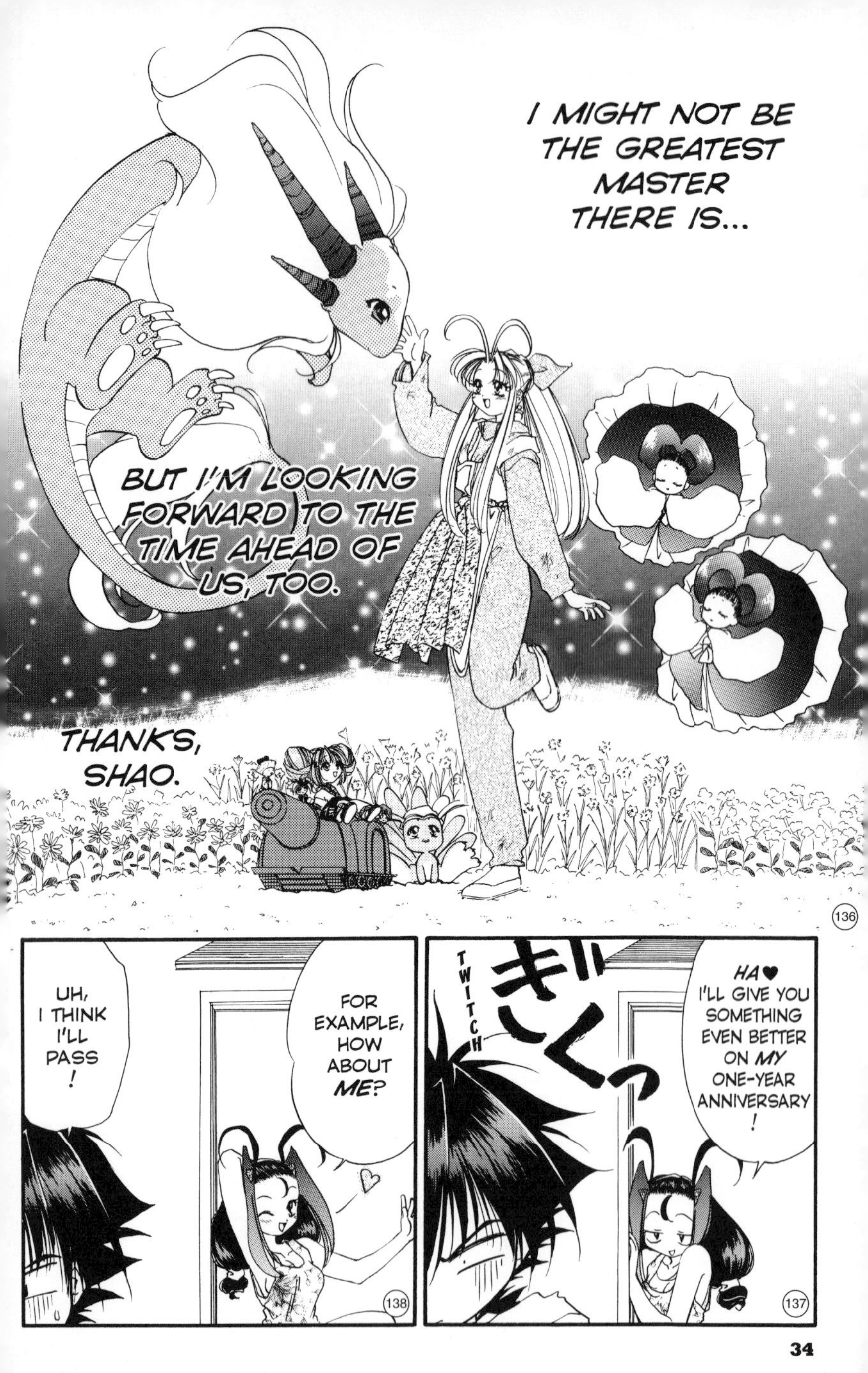
I MIGHT NOT BE THE GREATEST MASTER THERE IS...
BUT I'M LOOKING FORWARD TO THE TIME AHEAD OF US, TOO.
THANKS, SHAO.
136
TWITCH
ぎくっ
HA♥ I'LL GIVE YOU SOMETHING EVEN BETTER ON MY ONE-YEAR ANNIVERSARY!
137
FOR EXAMPLE, HOW ABOUT ME?
UH, I THINK I'LL PASS!
138

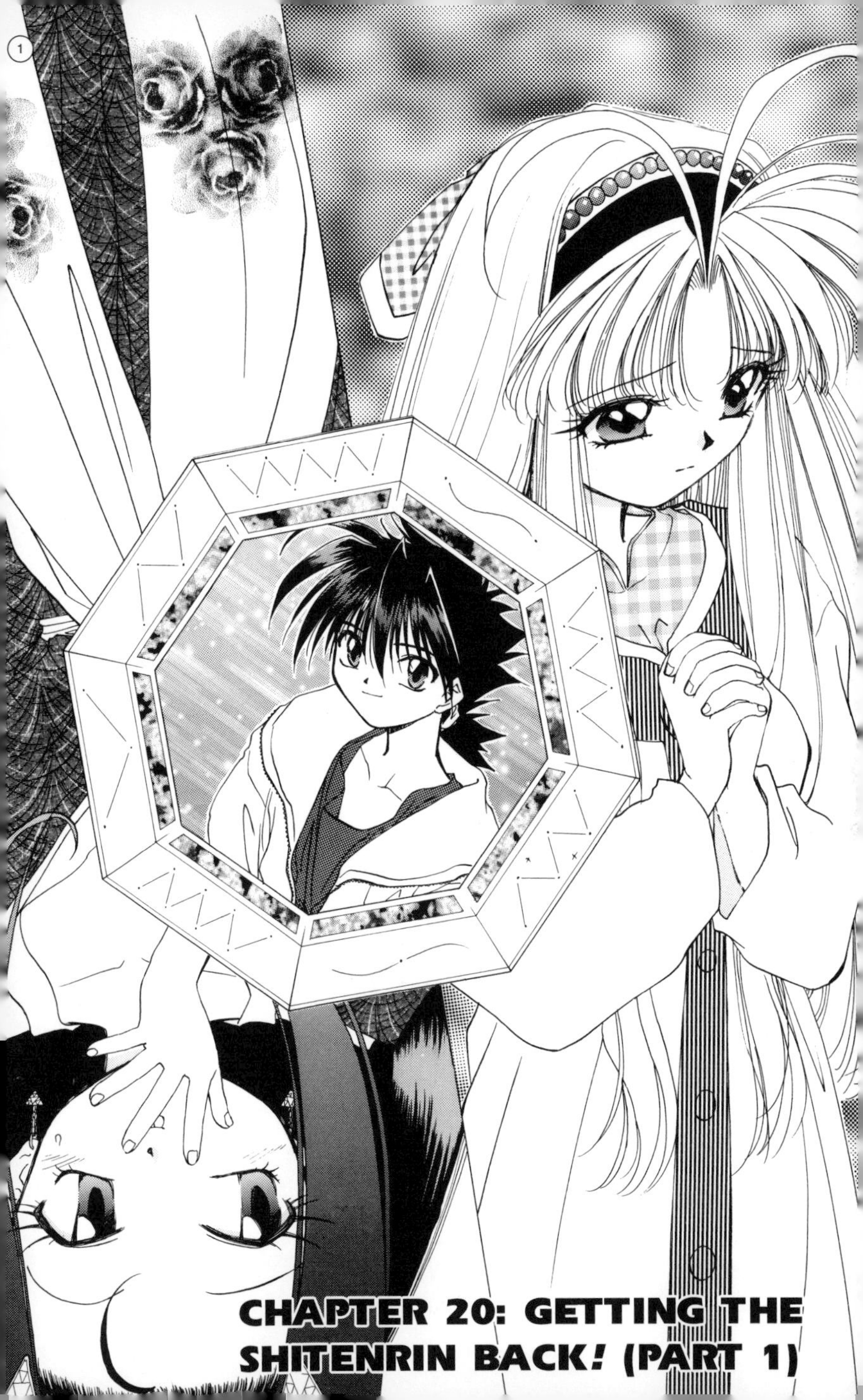
1
CHAPTER 20: GETTING THE
SHITENRIN BACK! (PART 1)

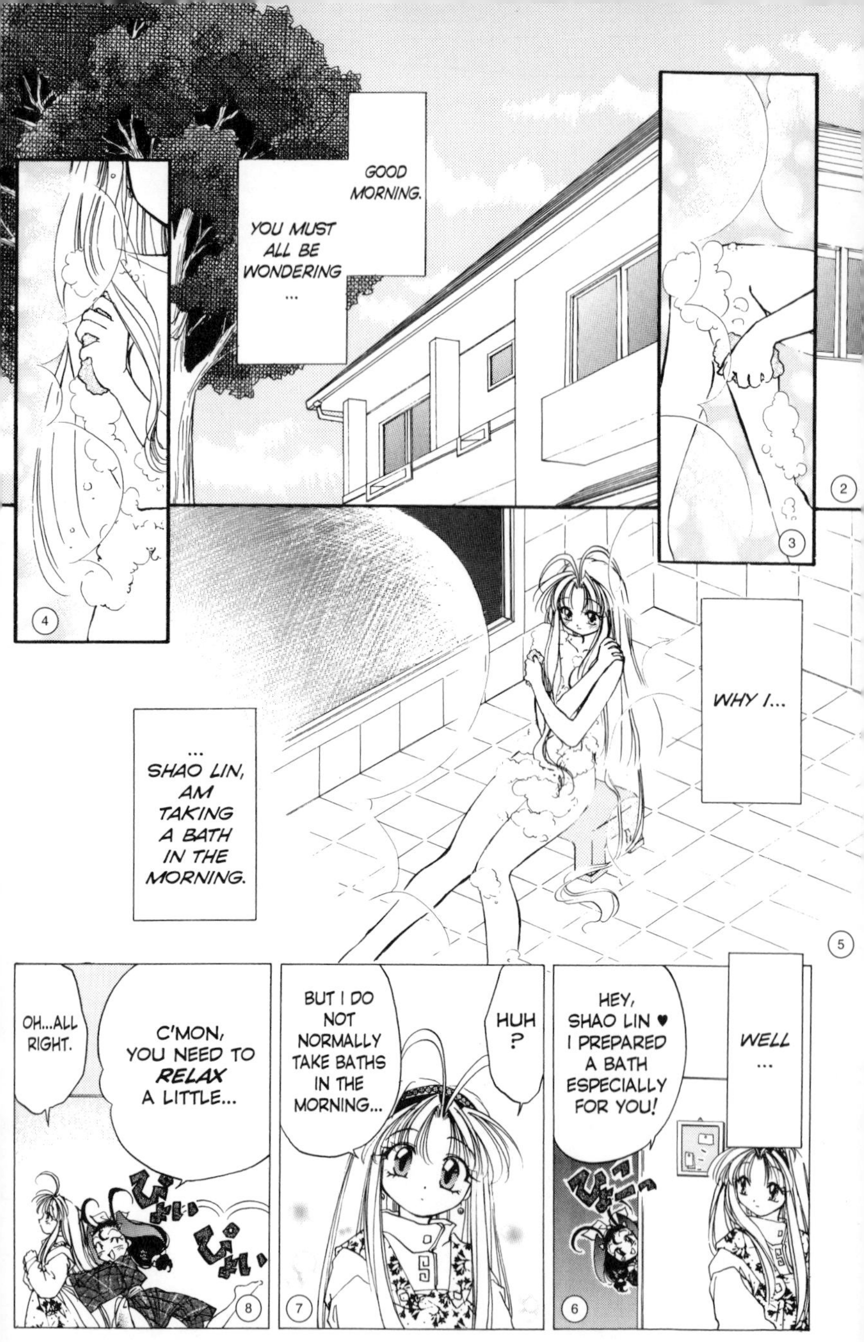
GOOD MORNING.
YOU MUST ALL BE WONDERING ...
WHY I...
... SHAO LIN, AM TAKING A BATH IN THE MORNING.
WELL ...
HEY, SHAO LIN ♥ I PREPARED A BATH ESPECIALLY FOR YOU!
HUH ?
BUT I DO NOT NORMALLY TAKE BATHS IN THE MORNING...
C'MON, YOU NEED TO RELAX A LITTLE...
OH...ALL RIGHT.

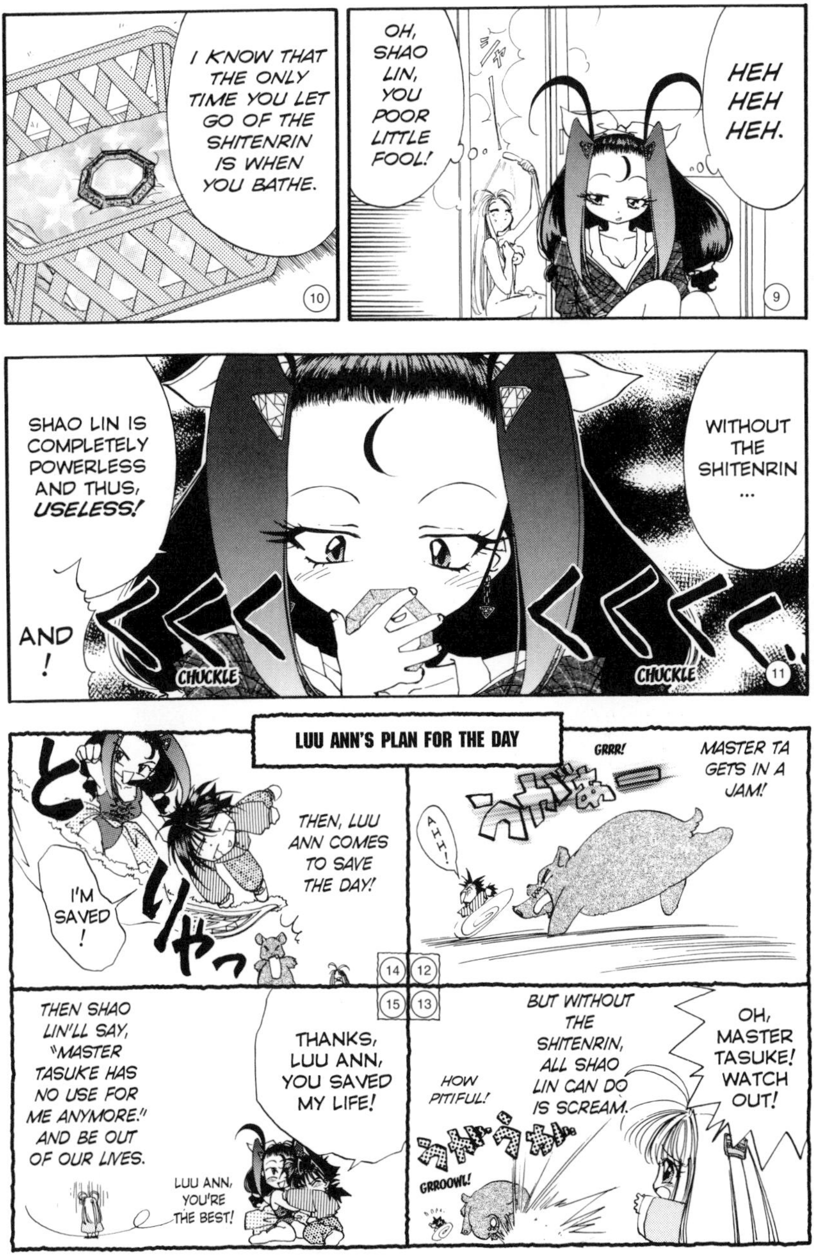
HEH HEH HEH.
OH, SHAO LIN, YOU POOR LITTLE FOOL!
I KNOW THAT THE ONLY TIME YOU LET GO OF THE SHITENRIN IS WHEN YOU BATHE.
WITHOUT THE SHITENRIN ...
SHAO LIN IS COMPLETELY POWERLESS AND THUS, USELESS!
AND !
CHUCKLE
CHUCKLE
LUU ANN'S PLAN FOR THE DAY
MASTER TA GETS IN A JAM!
GRRR!
AHH!
OH, MASTER TASUKE! WATCH OUT!
BUT WITHOUT THE SHITENRIN, ALL SHAO LIN CAN DO IS SCREAM.
HOW PITIFUL!
GRROOWL!
THEN, LUU ANN COMES TO SAVE THE DAY!
I'M SAVED !
THANKS, LUU ANN, YOU SAVED MY LIFE!
THEN SHAO LIN'LL SAY, "MASTER TASUKE HAS NO USE FOR ME ANYMORE." AND BE OUT OF OUR LIVES.
LUU ANN, YOU'RE THE BEST!

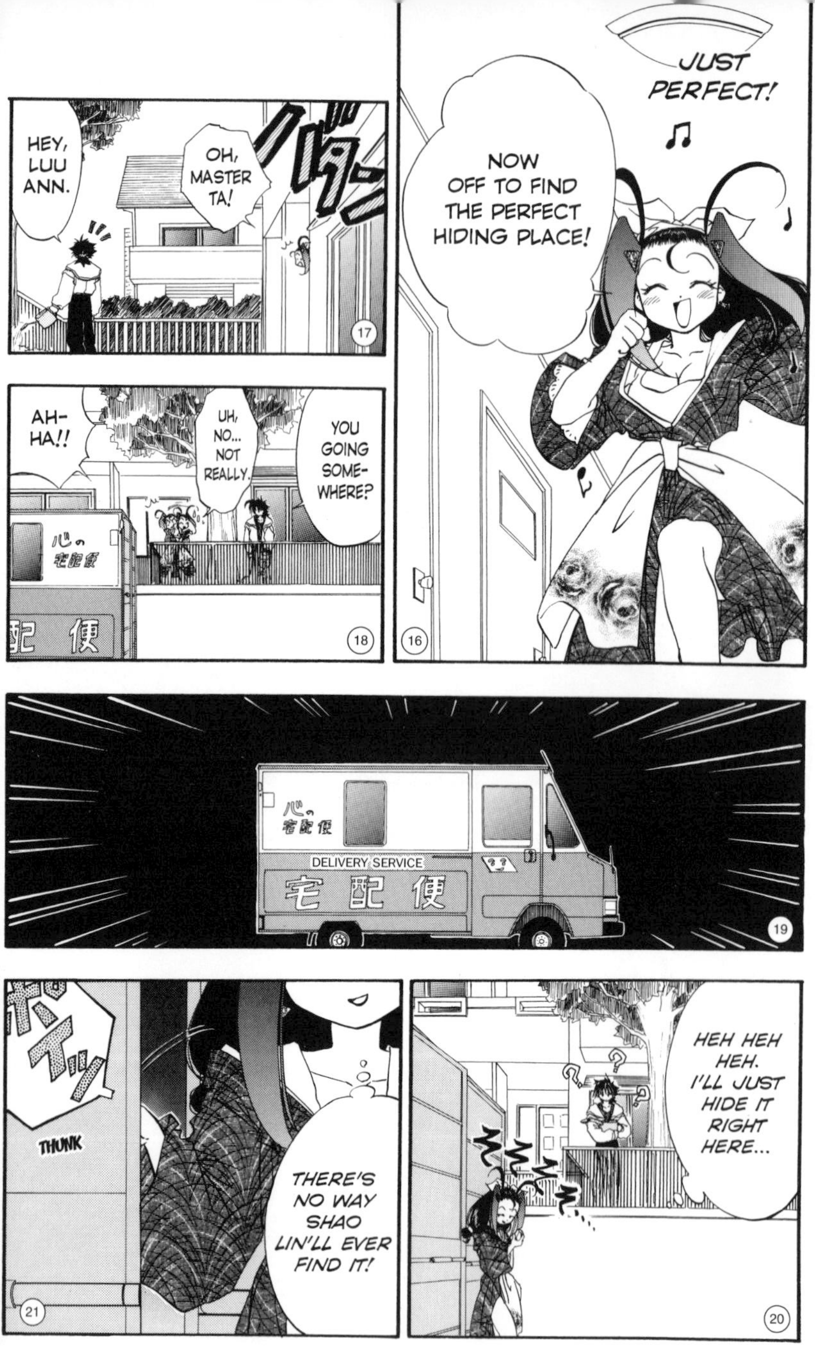
JUST PERFECT!
NOW OFF TO FIND THE PERFECT HIDING PLACE!
OH, MASTER TA!
HEY, LUU ANN.
YOU GOING SOME-WHERE?
UH, NO... NOT REALLY.
AH-HA!!
心の宅配便
宅配便
心の宅配便
DELIVERY SERVICE
宅配便
HEH HEH HEH. I'LL JUST HIDE IT RIGHT HERE...
THERE'S NO WAY SHAO LIN'LL EVER FIND IT!
THUNK

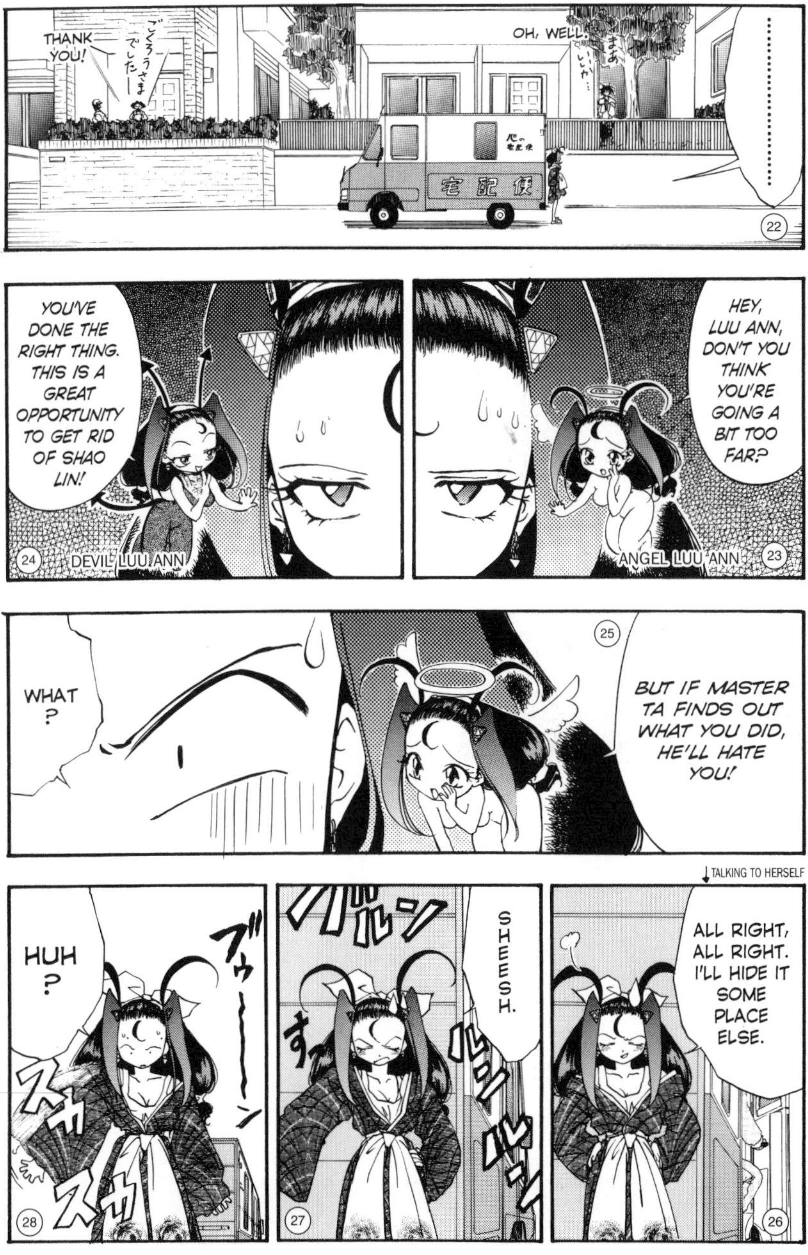

22
......
OH, WELL.
まあいいか…
THANK YOU!
ごくろうさまでした—
宅配便
23
HEY, LUU ANN, DON'T YOU THINK YOU'RE GOING A BIT TOO FAR?
ANGEL LUU ANN
24
YOU'VE DONE THE RIGHT THING. THIS IS A GREAT OPPORTUNITY TO GET RID OF SHAO LIN!
DEVIL LUU ANN
25
BUT IF MASTER TA FINDS OUT WHAT YOU DID, HE'LL HATE YOU!
WHAT ?
TALKING TO HERSELF
26
ALL RIGHT, ALL RIGHT. I'LL HIDE IT SOME PLACE ELSE.
27
SHEESH.
28
HUH ?

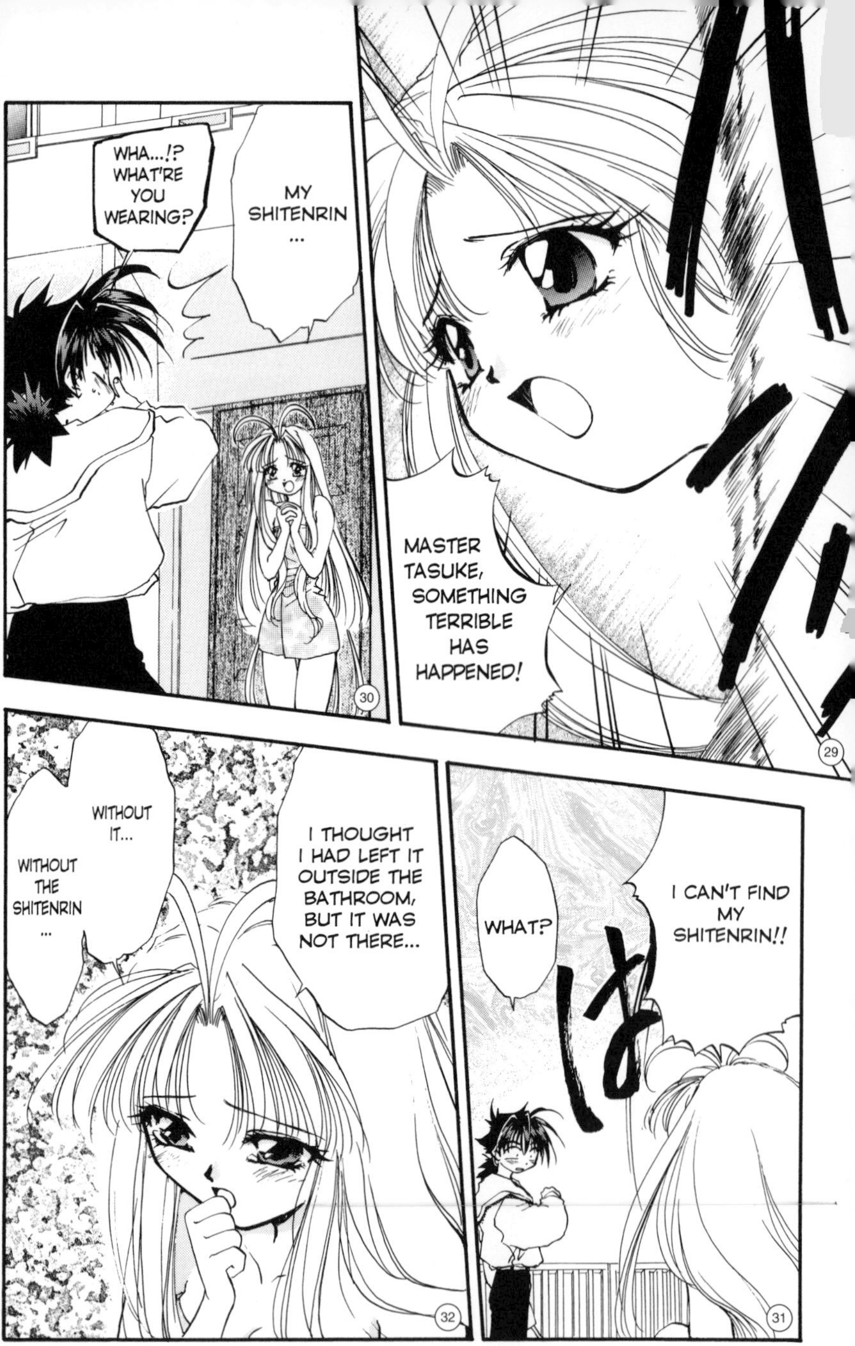
MASTER TASUKE, SOMETHING TERRIBLE HAS HAPPENED!
MY SHITENRIN ...
WHA...!? WHAT'RE YOU WEARING?
I CAN'T FIND MY SHITENRIN!!
は
WHAT?
I THOUGHT I HAD LEFT IT OUTSIDE THE BATHROOM, BUT IT WAS NOT THERE...
WITHOUT IT...
WITHOUT THE SHITENRIN ...

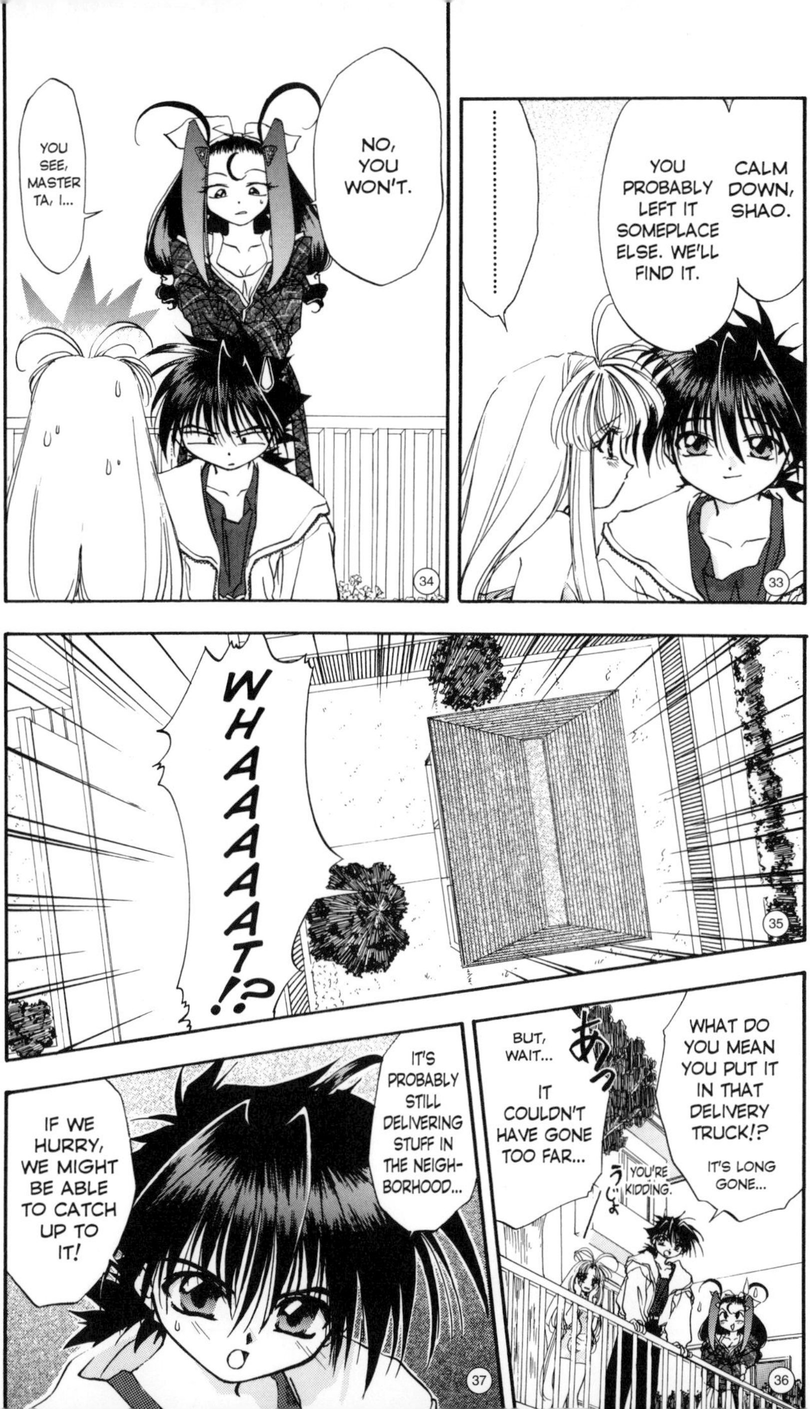
CALM DOWN, SHAO.
YOU PROBABLY LEFT IT SOMEPLACE ELSE. WE'LL FIND IT.
......
NO, YOU WON'T.
YOU SEE, MASTER TA, I...
WHAAAAAAT!?
WHAT DO YOU MEAN YOU PUT IT IN THAT DELIVERY TRUCK!?
IT'S LONG GONE...
YOU'RE KIDDING.
BUT, WAIT...
IT COULDN'T HAVE GONE TOO FAR...
IT'S PROBABLY STILL DELIVERING STUFF IN THE NEIGHBORHOOD...
IF WE HURRY, WE MIGHT BE ABLE TO CATCH UP TO IT!

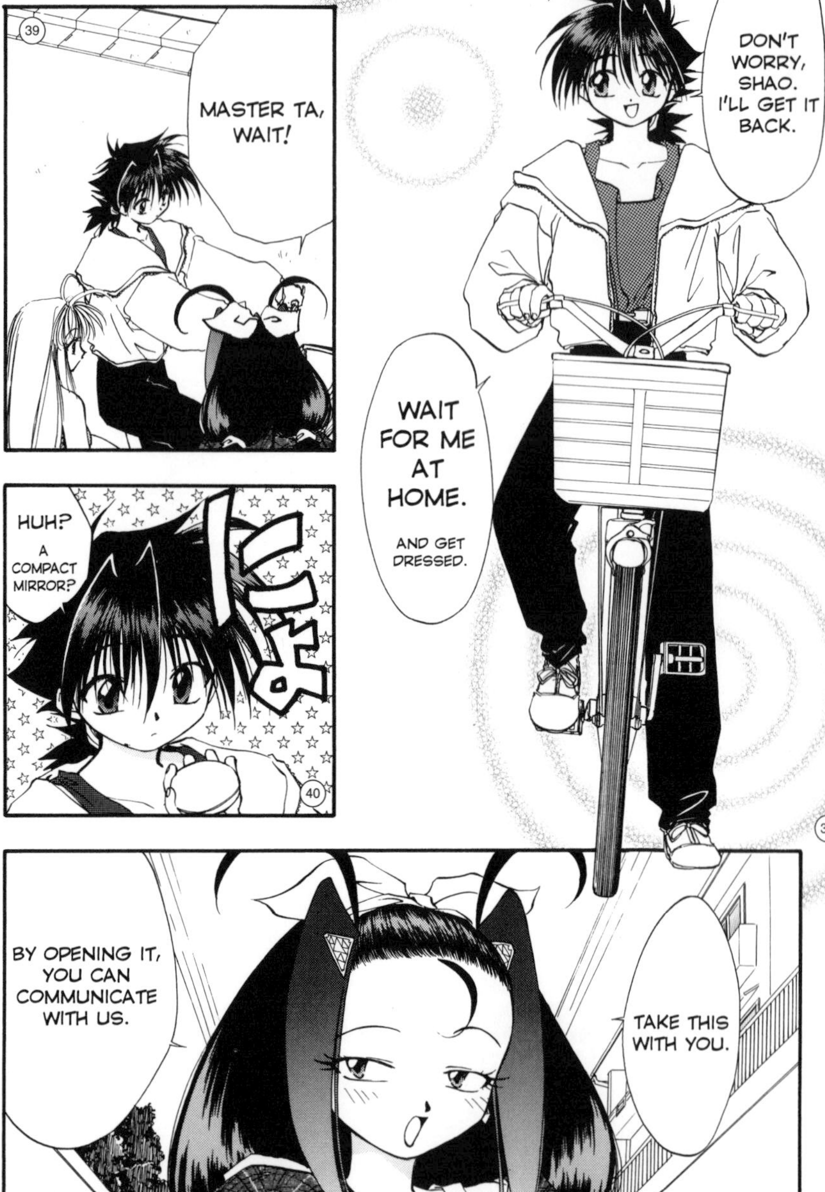
DON'T WORRY, SHAO. I'LL GET IT BACK.
WAIT FOR ME AT HOME.
AND GET DRESSED.
MASTER TA, WAIT!
HUH?
A COMPACT MIRROR?
TAKE THIS WITH YOU.
BY OPENING IT, YOU CAN COMMUNICATE WITH US.

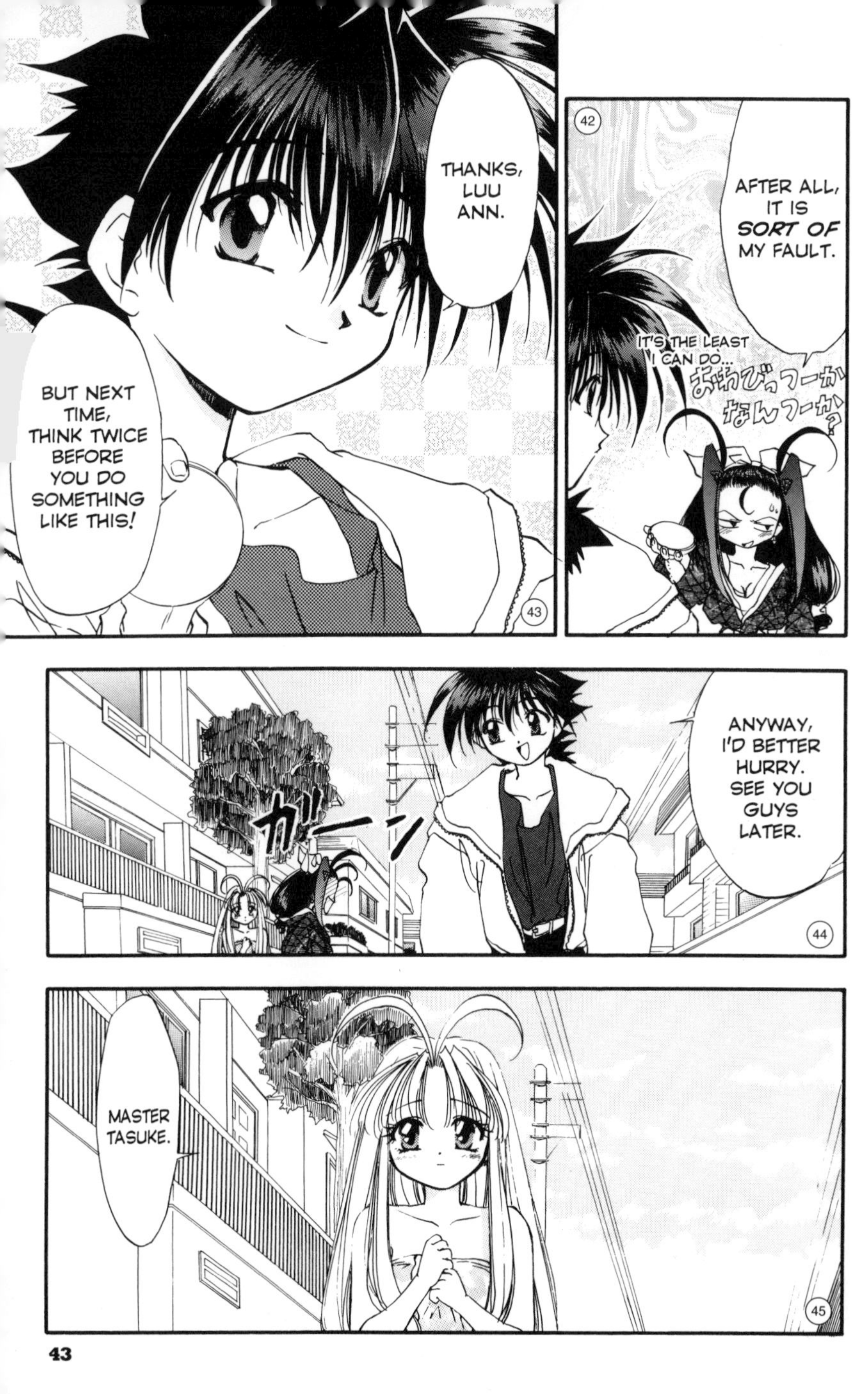
AFTER ALL, IT IS *SORT OF* MY FAULT.
IT'S THE LEAST I CAN DO...
おわびっつーか なんつーか?
THANKS, LUU ANN.
BUT NEXT TIME, THINK TWICE BEFORE YOU DO SOMETHING LIKE THIS!
ANYWAY, I'D BETTER HURRY. SEE YOU GUYS LATER.
ガーーン
MASTER TASUKE.

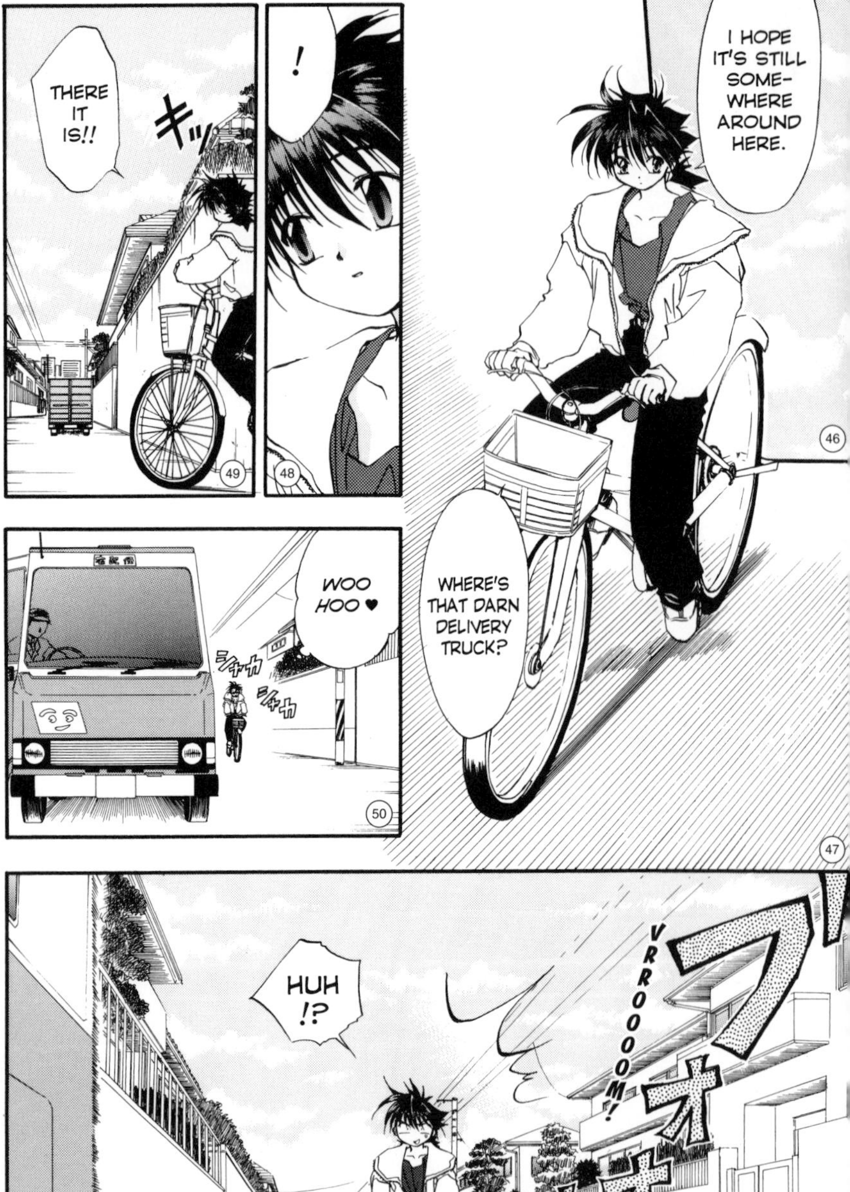
I HOPE IT'S STILL SOME-WHERE AROUND HERE.
WHERE'S THAT DARN DELIVERY TRUCK?
!
THERE IT IS!!
ギッ
WOO HOO ♥
シャカ
シャカ
HUH !?
VRROOOOOM!
ブオオオ

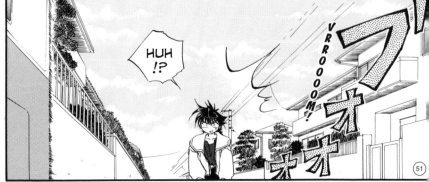

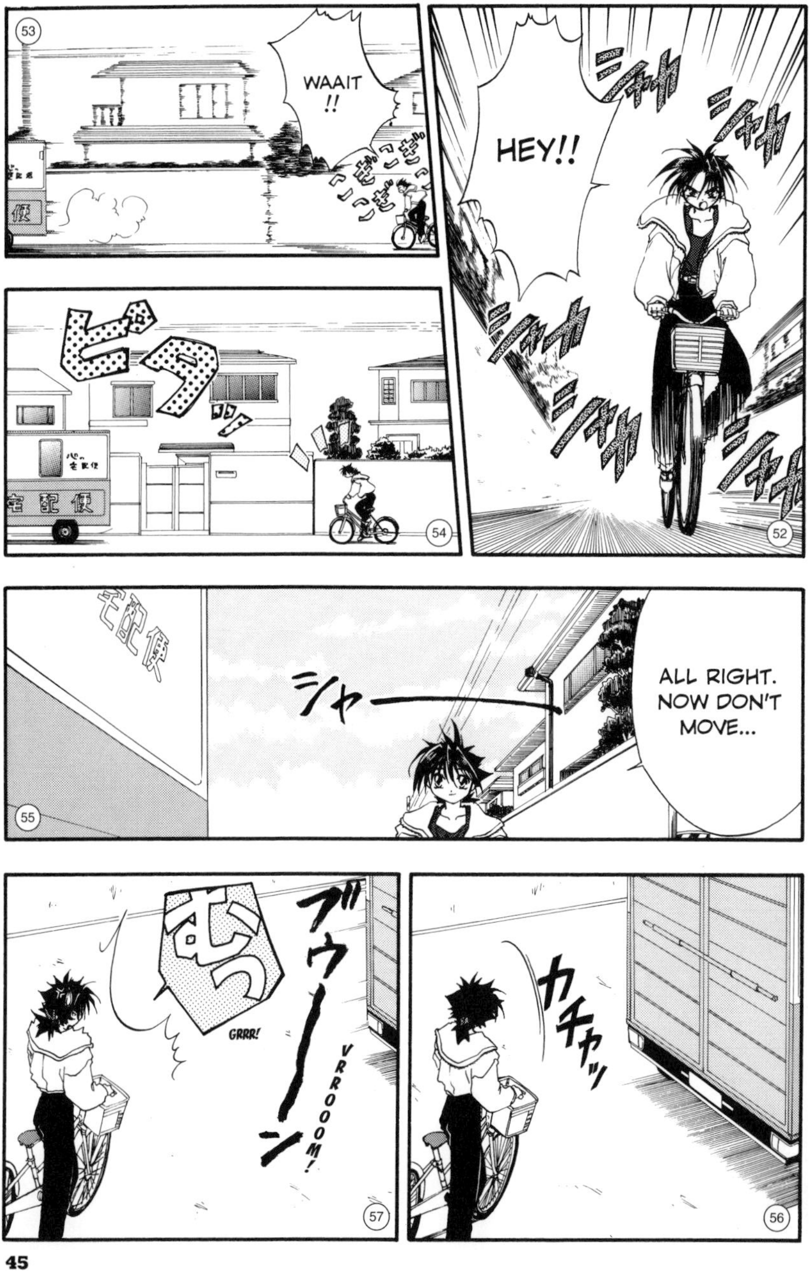

HEY!!
WAAIT!!
ALL RIGHT. NOW DON'T MOVE...
GRRR!
VRROOOOM!

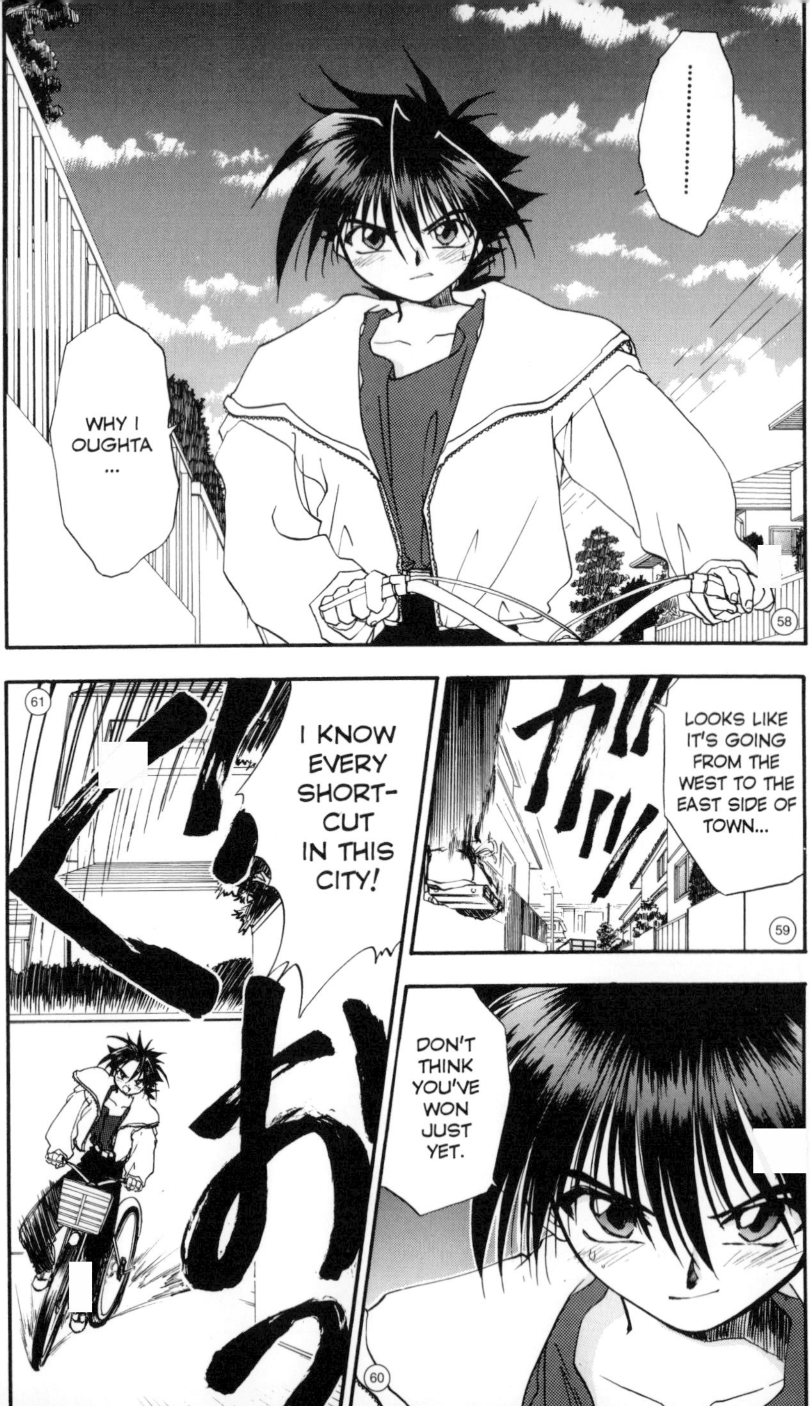
……
WHY I OUGHTA ...
LOOKS LIKE IT'S GOING FROM THE WEST TO THE EAST SIDE OF TOWN...
DON'T THINK YOU'VE WON JUST YET.
I KNOW EVERY SHORT-CUT IN THIS CITY!

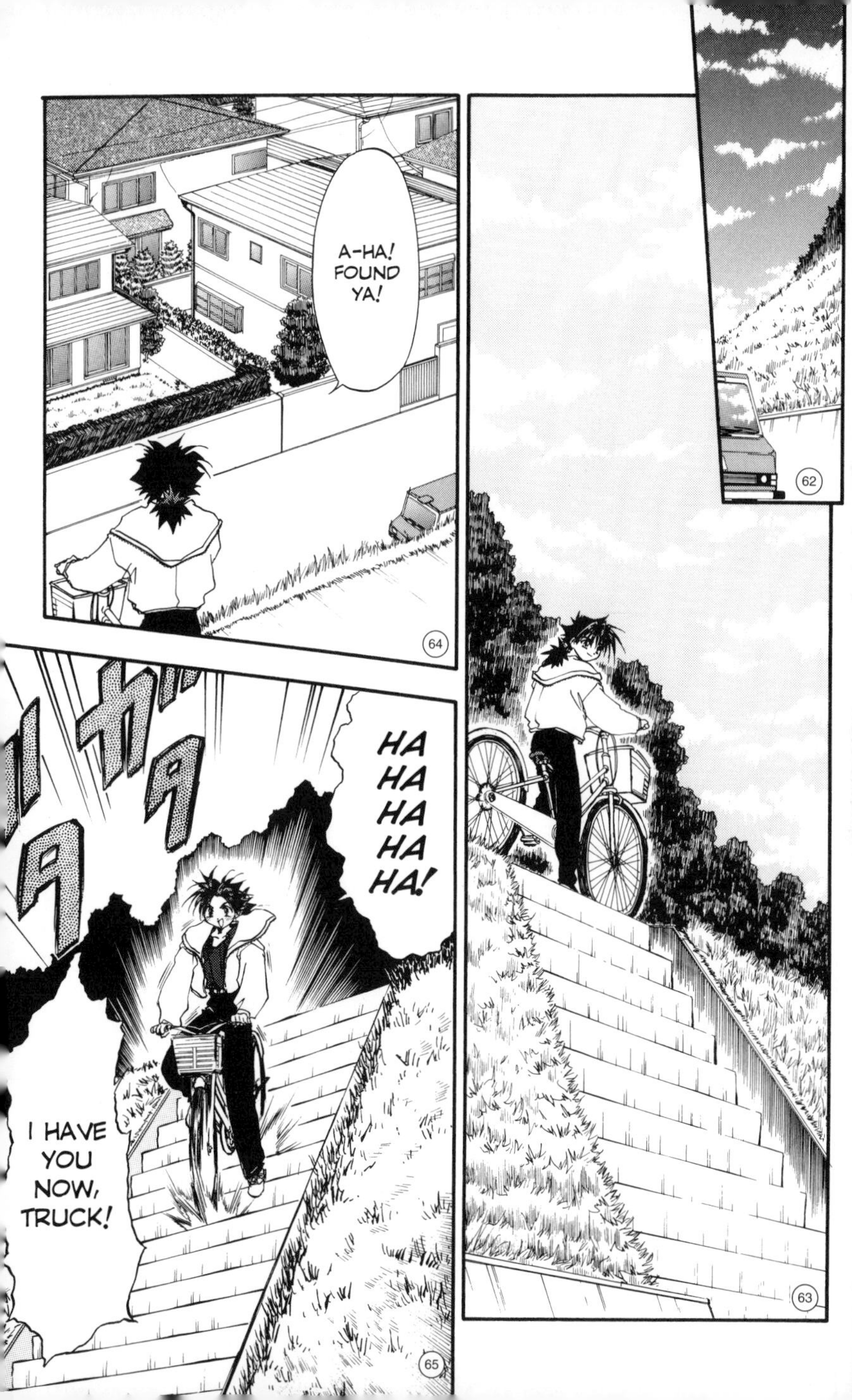
62
63
A-HA! FOUND YA!
64
HA HA HA HA HA!
I HAVE YOU NOW, TRUCK!
65

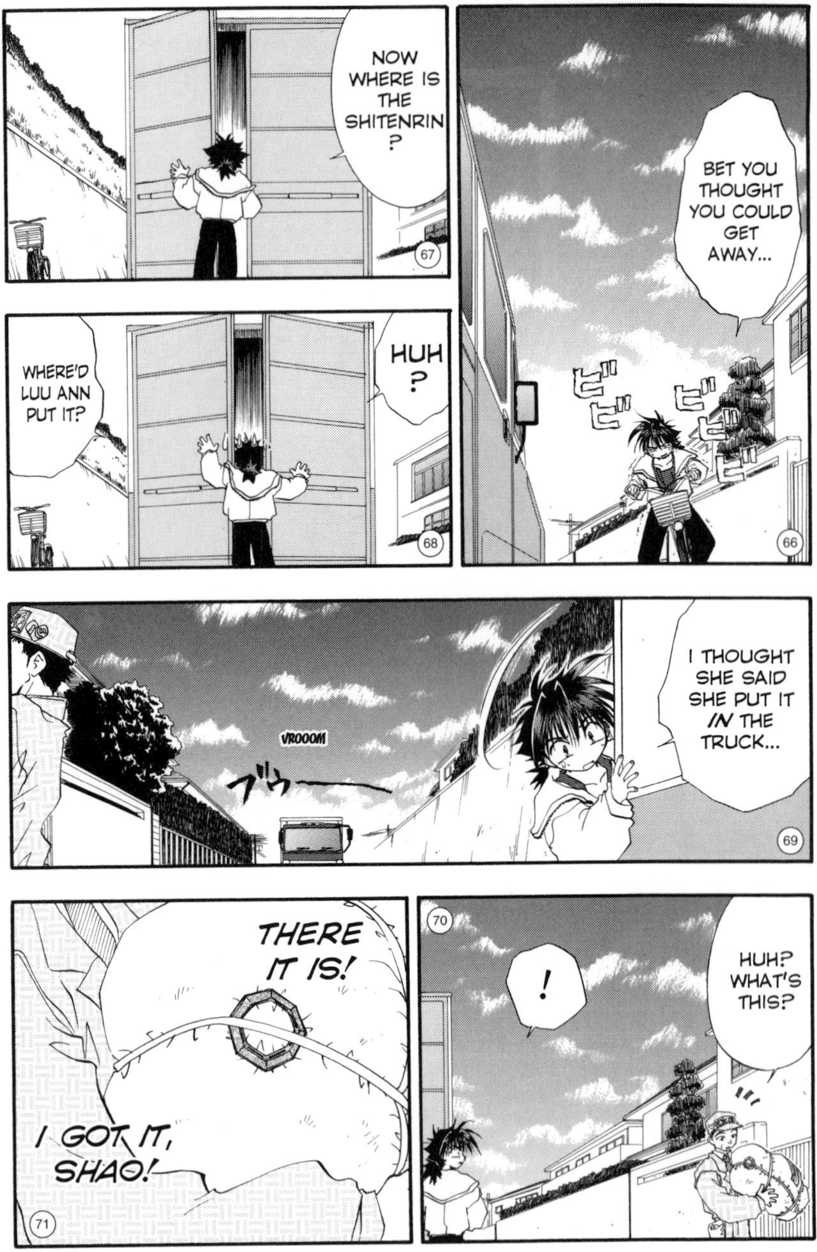
BET YOU THOUGHT YOU COULD GET AWAY...
NOW WHERE IS THE SHITENRIN?
HUH?
WHERE'D LUU ANN PUT IT?
I THOUGHT SHE SAID SHE PUT IT *IN* THE TRUCK...
VROOOM
HUH? WHAT'S THIS?
!
THERE IT IS!
I GOT IT, SHAO!

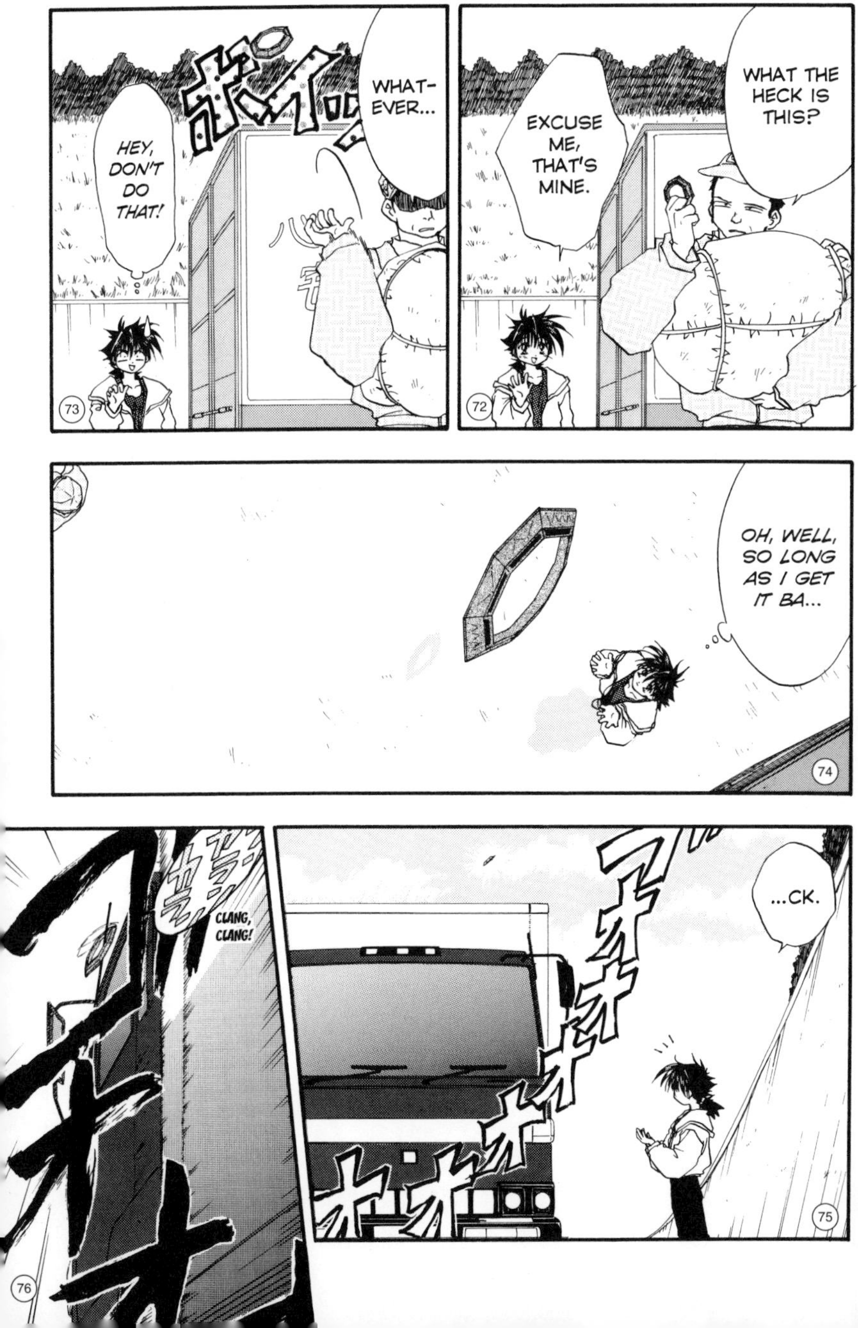
WHAT THE HECK IS THIS?
EXCUSE ME, THAT'S MINE.
WHAT-EVER...
HEY, DON'T DO THAT!
OH, WELL, SO LONG AS I GET IT BA...
...CK.
CLANG, CLANG!

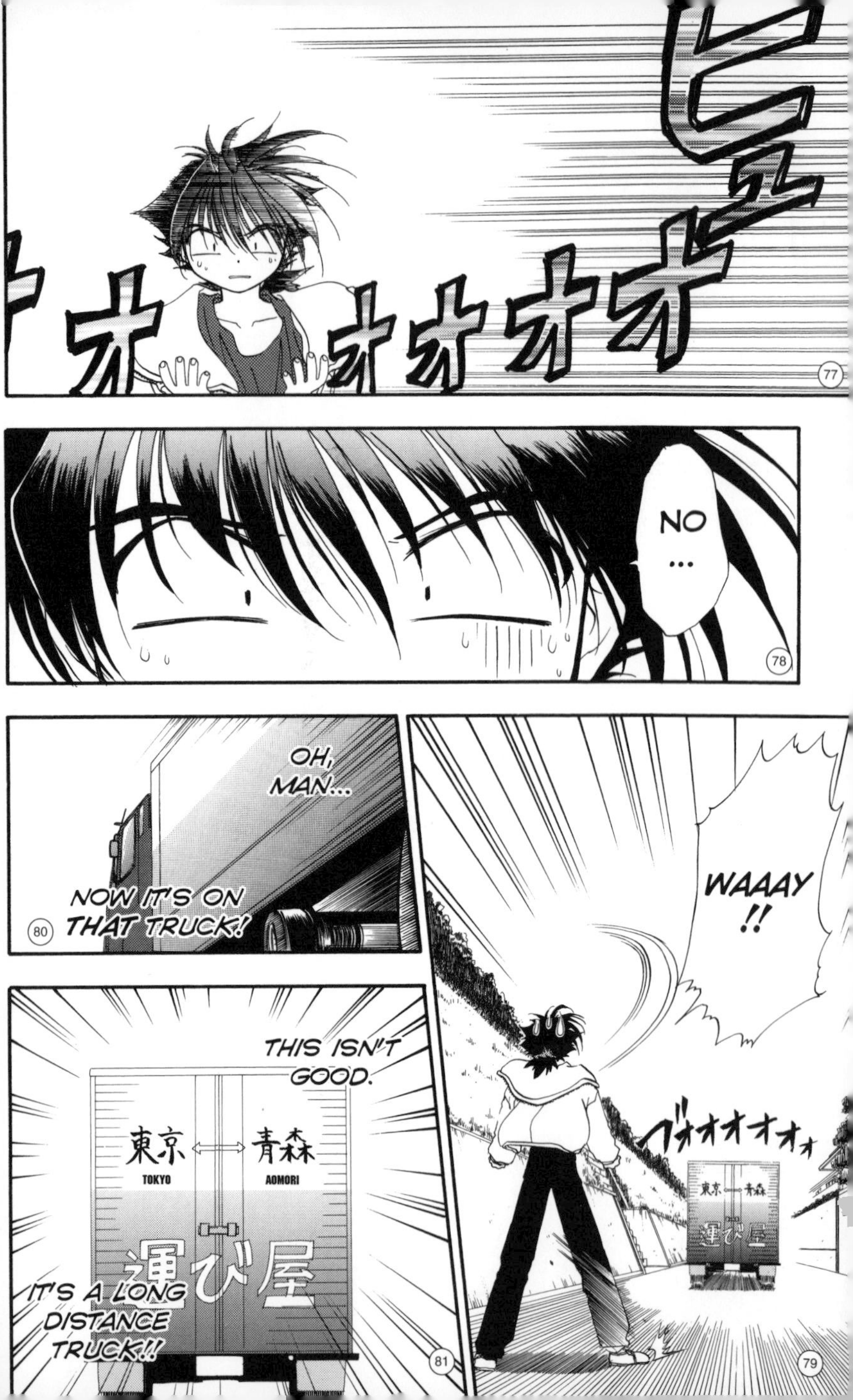

ヒュオオオオオ
77
NO ...
78
WAAAY !!
ブォオオオオオ
東京 青森
運び屋
79
OH, MAN...
NOW IT'S ON THAT TRUCK!
80
THIS ISN'T GOOD.
東京 ⟷ 青森
TOKYO AOMORI
運び屋
IT'S A LONG DISTANCE TRUCK!!
81

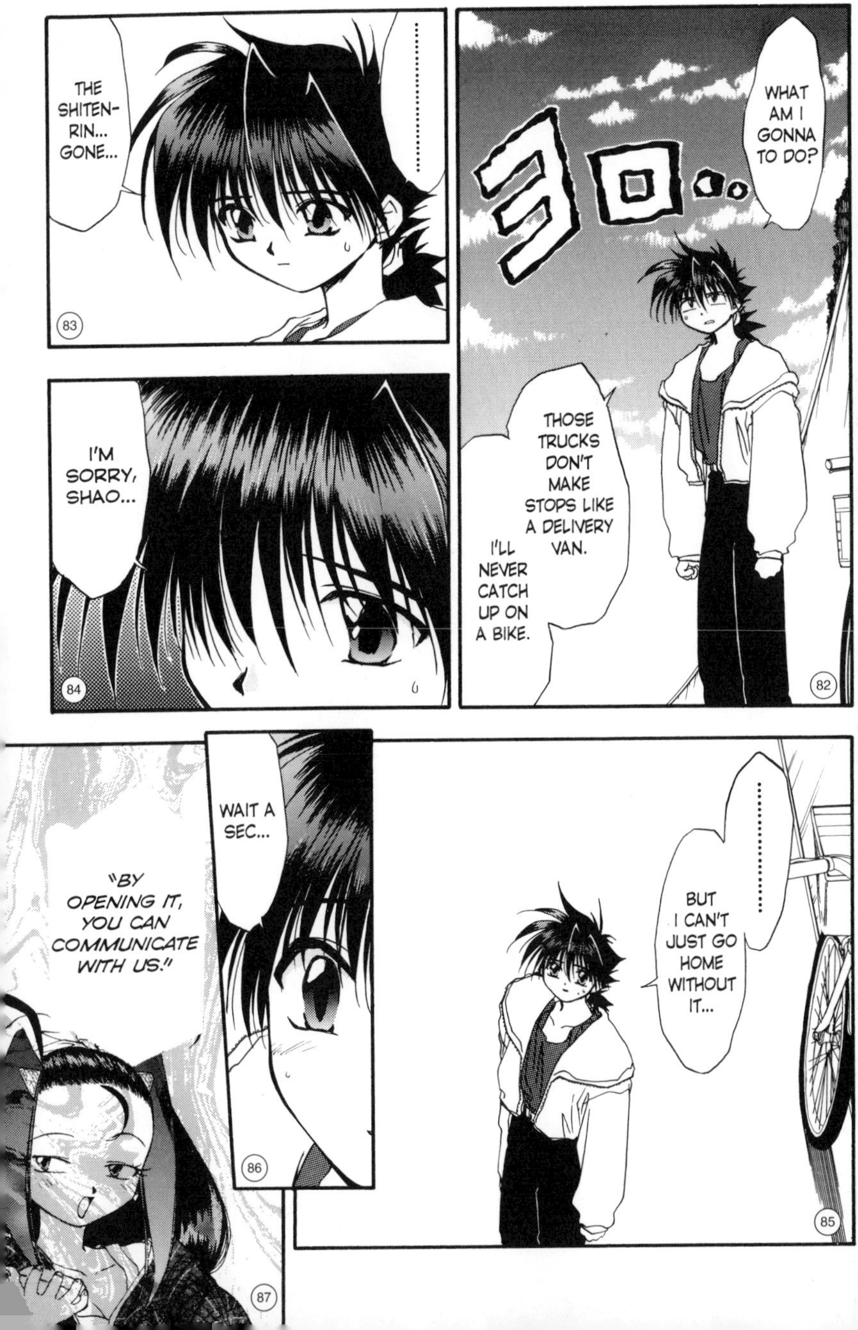
WHAT AM I GONNA TO DO?
ヨロ...
THOSE TRUCKS DON'T MAKE STOPS LIKE A DELIVERY VAN.
I'LL NEVER CATCH UP ON A BIKE.
......
THE SHITEN-RIN... GONE...
I'M SORRY, SHAO...
......
BUT I CAN'T JUST GO HOME WITHOUT IT...
WAIT A SEC...
"BY OPENING IT, YOU CAN COMMUNICATE WITH US."

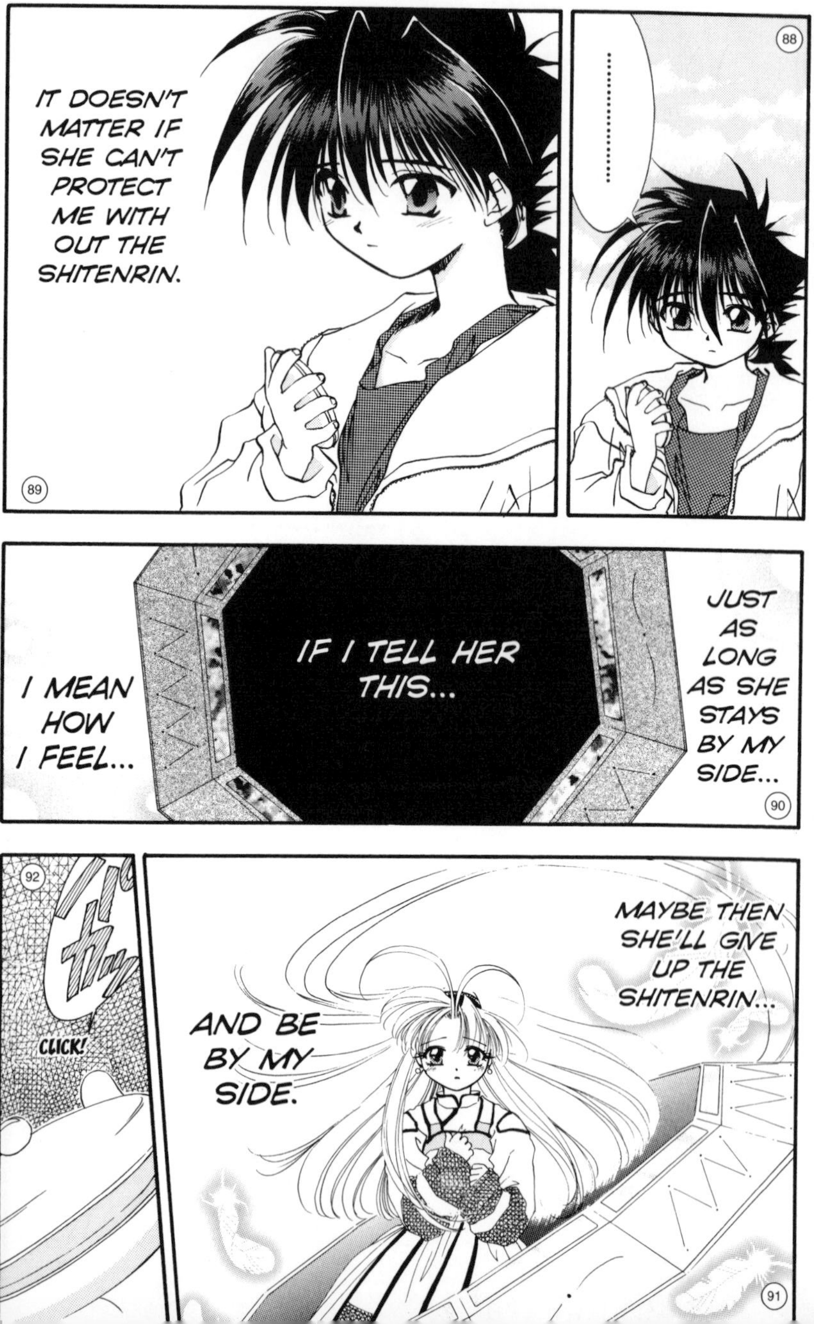
......
IT DOESN'T MATTER IF SHE CAN'T PROTECT ME WITH OUT THE SHITENRIN.
JUST AS LONG AS SHE STAYS BY MY SIDE...
IF I TELL HER THIS...
I MEAN HOW I FEEL...
MAYBE THEN SHE'LL GIVE UP THE SHITENRIN...
AND BE BY MY SIDE.
CLICK!

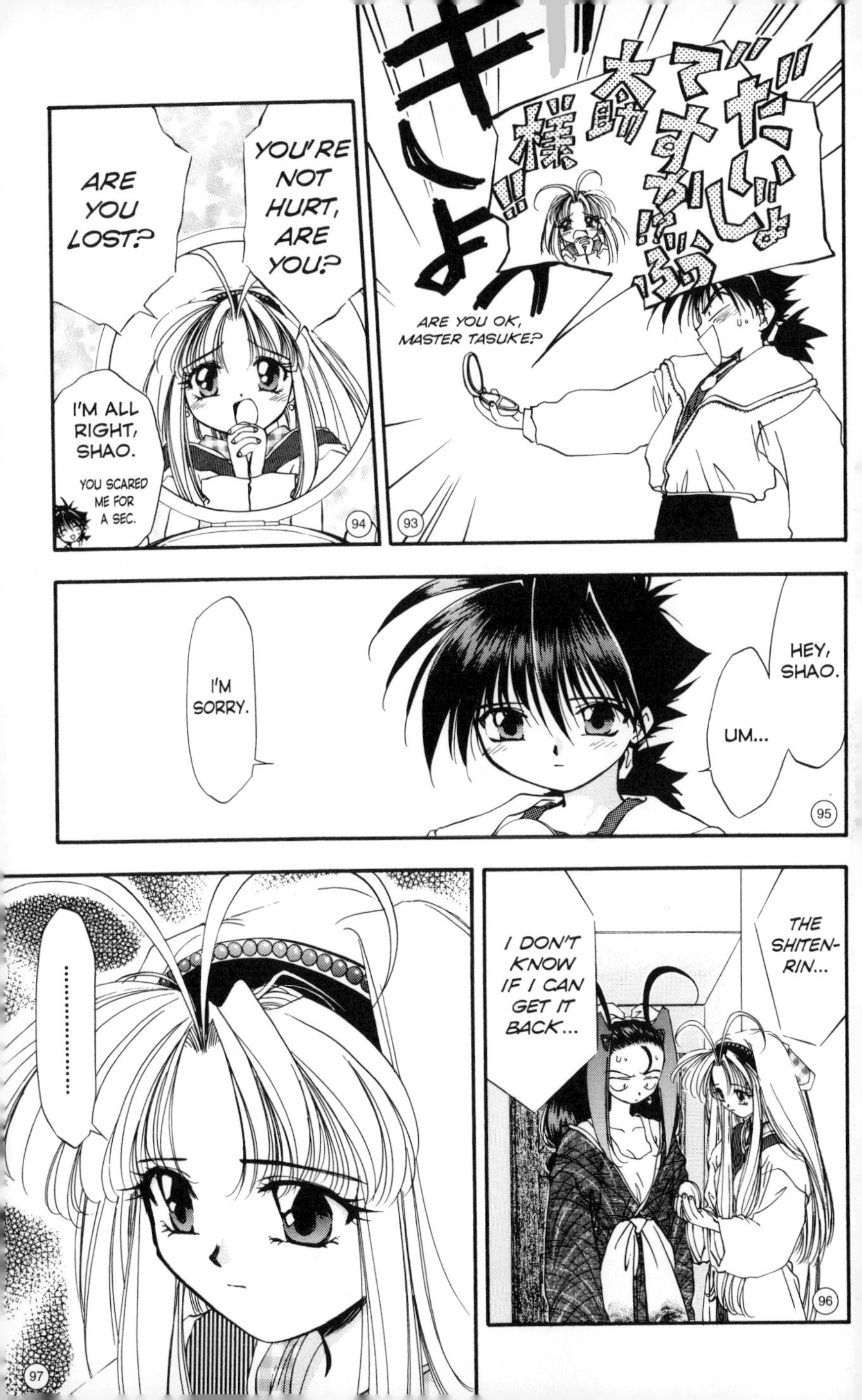
ぎしょっ
だいじょうぶですか太助様!!
ARE YOU OK, MASTER TASUKE?
YOU'RE NOT HURT, ARE YOU?
ARE YOU LOST?
I'M ALL RIGHT, SHAO.
YOU SCARED ME FOR A SEC.
HEY, SHAO.
UM...
I'M SORRY.
THE SHITEN-RIN...
I DON'T KNOW IF I CAN GET IT BACK...
....

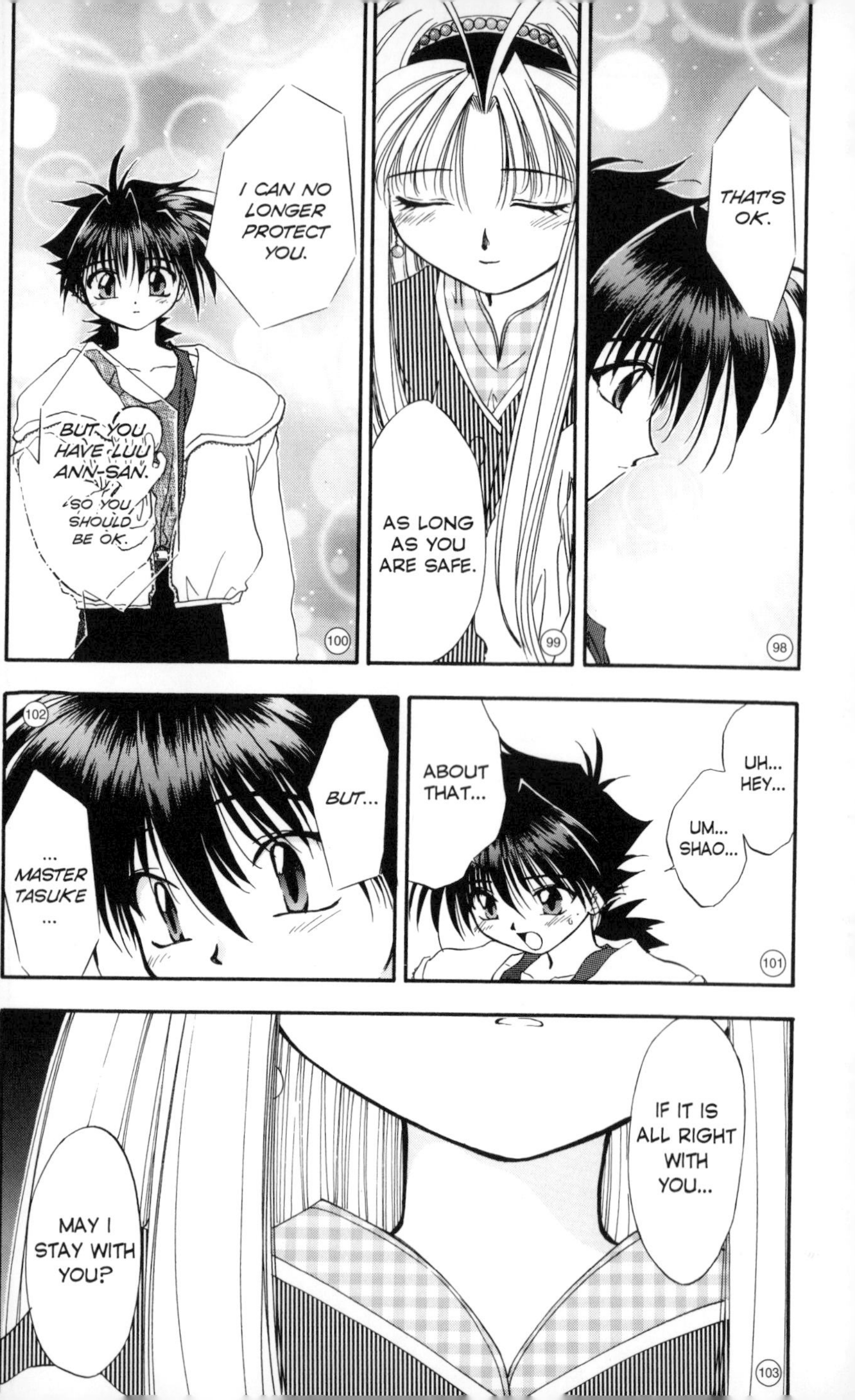
THAT'S OK.
AS LONG AS YOU ARE SAFE.
I CAN NO LONGER PROTECT YOU.
BUT YOU HAVE LUU ANN-SAN.
SO YOU SHOULD BE OK.
UH... HEY...
UM... SHAO...
ABOUT THAT...
BUT...
... MASTER TASUKE ...
IF IT IS ALL RIGHT WITH YOU...
MAY I STAY WITH YOU?

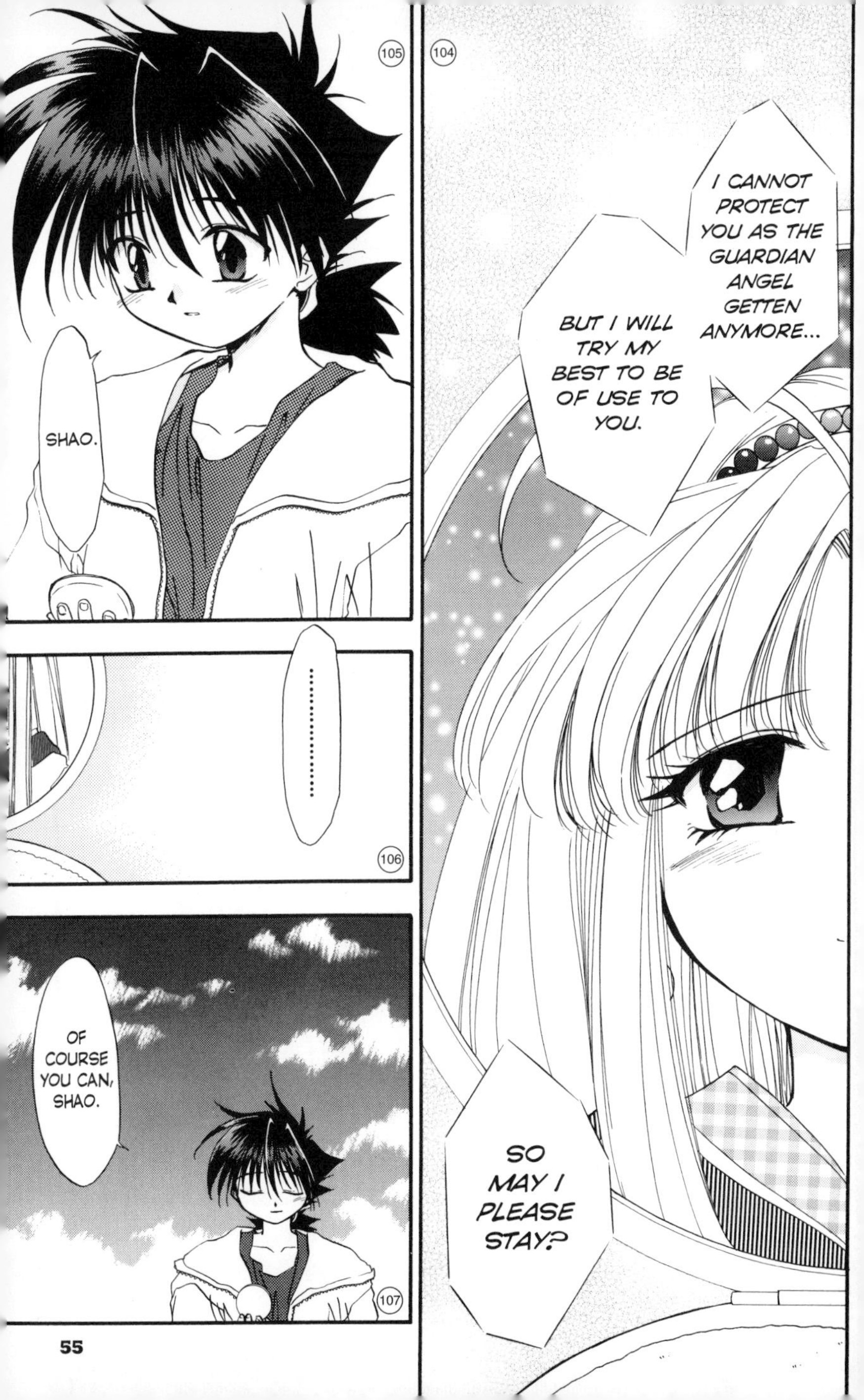
I CANNOT PROTECT YOU AS THE GUARDIAN ANGEL GETTEN ANYMORE...
BUT I WILL TRY MY BEST TO BE OF USE TO YOU.
SO MAY I PLEASE STAY?
SHAO.
....
OF COURSE YOU CAN, SHAO.

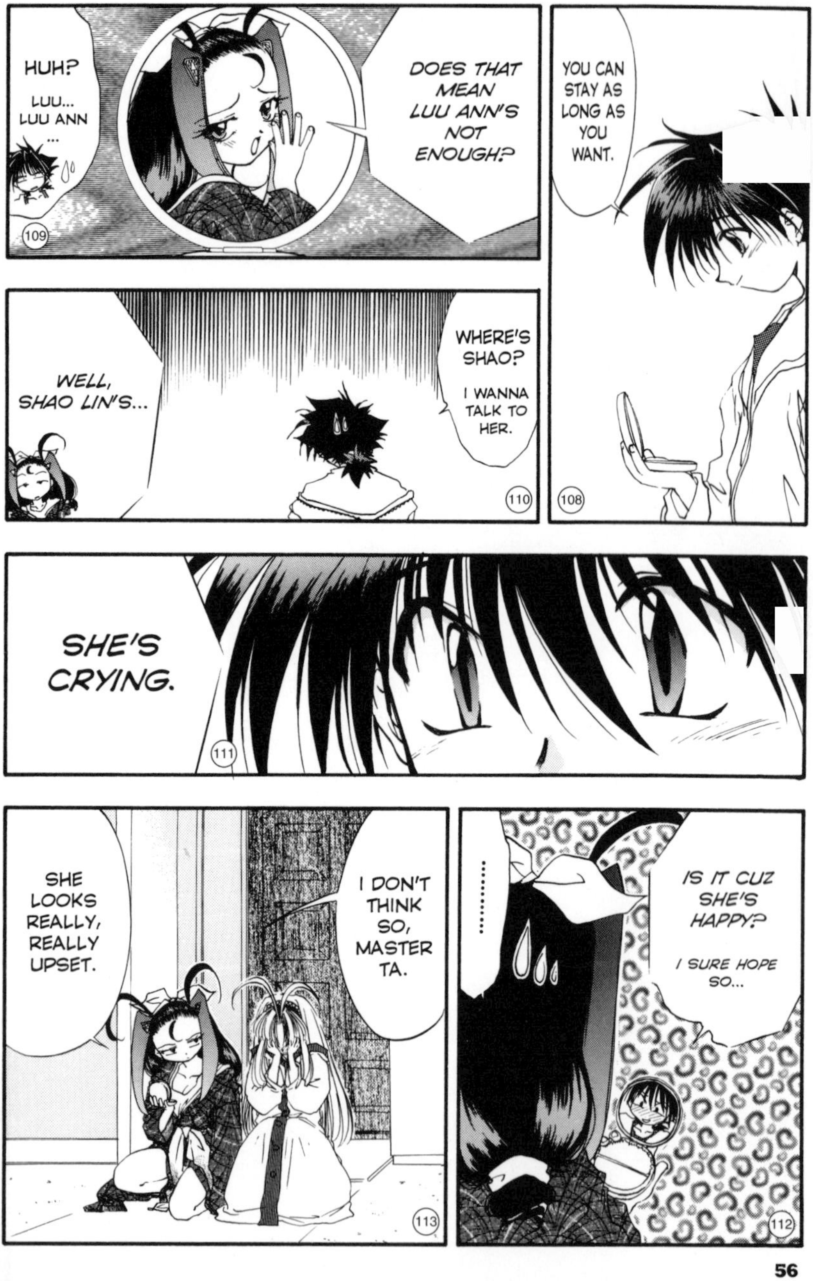
YOU CAN STAY AS LONG AS YOU WANT.
DOES THAT MEAN LUU ANN'S NOT ENOUGH?
HUH?
LUU... LUU ANN ...
WHERE'S SHAO?
I WANNA TALK TO HER.
WELL, SHAO LIN'S...
SHE'S CRYING.
IS IT CUZ SHE'S HAPPY?
I SURE HOPE SO...
....
I DON'T THINK SO, MASTER TA.
SHE LOOKS REALLY, REALLY UPSET.

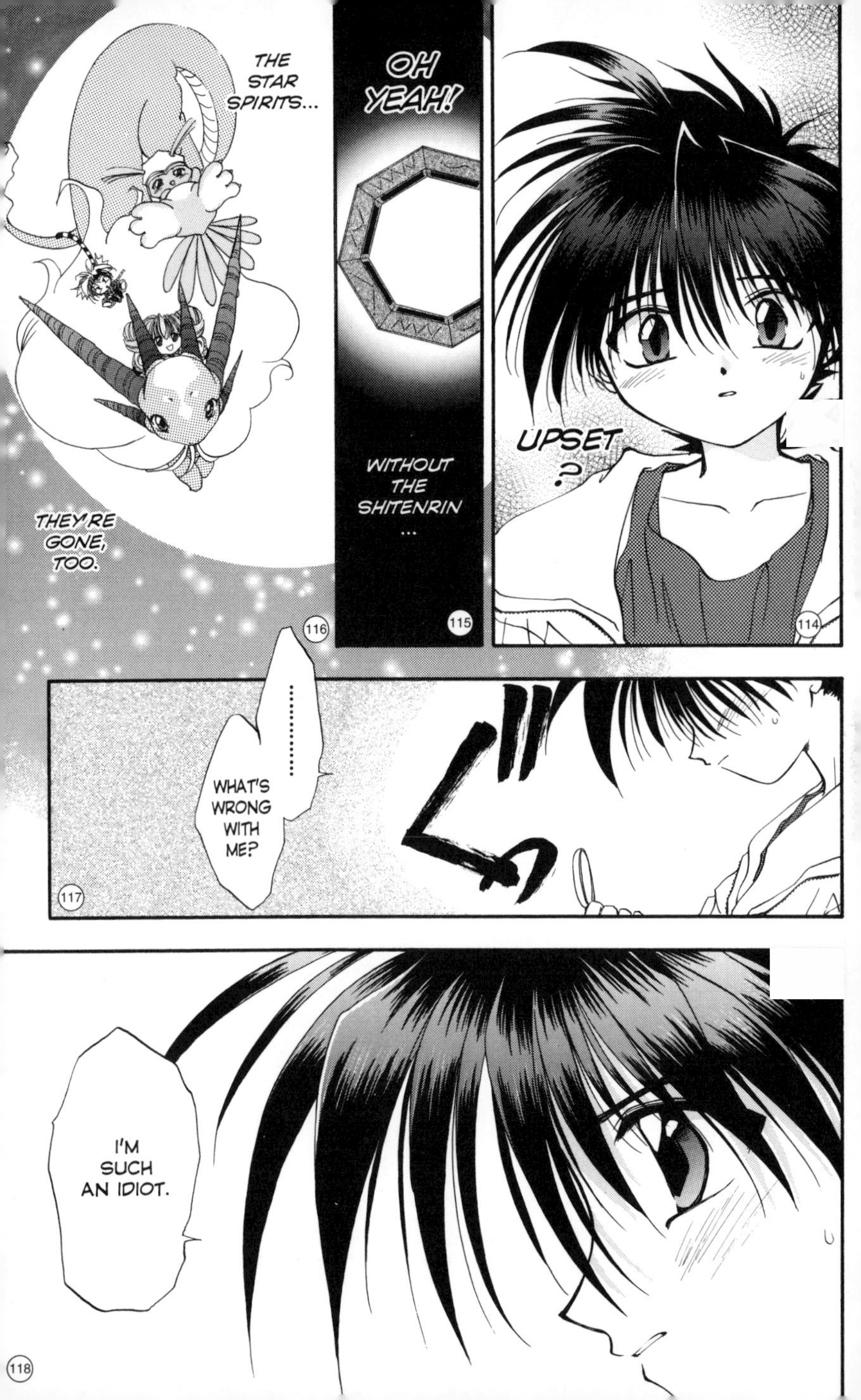
UPSET ?
OH YEAH!
WITHOUT THE SHITENRIN ...
THE STAR SPIRITS...
THEY'RE GONE, TOO.
....
WHAT'S WRONG WITH ME?
I'M SUCH AN IDIOT.

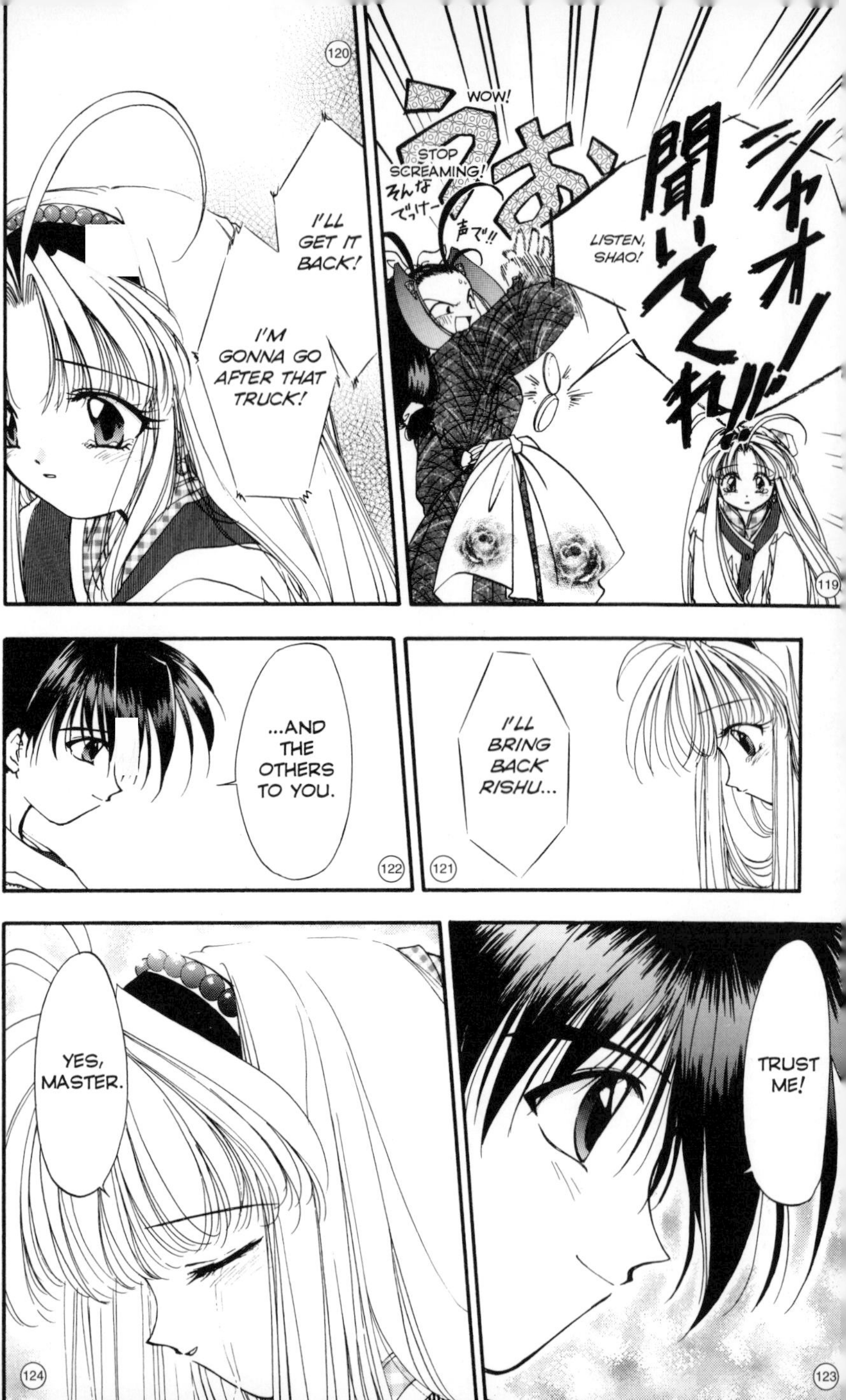

119
シャオ!!
聞いてくれ!!
LISTEN, SHAO!
うお
WOW!
STOP SCREAMING!
そんなでっけー声で!!
120
I'LL GET IT BACK!
I'M GONNA GO AFTER THAT TRUCK!
121
I'LL BRING BACK RISHU...
122
...AND THE OTHERS TO YOU.
123
TRUST ME!
124
YES, MASTER.

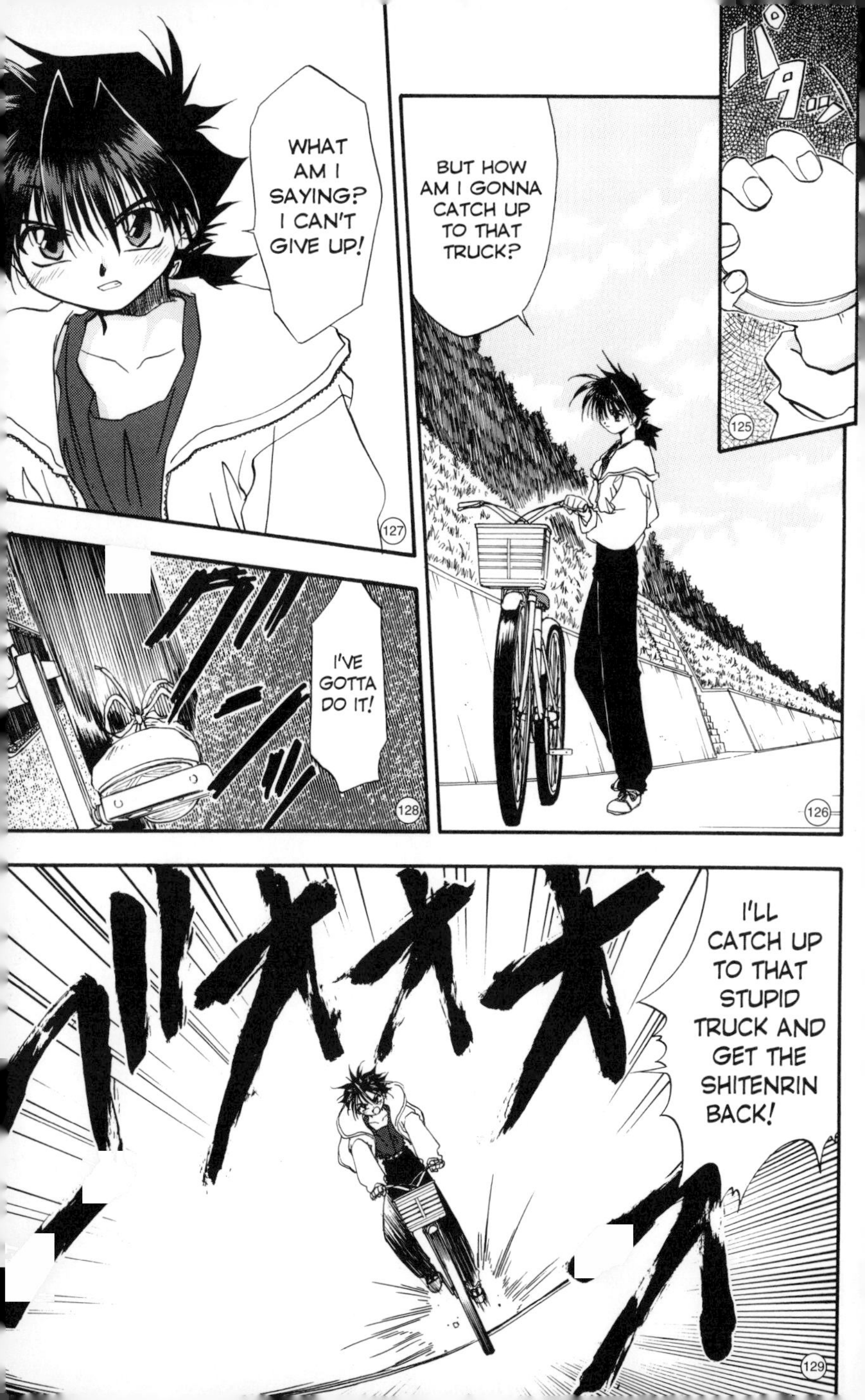
BUT HOW AM I GONNA CATCH UP TO THAT TRUCK?
WHAT AM I SAYING? I CAN'T GIVE UP!
I'VE GOTTA DO IT!
I'LL CATCH UP TO THAT STUPID TRUCK AND GET THE SHITENRIN BACK!

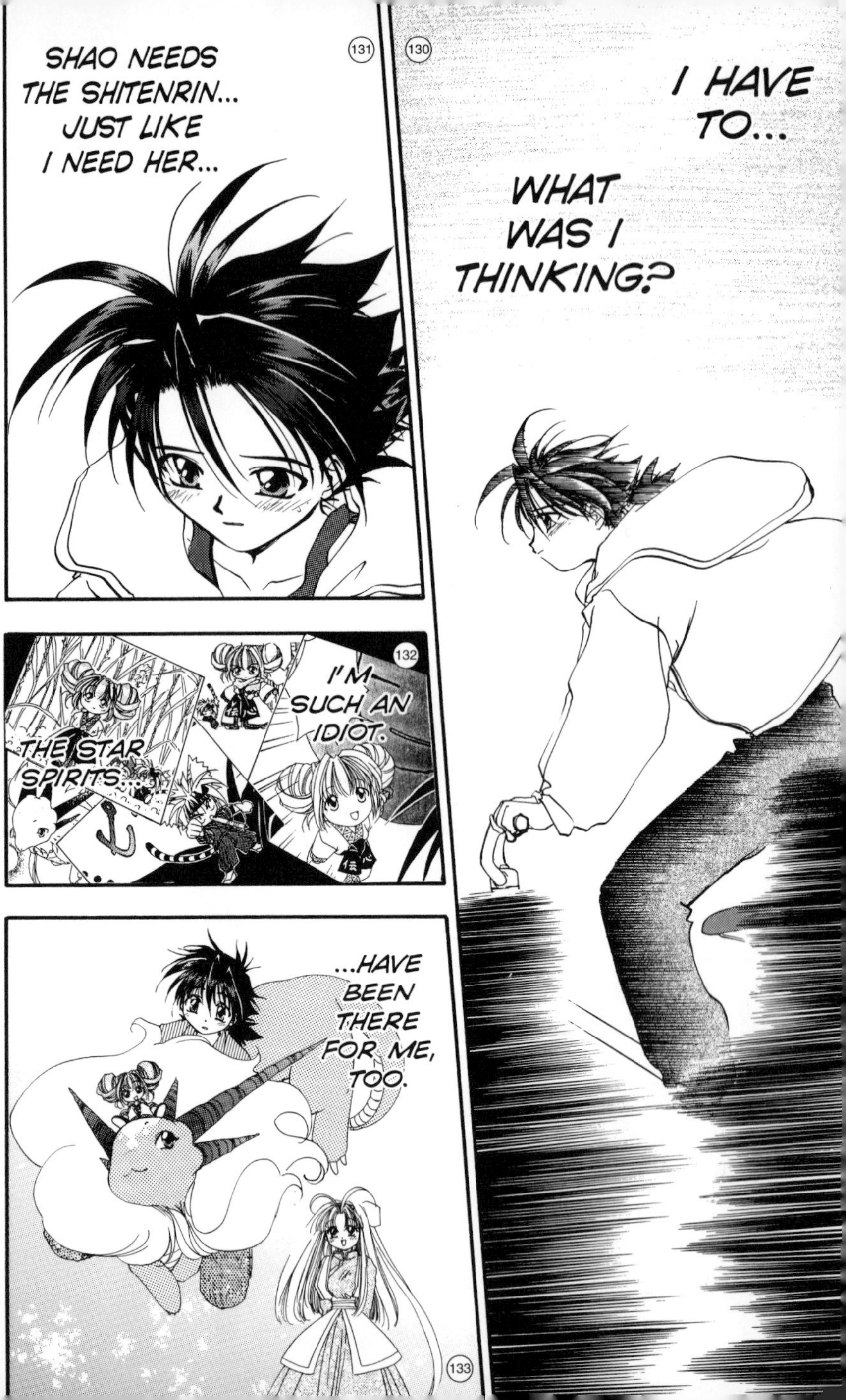
I HAVE TO...
WHAT WAS I THINKING?
SHAO NEEDS THE SHITENRIN... JUST LIKE I NEED HER...
I'M SUCH AN IDIOT.
THE STAR SPIRITS...
...HAVE BEEN THERE FOR ME, TOO.

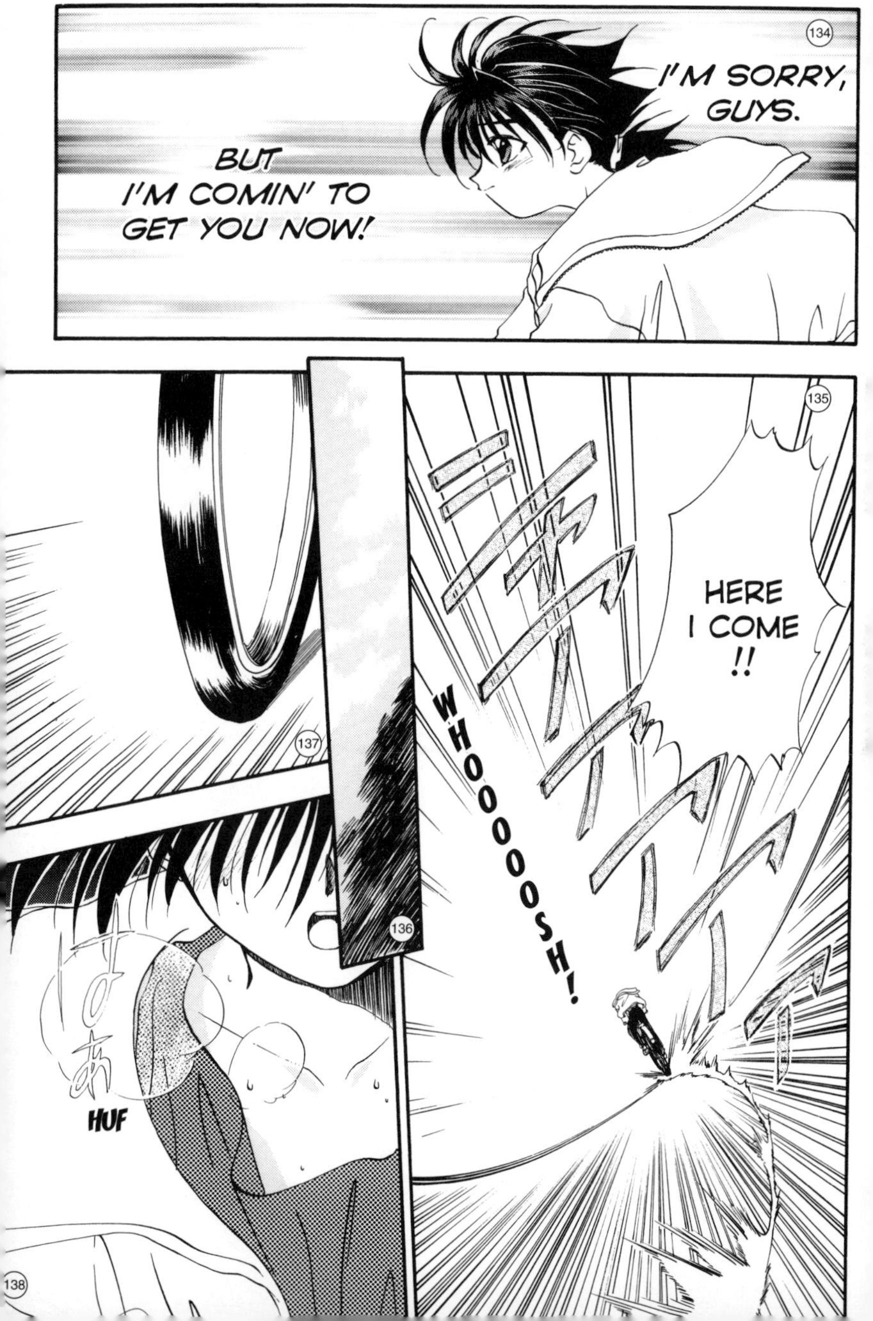
I'M SORRY, GUYS.
BUT I'M COMIN' TO GET YOU NOW!
HERE I COME!!
WHOOOOOOSH!
HUF

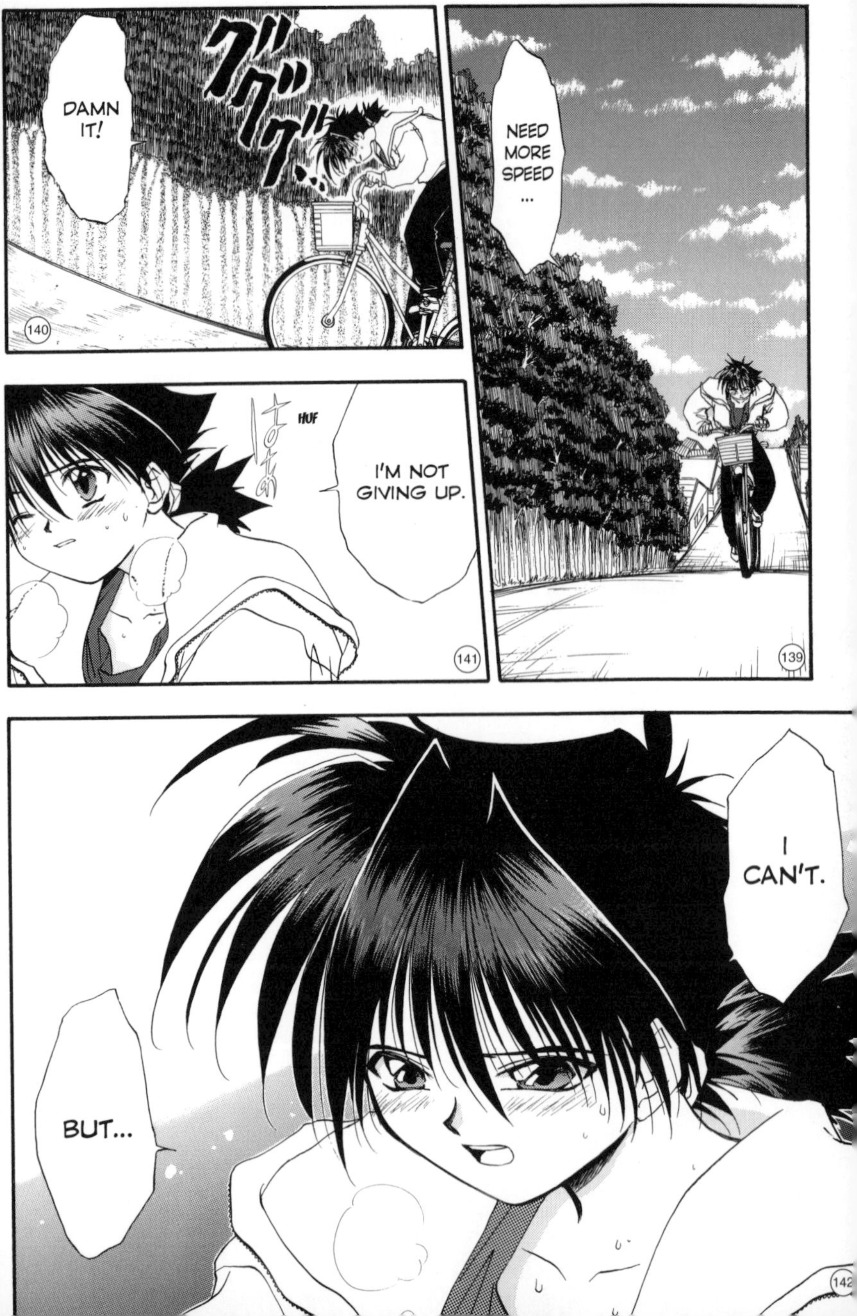
NEED MORE SPEED ...
DAMN IT!
HUF
I'M NOT GIVING UP.
I CAN'T.
BUT...

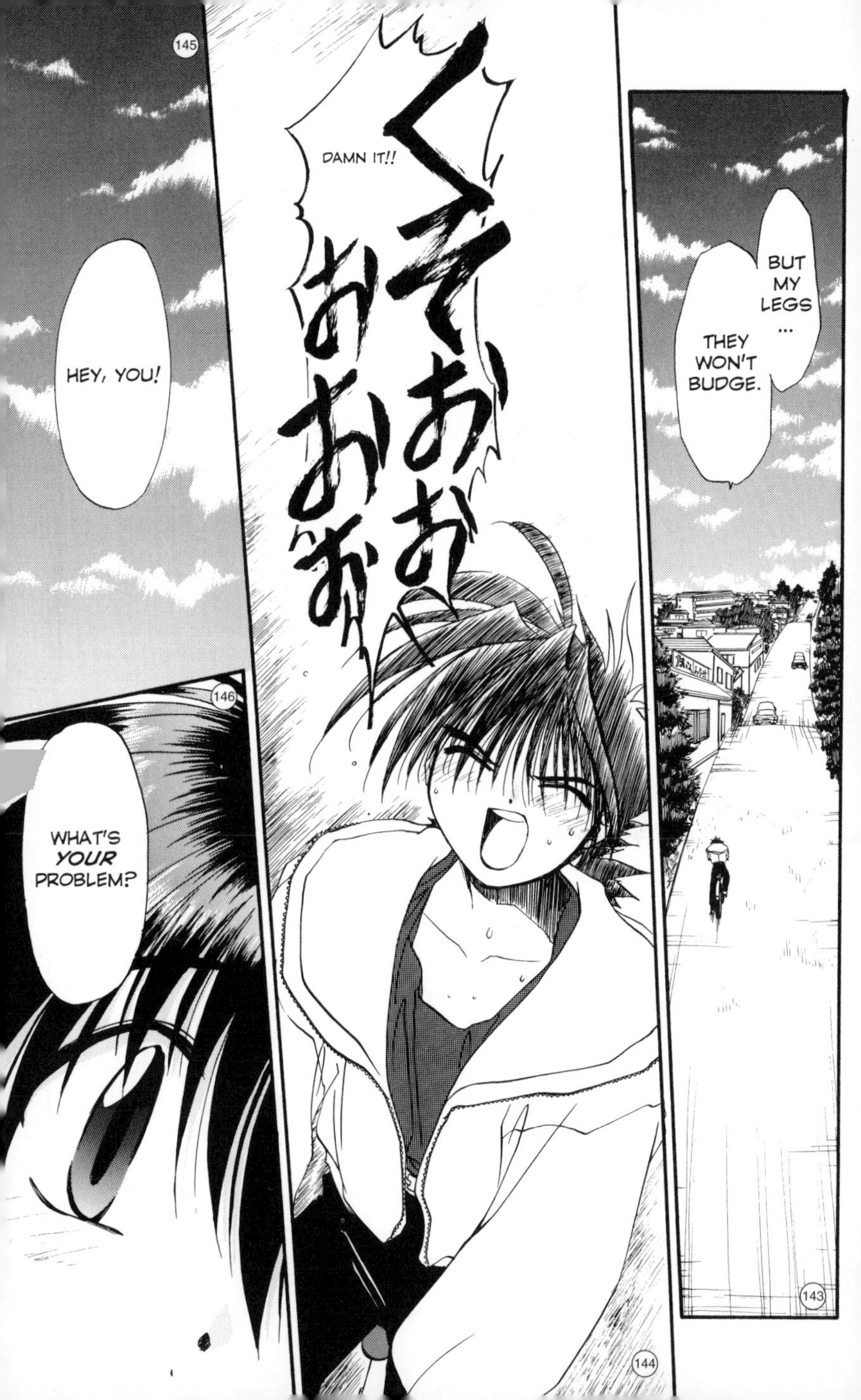
BUT MY LEGS ...
THEY WON'T BUDGE.
くそおおおおお
DAMN IT!!
HEY, YOU!
WHAT'S YOUR PROBLEM?

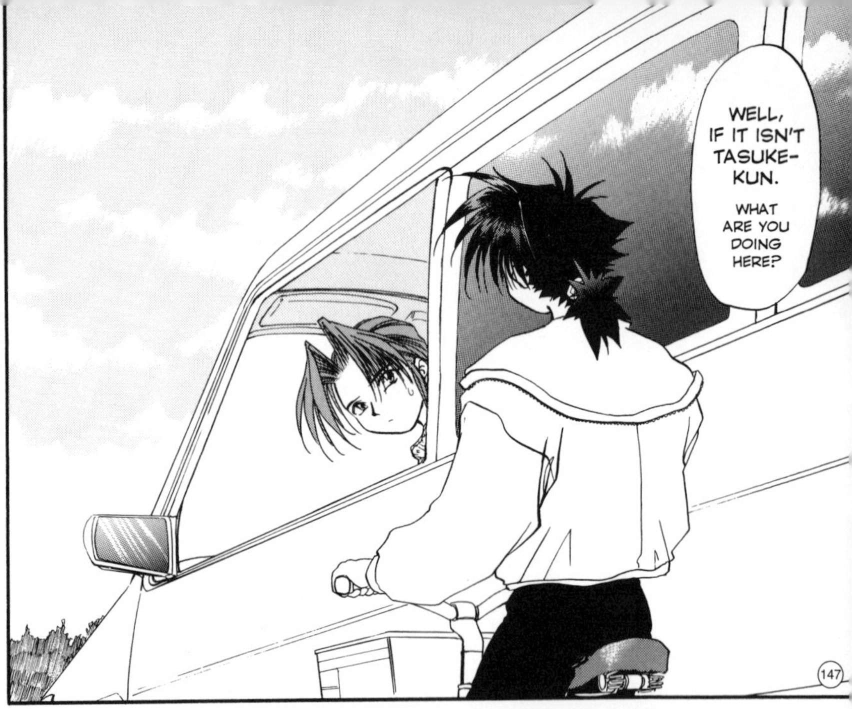
WELL, IF IT ISN'T TASUKE-KUN.
WHAT ARE YOU DOING HERE?
147

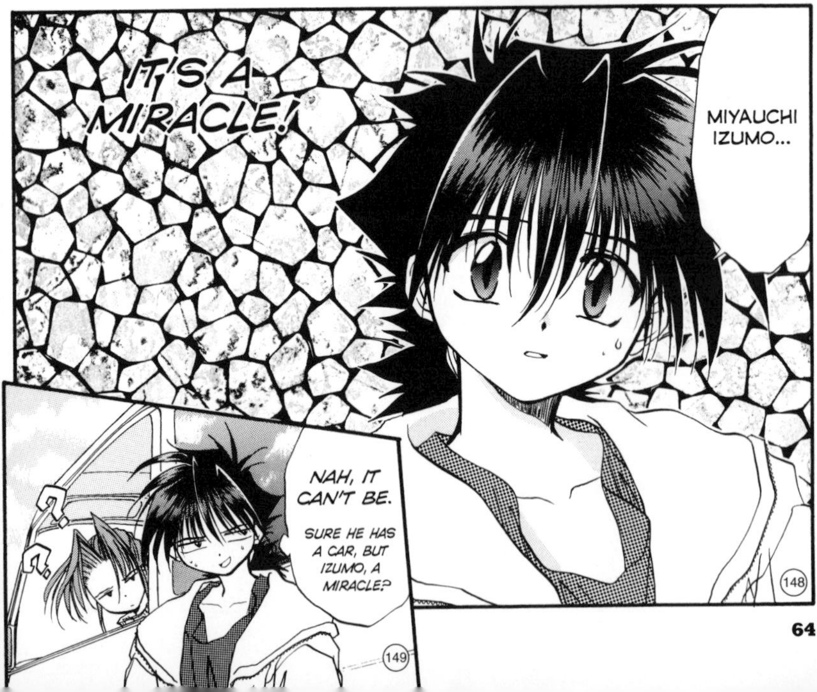
MIYAUCHI IZUMO...
IT'S A MIRACLE!
148
NAH, IT CAN'T BE.
SURE HE HAS A CAR, BUT IZUMO, A MIRACLE?
149

CHAPTER 21: GETTING THE SHITENRIN BACK! (PART 2)

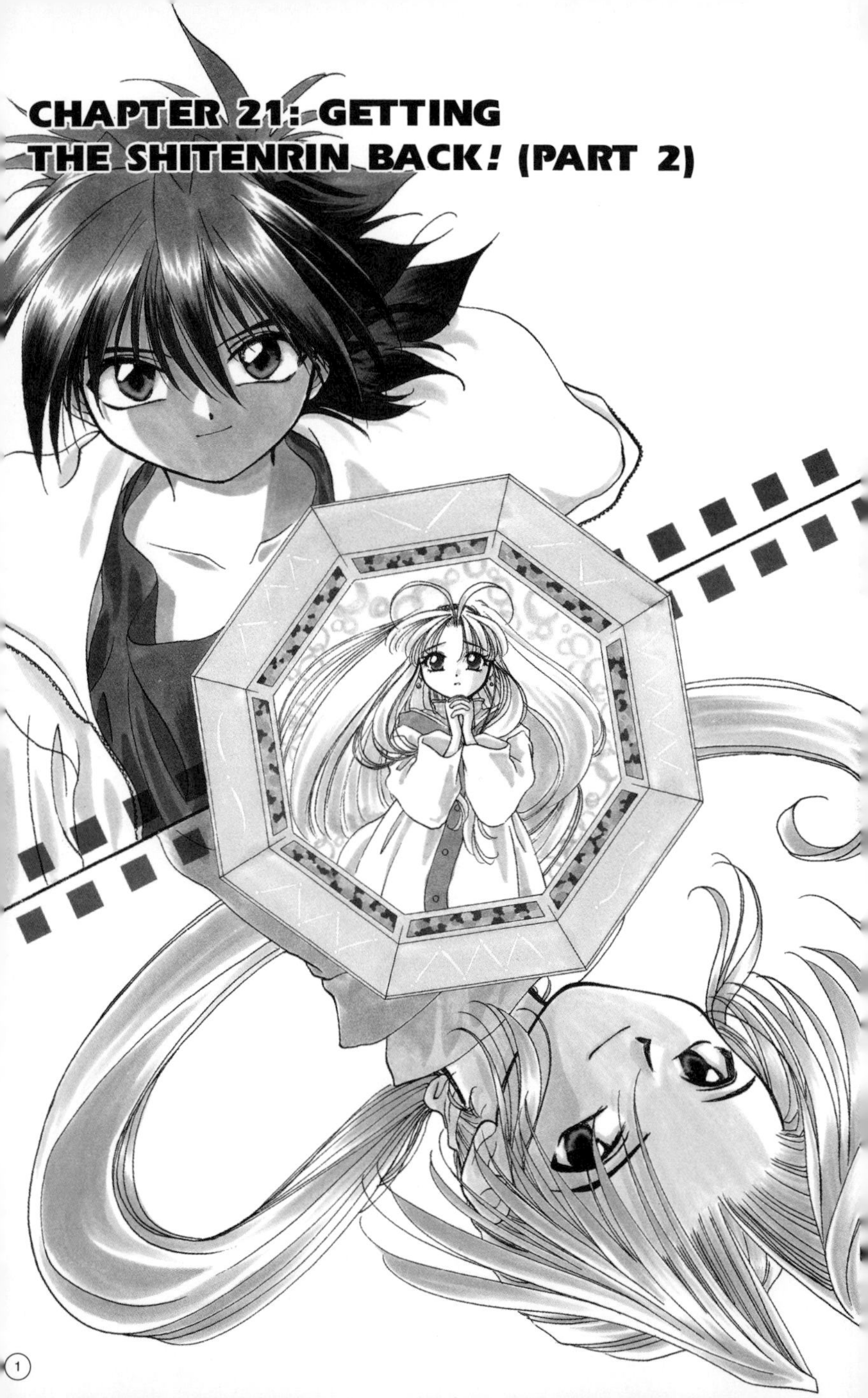

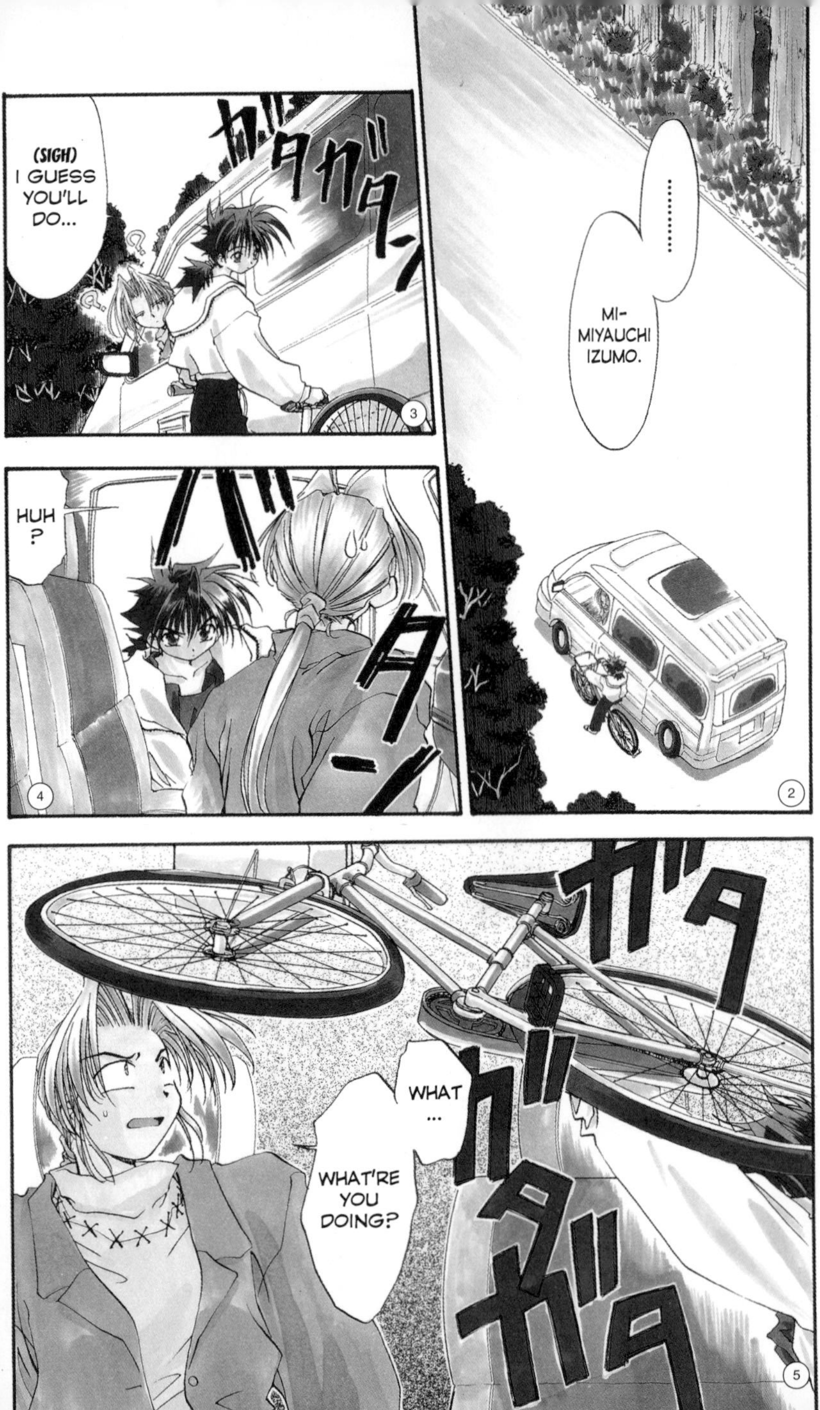
......
MI- MIYAUCHI IZUMO.
(SIGH) I GUESS YOU'LL DO...
HUH ?
WHAT ...
WHAT'RE YOU DOING?

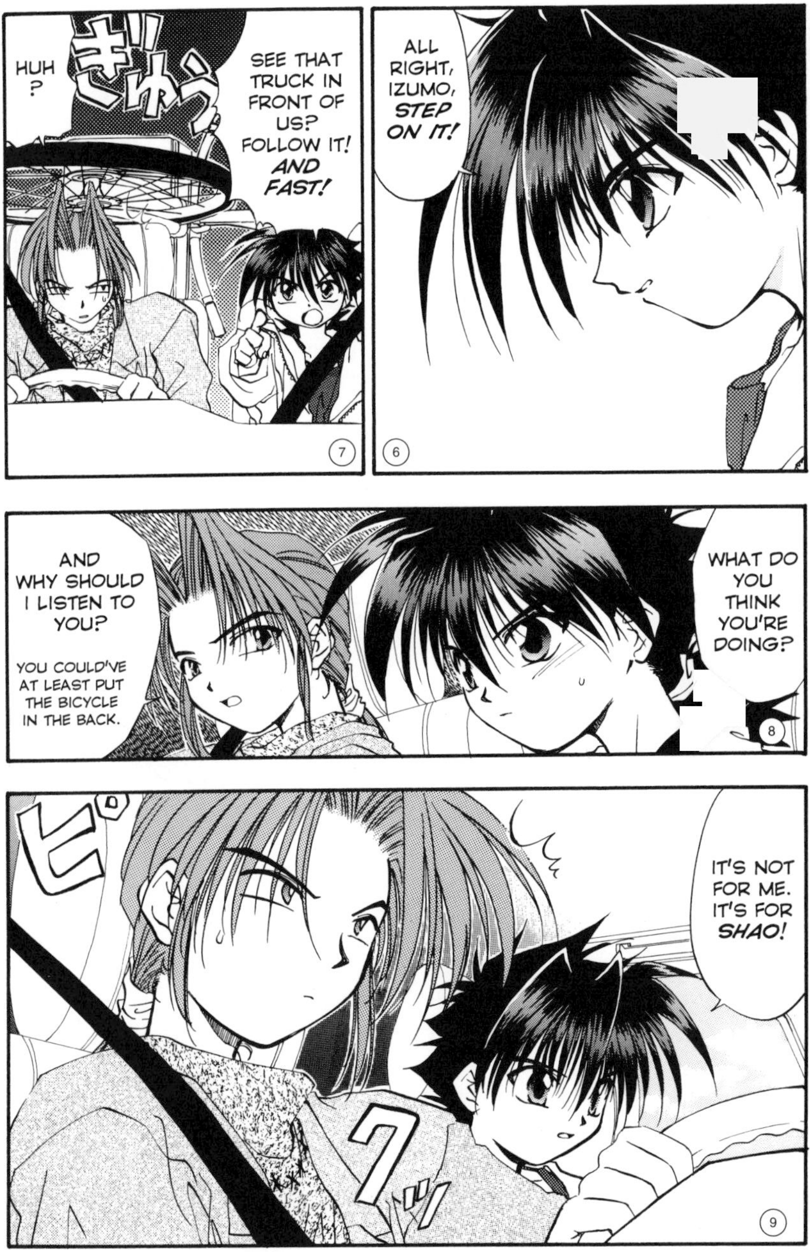
ALL RIGHT, IZUMO, STEP ON IT!
SEE THAT TRUCK IN FRONT OF US? FOLLOW IT! AND FAST!
HUH?
WHAT DO YOU THINK YOU'RE DOING?
AND WHY SHOULD I LISTEN TO YOU?
YOU COULD'VE AT LEAST PUT THE BICYCLE IN THE BACK.
IT'S NOT FOR ME. IT'S FOR SHAO!

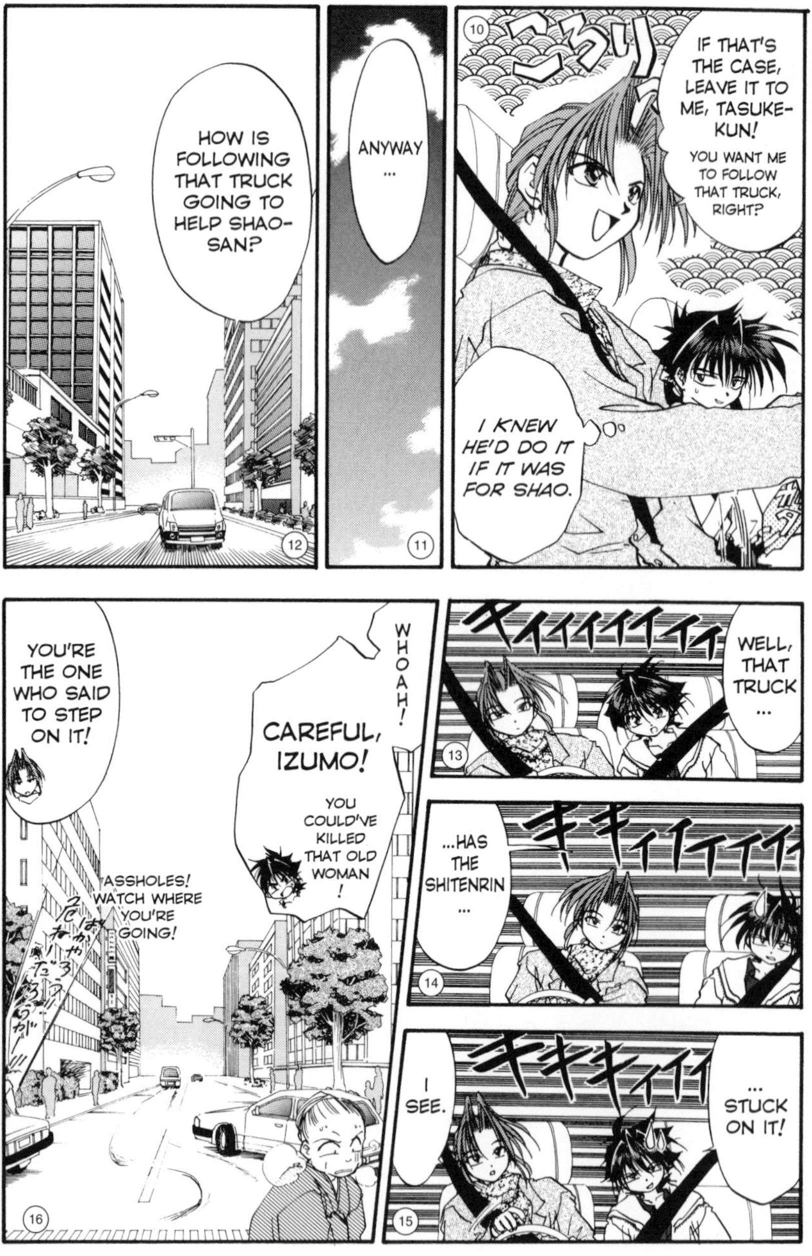
IF THAT'S THE CASE, LEAVE IT TO ME, TASUKE-KUN!
YOU WANT ME TO FOLLOW THAT TRUCK, RIGHT?
I KNEW HE'D DO IT IF IT WAS FOR SHAO.
ANYWAY ...
HOW IS FOLLOWING THAT TRUCK GOING TO HELP SHAO-SAN?
WELL, THAT TRUCK ...
...HAS THE SHITENRIN ...
... STUCK ON IT!
I SEE.
WHOAH!
CAREFUL, IZUMO!
YOU COULD'VE KILLED THAT OLD WOMAN!
YOU'RE THE ONE WHO SAID TO STEP ON IT!
ASSHOLES! WATCH WHERE YOU'RE GOING!

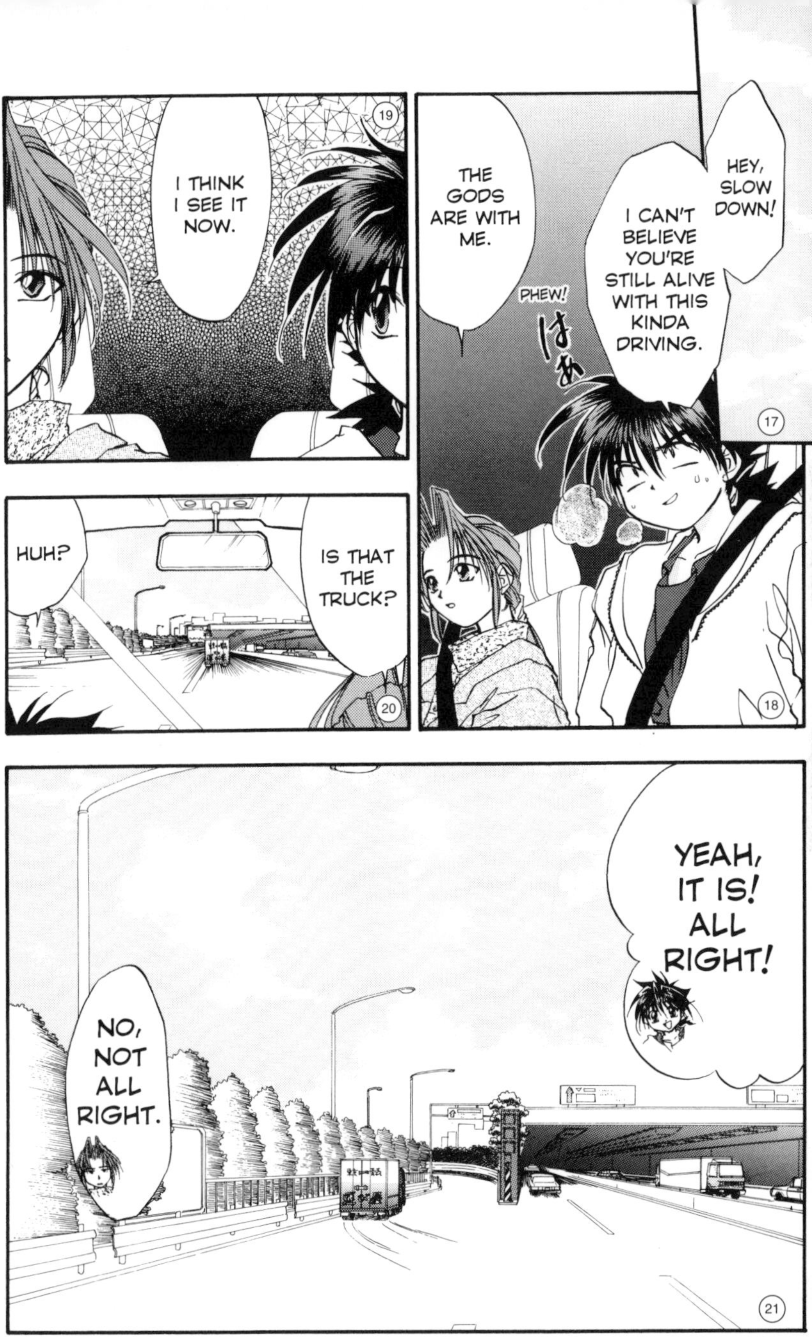
HEY, SLOW DOWN!
I CAN'T BELIEVE YOU'RE STILL ALIVE WITH THIS KINDA DRIVING.
THE GODS ARE WITH ME.
PHEW! はぁ
I THINK I SEE IT NOW.
IS THAT THE TRUCK?
HUH?
YEAH, IT IS! ALL RIGHT!
NO, NOT ALL RIGHT.

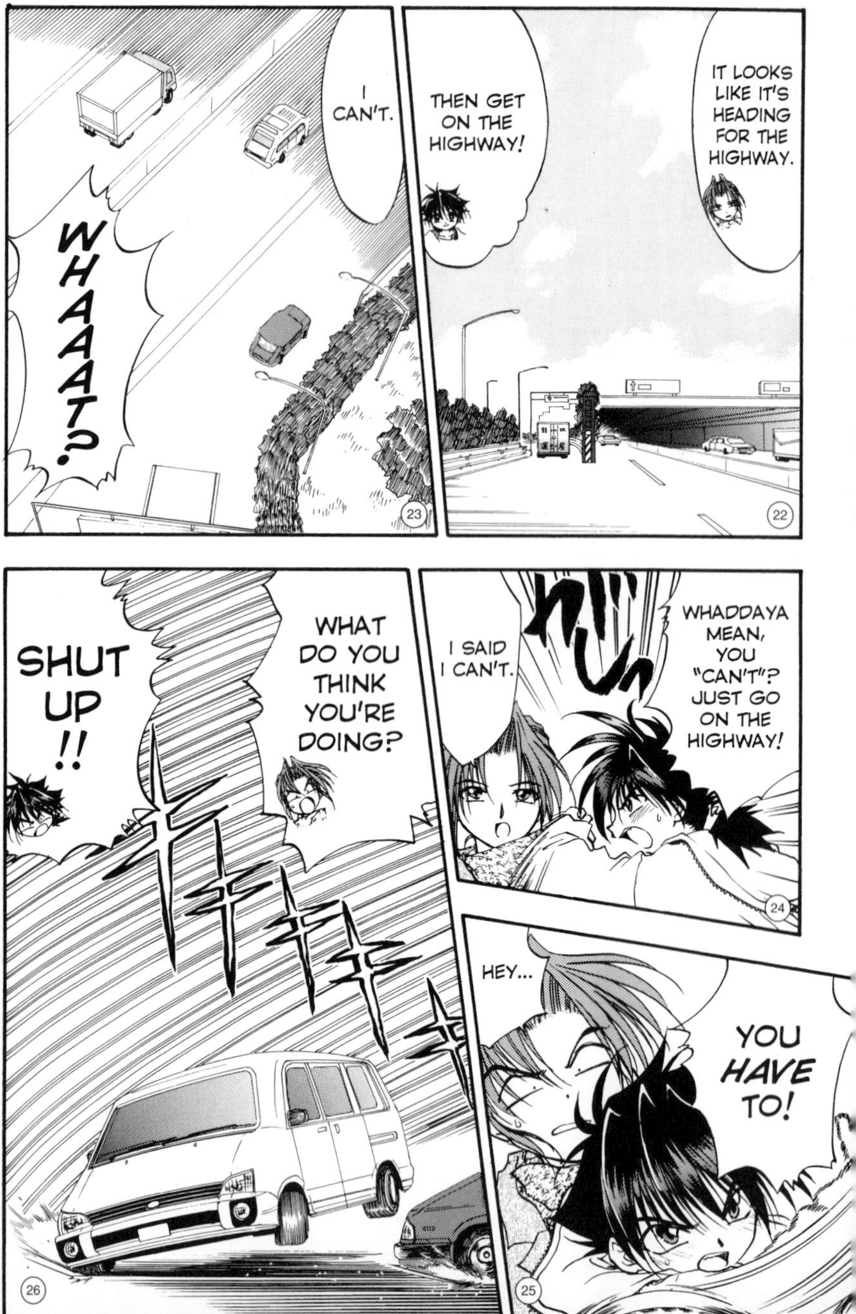
IT LOOKS LIKE IT'S HEADING FOR THE HIGHWAY.
THEN GET ON THE HIGHWAY!
I CAN'T.
WHAAAAT?
WHADDAYA MEAN, YOU "CAN'T"? JUST GO ON THE HIGHWAY!
I SAID I CAN'T.
HEY...
YOU HAVE TO!
WHAT DO YOU THINK YOU'RE DOING?
SHUT UP!!

(PHEW!) NOW ALL WE'VE GOTTA DO IS WAIT FOR THAT TRUCK TO STOP.

I SURE HOPE TO GOD IT DOES THAT SOON.

HUH?

?

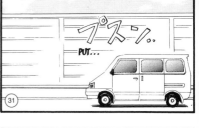

PUT...

SIGH...

STOP

HUH?

PUT, PUT

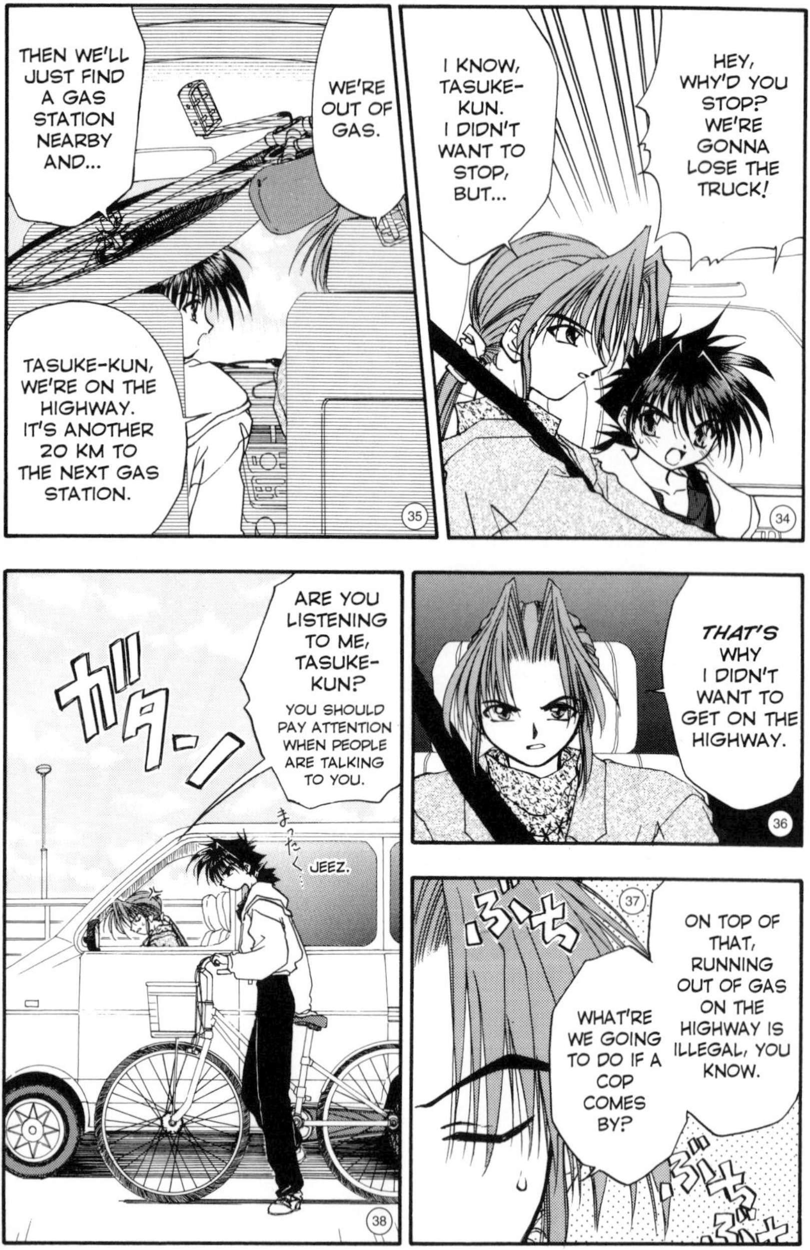
HEY, WHY'D YOU STOP? WE'RE GONNA LOSE THE TRUCK!
I KNOW, TASUKE-KUN. I DIDN'T WANT TO STOP, BUT...
WE'RE OUT OF GAS.
THEN WE'LL JUST FIND A GAS STATION NEARBY AND...
TASUKE-KUN, WE'RE ON THE HIGHWAY. IT'S ANOTHER 20 KM TO THE NEXT GAS STATION.
THAT'S WHY I DIDN'T WANT TO GET ON THE HIGHWAY.
ON TOP OF THAT, RUNNING OUT OF GAS ON THE HIGHWAY IS ILLEGAL, YOU KNOW.
WHAT'RE WE GOING TO DO IF A COP COMES BY?
ガタ-ン
ARE YOU LISTENING TO ME, TASUKE-KUN? YOU SHOULD PAY ATTENTION WHEN PEOPLE ARE TALKING TO YOU.
まったく…
JEEZ.

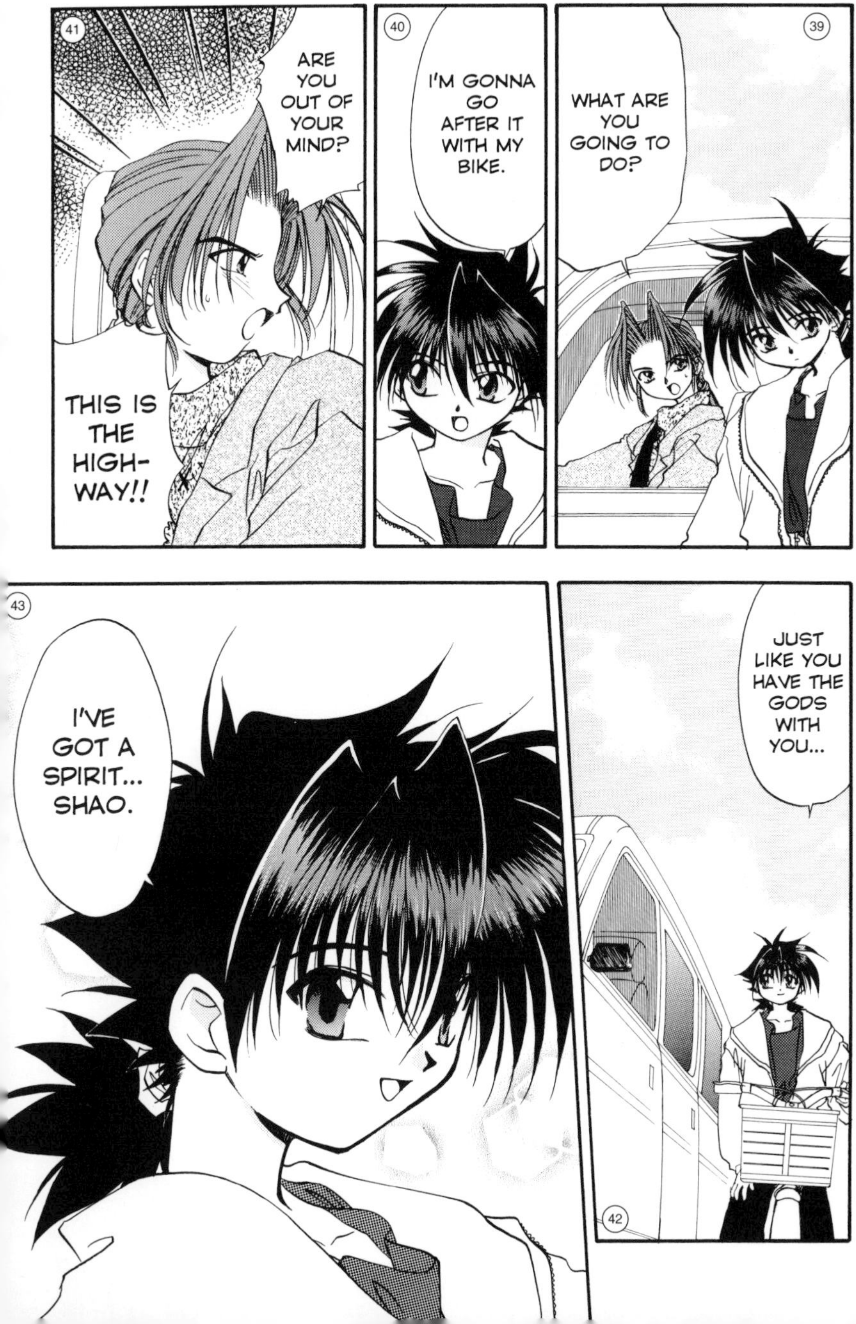
WHAT ARE YOU GOING TO DO?
I'M GONNA GO AFTER IT WITH MY BIKE.
ARE YOU OUT OF YOUR MIND?
THIS IS THE HIGH-WAY!!
JUST LIKE YOU HAVE THE GODS WITH YOU...
I'VE GOT A SPIRIT... SHAO.

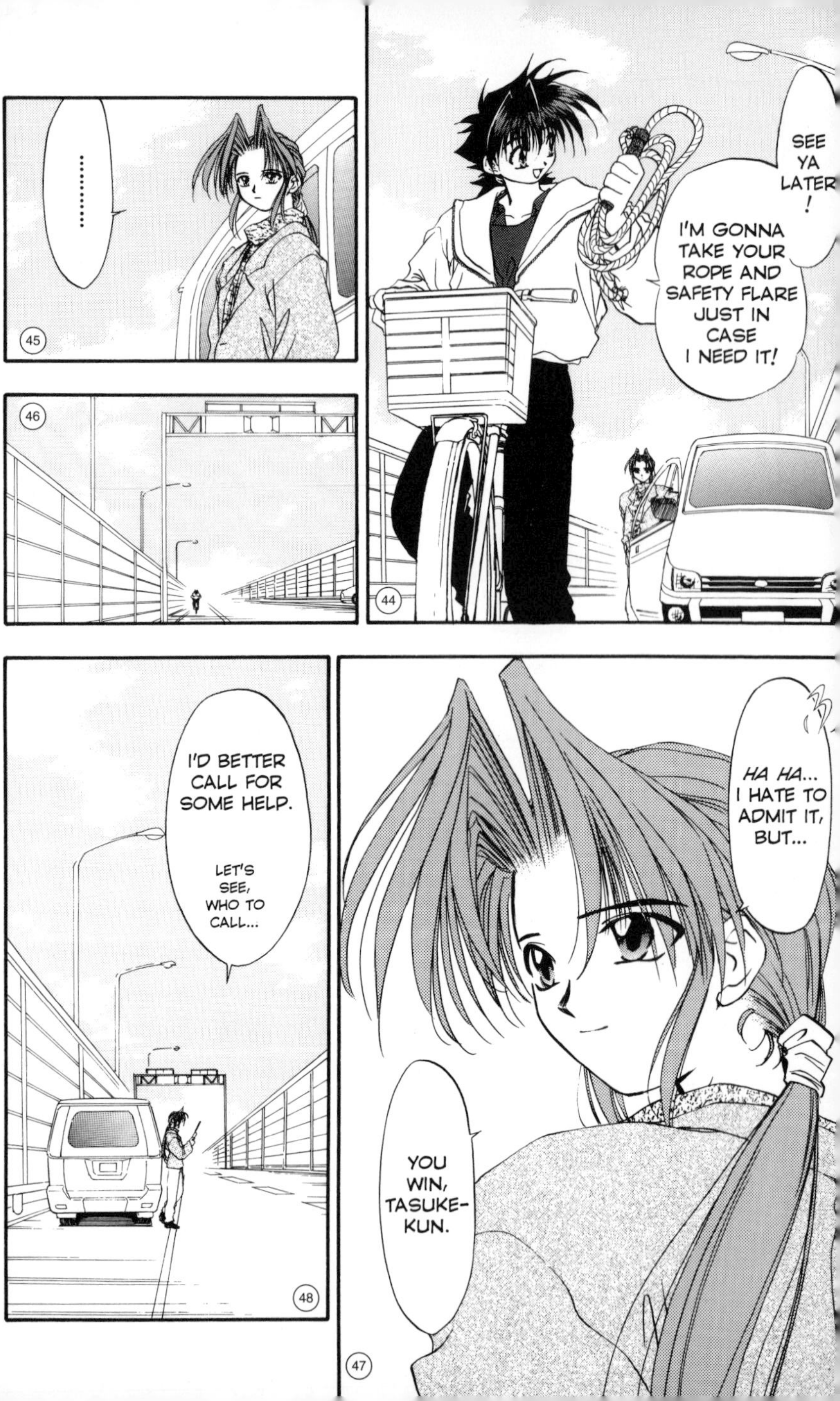
SEE YA LATER!
I'M GONNA TAKE YOUR ROPE AND SAFETY FLARE JUST IN CASE I NEED IT!
....
HA HA... I HATE TO ADMIT IT, BUT...
YOU WIN, TASUKE-KUN.
I'D BETTER CALL FOR SOME HELP.
LET'S SEE, WHO TO CALL...

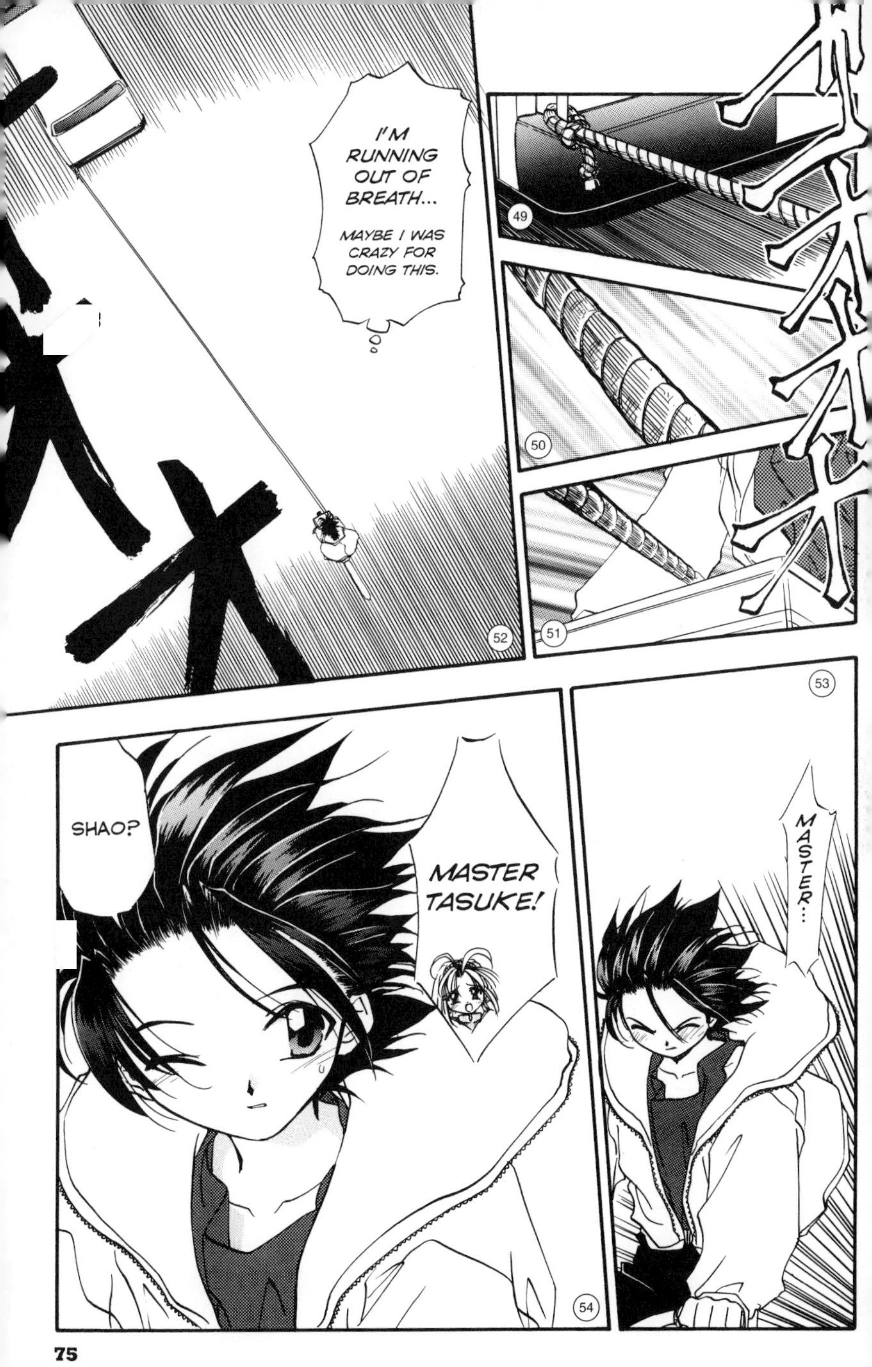
I'M RUNNING OUT OF BREATH...
MAYBE I WAS CRAZY FOR DOING THIS.
MASTER...
MASTER TASUKE!
SHAO?

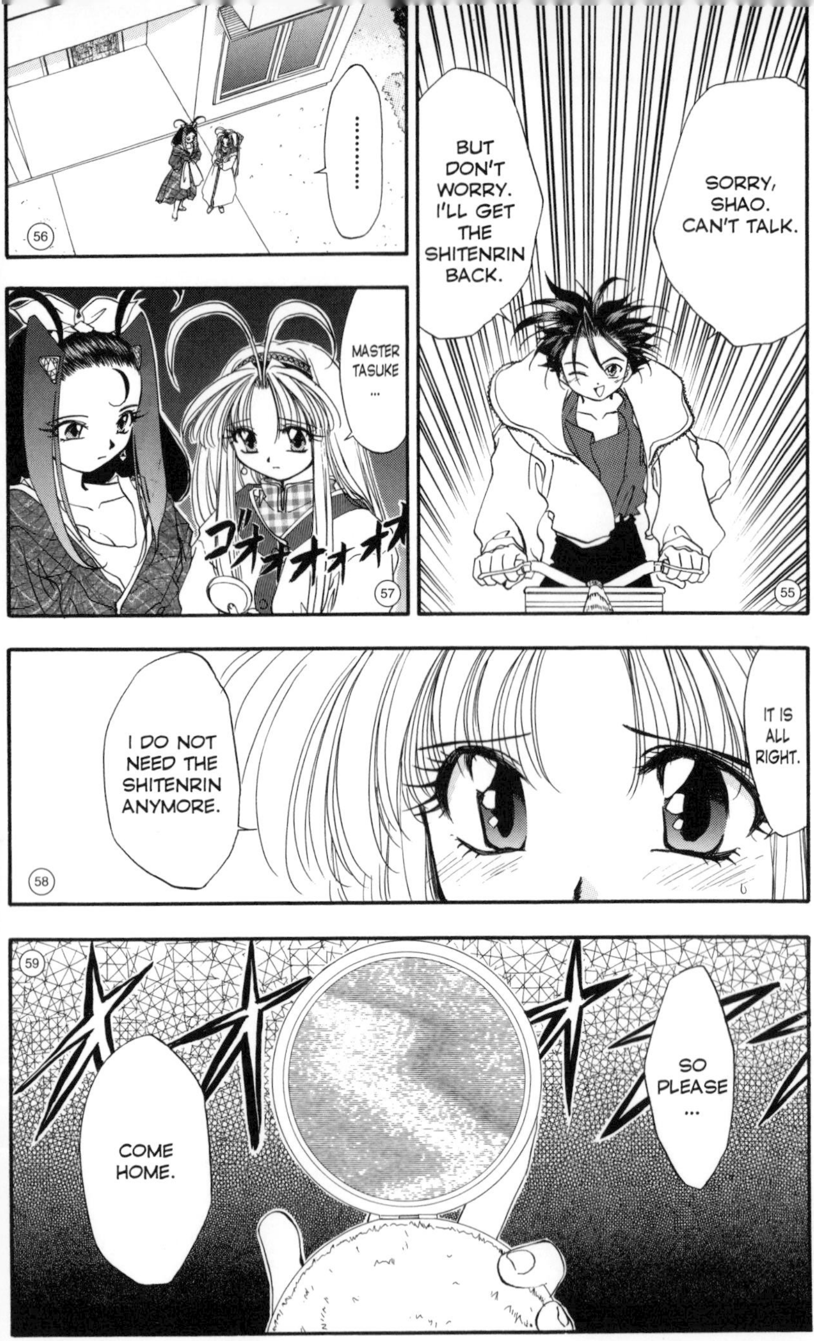
SORRY, SHAO. CAN'T TALK.
BUT DON'T WORRY. I'LL GET THE SHITENRIN BACK.
....
MASTER TASUKE ...
IT IS ALL RIGHT.
I DO NOT NEED THE SHITENRIN ANYMORE.
SO PLEASE ...
COME HOME.

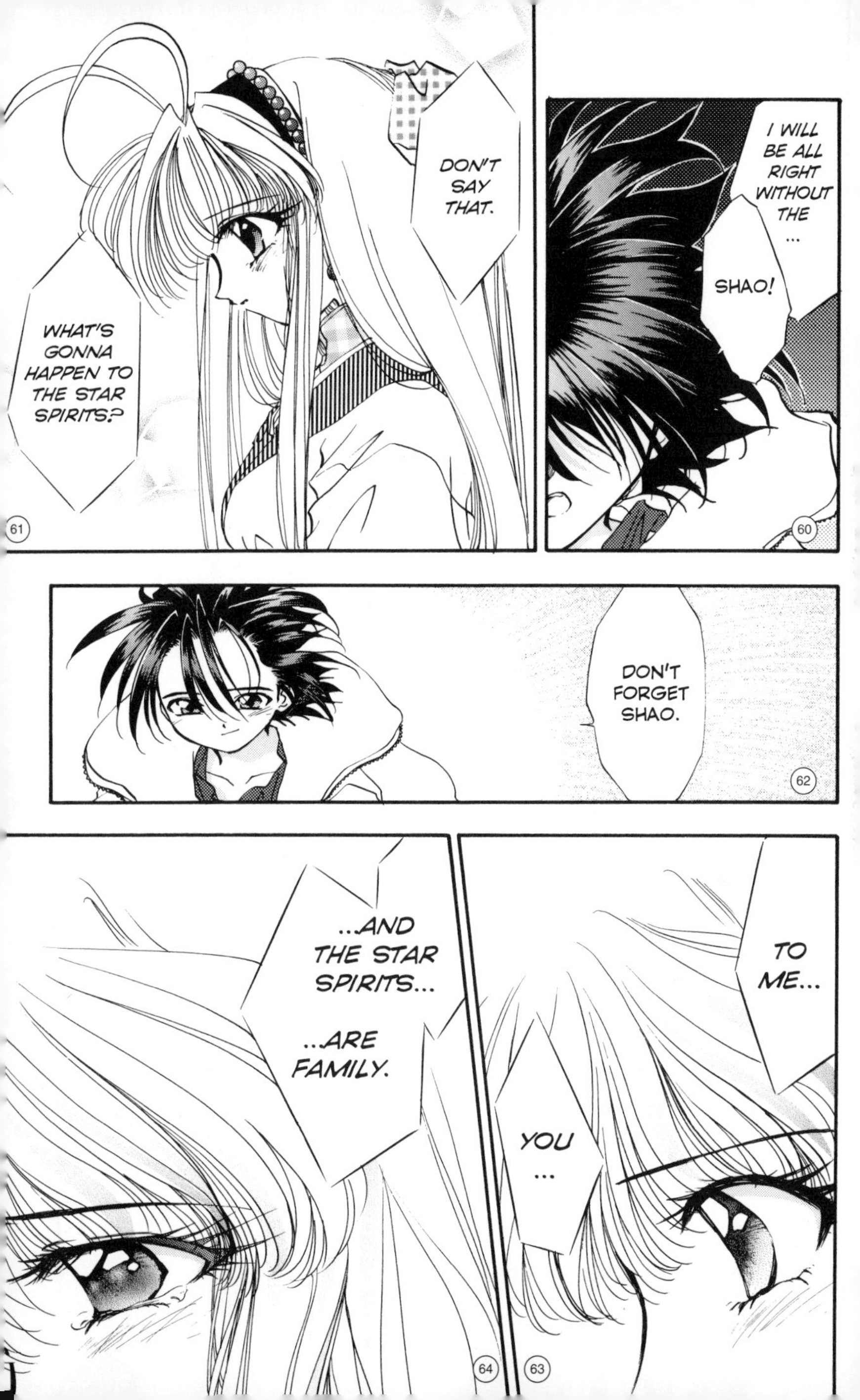
I WILL BE ALL RIGHT WITHOUT THE ...
SHAO!
DON'T SAY THAT.
WHAT'S GONNA HAPPEN TO THE STAR SPIRITS?
DON'T FORGET SHAO.
TO ME...
YOU ...
...AND THE STAR SPIRITS...
...ARE FAMILY.

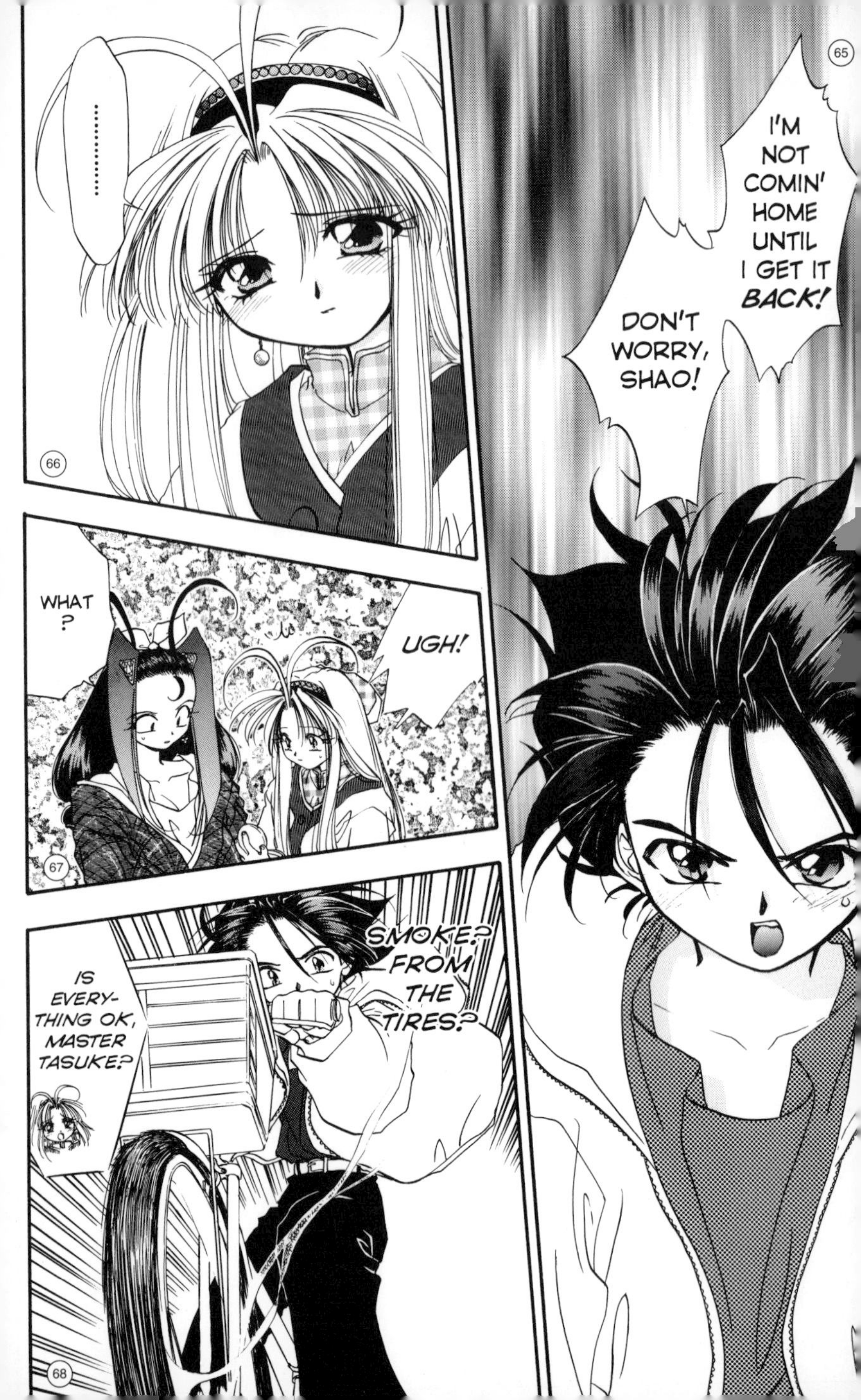
I'M NOT COMIN' HOME UNTIL I GET IT BACK!
DON'T WORRY, SHAO!
....
UGH!
WHAT?
SMOKE? FROM THE TIRES?
IS EVERY-THING OK, MASTER TASUKE?

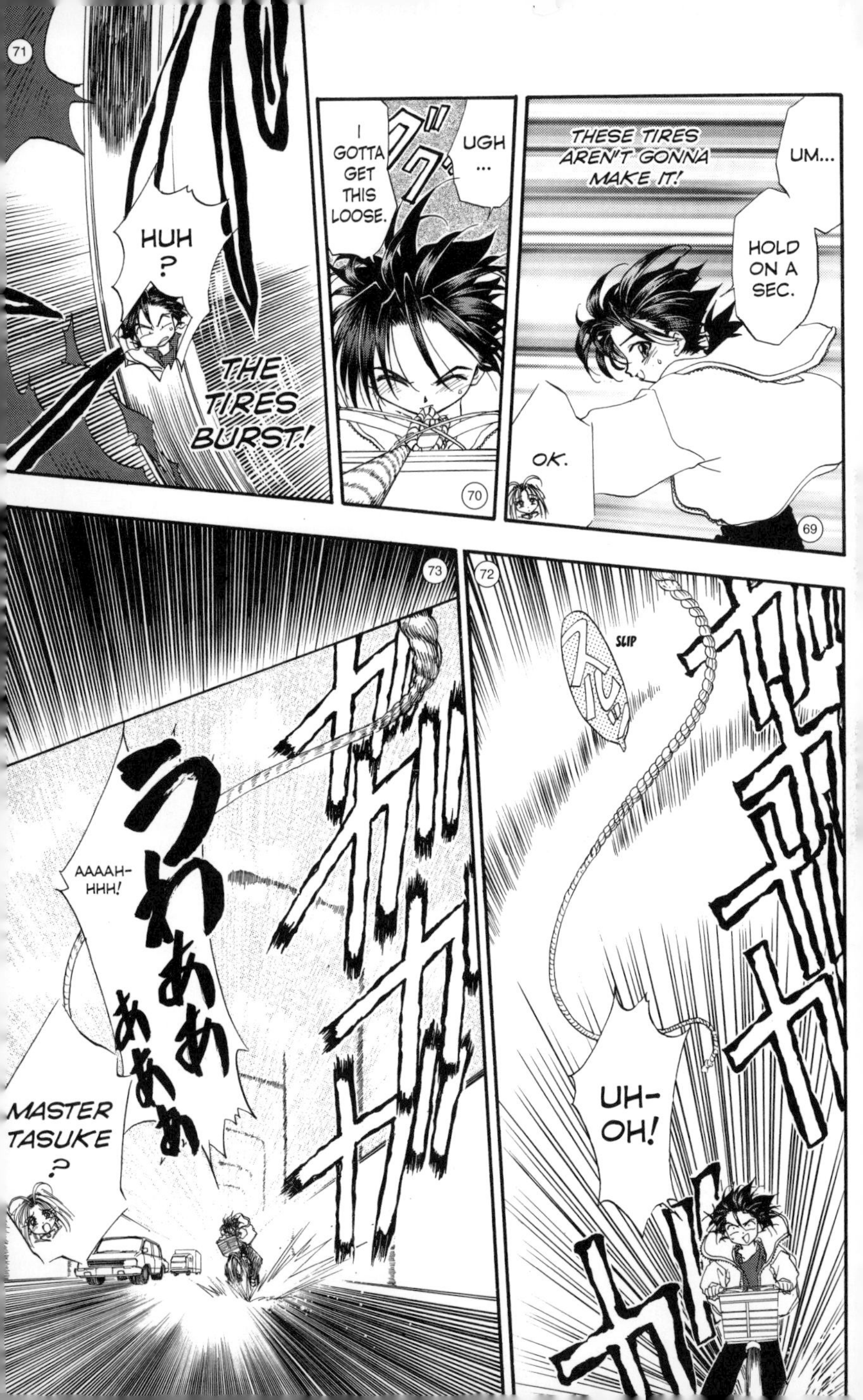

UM...
HOLD ON A SEC.
THESE TIRES AREN'T GONNA MAKE IT!
OK.
UGH ...
I GOTTA GET THIS LOOSE.
HUH ?
THE TIRES BURST!
SLIP
UH-OH!
AAAAH-HHH!
MASTER TASUKE ?

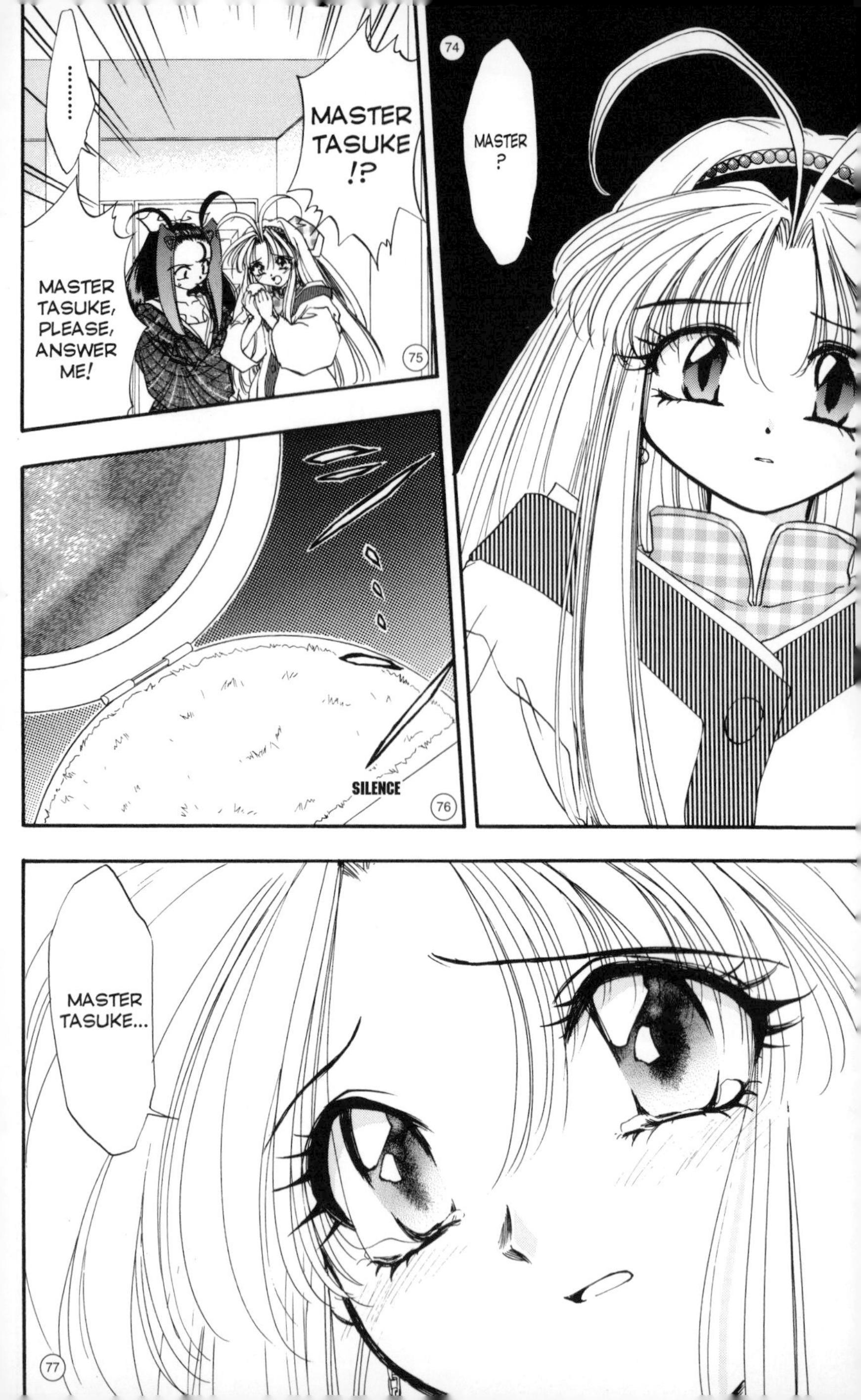
MASTER ?
MASTER TASUKE !?
....
MASTER TASUKE, PLEASE, ANSWER ME!
SILENCE
MASTER TASUKE...

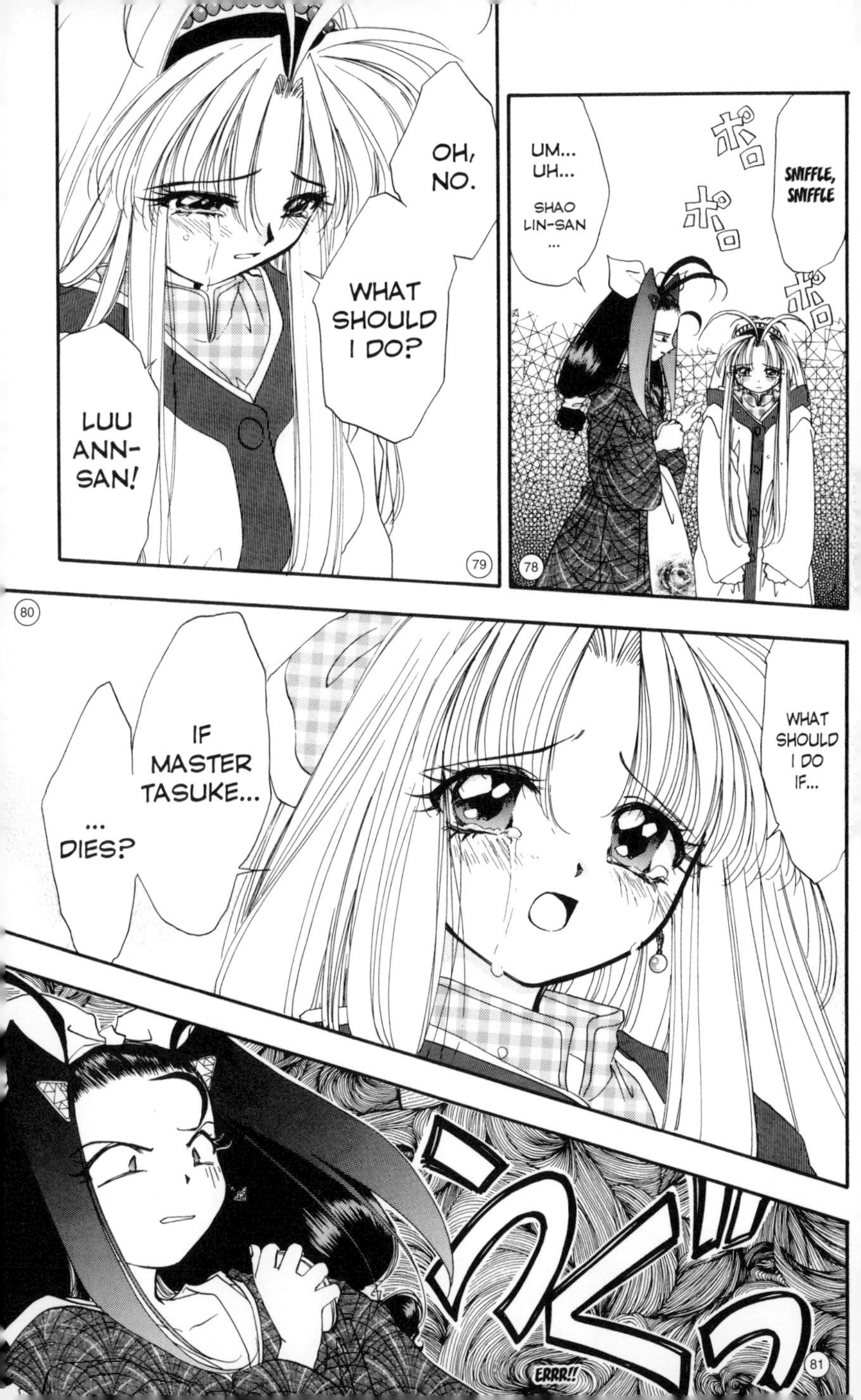
ポロ
ポロ
ポロ
SNIFFLE, SNIFFLE
UM... UH...
SHAO LIN-SAN ...
78
OH, NO.
WHAT SHOULD I DO?
LUU ANN-SAN!
79
80
WHAT SHOULD I DO IF...
IF MASTER TASUKE...
... DIES?
ERRR!!
81

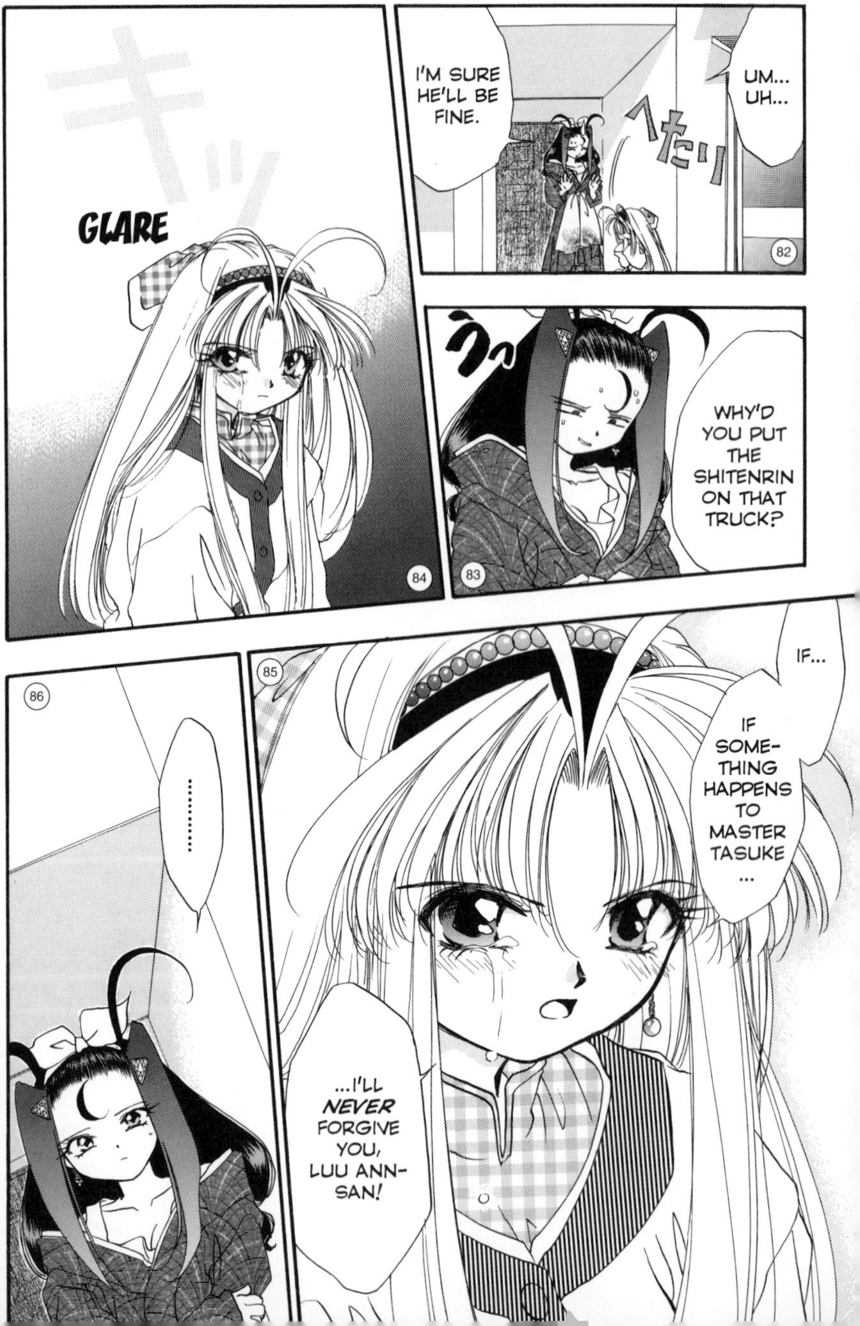
UM... UH...
I'M SURE HE'LL BE FINE.
へたり
うっ
WHY'D YOU PUT THE SHITENRIN ON THAT TRUCK?
キッ
GLARE
IF...
IF SOME-THING HAPPENS TO MASTER TASUKE ...
...I'LL *NEVER* FORGIVE YOU, LUU ANN-SAN!
....

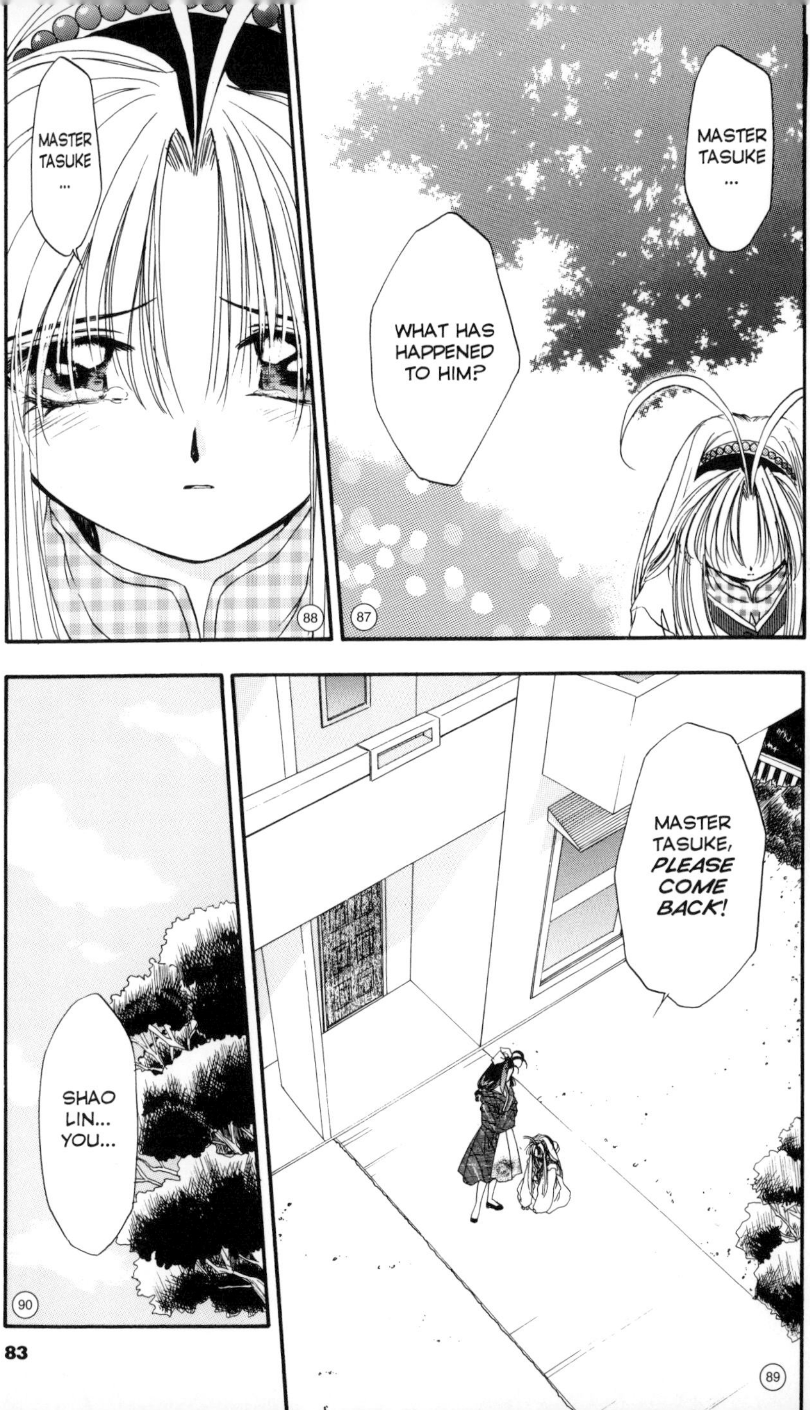

MASTER TASUKE ...
WHAT HAS HAPPENED TO HIM?
MASTER TASUKE ...
MASTER TASUKE, *PLEASE COME BACK!*
SHAO LIN... YOU...

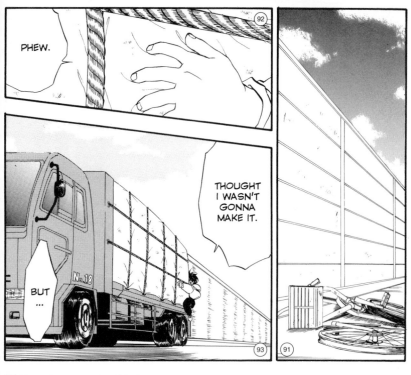

PHEW.

THOUGHT I WASN'T GONNA MAKE IT.

BUT...

CLANK, CLANK

...I'M ALMOST CAUGHT UP!

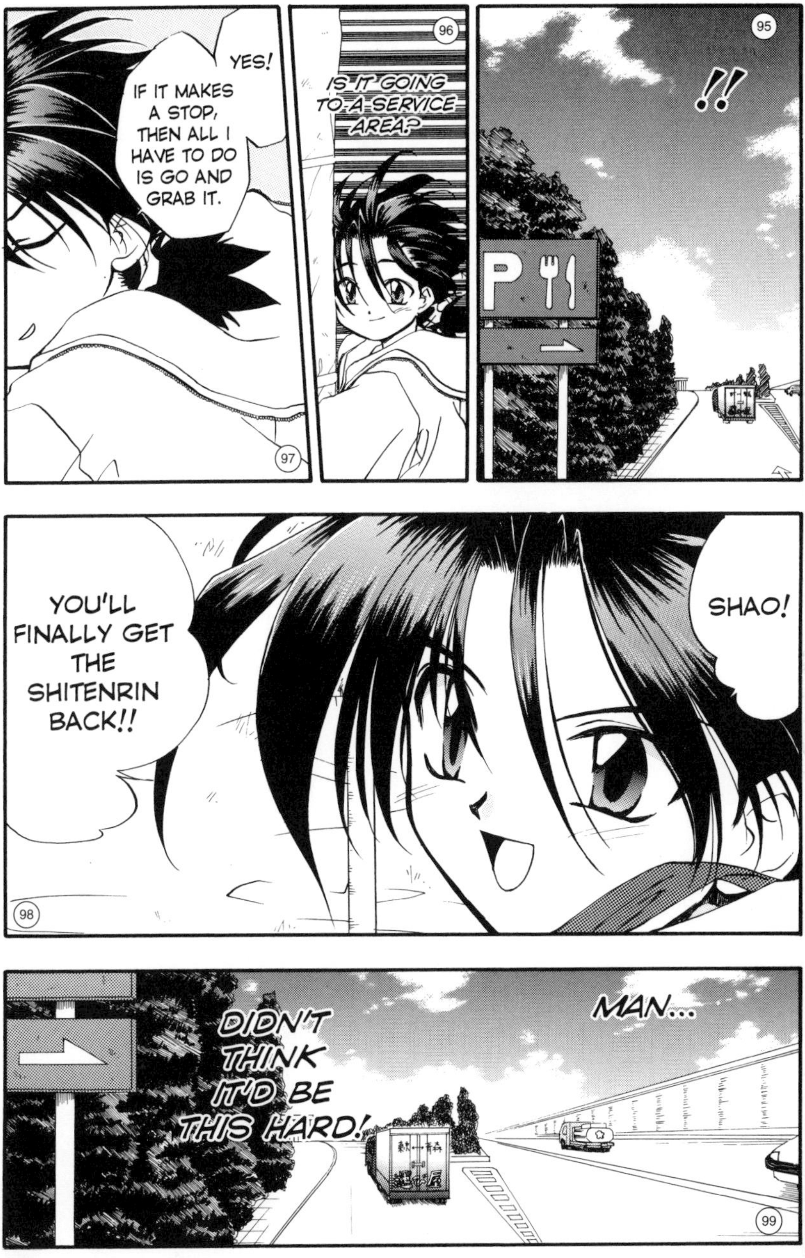
!!
IS IT GOING TO A SERVICE AREA?
YES!
IF IT MAKES A STOP, THEN ALL I HAVE TO DO IS GO AND GRAB IT.
SHAO!
YOU'LL FINALLY GET THE SHITENRIN BACK!!
MAN...
DIDN'T THINK IT'D BE THIS HARD!

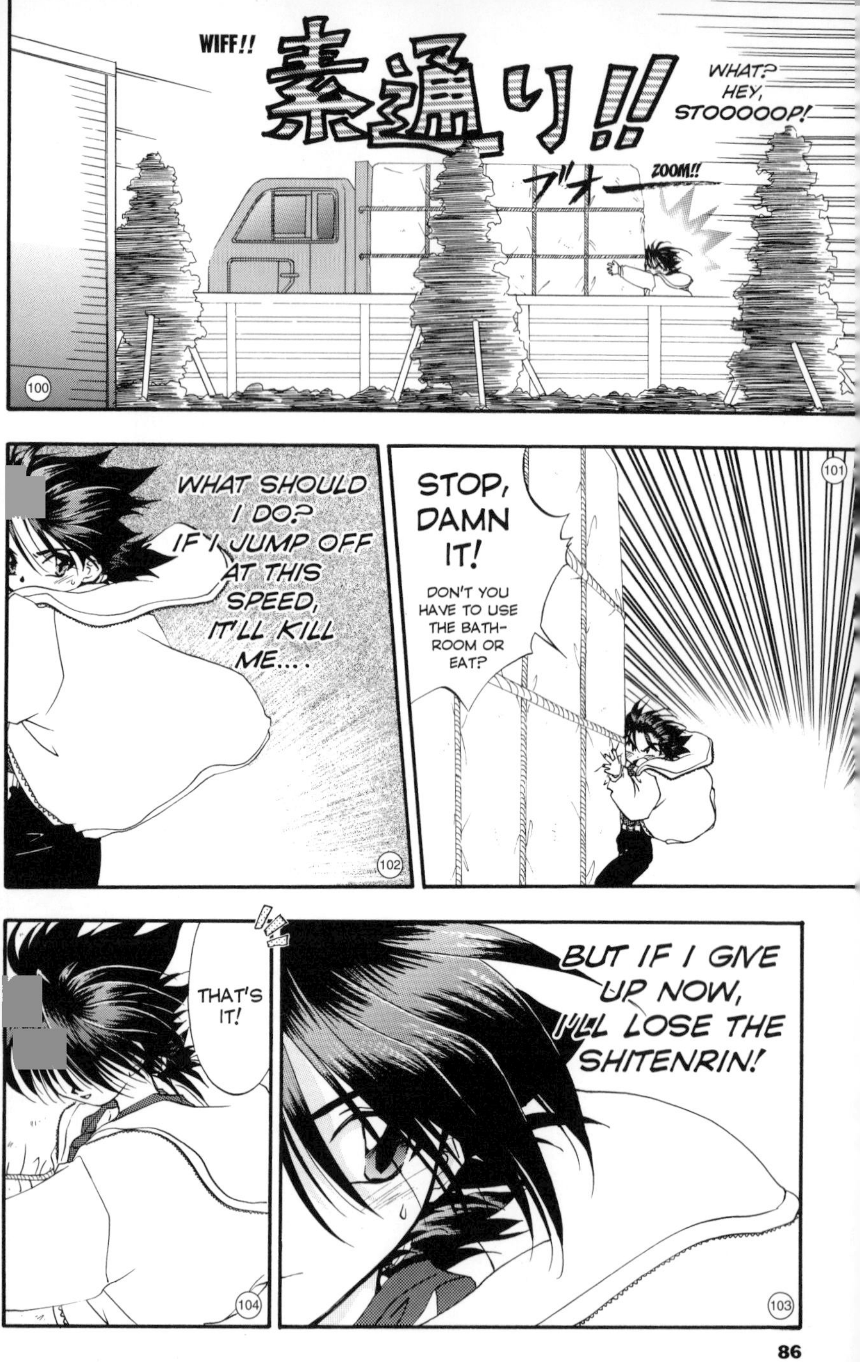
WHAT? HEY, STOOOOOP!
素通り!!
WIFF!!
ブオー
ZOOM!!
STOP, DAMN IT!
DON'T YOU HAVE TO USE THE BATH-ROOM OR EAT?
WHAT SHOULD I DO? IF I JUMP OFF AT THIS SPEED, IT'LL KILL ME....
BUT IF I GIVE UP NOW, I'LL LOSE THE SHITENRIN!
THAT'S IT!

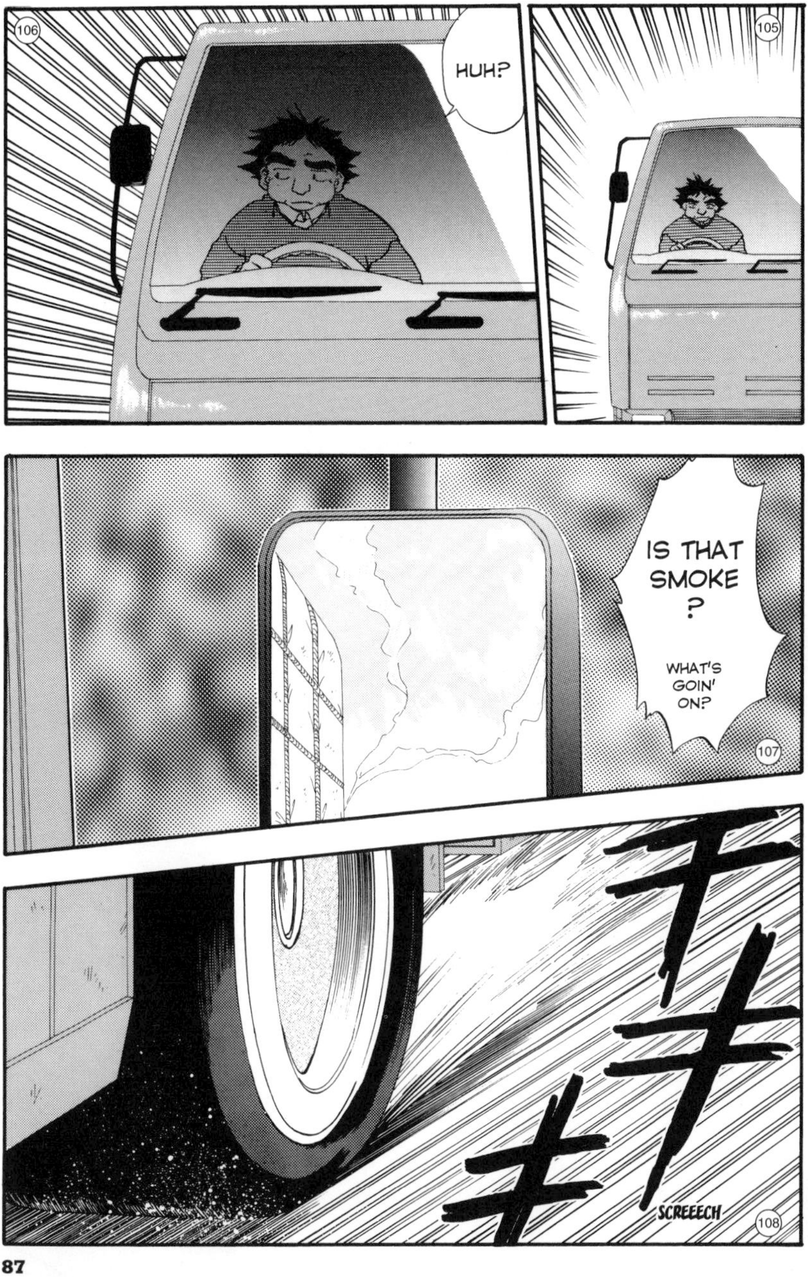
105
106
HUH?
107
IS THAT SMOKE?
WHAT'S GOIN' ON?
108
SCREEECH

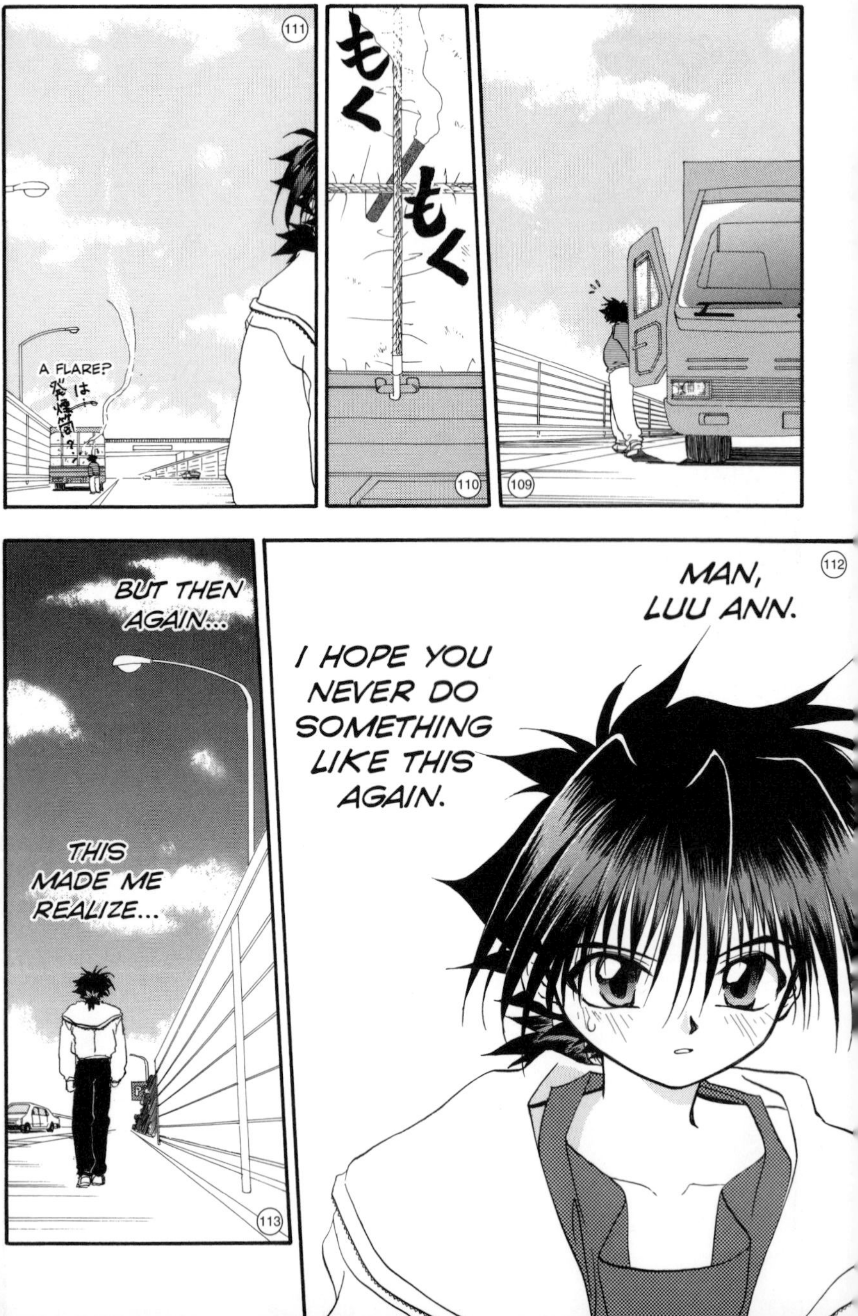
もく
もく
A FLARE?
は…発煙筒？
MAN, LUU ANN.
I HOPE YOU NEVER DO SOMETHING LIKE THIS AGAIN.
BUT THEN AGAIN...
THIS MADE ME REALIZE...

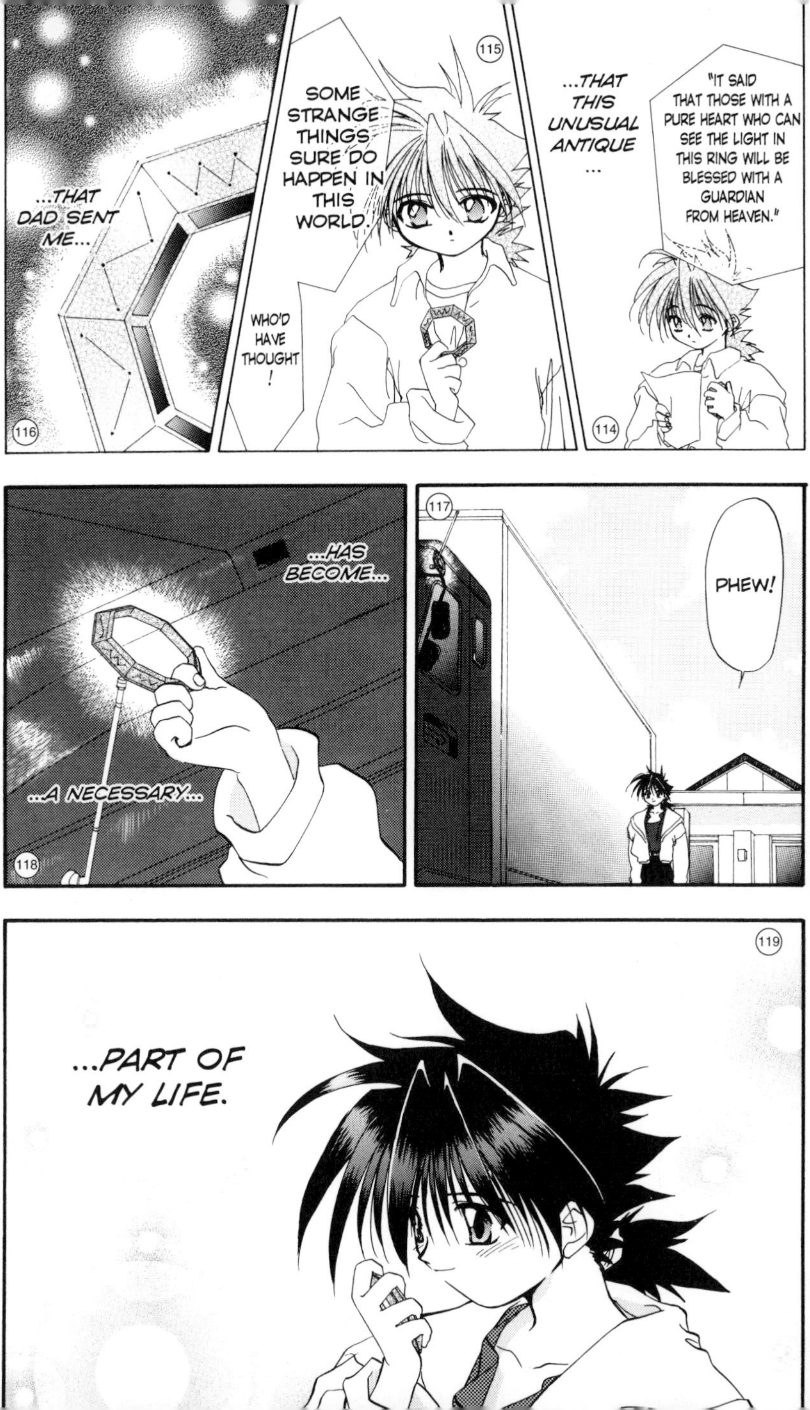
"IT SAID THAT THOSE WITH A PURE HEART WHO CAN SEE THE LIGHT IN THIS RING WILL BE BLESSED WITH A GUARDIAN FROM HEAVEN."
...THAT THIS UNUSUAL ANTIQUE ...
SOME STRANGE THINGS SURE DO HAPPEN IN THIS WORLD.
WHO'D HAVE THOUGHT!
...THAT DAD SENT ME...
PHEW!
...HAS BECOME...
...A NECESSARY...
...PART OF MY LIFE.

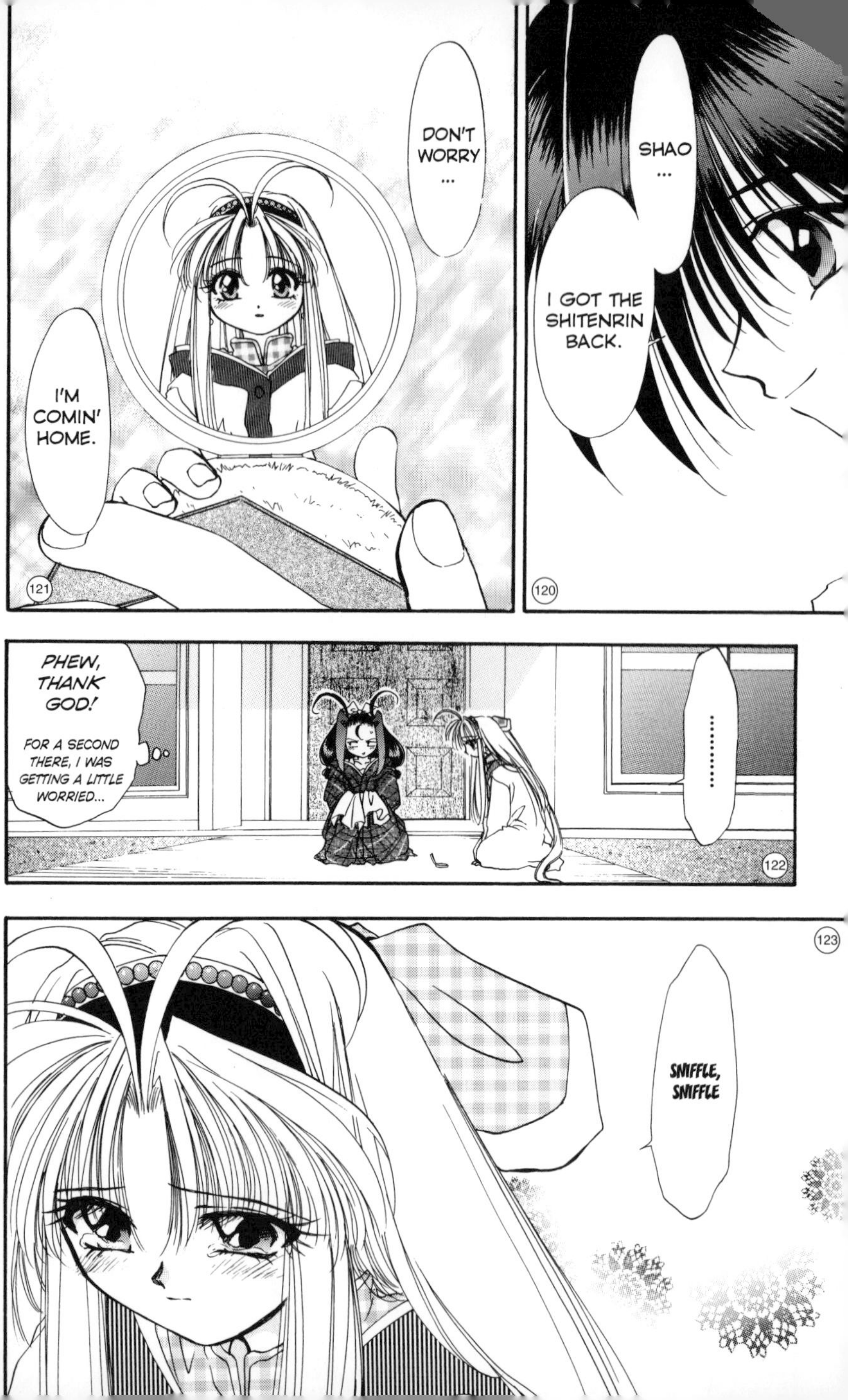
SHAO ...
I GOT THE SHITENRIN BACK.
DON'T WORRY ...
I'M COMIN' HOME.
....
PHEW, THANK GOD!
FOR A SECOND THERE, I WAS GETTING A LITTLE WORRIED...
SNIFFLE, SNIFFLE

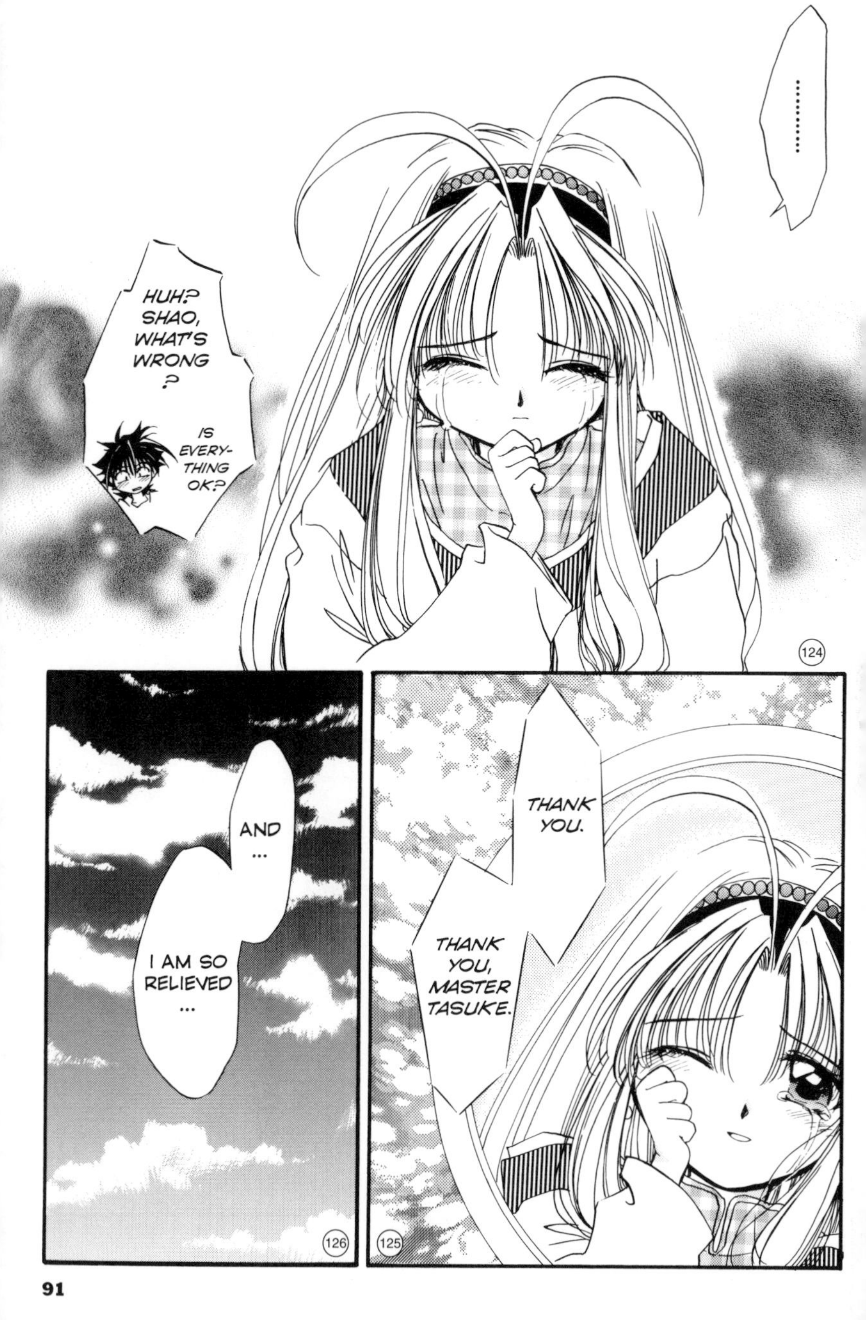
......
HUH? SHAO, WHAT'S WRONG?
IS EVERYTHING OK?
THANK YOU.
THANK YOU, MASTER TASUKE.
AND ...
I AM SO RELIEVED ...

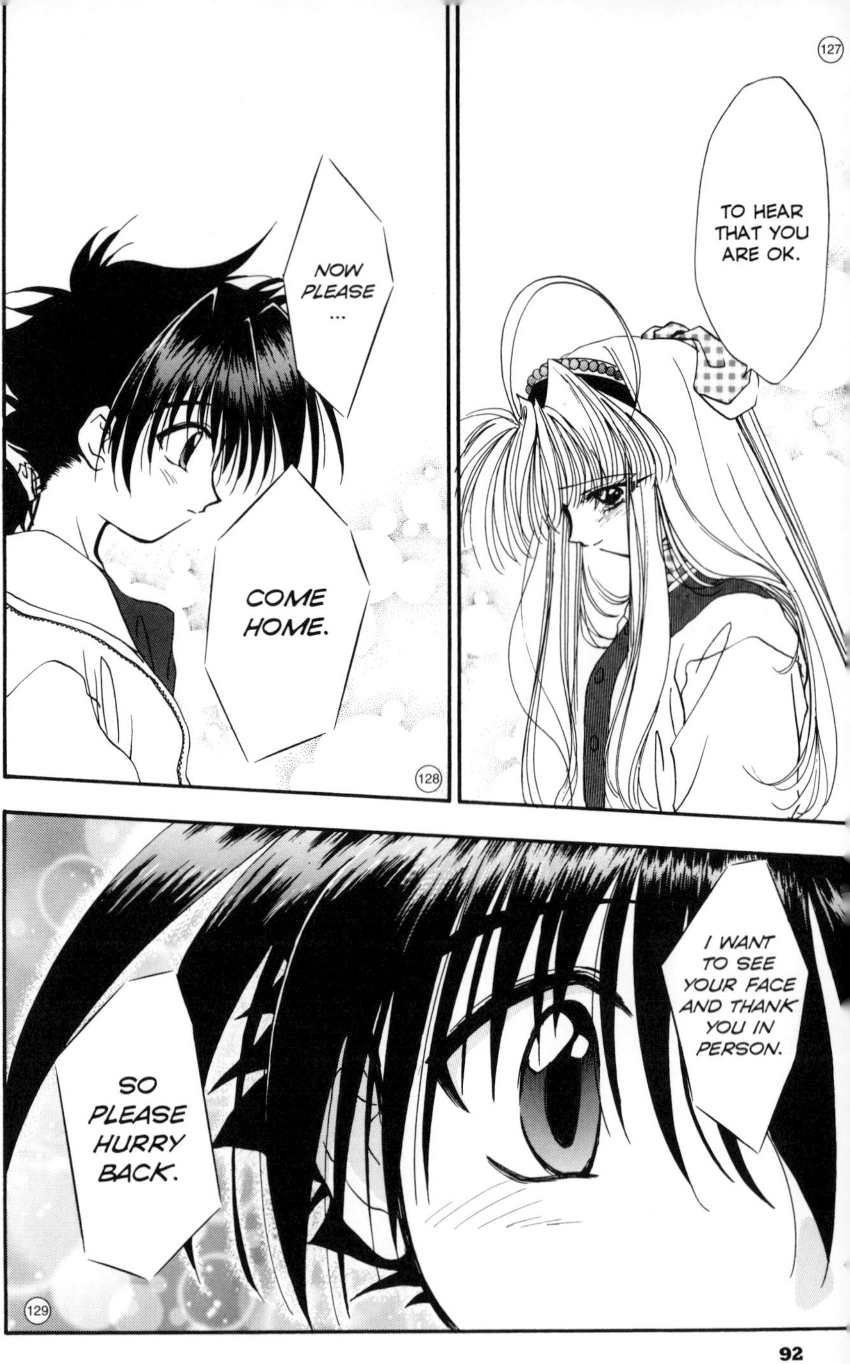
TO HEAR THAT YOU ARE OK.
NOW PLEASE ...
COME HOME.
I WANT TO SEE YOUR FACE AND THANK YOU IN PERSON.
SO PLEASE HURRY BACK.

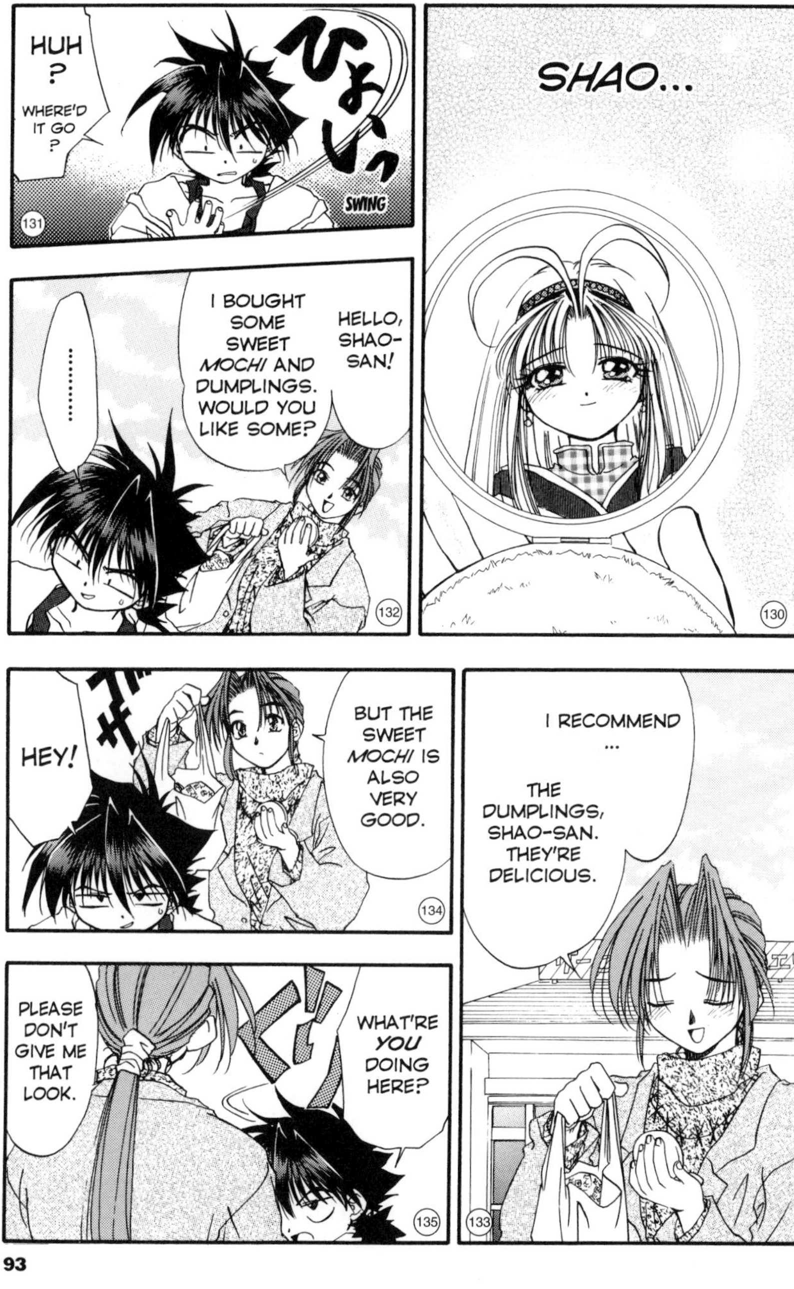
SHAO...
ひょいっ
SWING
HUH ?
WHERE'D IT GO ?
HELLO, SHAO-SAN!
I BOUGHT SOME SWEET MOCHI AND DUMPLINGS. WOULD YOU LIKE SOME?
....
I RECOMMEND ...
THE DUMPLINGS, SHAO-SAN. THEY'RE DELICIOUS.
BUT THE SWEET MOCHI IS ALSO VERY GOOD.
HEY!
WHAT'RE YOU DOING HERE?
PLEASE DON'T GIVE ME THAT LOOK.

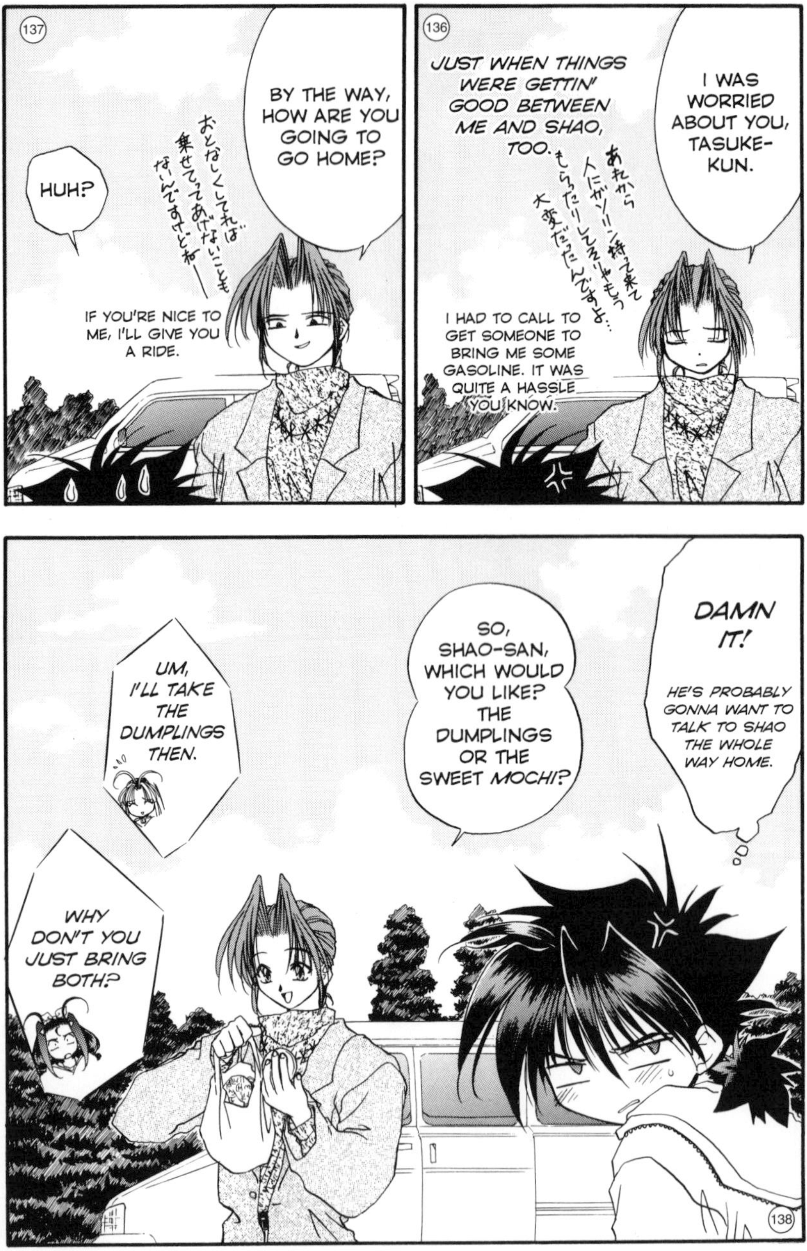
136
I WAS WORRIED ABOUT YOU, TASUKE-KUN.
JUST WHEN THINGS WERE GETTIN' GOOD BETWEEN ME AND SHAO, TOO.
あれから人にガソリン持って来てもらったりしてそりゃもう大変だったんですよ…
I HAD TO CALL TO GET SOMEONE TO BRING ME SOME GASOLINE. IT WAS QUITE A HASSLE YOU KNOW.
137
BY THE WAY, HOW ARE YOU GOING TO GO HOME?
HUH?
おとなしくしてれば乗せてってあげないこともないんですけどね——
IF YOU'RE NICE TO ME, I'LL GIVE YOU A RIDE.
DAMN IT!
HE'S PROBABLY GONNA WANT TO TALK TO SHAO THE WHOLE WAY HOME.
SO, SHAO-SAN, WHICH WOULD YOU LIKE? THE DUMPLINGS OR THE SWEET *MOCHI*?
UM, I'LL TAKE THE DUMPLINGS THEN.
WHY DON'T YOU JUST BRING BOTH?
138

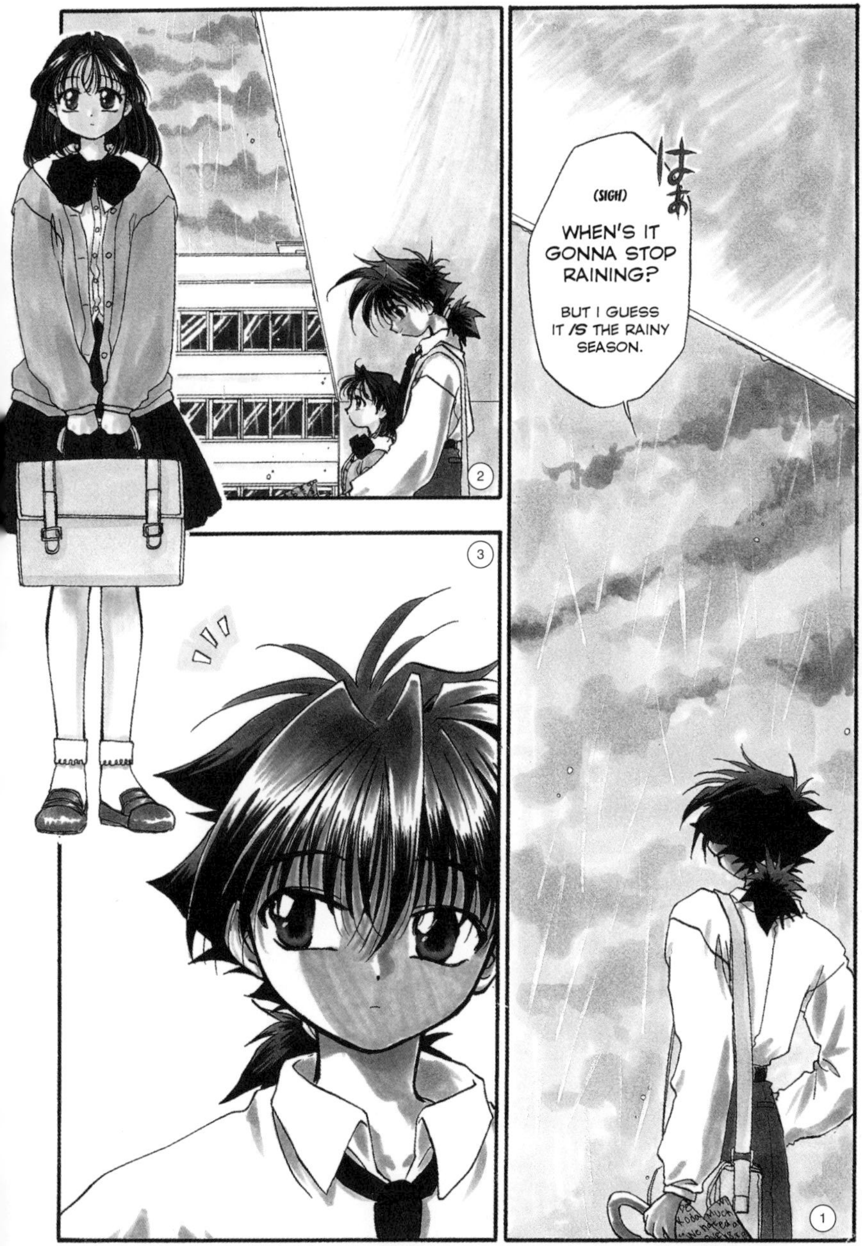
はあ
(SIGH)
WHEN'S IT GONNA STOP RAINING?
BUT I GUESS IT *IS* THE RAINY SEASON.

CHAPTER 22: TASUKE'S NEW CRUSH (PART 1)

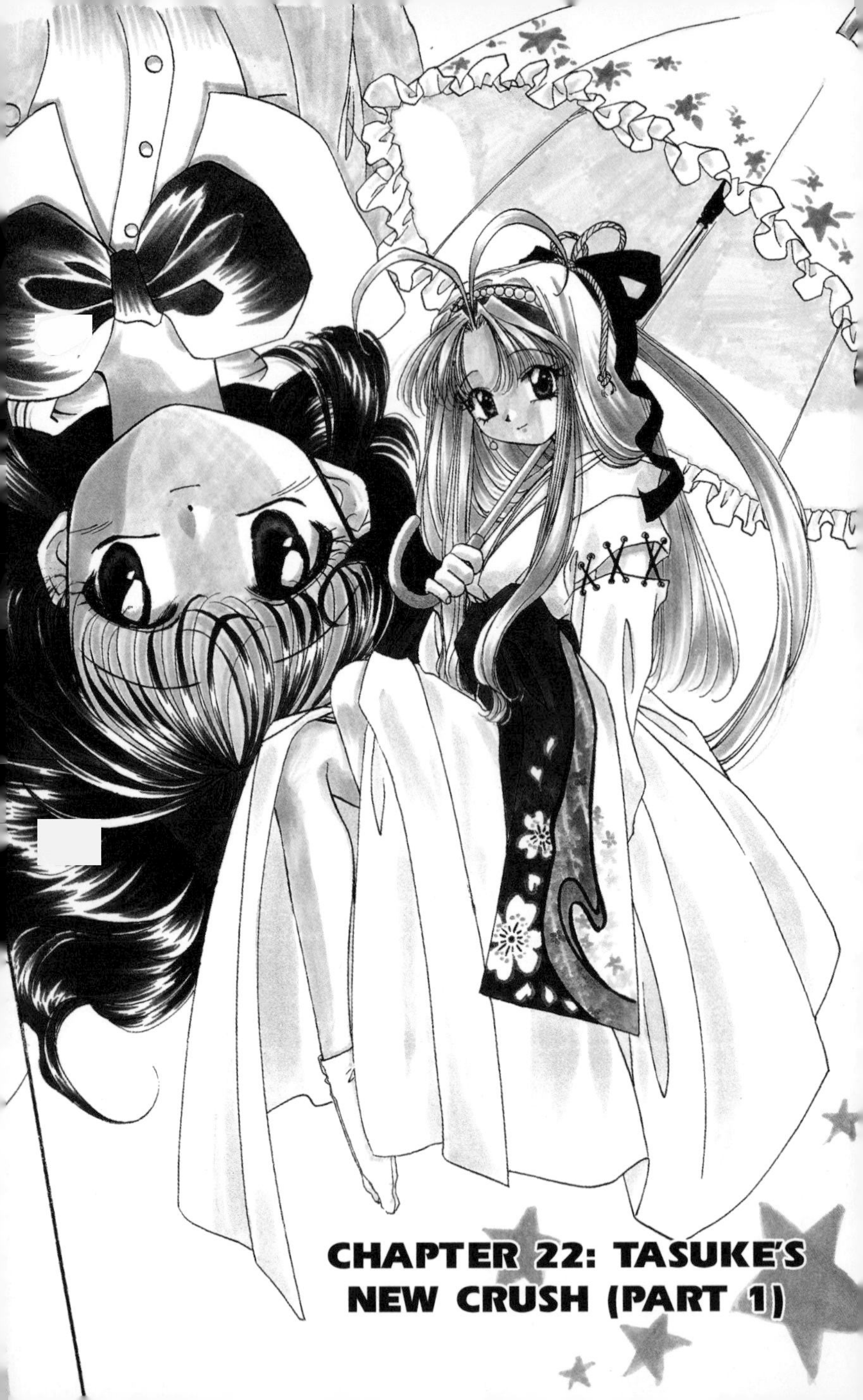
CHAPTER 22: TASUKE'S
NEW CRUSH (PART 1)

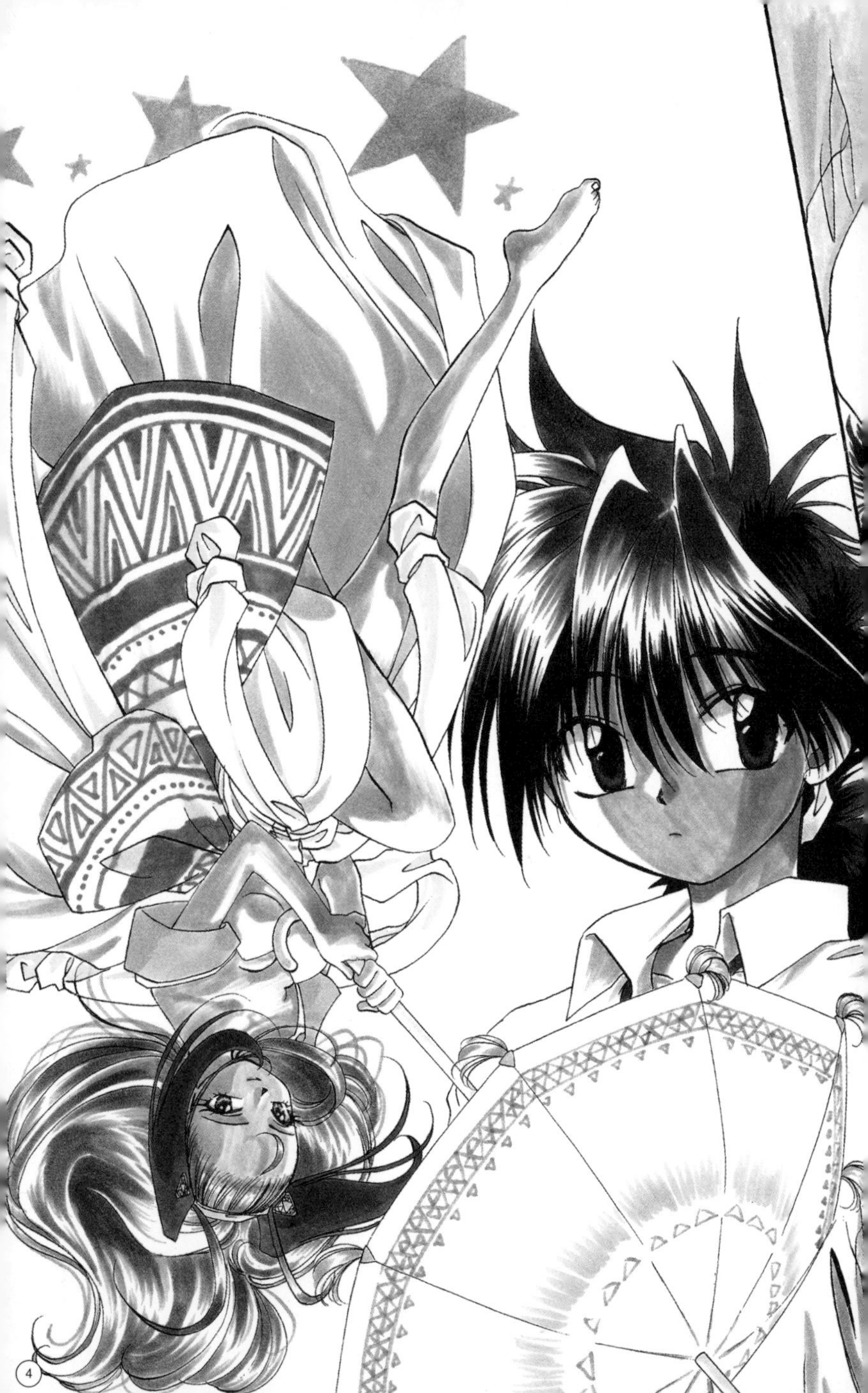

Guardian Angel
GETTEN
守護月天!
™

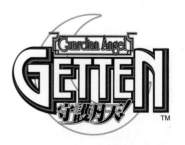

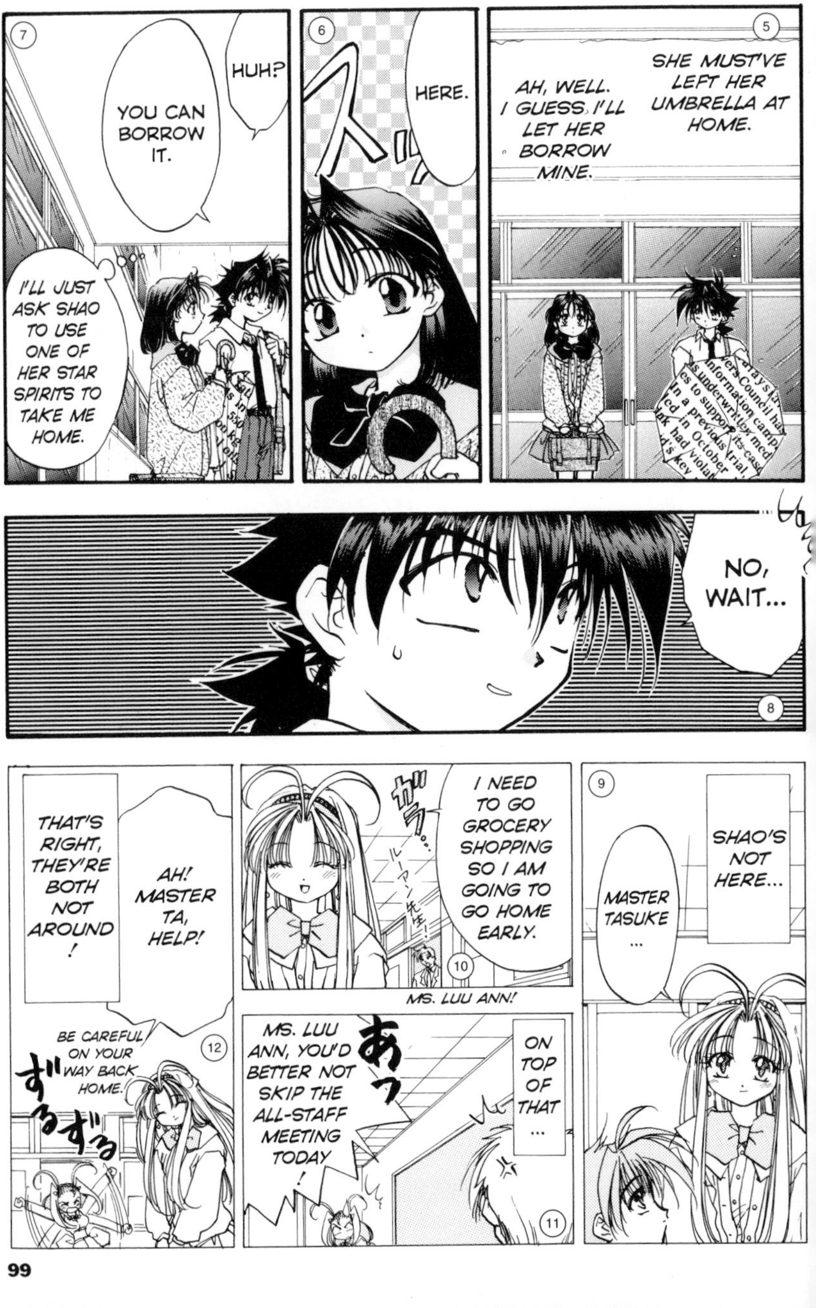
SHE MUST'VE LEFT HER UMBRELLA AT HOME.
AH, WELL. I GUESS I'LL LET HER BORROW MINE.
HERE.
HUH?
YOU CAN BORROW IT.
I'LL JUST ASK SHAO TO USE ONE OF HER STAR SPIRITS TO TAKE ME HOME.
NO, WAIT...
SHAO'S NOT HERE...
MASTER TASUKE ...
I NEED TO GO GROCERY SHOPPING SO I AM GOING TO GO HOME EARLY.
ルーアン先生!
MS. LUU ANN!
ON TOP OF THAT ...
MS. LUU ANN, YOU'D BETTER NOT SKIP THE ALL-STAFF MEETING TODAY!
あっ
THAT'S RIGHT, THEY'RE BOTH NOT AROUND!
AH! MASTER TA, HELP!
BE CAREFUL ON YOUR WAY BACK HOME.
ずるずる

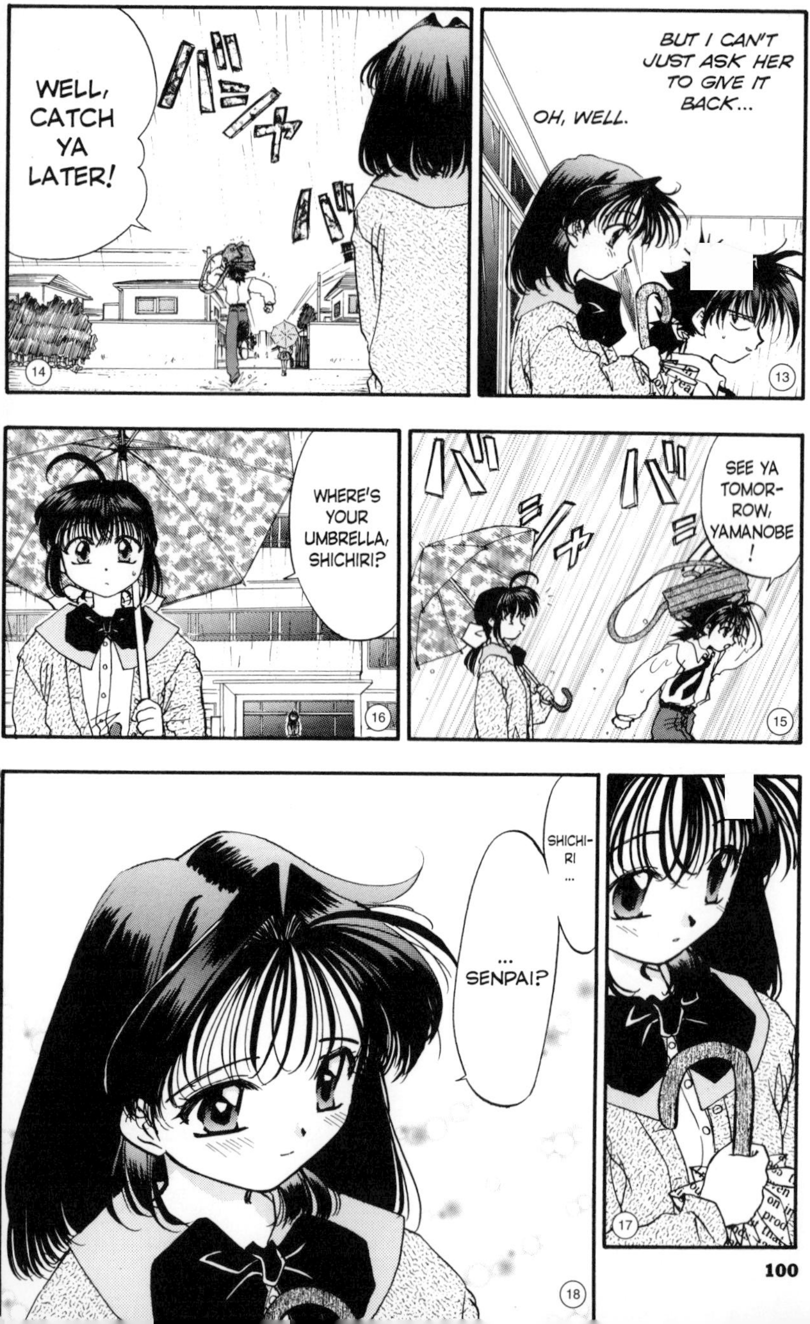
BUT I CAN'T JUST ASK HER TO GIVE IT BACK...
OH, WELL.
WELL, CATCH YA LATER!
SEE YA TOMORROW, YAMANOBE!
WHERE'S YOUR UMBRELLA, SHICHIRI?
SHICHIRI ...
... SENPAI?

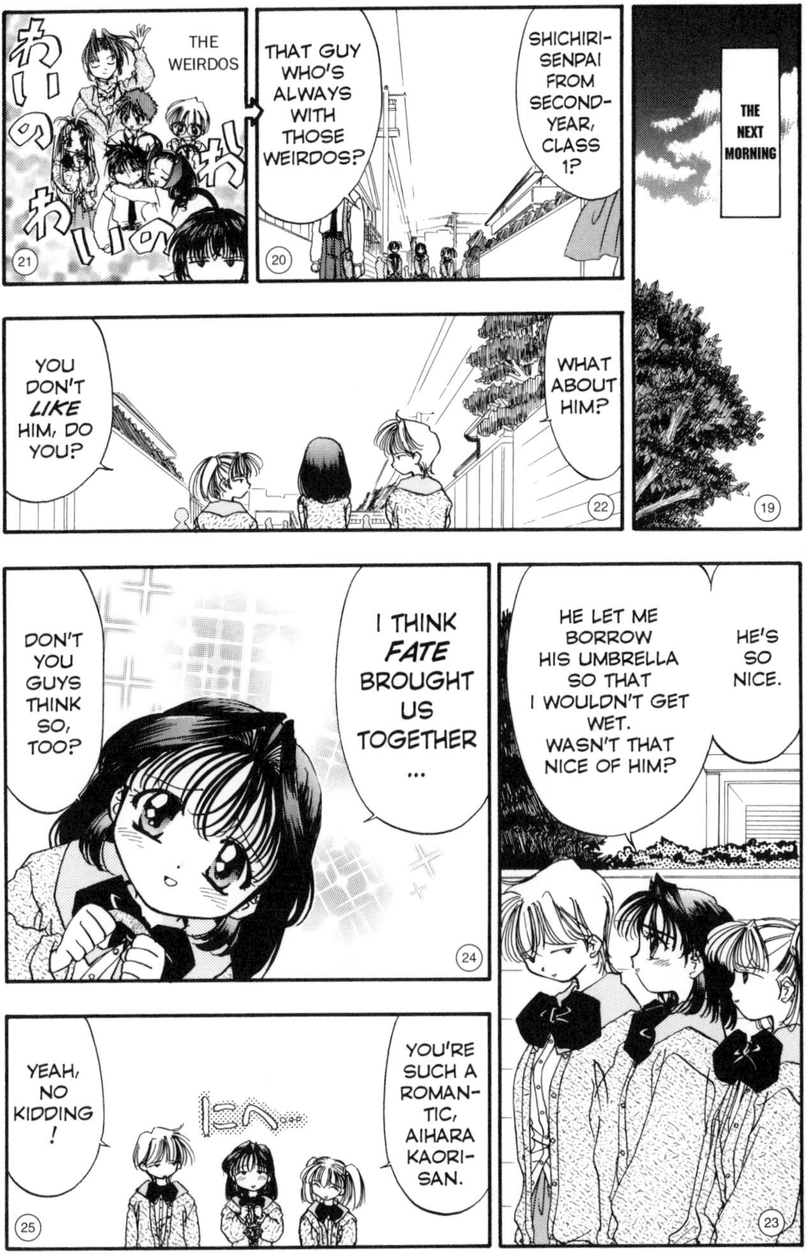
THE NEXT MORNING
SHICHIRI-SENPAI FROM SECOND-YEAR, CLASS 1?
THAT GUY WHO'S ALWAYS WITH THOSE WEIRDOS?
THE WEIRDOS
WHAT ABOUT HIM?
YOU DON'T *LIKE* HIM, DO YOU?
HE'S SO NICE.
HE LET ME BORROW HIS UMBRELLA SO THAT I WOULDN'T GET WET. WASN'T THAT NICE OF HIM?
I THINK *FATE* BROUGHT US TOGETHER...
DON'T YOU GUYS THINK SO, TOO?
YOU'RE SUCH A ROMANTIC, AIHARA KAORI-SAN.
にへ
YEAH, NO KIDDING!

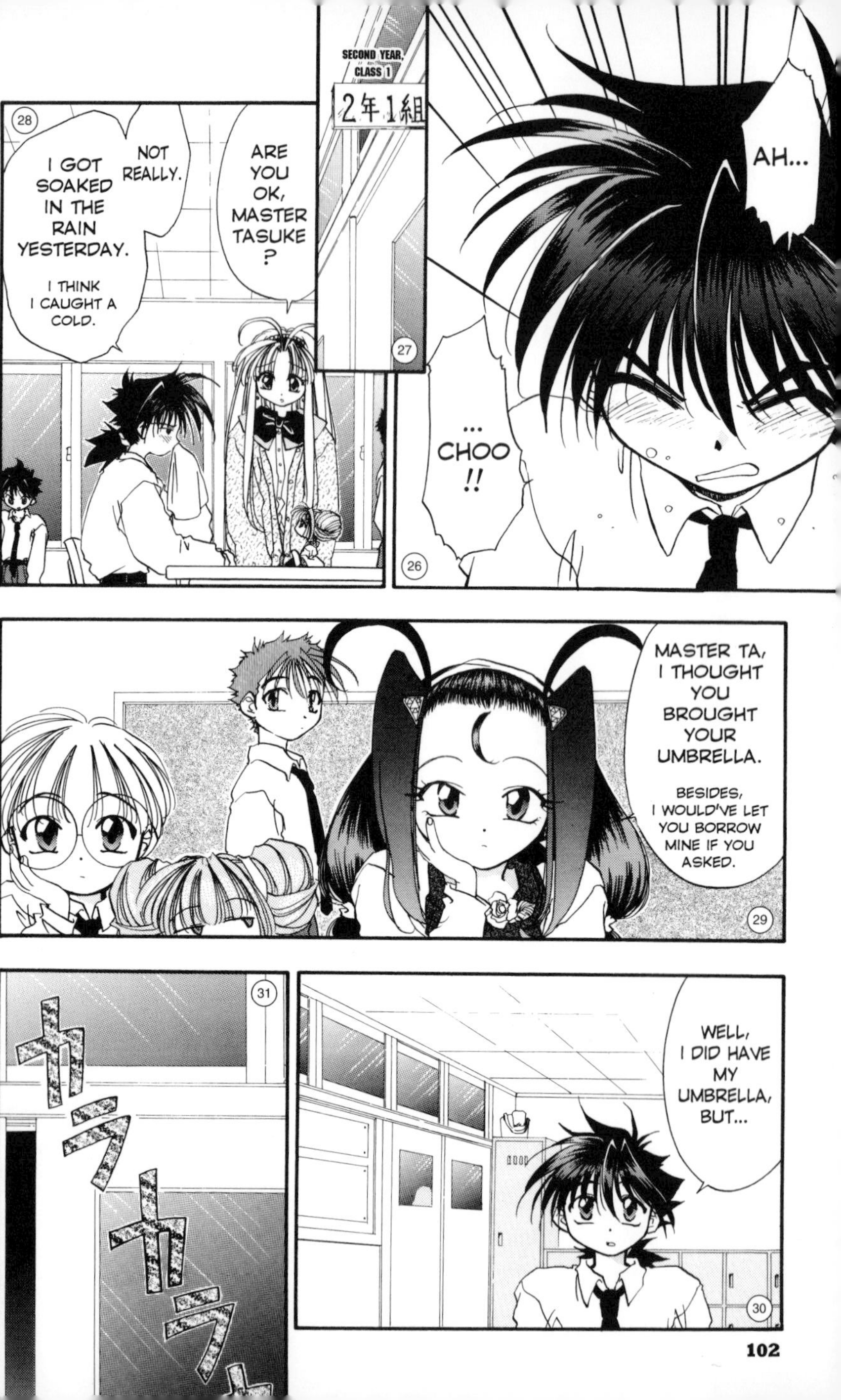
AH...
...CHOO!!
SECOND YEAR, CLASS 1
2年1組
ARE YOU OK, MASTER TASUKE?
NOT REALLY.
I GOT SOAKED IN THE RAIN YESTERDAY.
I THINK I CAUGHT A COLD.
MASTER TA, I THOUGHT YOU BROUGHT YOUR UMBRELLA.
BESIDES, I WOULD'VE LET YOU BORROW MINE IF YOU ASKED.
WELL, I DID HAVE MY UMBRELLA, BUT...

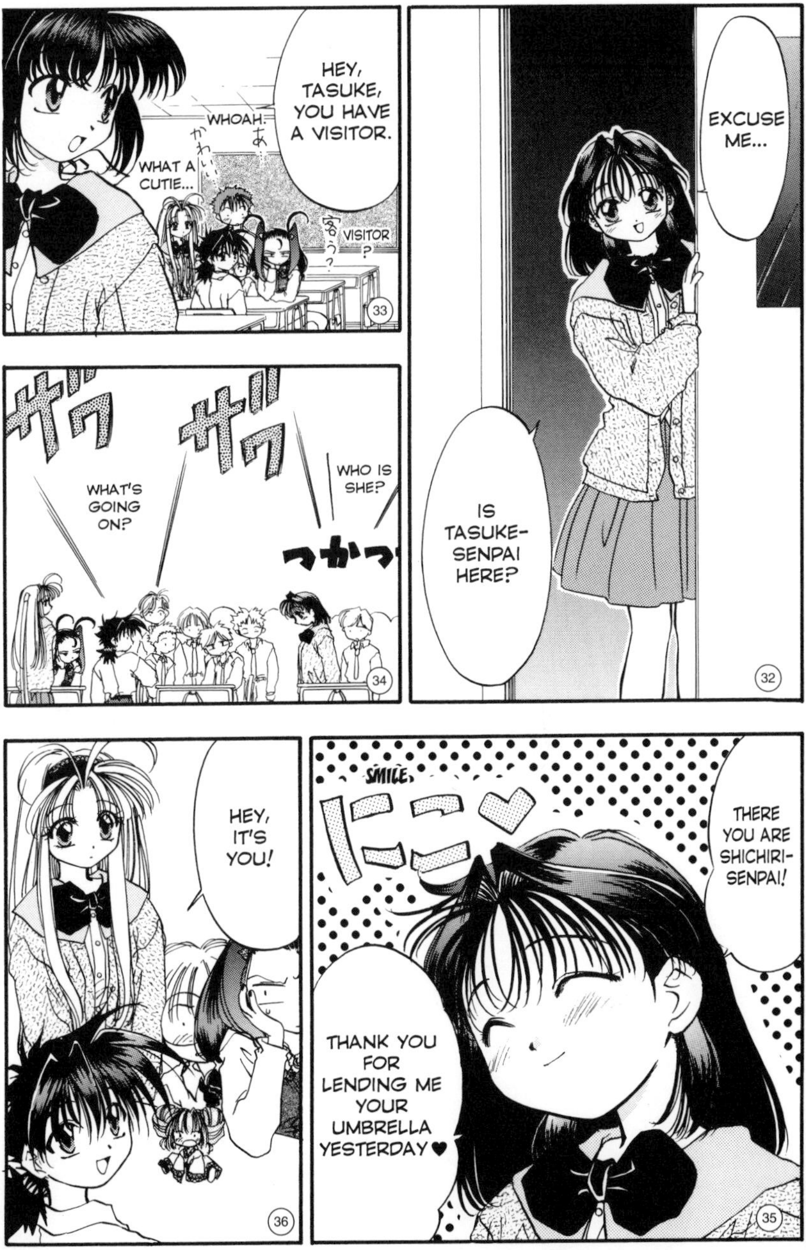
EXCUSE ME...
IS TASUKE-SENPAI HERE?
HEY, TASUKE, YOU HAVE A VISITOR.
WHOAH.
WHAT A CUTIE...
VISITOR?
WHAT'S GOING ON?
WHO IS SHE?
SMILE
THERE YOU ARE SHICHIRI-SENPAI!
THANK YOU FOR LENDING ME YOUR UMBRELLA YESTERDAY♥
HEY, IT'S YOU!

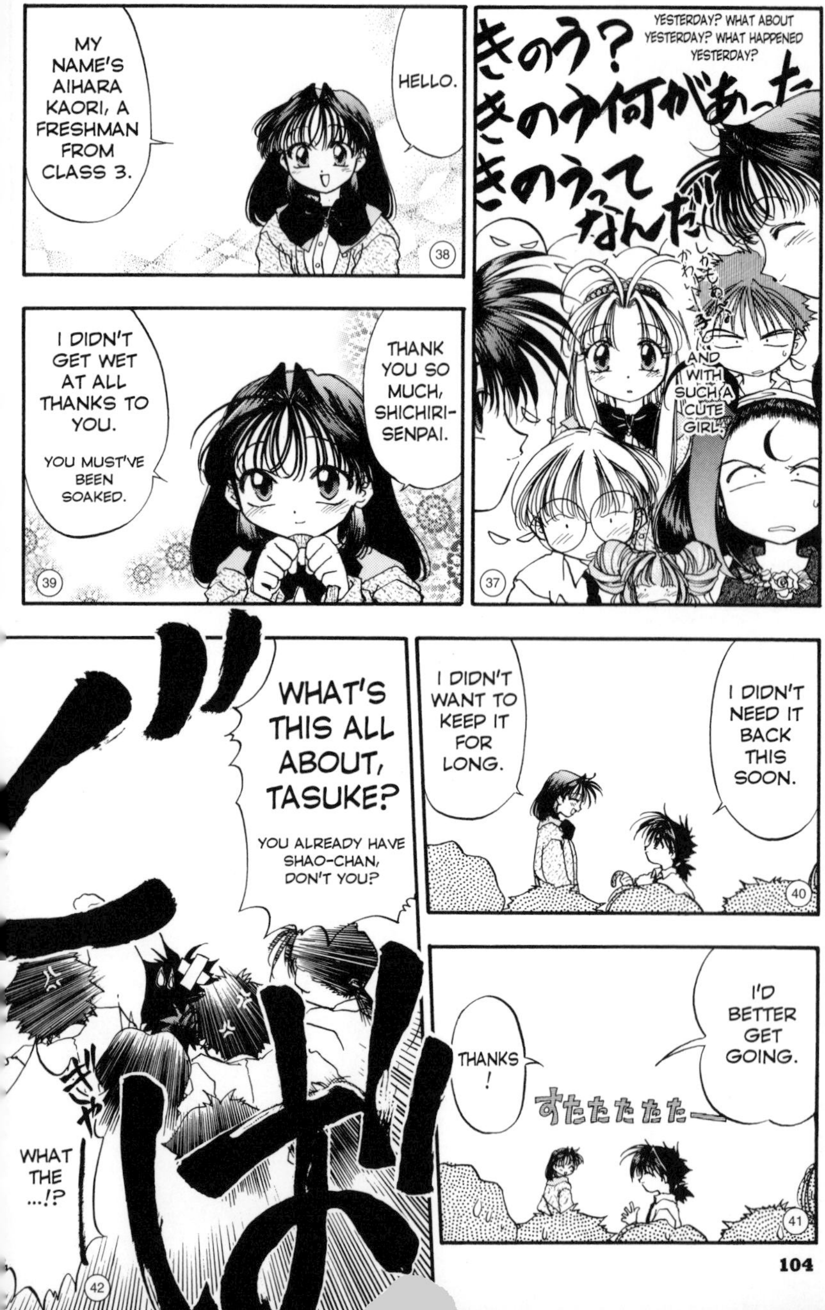

きのう？
きのう何があった
きのうってなんだ
YESTERDAY? WHAT ABOUT YESTERDAY? WHAT HAPPENED YESTERDAY?
AND WITH SUCH A CUTE GIRL.
HELLO.
MY NAME'S AIHARA KAORI, A FRESHMAN FROM CLASS 3.
THANK YOU SO MUCH, SHICHIRI-SENPAI.
I DIDN'T GET WET AT ALL THANKS TO YOU.
YOU MUST'VE BEEN SOAKED.
I DIDN'T NEED IT BACK THIS SOON.
I DIDN'T WANT TO KEEP IT FOR LONG.
I'D BETTER GET GOING.
THANKS!
すたたたたたー
WHAT'S THIS ALL ABOUT, TASUKE?
YOU ALREADY HAVE SHAO-CHAN, DON'T YOU?
WHAT THE ...!?

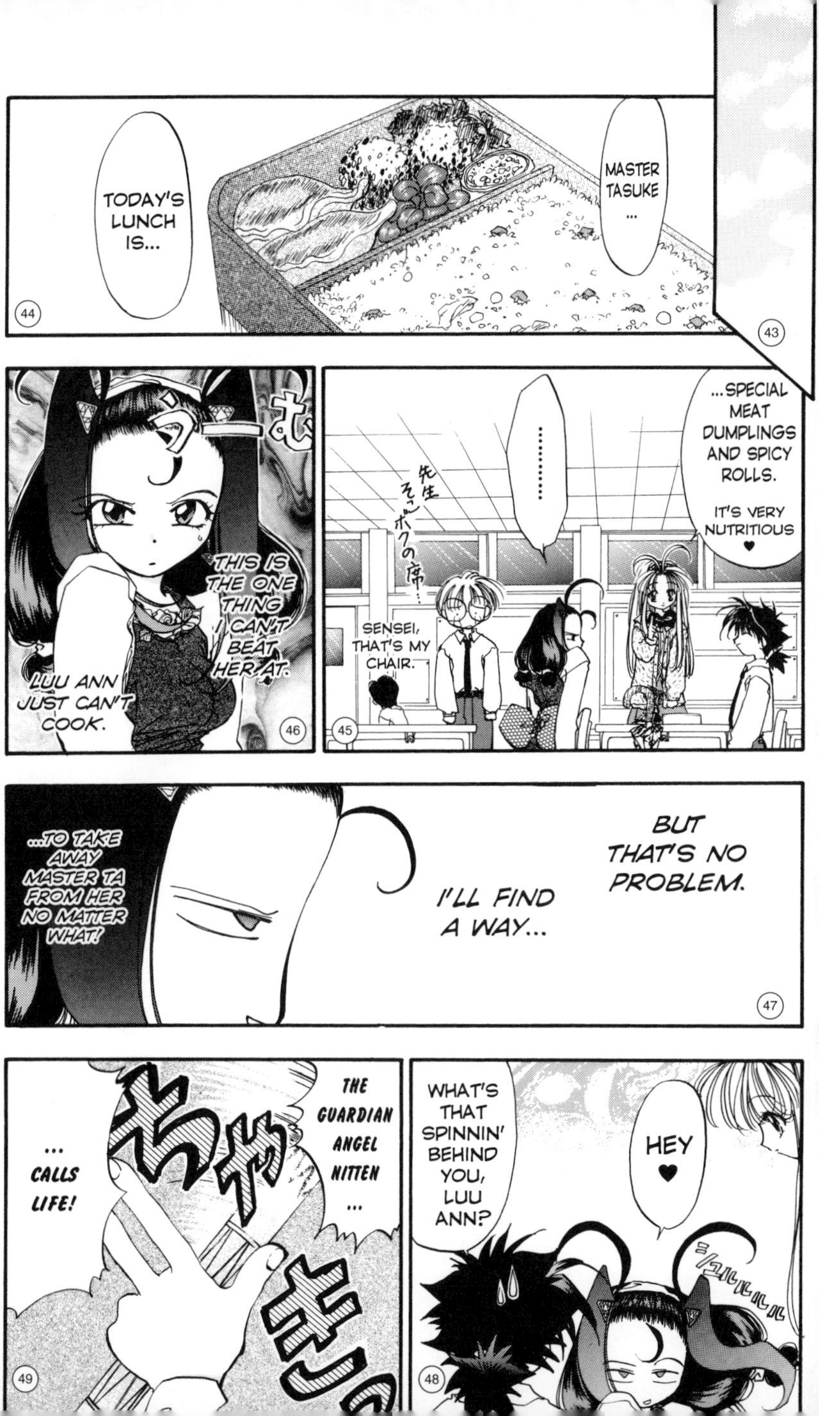
MASTER TASUKE ...
TODAY'S LUNCH IS...
...SPECIAL MEAT DUMPLINGS AND SPICY ROLLS.
IT'S VERY NUTRITIOUS ♥
....
先生 そこボクの席…
SENSEI, THAT'S MY CHAIR.
THIS IS THE ONE THING I CAN'T BEAT HER AT.
LUU ANN JUST CAN'T COOK.
BUT THAT'S NO PROBLEM.
I'LL FIND A WAY...
...TO TAKE AWAY MASTER TA FROM HER NO MATTER WHAT!
HEY ♥
WHAT'S THAT SPINNIN' BEHIND YOU, LUU ANN?
シュルルルル
THE GUARDIAN ANGEL NITTEN ...
... CALLS LIFE!

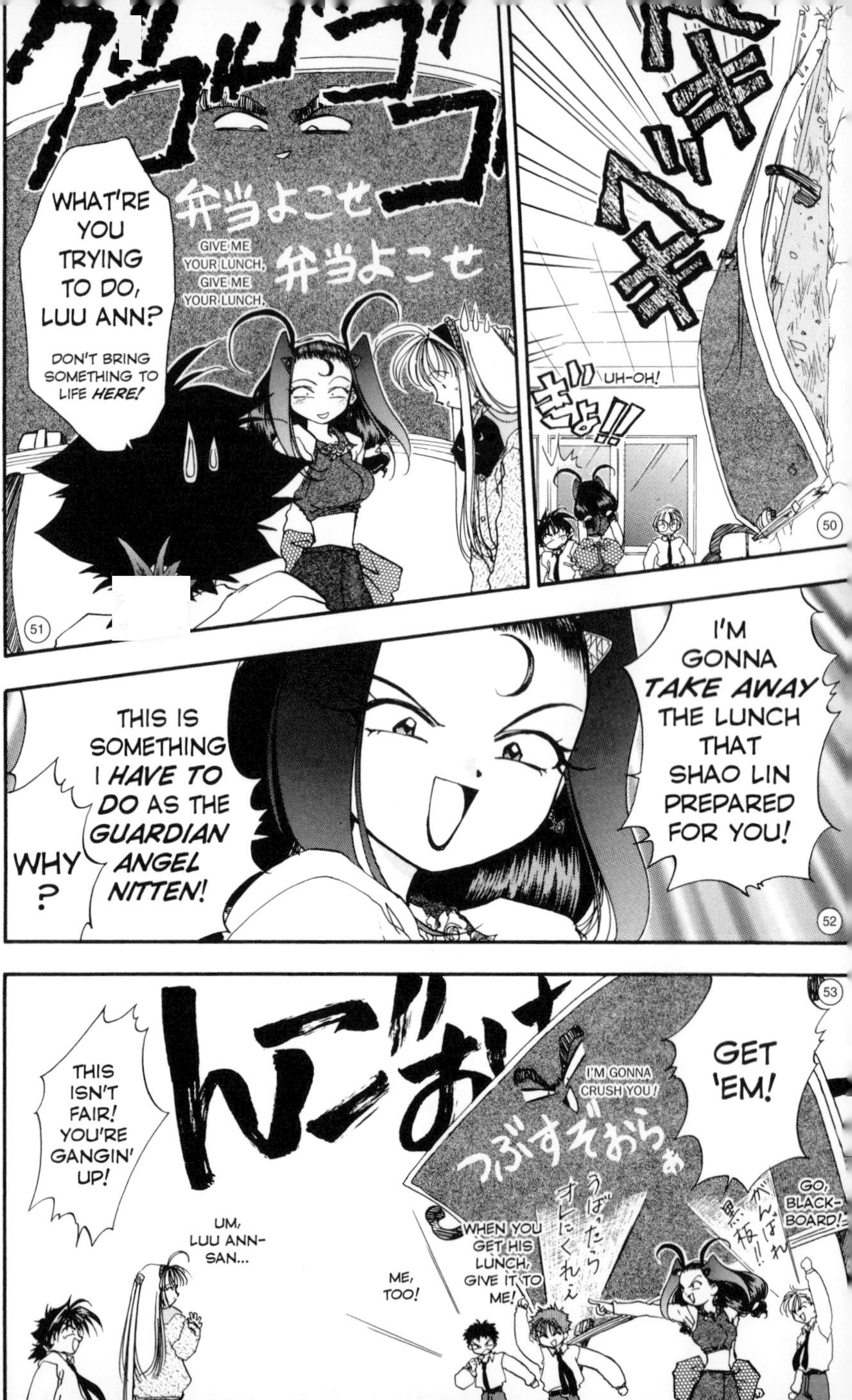

ぎょ!!
UH-OH!
50
弁当よこせ 弁当よこせ
GIVE ME YOUR LUNCH, GIVE ME YOUR LUNCH.
WHAT'RE YOU TRYING TO DO, LUU ANN?
DON'T BRING SOMETHING TO LIFE *HERE!*
51
I'M GONNA *TAKE AWAY* THE LUNCH THAT SHAO LIN PREPARED FOR YOU!
WHY?
THIS IS SOMETHING I *HAVE TO DO* AS THE *GUARDIAN ANGEL NITTEN!*
52
53
GET 'EM!
黒板!! がんばれ
GO, BLACKBOARD!
つぶすぞおらぁ
I'M GONNA CRUSH YOU!
うばったらオレにくれぇ
WHEN YOU GET HIS LUNCH, GIVE IT TO ME!
ME, TOO!
THIS ISN'T FAIR! YOU'RE GANGIN' UP!
UM, LUU ANN-SAN...

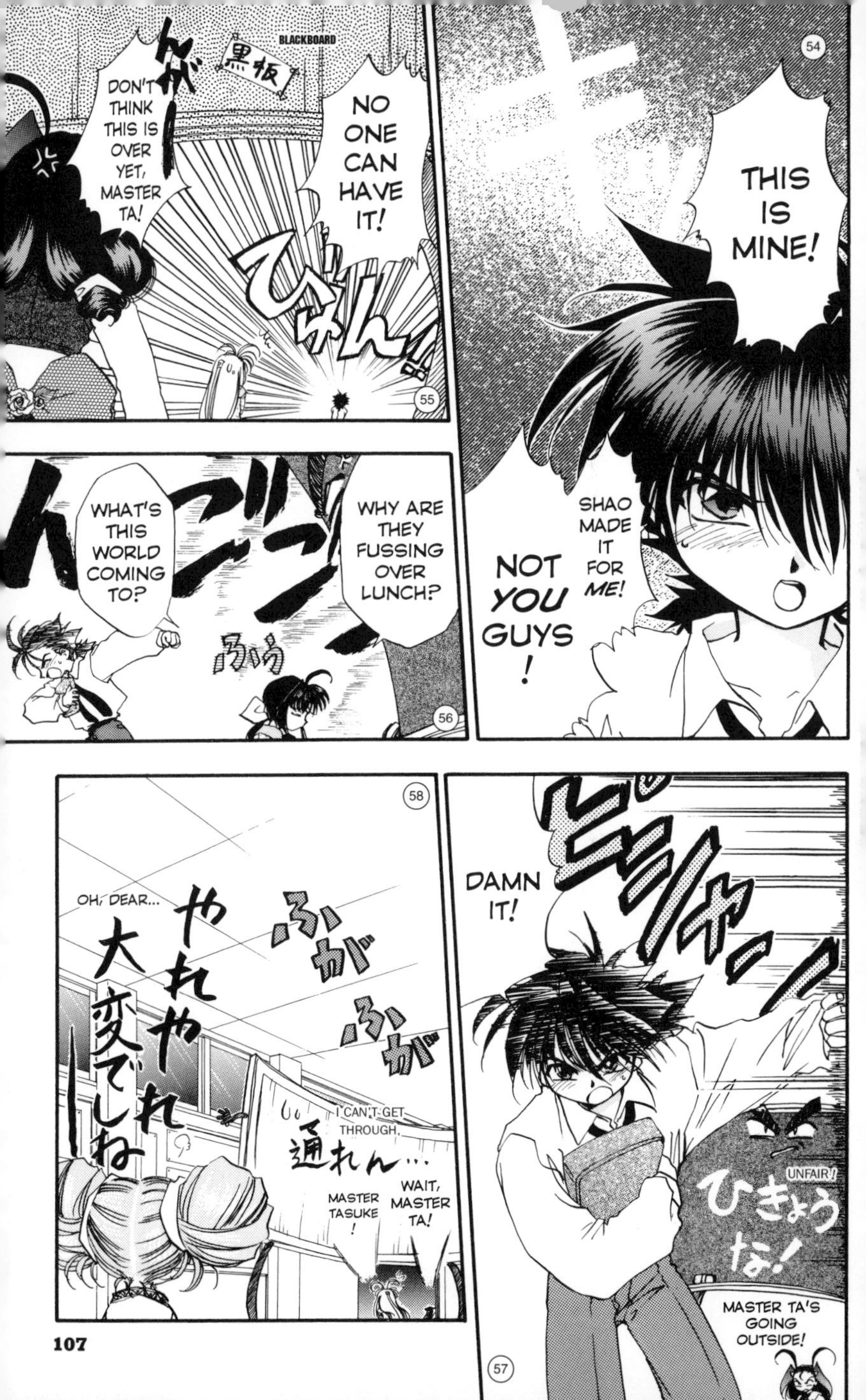

THIS IS MINE!
SHAO MADE IT FOR ME!
NOT YOU GUYS!
黒板
BLACKBOARD
NO ONE CAN HAVE IT!
DON'T THINK THIS IS OVER YET, MASTER TA!
ひゅん!!
WHY ARE THEY FUSSING OVER LUNCH?
WHAT'S THIS WORLD COMING TO?
ふぅ
DAMN IT!
ひきょうな!
UNFAIR!
MASTER TA'S GOING OUTSIDE!
ふが ふが
通れん…
I CAN'T GET THROUGH.
WAIT, MASTER TA!
MASTER TASUKE!
やれやれ 大変でしね
OH, DEAR...

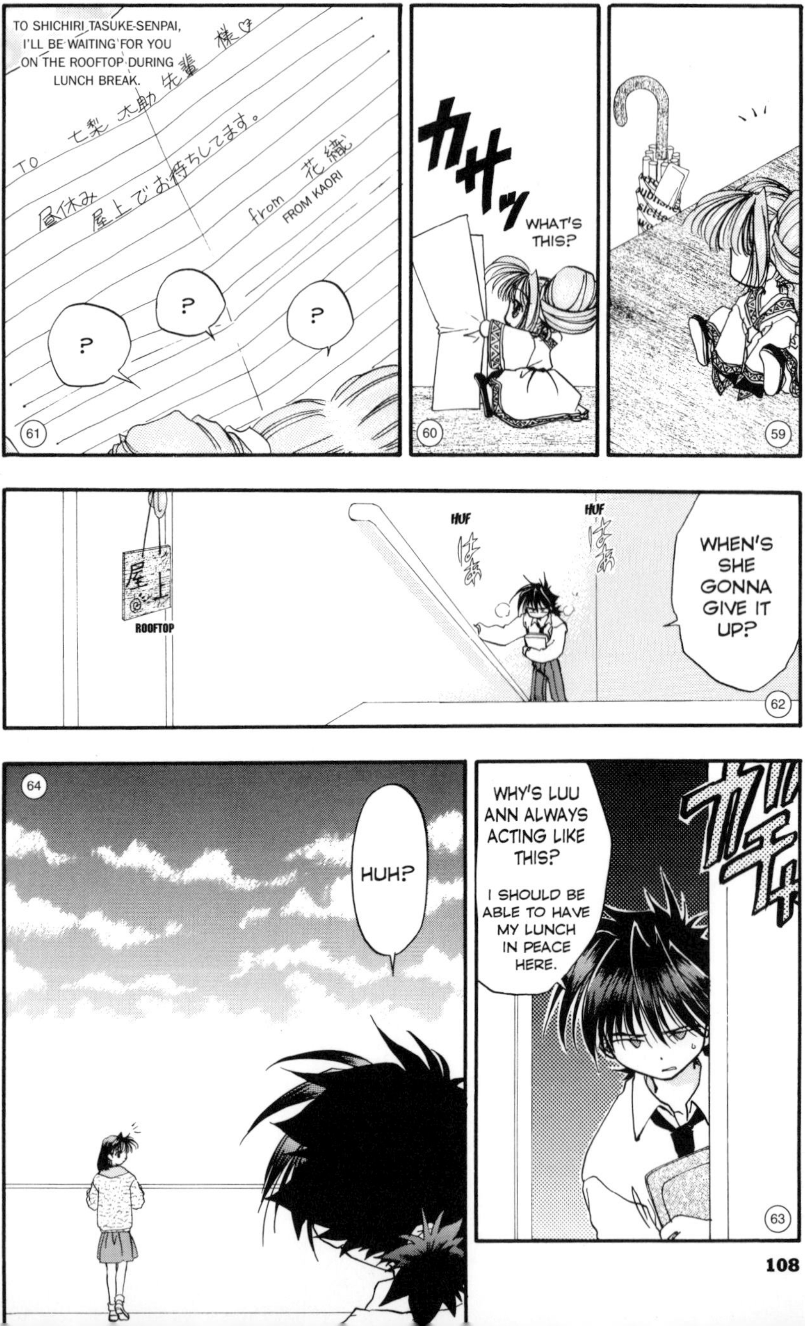

カサッ
WHAT'S THIS?
To 七梨 太助 先輩 様♡
昼休み 屋上でお待ちしてます。
from 花織
TO SHICHIRI TASUKE-SENPAI, I'LL BE WAITING FOR YOU ON THE ROOFTOP DURING LUNCH BREAK.
FROM KAORI
?
?
?
はぁ
HUF
はぁ
HUF
WHEN'S SHE GONNA GIVE IT UP?
屋上
ROOFTOP
WHY'S LUU ANN ALWAYS ACTING LIKE THIS?
I SHOULD BE ABLE TO HAVE MY LUNCH IN PEACE HERE.
HUH?

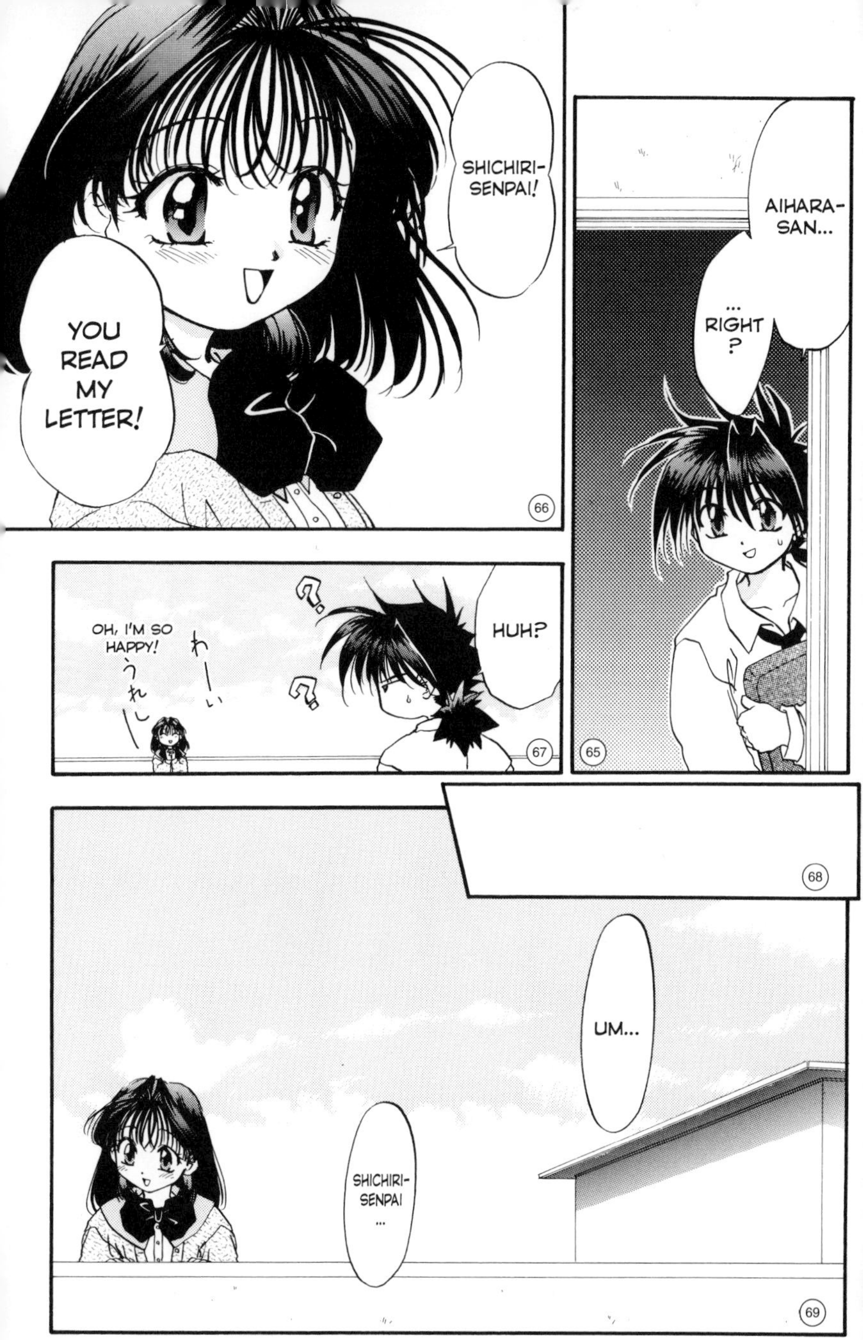
AIHARA-SAN...
... RIGHT?
SHICHIRI-SENPAI!
YOU READ MY LETTER!
HUH?
OH, I'M SO HAPPY!
わーい
うれし
UM...
SHICHIRI-SENPAI ...

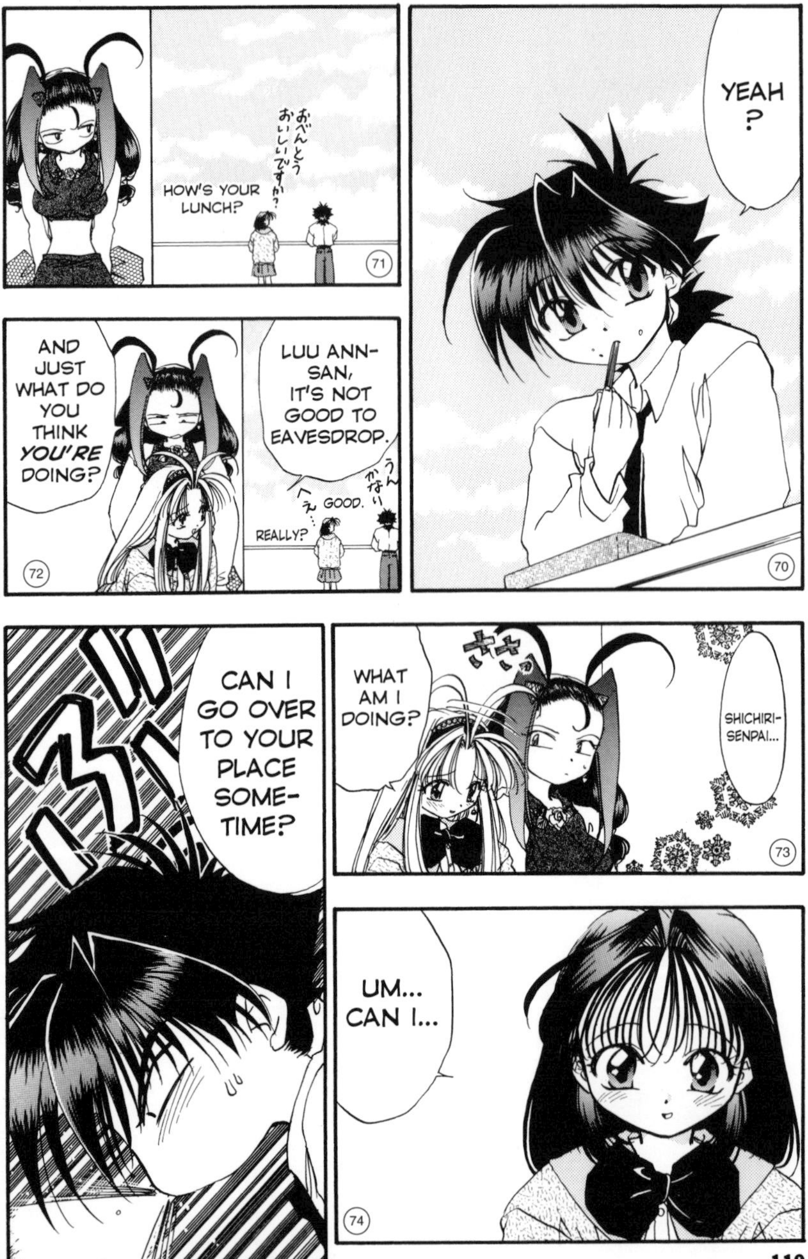
YEAH?
おべんとう
おいしいですか？
HOW'S YOUR LUNCH?
LUU ANN-SAN, IT'S NOT GOOD TO EAVESDROP.
うん かなり
GOOD.
へぇ…
REALLY?
AND JUST WHAT DO YOU THINK *YOU'RE* DOING?
SHICHIRI-SENPAI...
WHAT AM I DOING?
UM... CAN I...
CAN I GO OVER TO YOUR PLACE SOME-TIME?

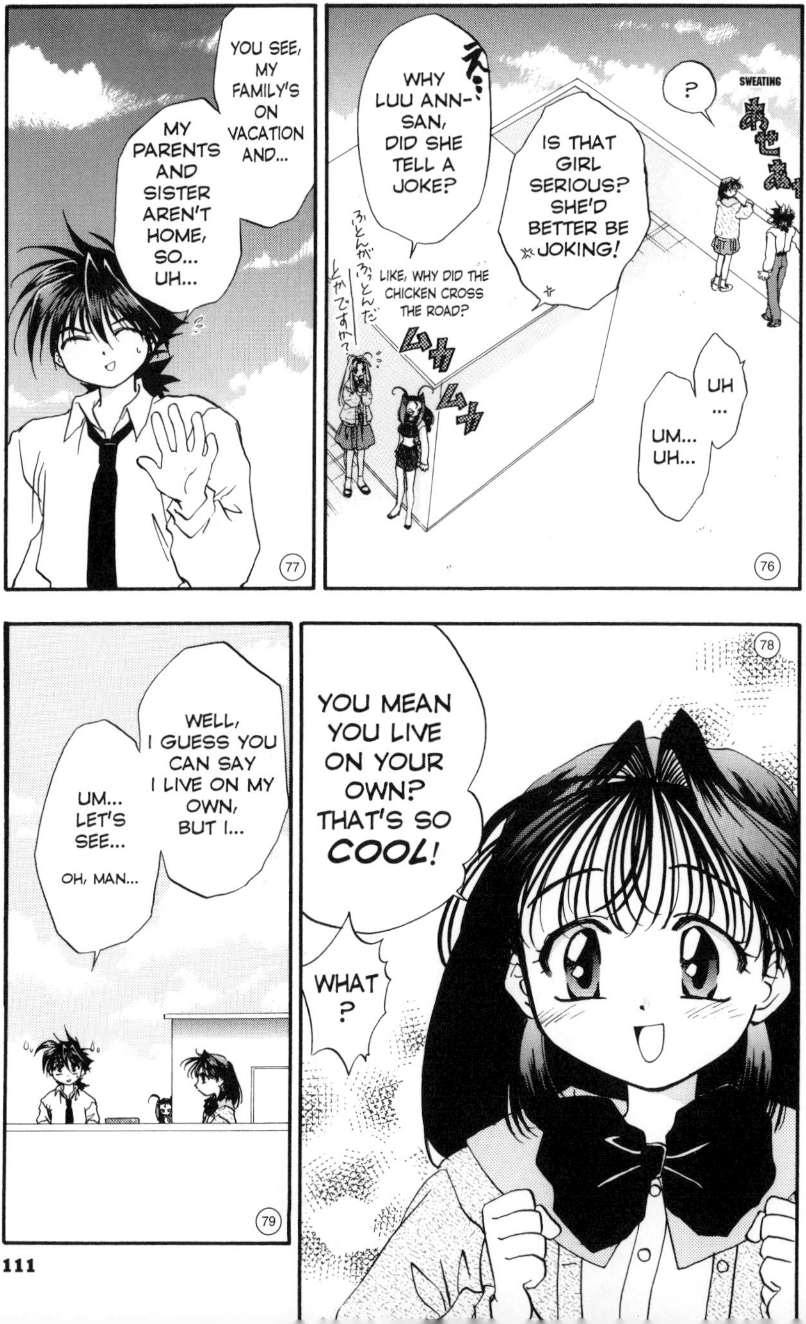
?
SWEATING
IS THAT GIRL SERIOUS? SHE'D BETTER BE JOKING!
UH ... UM... UH...
WHY LUU ANN-SAN, DID SHE TELL A JOKE?
LIKE, WHY DID THE CHICKEN CROSS THE ROAD?
YOU SEE, MY FAMILY'S ON VACATION AND...
MY PARENTS AND SISTER AREN'T HOME, SO... UH...
YOU MEAN YOU LIVE ON YOUR OWN? THAT'S SO COOL!
WHAT ?
WELL, I GUESS YOU CAN SAY I LIVE ON MY OWN, BUT I...
UM... LET'S SEE...
OH, MAN...

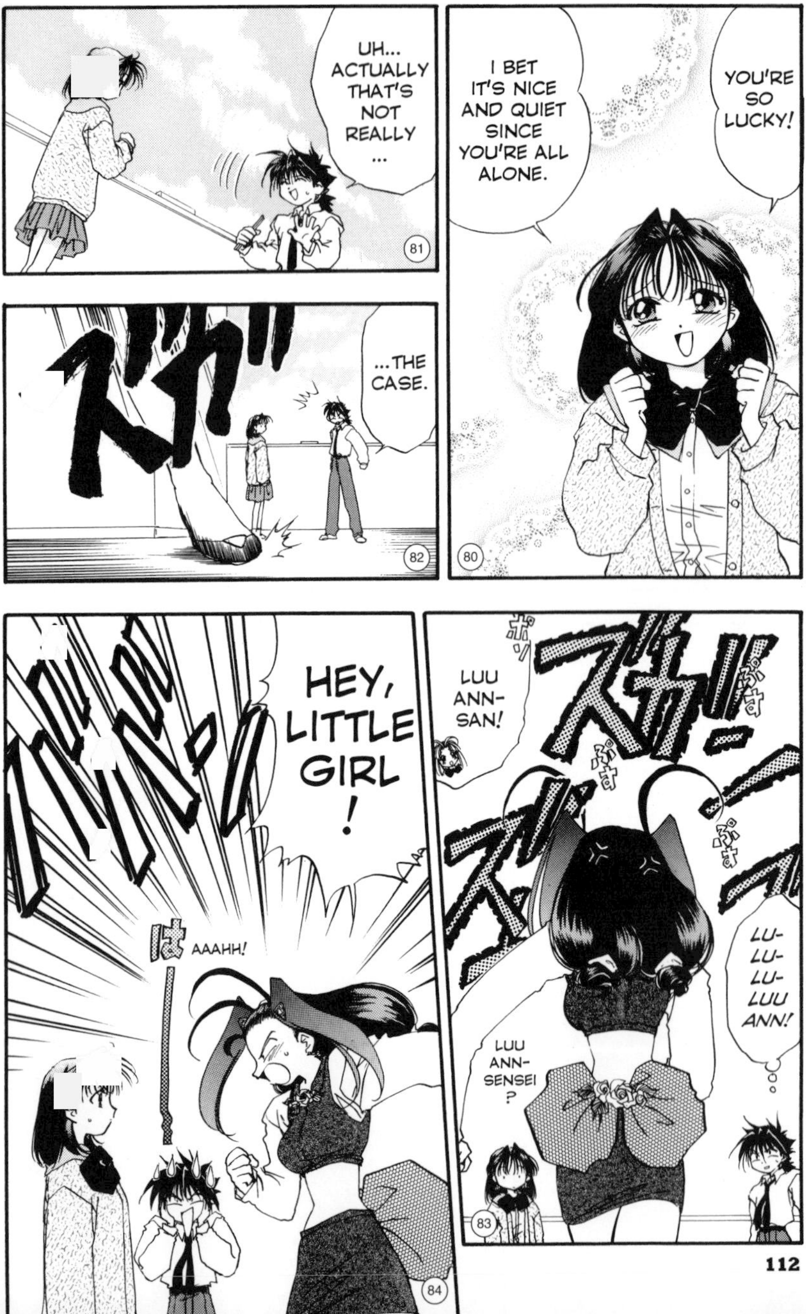
YOU'RE SO LUCKY!
I BET IT'S NICE AND QUIET SINCE YOU'RE ALL ALONE.
UH... ACTUALLY THAT'S NOT REALLY ...
...THE CASE.
LUU ANN-SAN!
LU-LU-LU-LUU ANN!
LUU ANN-SENSEI ?
HEY, LITTLE GIRL !
AAAHH!

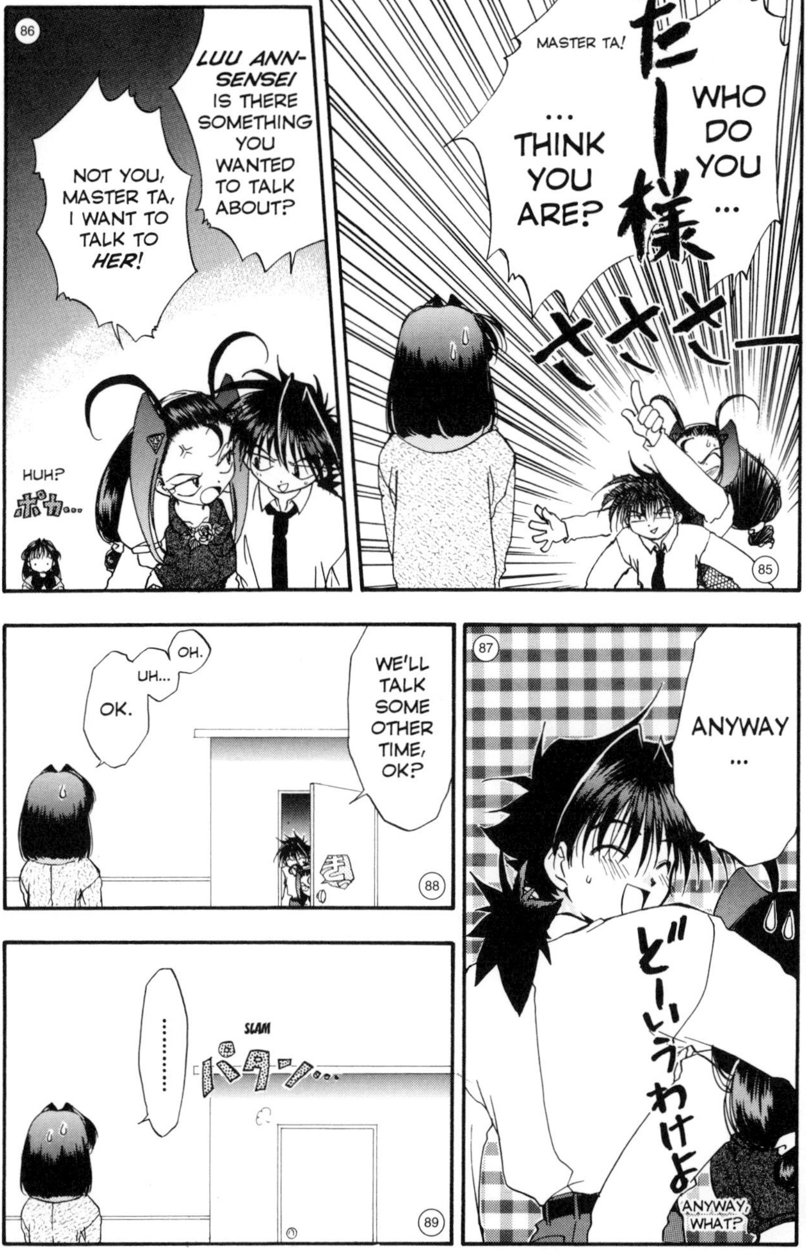
85
MASTER TA!
たー様
WHO DO YOU ...
... THINK YOU ARE?
ささー
86
LUU ANN-SENSEI IS THERE SOMETHING YOU WANTED TO TALK ABOUT?
NOT YOU, MASTER TA, I WANT TO TALK TO HER!
HUH?
ポカ...
87
ANYWAY ...
どーいうわけよ
ANYWAY, WHAT?
88
WE'LL TALK SOME OTHER TIME, OK?
OH.
UH...
OK.
89
SLAM
バタン...
....

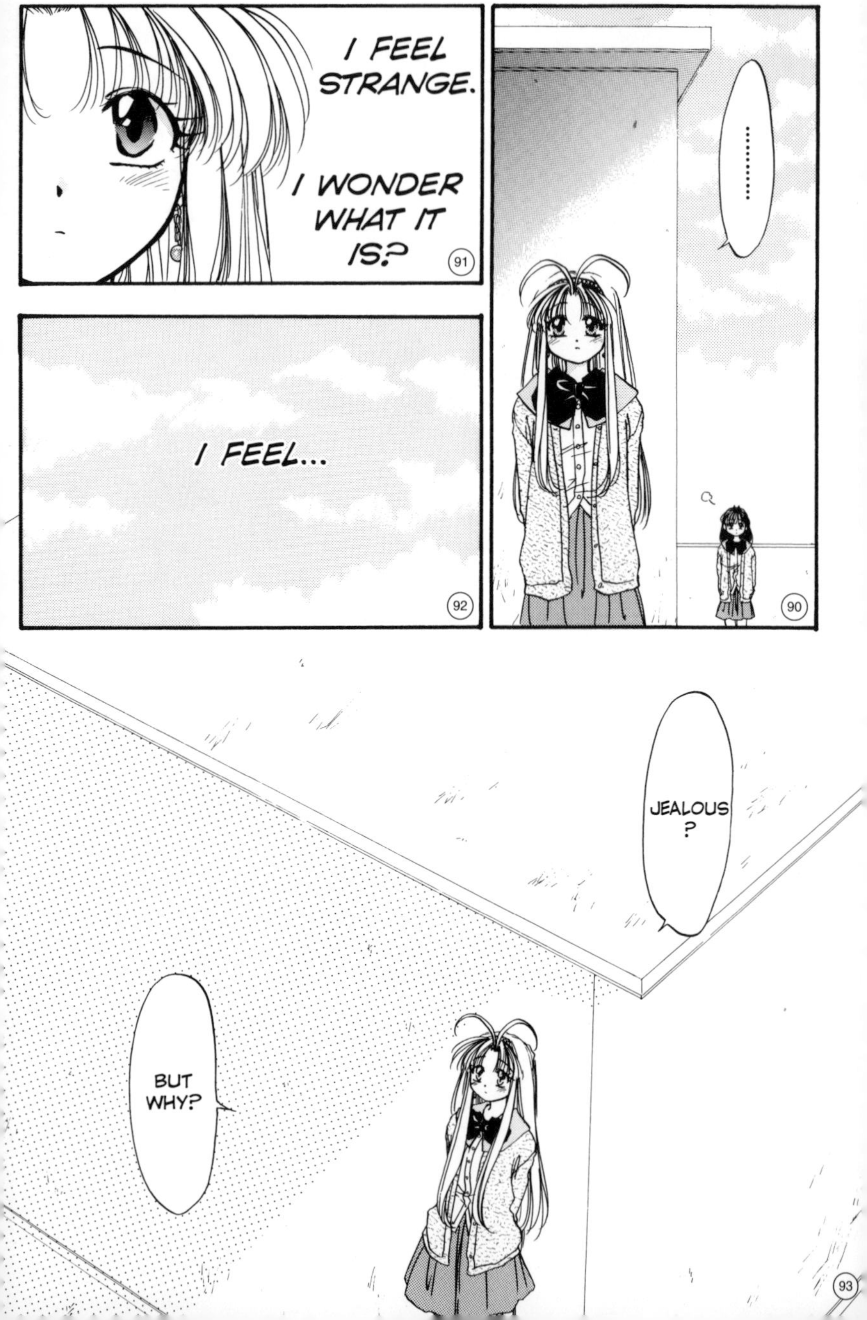
......
I FEEL STRANGE.
I WONDER WHAT IT IS?
I FEEL...
JEALOUS?
BUT WHY?

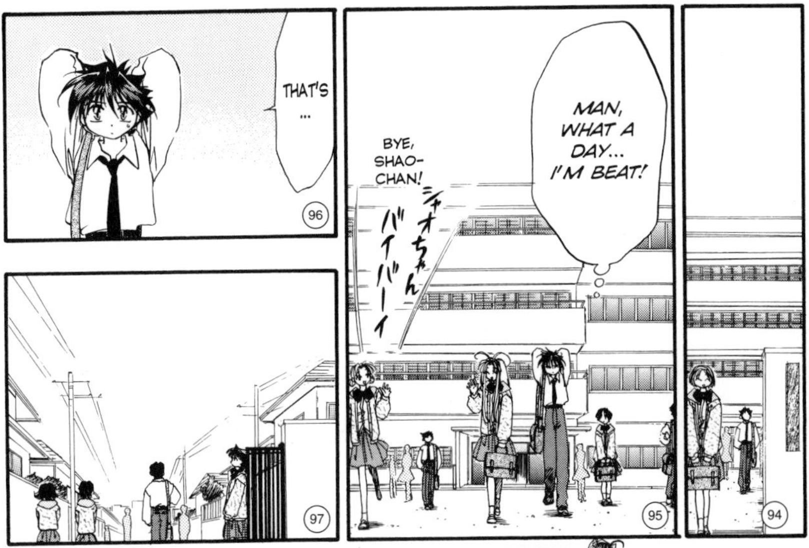
MAN, WHAT A DAY... I'M BEAT!
BYE, SHAO-CHAN!
シャオちゃんバイバーイ
THAT'S ...

LUU ANN'S STUCK IN AN ALL-STAFF MEETING AGAIN.

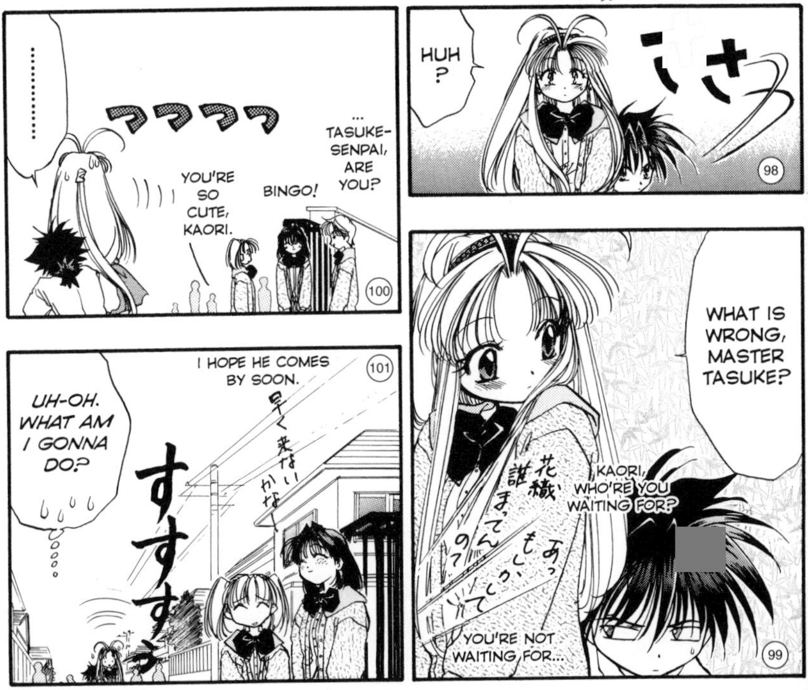
HUH?
WHAT IS WRONG, MASTER TASUKE?
KAORI, WHO'RE YOU WAITING FOR?
花織誰まってんの?
あっもしかして
YOU'RE NOT WAITING FOR...
... TASUKE-SENPAI, ARE YOU?
BINGO!
YOU'RE SO CUTE, KAORI.
....
I HOPE HE COMES BY SOON.
早く来ないかな
UH-OH. WHAT AM I GONNA DO?
すすす

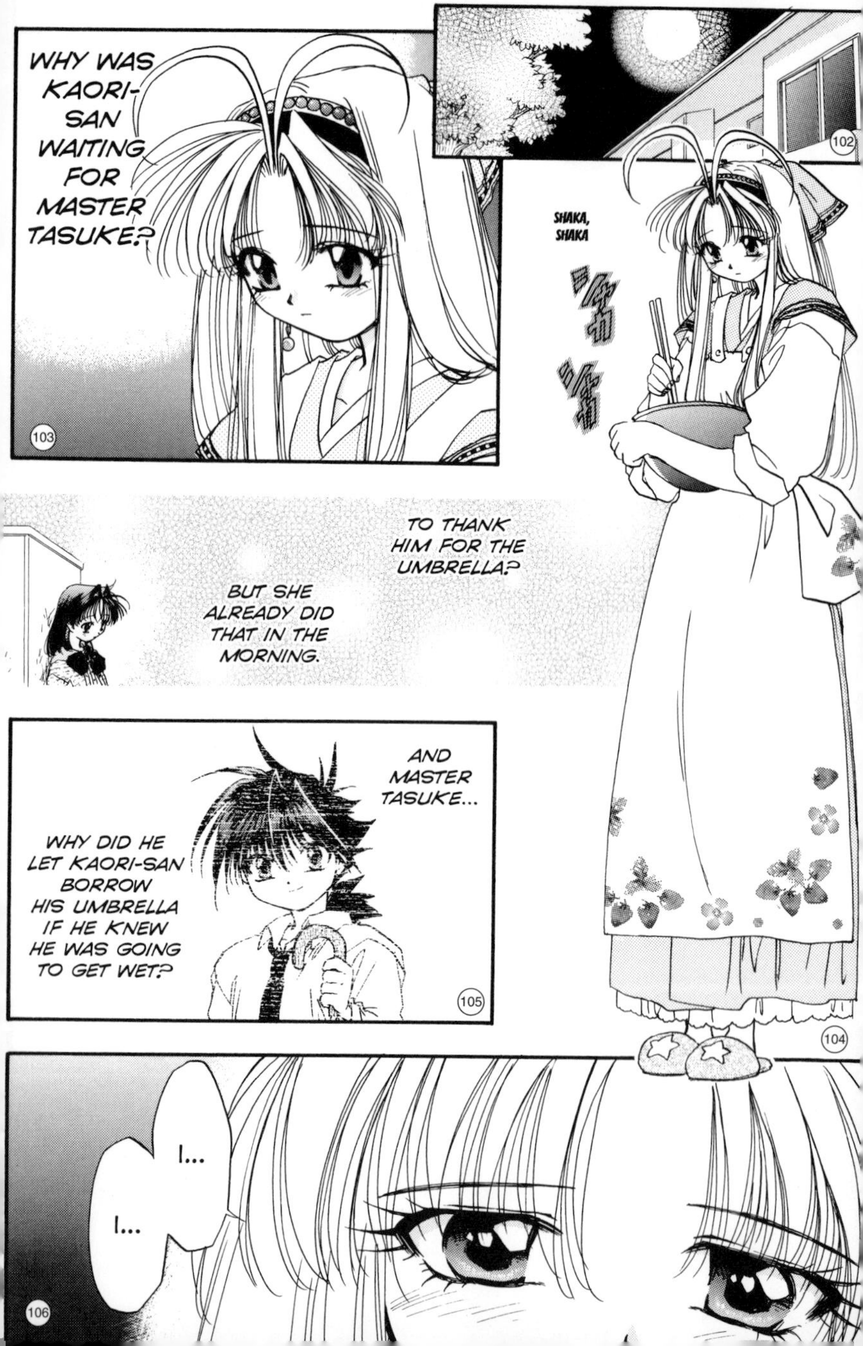
WHY WAS KAORI-SAN WAITING FOR MASTER TASUKE?
SHAKA, SHAKA
TO THANK HIM FOR THE UMBRELLA?
BUT SHE ALREADY DID THAT IN THE MORNING.
AND MASTER TASUKE...
WHY DID HE LET KAORI-SAN BORROW HIS UMBRELLA IF HE KNEW HE WAS GOING TO GET WET?
I...
I...

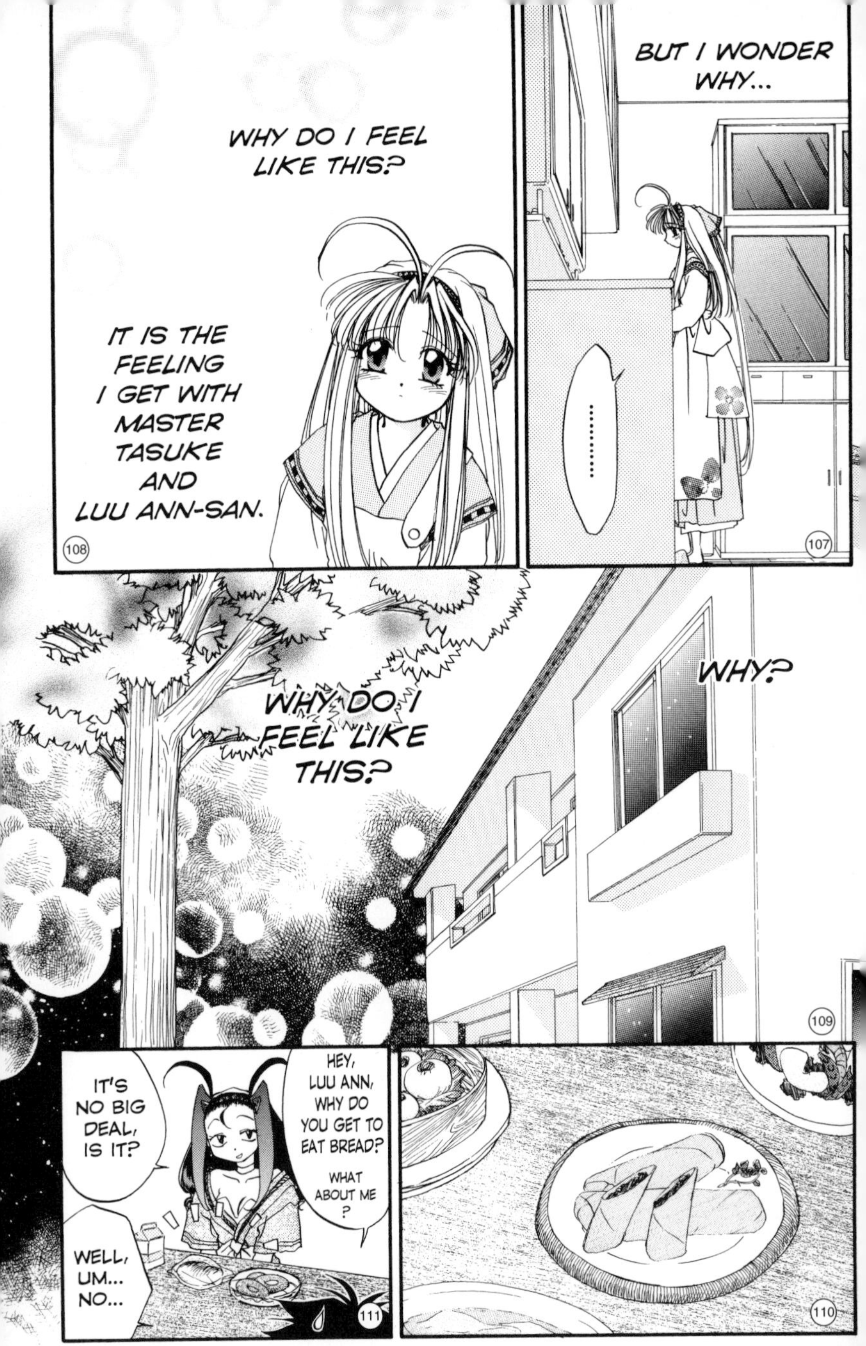
BUT I WONDER WHY...
....
WHY DO I FEEL LIKE THIS?
IT IS THE FEELING I GET WITH MASTER TASUKE AND LUU ANN-SAN.
WHY?
WHY DO I FEEL LIKE THIS?
HEY, LUU ANN, WHY DO YOU GET TO EAT BREAD?
WHAT ABOUT ME?
IT'S NO BIG DEAL, IS IT?
WELL, UM... NO...

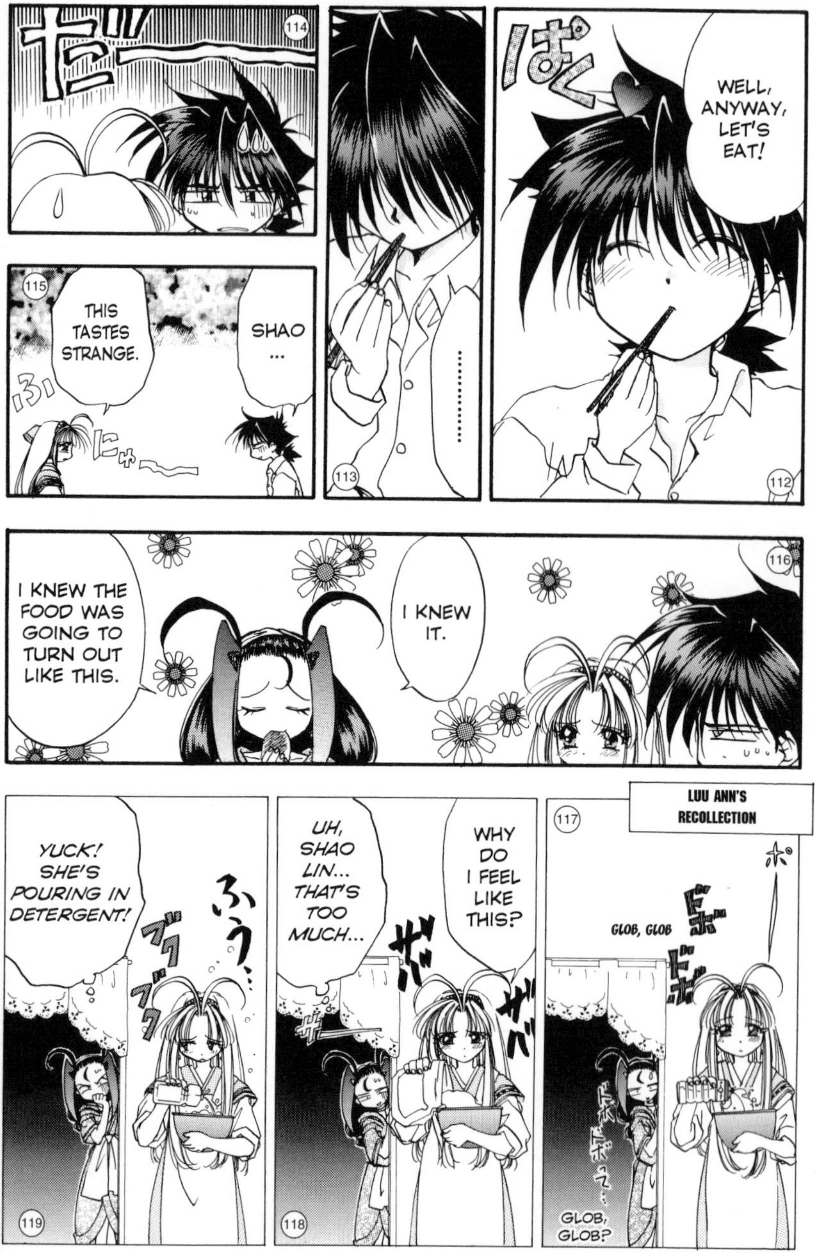
ぱく
WELL, ANYWAY, LET'S EAT!
......
SHAO ...
THIS TASTES STRANGE.
I KNEW IT.
I KNEW THE FOOD WAS GOING TO TURN OUT LIKE THIS.
LUU ANN'S RECOLLECTION
GLOB, GLOB
GLOB, GLOB?
WHY DO I FEEL LIKE THIS?
UH, SHAO LIN... THAT'S TOO MUCH...
YUCK! SHE'S POURING IN DETERGENT!

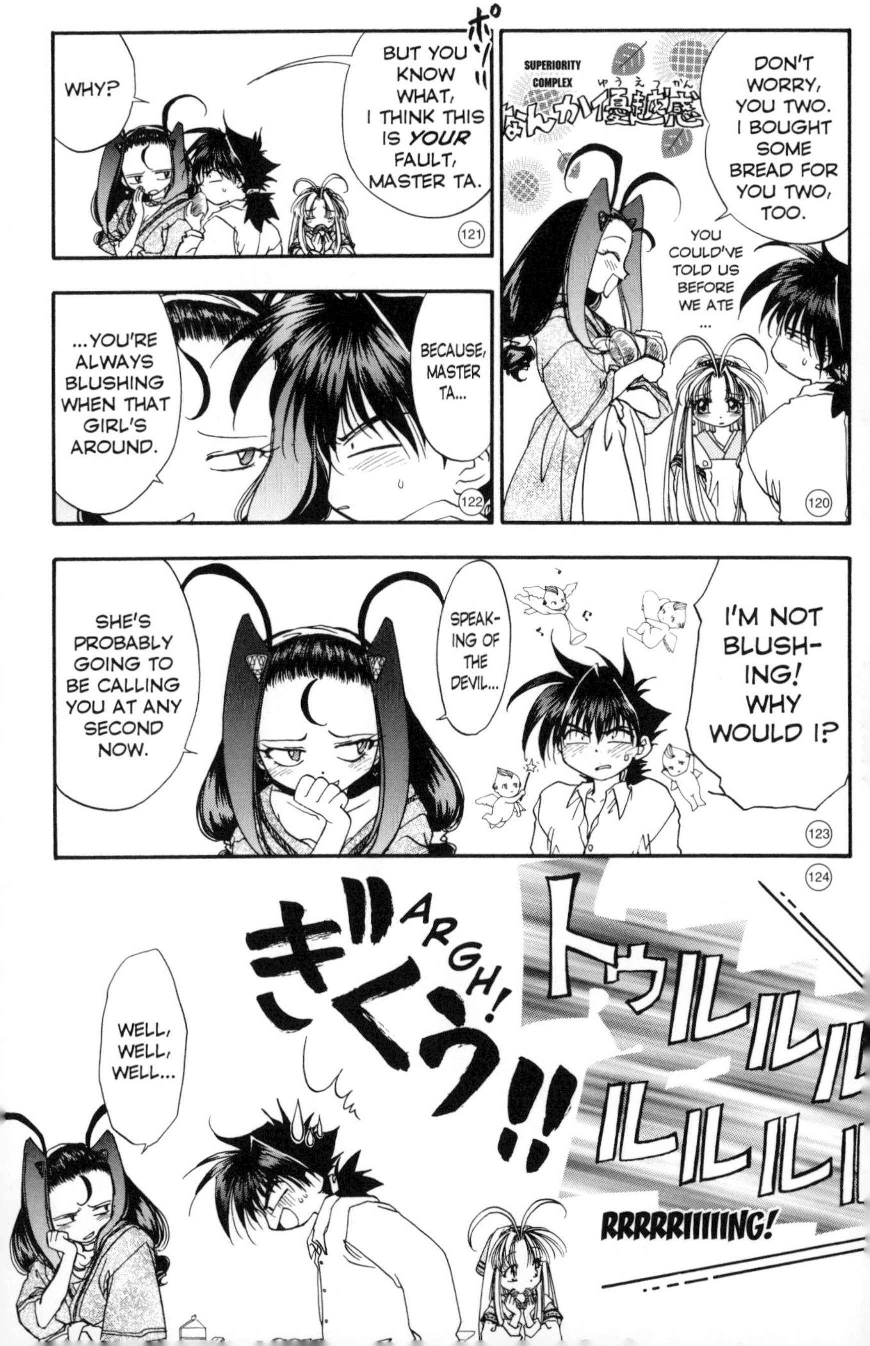
SUPERIORITY COMPLEX
なんか優越感
ゆうえつかん
DON'T WORRY, YOU TWO. I BOUGHT SOME BREAD FOR YOU TWO, TOO.
YOU COULD'VE TOLD US BEFORE WE ATE ...
120
BUT YOU KNOW WHAT, I THINK THIS IS *YOUR* FAULT, MASTER TA.
WHY?
121
BECAUSE, MASTER TA...
...YOU'RE ALWAYS BLUSHING WHEN THAT GIRL'S AROUND.
122
I'M NOT BLUSHING! WHY WOULD I?
SPEAKING OF THE DEVIL...
SHE'S PROBABLY GOING TO BE CALLING YOU AT ANY SECOND NOW.
123
124
トゥルルルルルルル
RRRRRIIIIIING!
ぎくぅ!!
ARGH!
WELL, WELL, WELL...

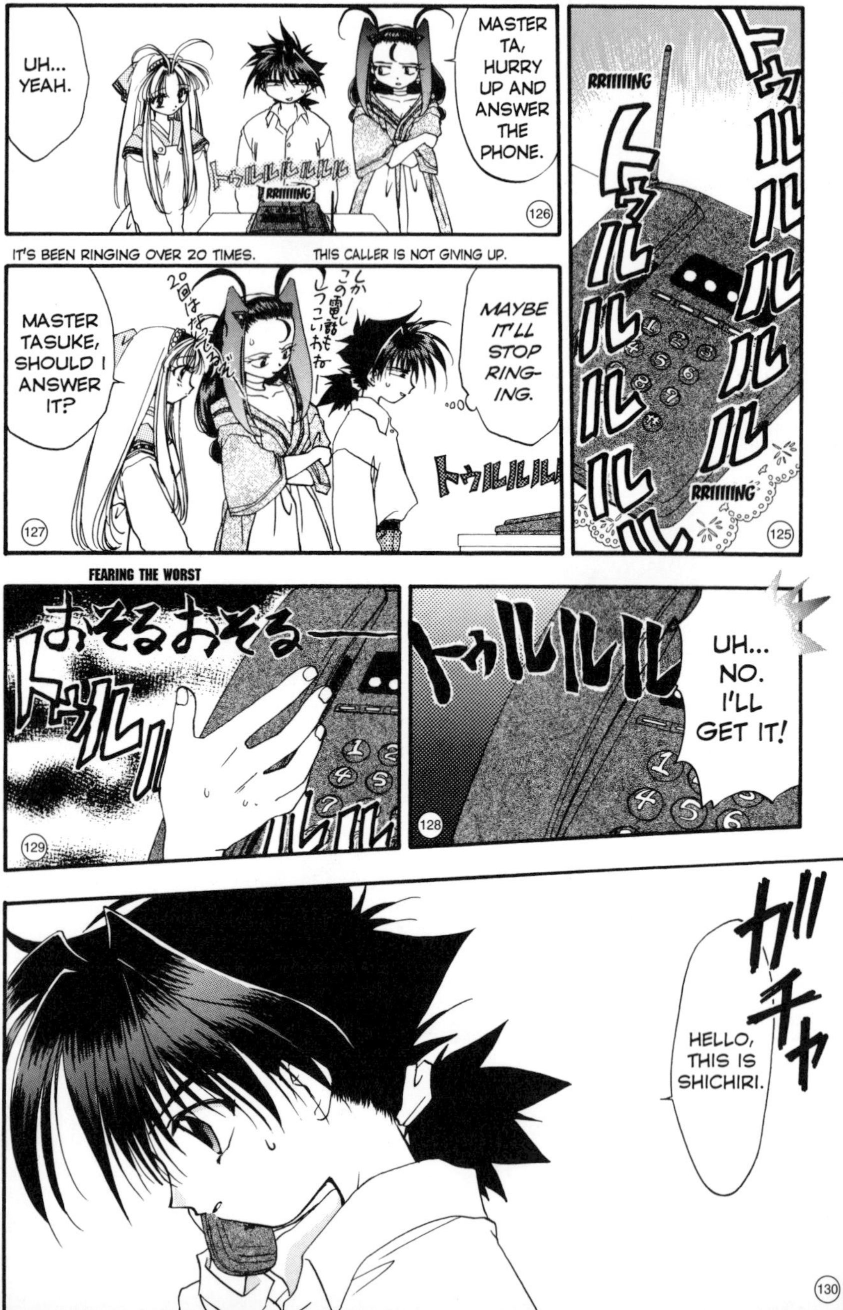
RRIIIIING
RRIIIIING
MASTER TA, HURRY UP AND ANSWER THE PHONE.
UH... YEAH.
RRIIIING
THIS CALLER IS NOT GIVING UP.
IT'S BEEN RINGING OVER 20 TIMES.
MAYBE IT'LL STOP RINGING.
MASTER TASUKE, SHOULD I ANSWER IT?
UH... NO. I'LL GET IT!
FEARING THE WORST
おそるおそる
HELLO, THIS IS SHICHIRI.
ガチャ

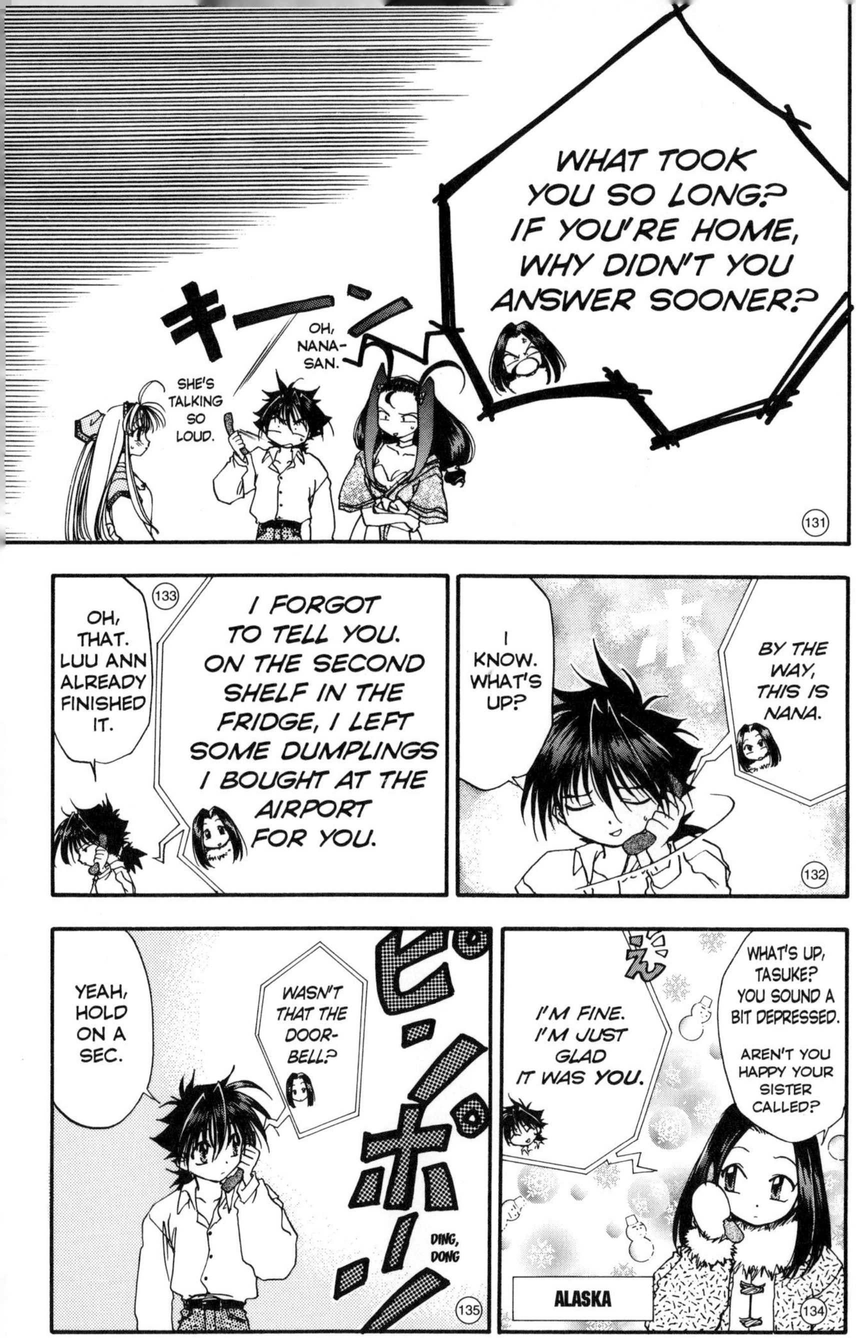

WHAT TOOK YOU SO LONG? IF YOU'RE HOME, WHY DIDN'T YOU ANSWER SOONER?
キーン
OH, NANA-SAN.
SHE'S TALKING SO LOUD.
131
BY THE WAY, THIS IS NANA.
I KNOW. WHAT'S UP?
132
I FORGOT TO TELL YOU. ON THE SECOND SHELF IN THE FRIDGE, I LEFT SOME DUMPLINGS I BOUGHT AT THE AIRPORT FOR YOU.
133
OH, THAT. LUU ANN ALREADY FINISHED IT.
WHAT'S UP, TASUKE? YOU SOUND A BIT DEPRESSED.
AREN'T YOU HAPPY YOUR SISTER CALLED?
I'M FINE. I'M JUST GLAD IT WAS YOU.
ALASKA
134
ピンポーン
DING, DONG
WASN'T THAT THE DOOR-BELL?
YEAH, HOLD ON A SEC.
135

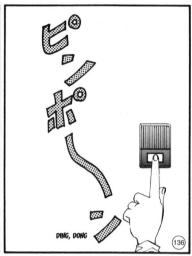

DING, DONG

SORRY IT TOOK SO LONG...

GEH!

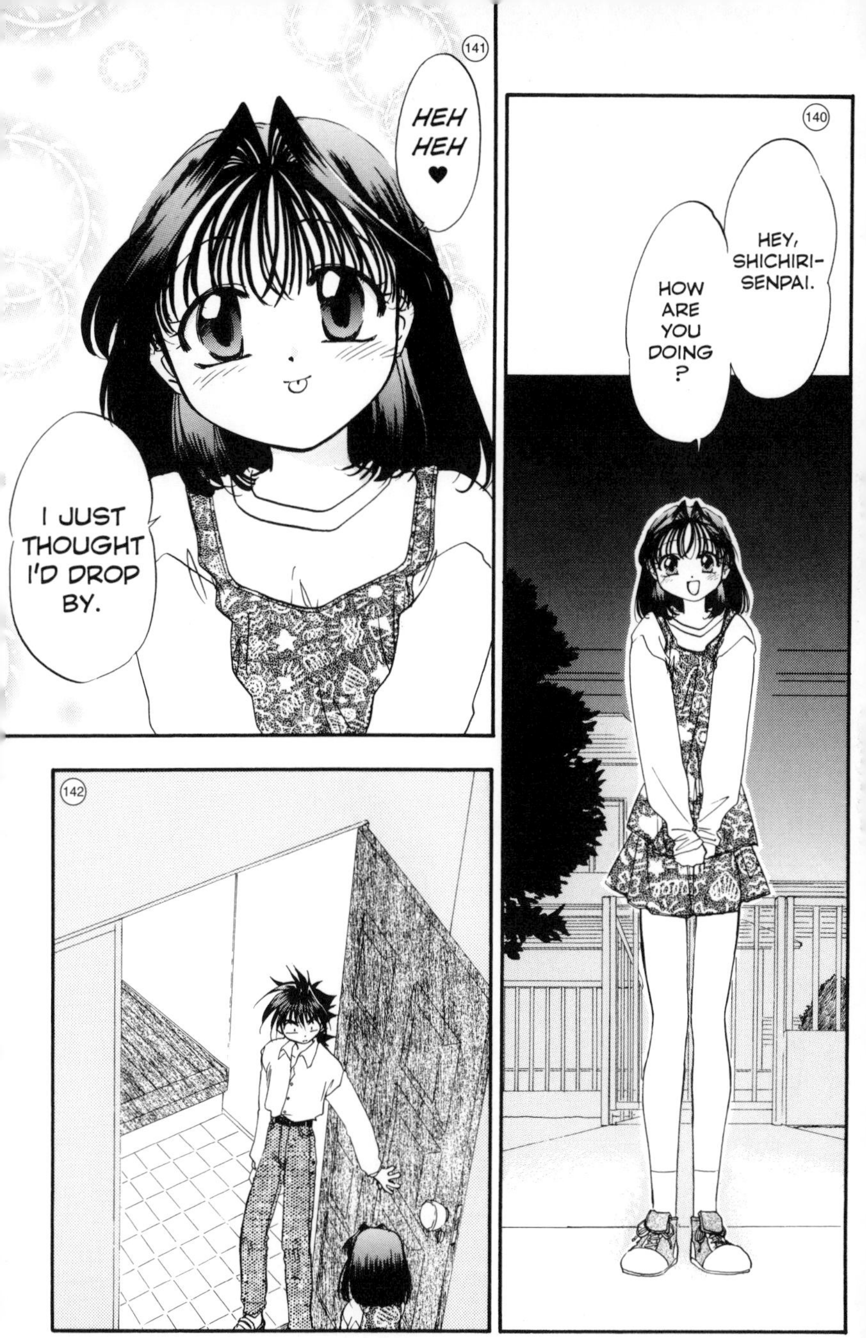
140
HEY, SHICHIRI-SENPAI.
HOW ARE YOU DOING?
141
HEH HEH ♥
I JUST THOUGHT I'D DROP BY.
142

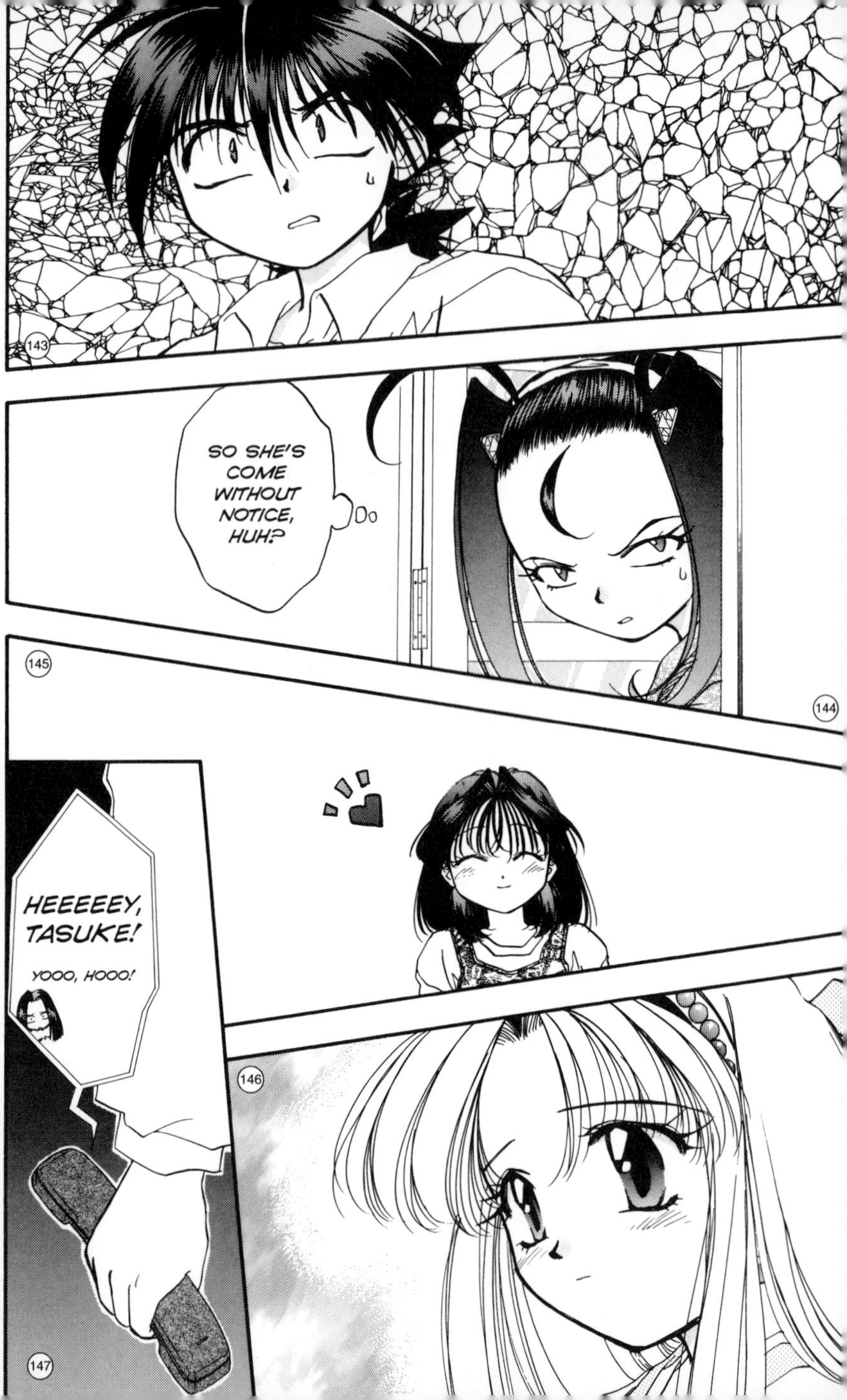
SO SHE'S COME WITHOUT NOTICE, HUH?
HEEEEEY, TASUKE!
YOOO, HOOO!

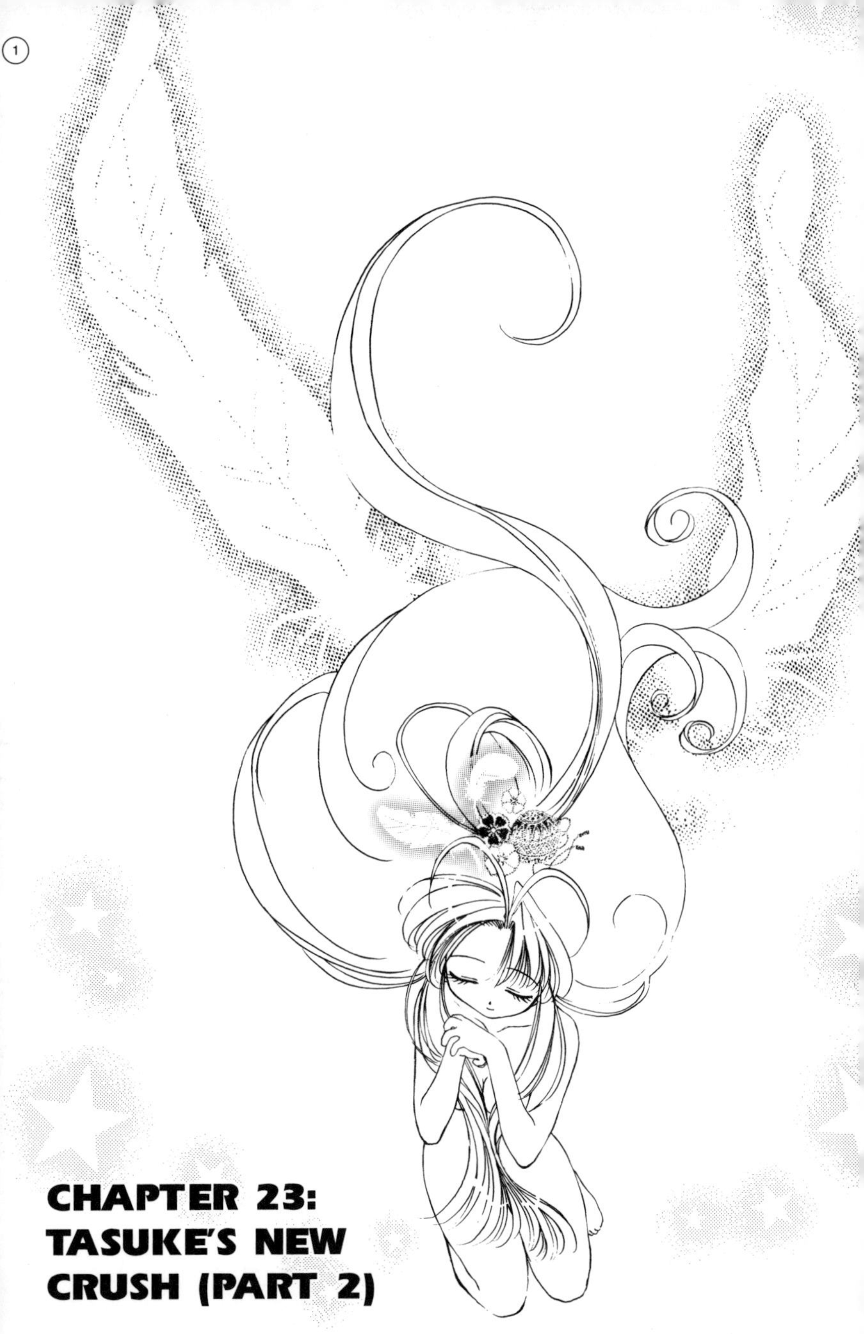

CHAPTER 23: TASUKE'S NEW CRUSH (PART 2)

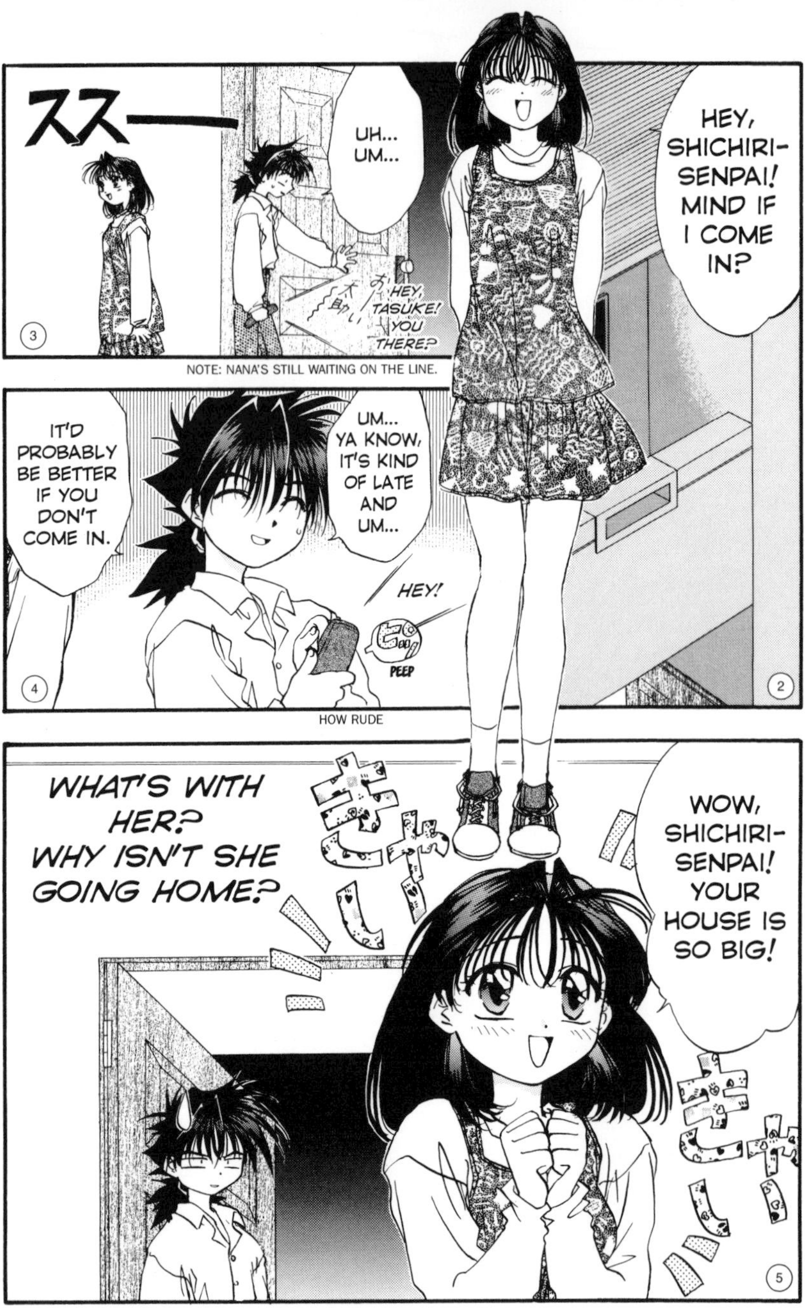

HEY, SHICHIRI-SENPAI! MIND IF I COME IN?
スス—
UH... UM...
HEY, TASUKE! YOU THERE?
NOTE: NANA'S STILL WAITING ON THE LINE.
UM... YA KNOW, IT'S KIND OF LATE AND UM...
IT'D PROBABLY BE BETTER IF YOU DON'T COME IN.
HEY!
PEEP
HOW RUDE
WOW, SHICHIRI-SENPAI! YOUR HOUSE IS SO BIG!
WHAT'S WITH HER? WHY ISN'T SHE GOING HOME?

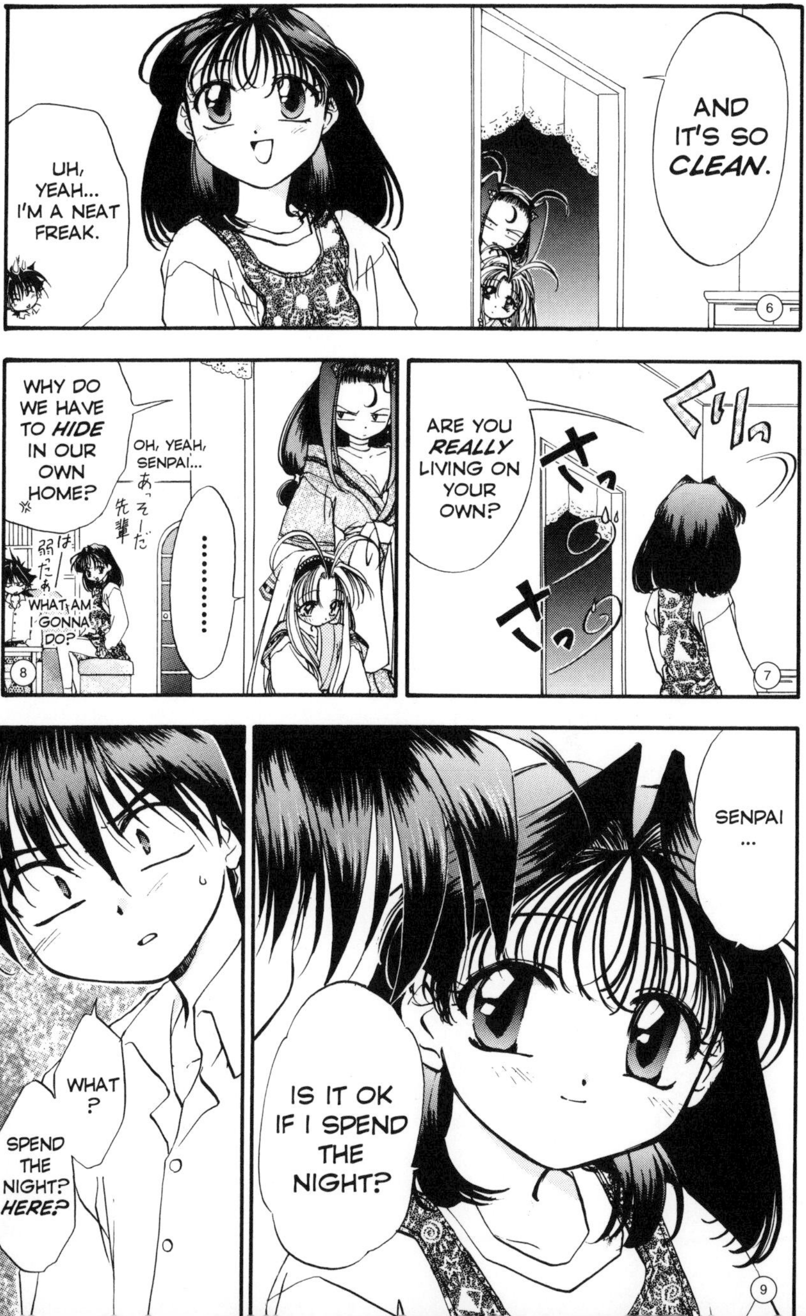
AND IT'S SO CLEAN.
UH, YEAH... I'M A NEAT FREAK.
くりっ
ARE YOU REALLY LIVING ON YOUR OWN?
さっ
さっ
....
OH, YEAH, SENPAI...
あっそーだ先輩
WHY DO WE HAVE TO HIDE IN OUR OWN HOME?
はー弱ったぁ
WHAT AM I GONNA DO?
SENPAI ...
IS IT OK IF I SPEND THE NIGHT?
WHAT?
SPEND THE NIGHT? HERE?

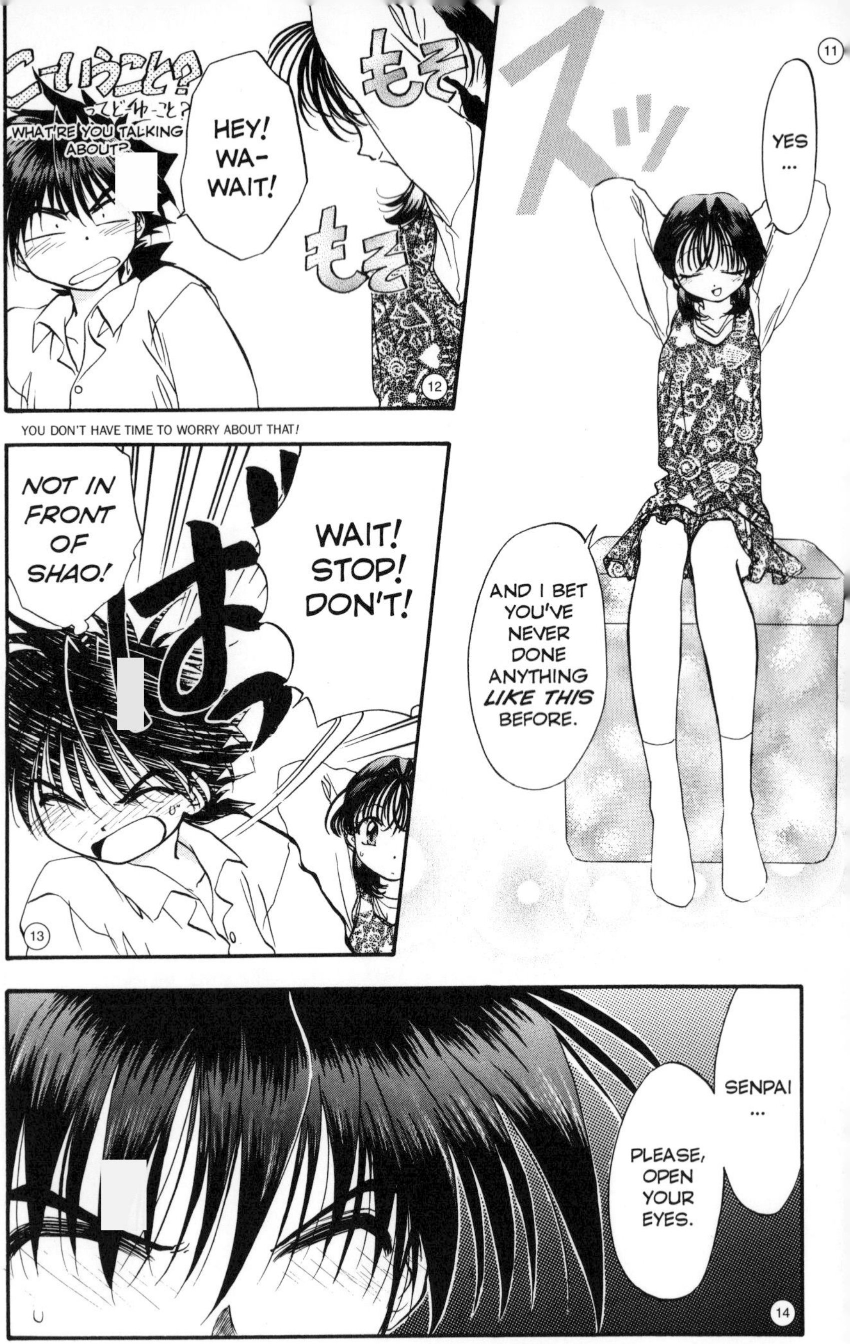
YES ...
AND I BET YOU'VE NEVER DONE ANYTHING *LIKE THIS* BEFORE.
HEY! WA-WAIT!
もぞ
もぞ
WHAT'RE YOU TALKING ABOUT?
YOU DON'T HAVE TIME TO WORRY ABOUT THAT!
WAIT! STOP! DON'T!
NOT IN FRONT OF SHAO!
SENPAI ...
PLEASE, OPEN YOUR EYES.

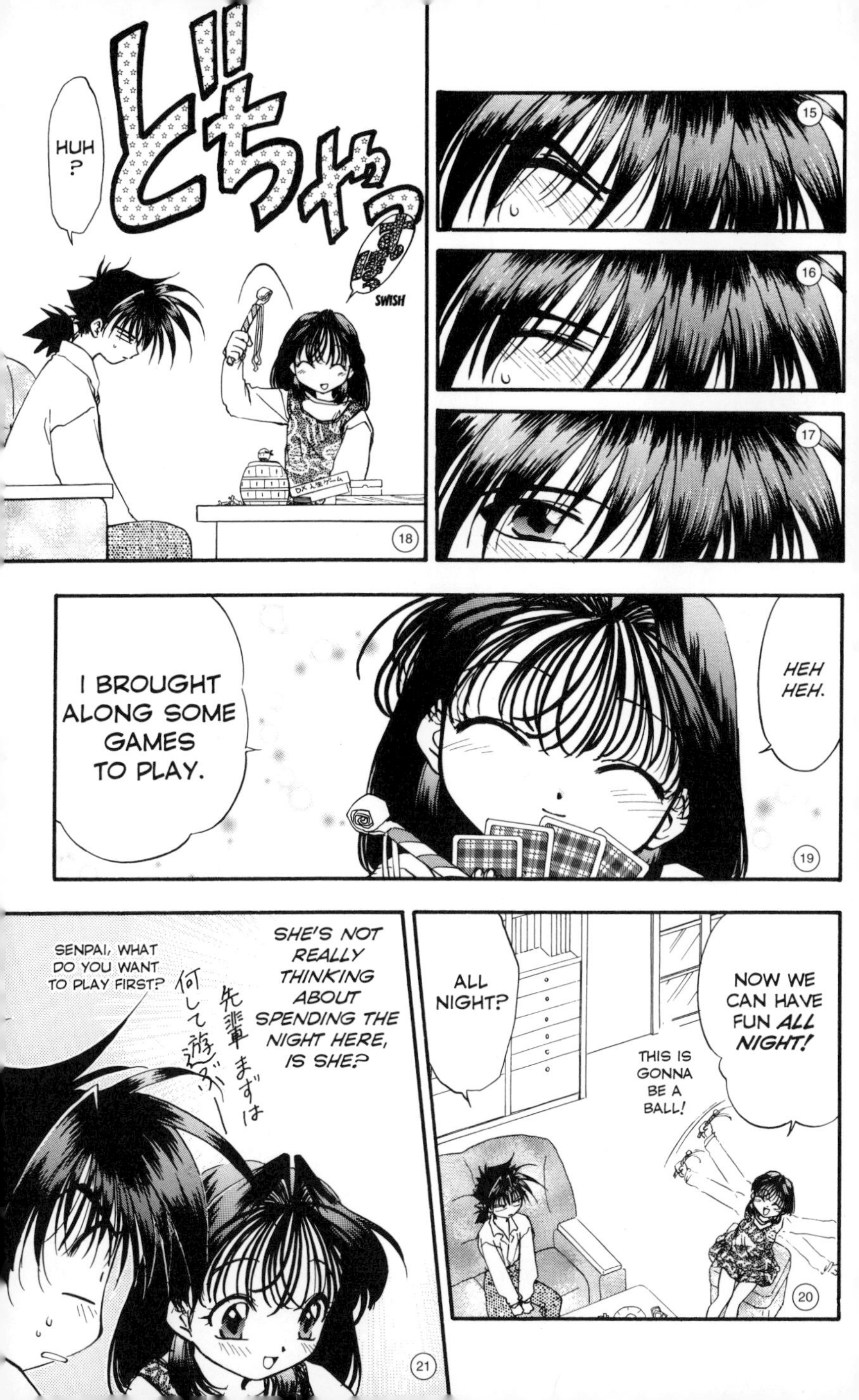
15
16
17
どちゃっ
HUH ?
SWISH
18
HEH HEH.
I BROUGHT ALONG SOME GAMES TO PLAY.
19
NOW WE CAN HAVE FUN ALL NIGHT!
THIS IS GONNA BE A BALL!
ALL NIGHT?
20
SHE'S NOT REALLY THINKING ABOUT SPENDING THE NIGHT HERE, IS SHE?
先輩まずは何して遊ぶ～
SENPAI, WHAT DO YOU WANT TO PLAY FIRST?
21

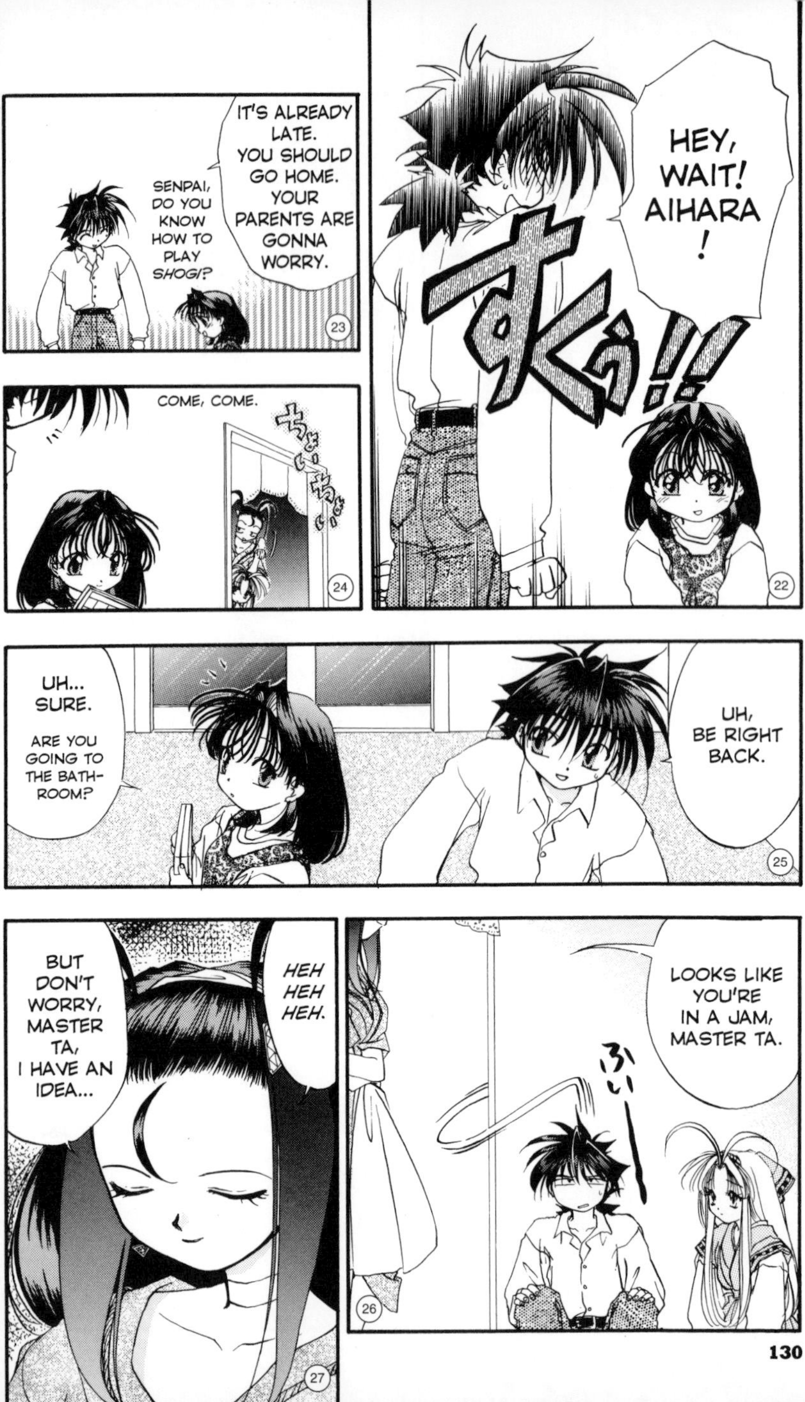
HEY, WAIT! AIHARA !
IT'S ALREADY LATE. YOU SHOULD GO HOME. YOUR PARENTS ARE GONNA WORRY.
SENPAI, DO YOU KNOW HOW TO PLAY SHOGI?
COME, COME.
UH, BE RIGHT BACK.
UH... SURE.
ARE YOU GOING TO THE BATH-ROOM?
LOOKS LIKE YOU'RE IN A JAM, MASTER TA.
HEH HEH HEH.
BUT DON'T WORRY, MASTER TA, I HAVE AN IDEA...

LUU ANN'S PLAN

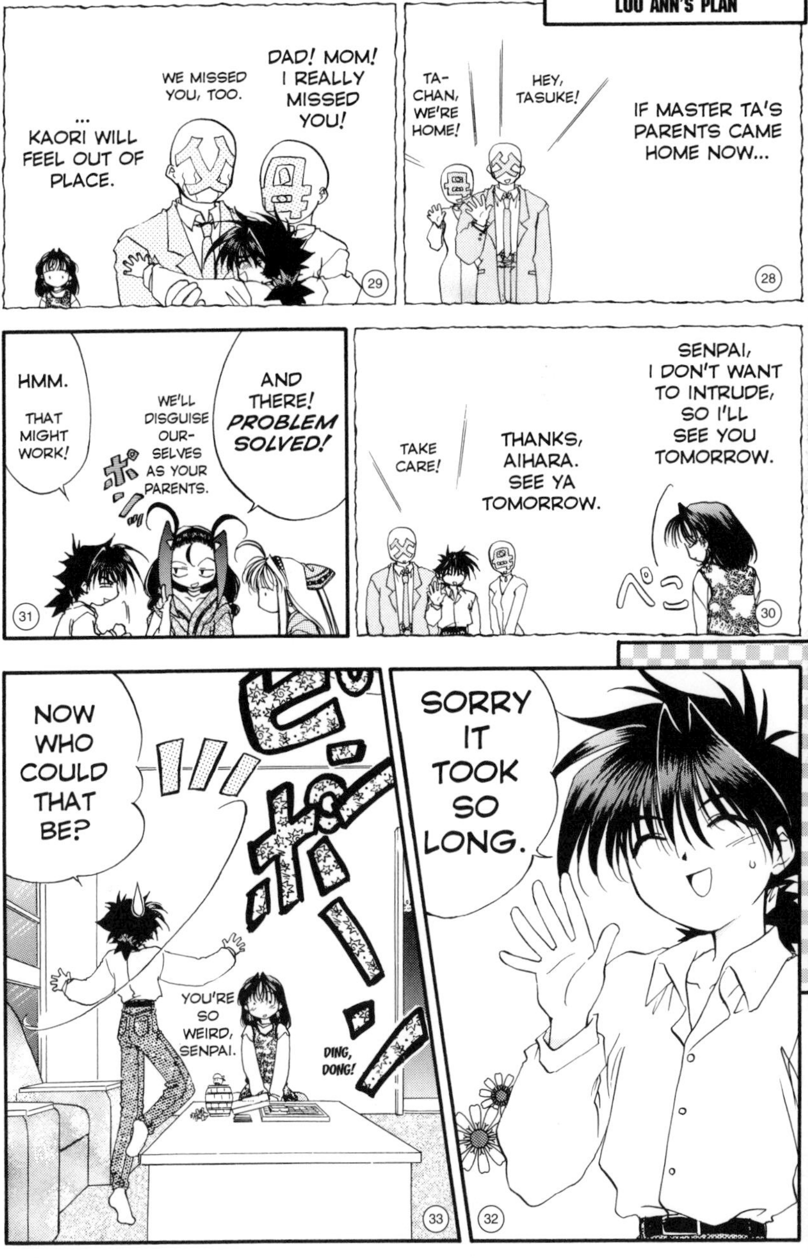
IF MASTER TA'S PARENTS CAME HOME NOW...
HEY, TASUKE!
TA-CHAN, WE'RE HOME!
28
DAD! MOM! I REALLY MISSED YOU!
WE MISSED YOU, TOO.
... KAORI WILL FEEL OUT OF PLACE.
29
SENPAI, I DON'T WANT TO INTRUDE, SO I'LL SEE YOU TOMORROW.
THANKS, AIHARA. SEE YA TOMORROW.
TAKE CARE!
30
AND THERE! PROBLEM SOLVED!
WE'LL DISGUISE OUR-SELVES AS YOUR PARENTS.
HMM.
THAT MIGHT WORK!
31
SORRY IT TOOK SO LONG.
32
DING, DONG!
NOW WHO COULD THAT BE?
YOU'RE SO WEIRD, SENPAI.
33

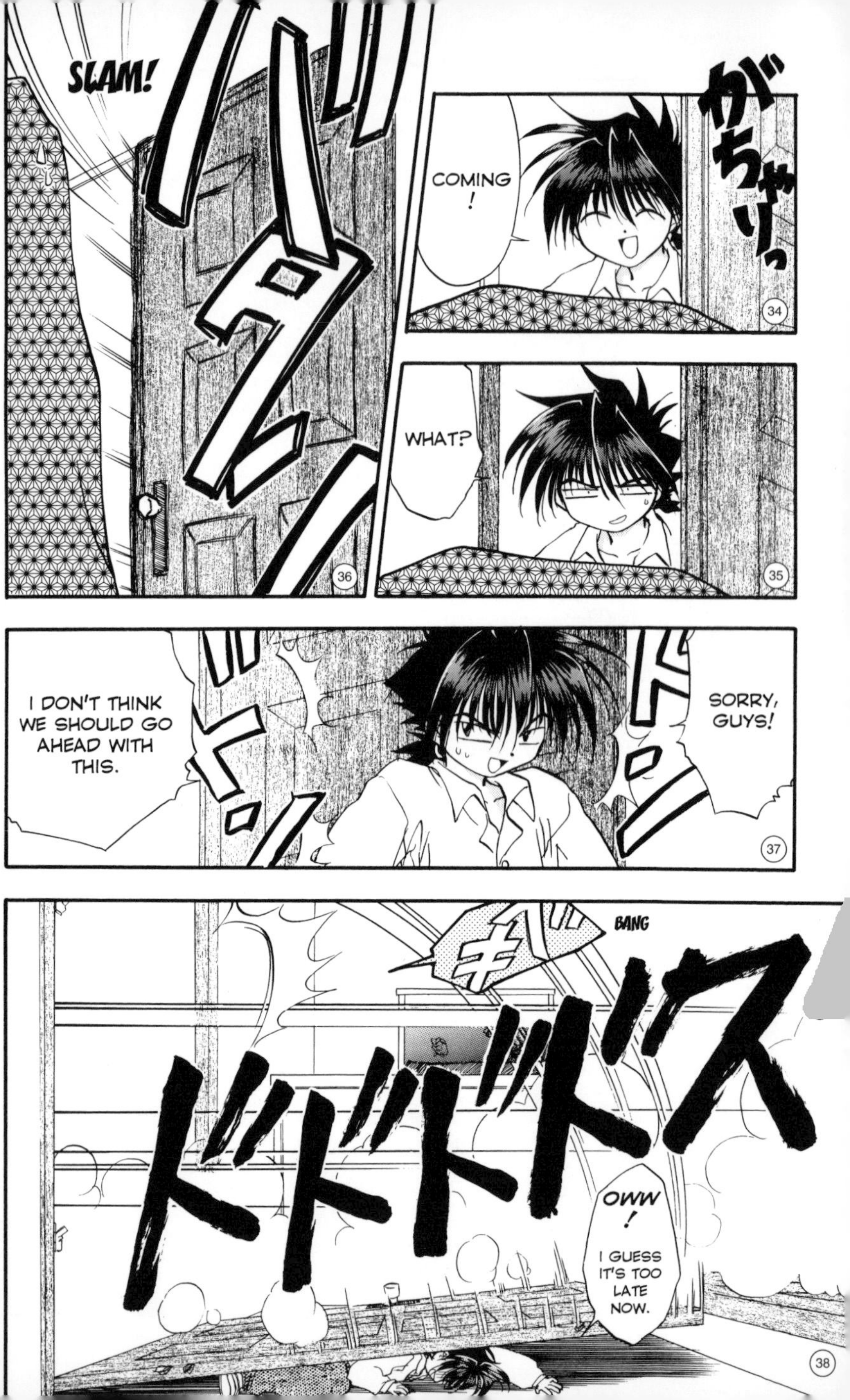

がちゃりっ
COMING!
WHAT?
SLAM!
SORRY, GUYS!
I DON'T THINK WE SHOULD GO AHEAD WITH THIS.
BANG
OWW!
I GUESS IT'S TOO LATE NOW.

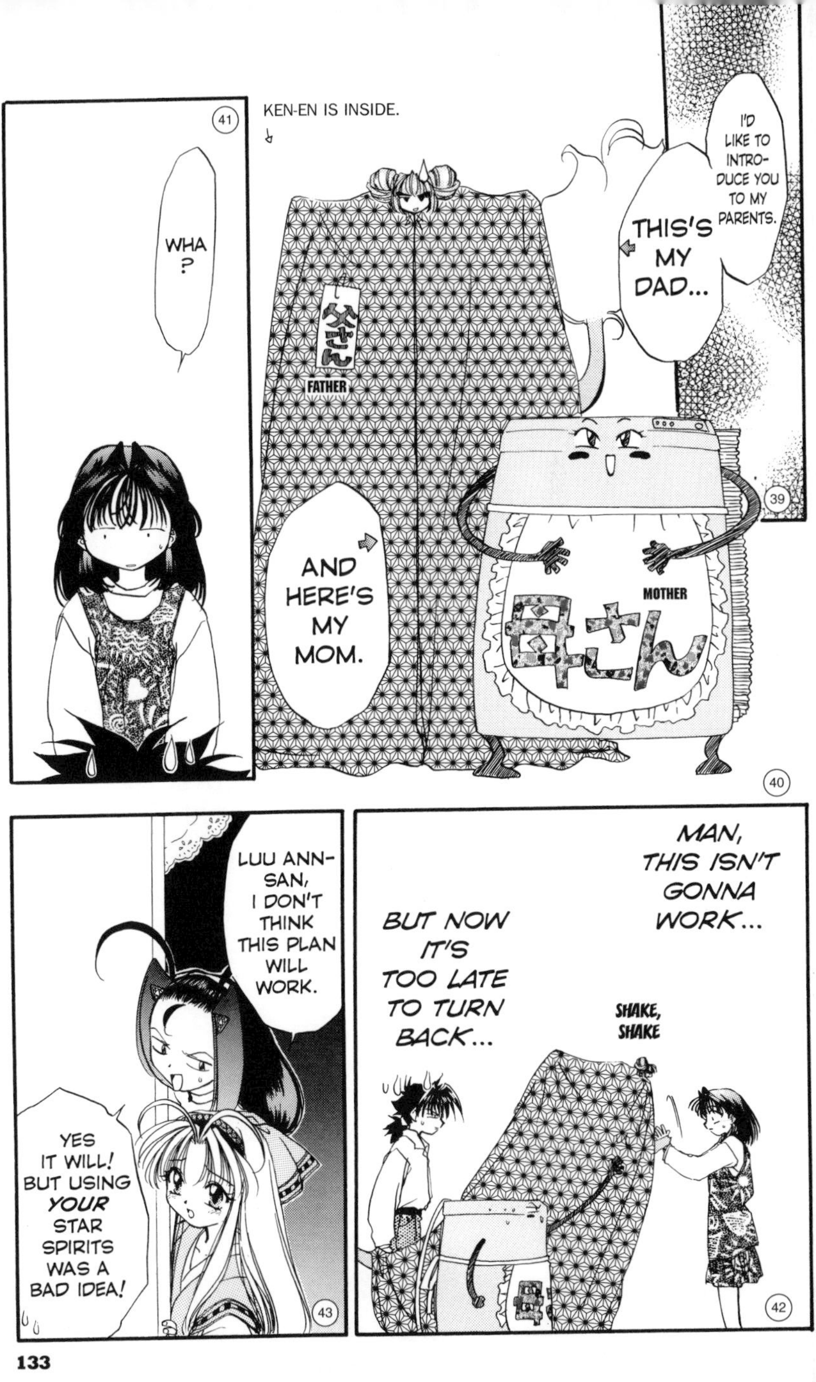

I'D LIKE TO INTRODUCE YOU TO MY PARENTS.
KEN-EN IS INSIDE.
THIS'S MY DAD...
父さん
FATHER
AND HERE'S MY MOM.
母さん
MOTHER
WHA ?
MAN, THIS ISN'T GONNA WORK...
BUT NOW IT'S TOO LATE TO TURN BACK...
SHAKE, SHAKE
LUU ANN-SAN, I DON'T THINK THIS PLAN WILL WORK.
YES IT WILL! BUT USING *YOUR* STAR SPIRITS WAS A BAD IDEA!

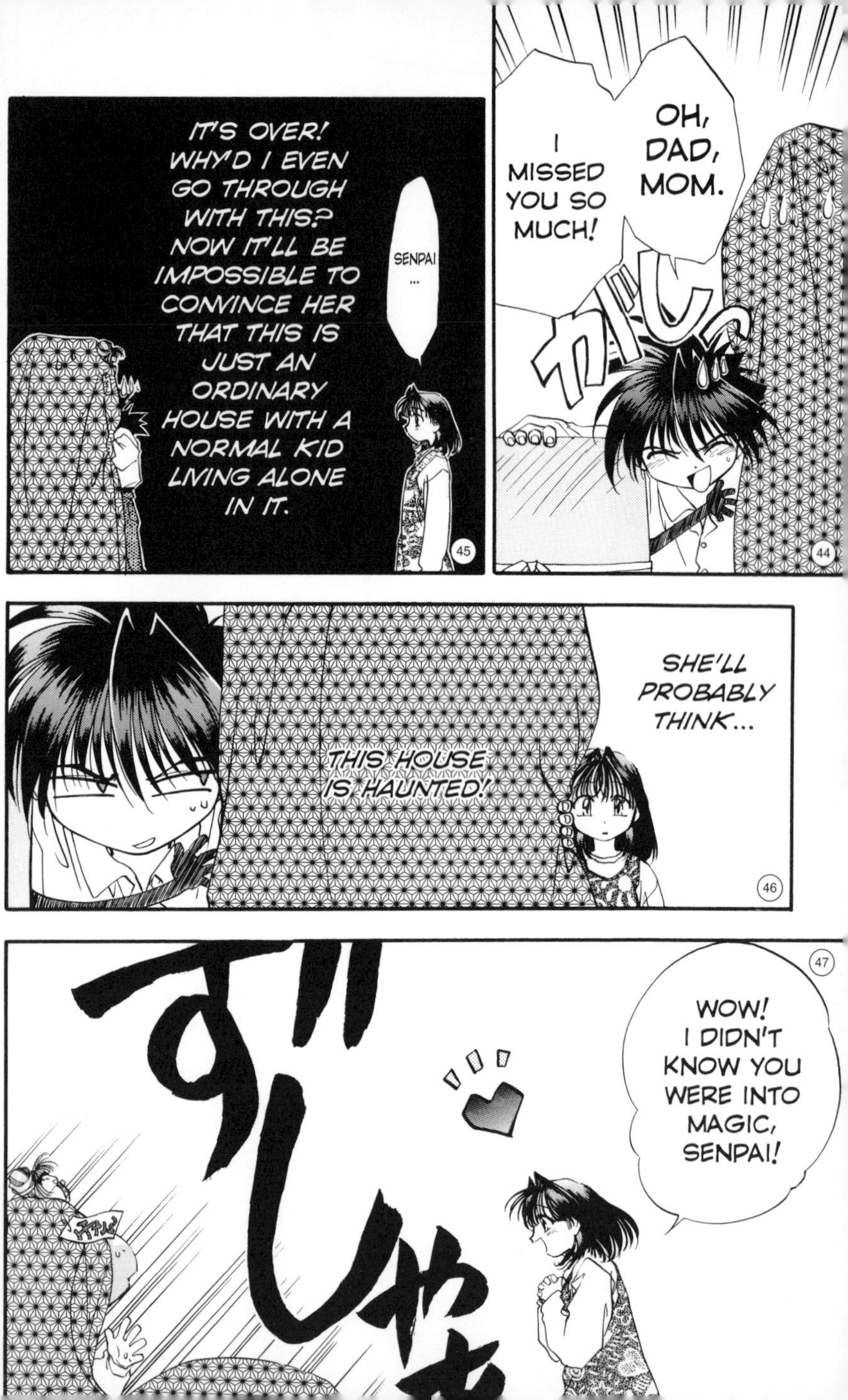
OH, DAD, MOM.
I MISSED YOU SO MUCH!
44
SENPAI...
IT'S OVER! WHY'D I EVEN GO THROUGH WITH THIS? NOW IT'LL BE IMPOSSIBLE TO CONVINCE HER THAT THIS IS JUST AN ORDINARY HOUSE WITH A NORMAL KID LIVING ALONE IN IT.
45
SHE'LL PROBABLY THINK...
THIS HOUSE IS HAUNTED!
46
WOW! I DIDN'T KNOW YOU WERE INTO MAGIC, SENPAI!
47

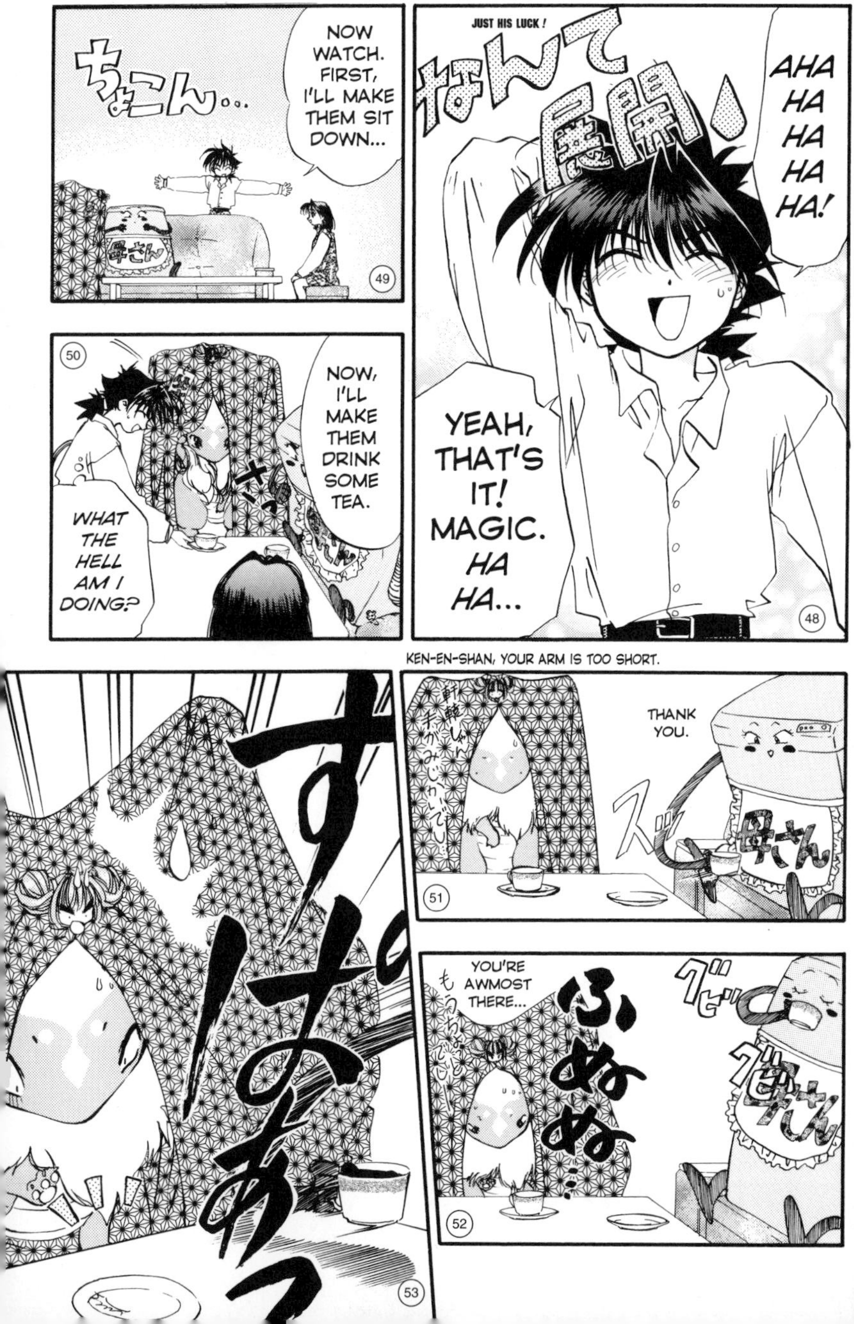
JUST HIS LUCK!
なんて展開!
AHA HA HA HA HA!
YEAH, THAT'S IT! MAGIC. HA HA...
ちょこん...
NOW WATCH. FIRST, I'LL MAKE THEM SIT DOWN...
NOW, I'LL MAKE THEM DRINK SOME TEA.
WHAT THE HELL AM I DOING?
KEN-EN-SHAN, YOUR ARM IS TOO SHORT.
THANK YOU.
YOU'RE AWMOST THERE...
ふぬぬぬ...

AH-HAH!

YOU HAD IT, TOO.

54

55

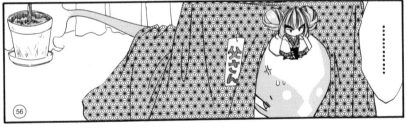

56

57

CRASH!

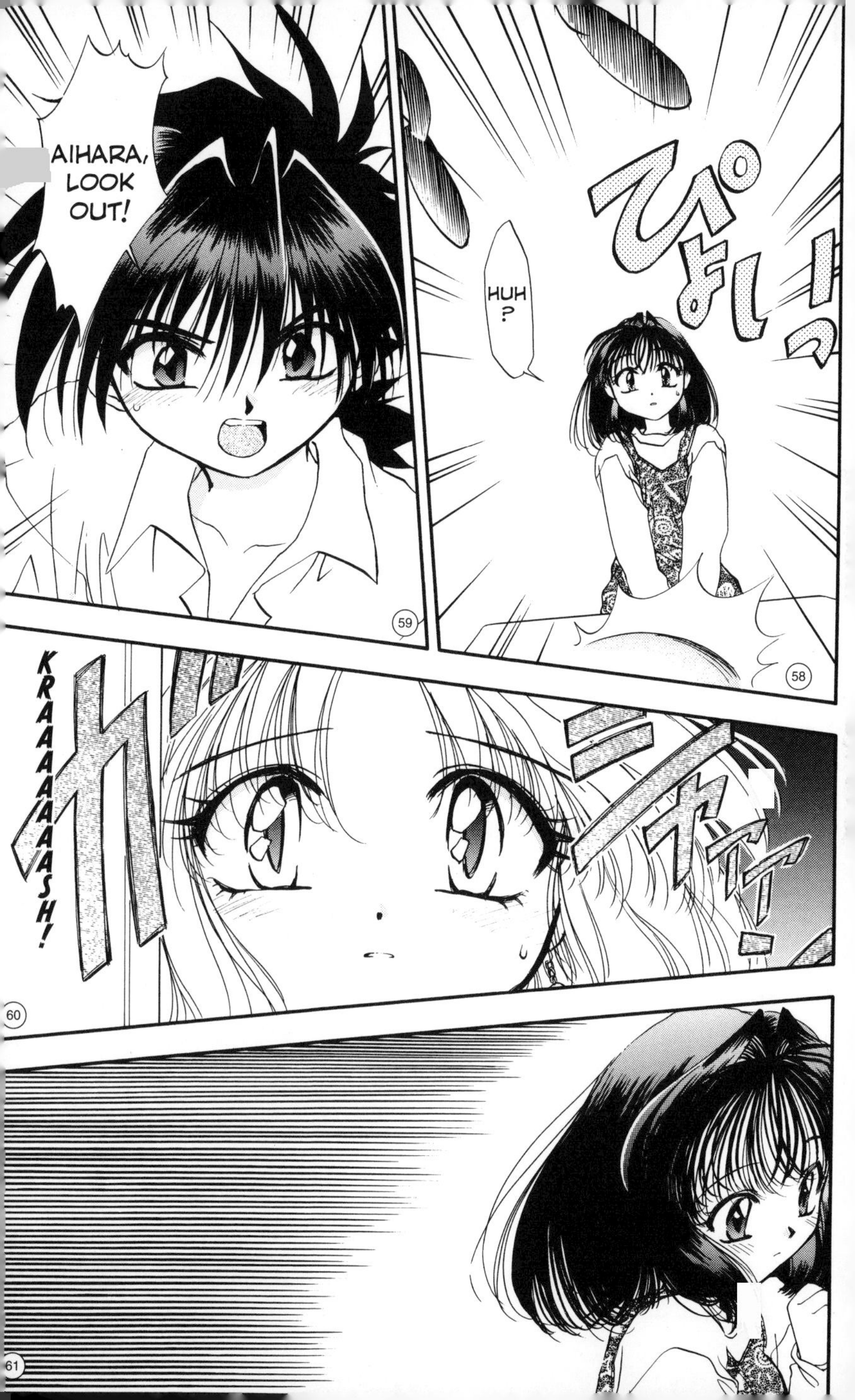
HUH ?
58
AIHARA, LOOK OUT!
59
KRAAAAAAAASH!
60
61

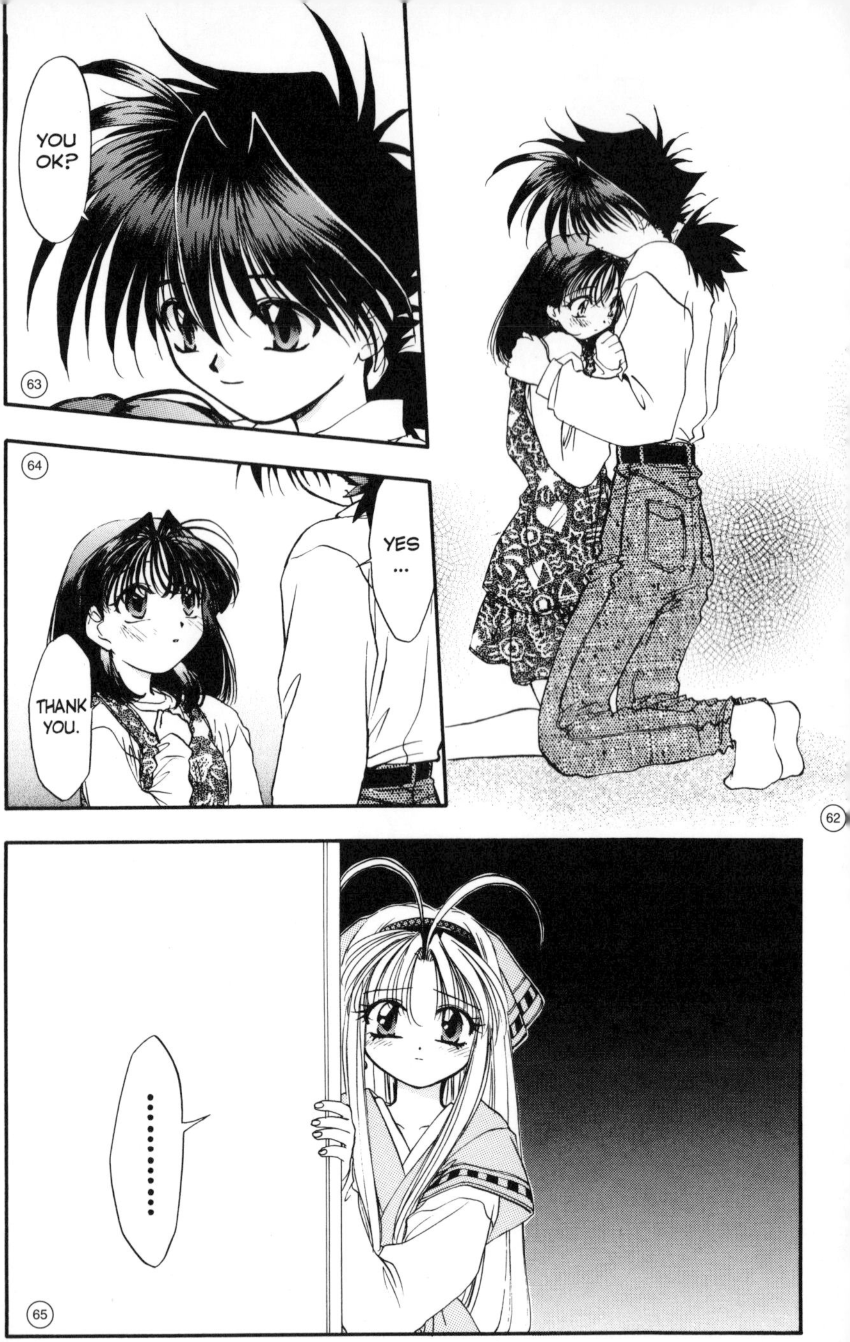
YOU OK?
YES ...
THANK YOU.
....

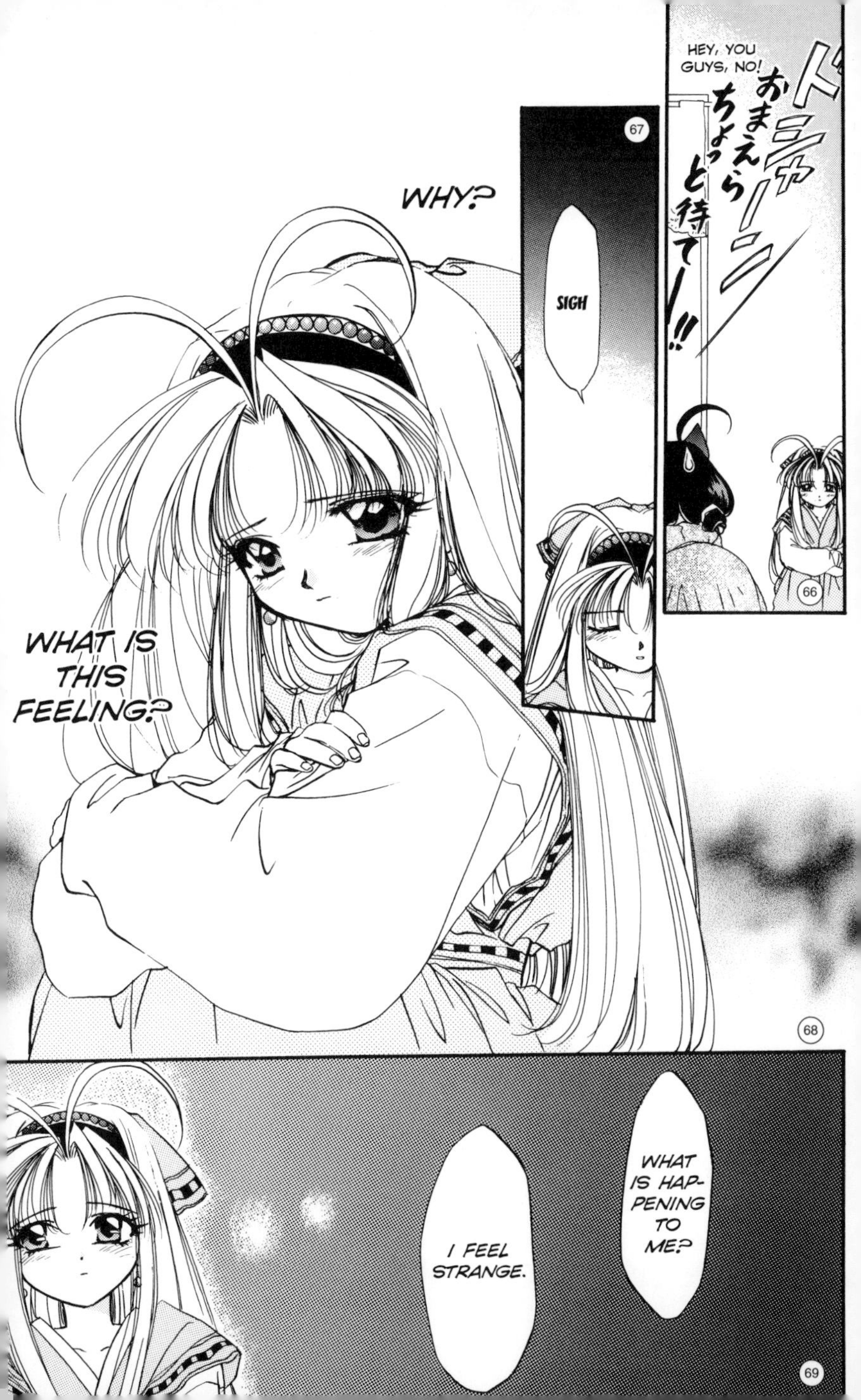

ドシャーン
HEY, YOU GUYS, NO!
おまえらちょっと待てー!!
SIGH
WHY?
WHAT IS THIS FEELING?
WHAT IS HAP-PENING TO ME?
I FEEL STRANGE.

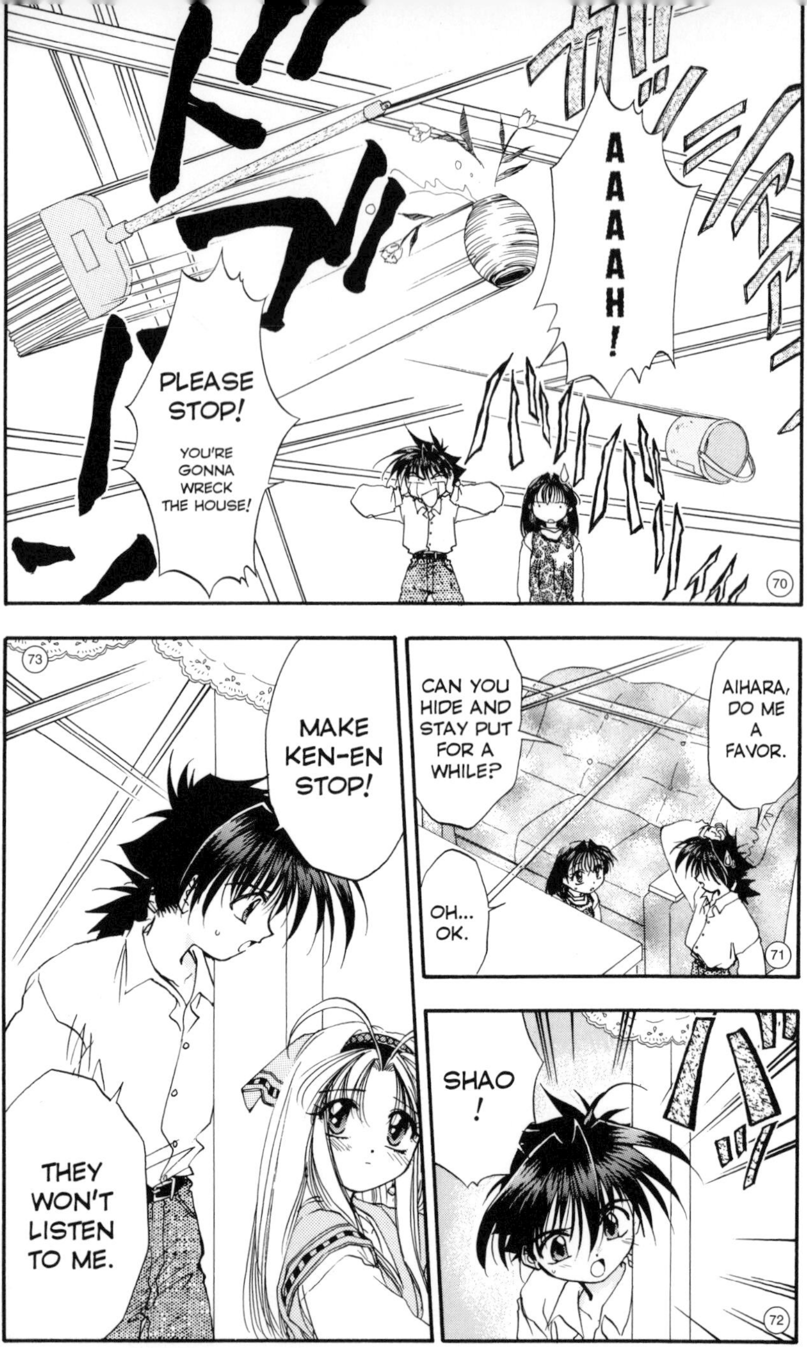

AAAAAH!
PLEASE STOP!
YOU'RE GONNA WRECK THE HOUSE!
AIHARA, DO ME A FAVOR.
CAN YOU HIDE AND STAY PUT FOR A WHILE?
OH... OK.
SHAO!
MAKE KEN-EN STOP!
THEY WON'T LISTEN TO ME.

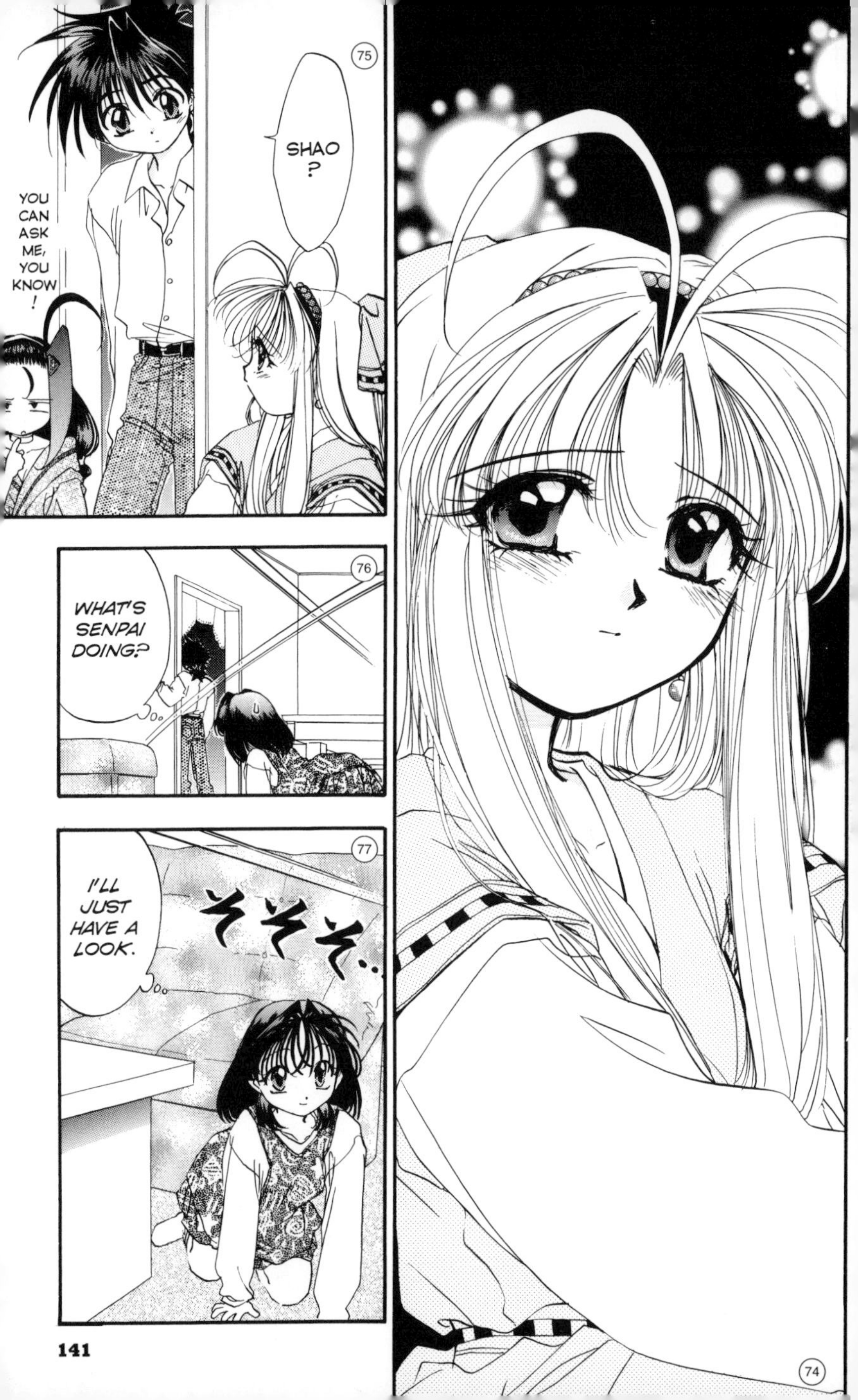
74
75
SHAO ?
YOU CAN ASK ME, YOU KNOW!
76
WHAT'S SENPAI DOING?
77
I'LL JUST HAVE A LOOK.
そそそ…

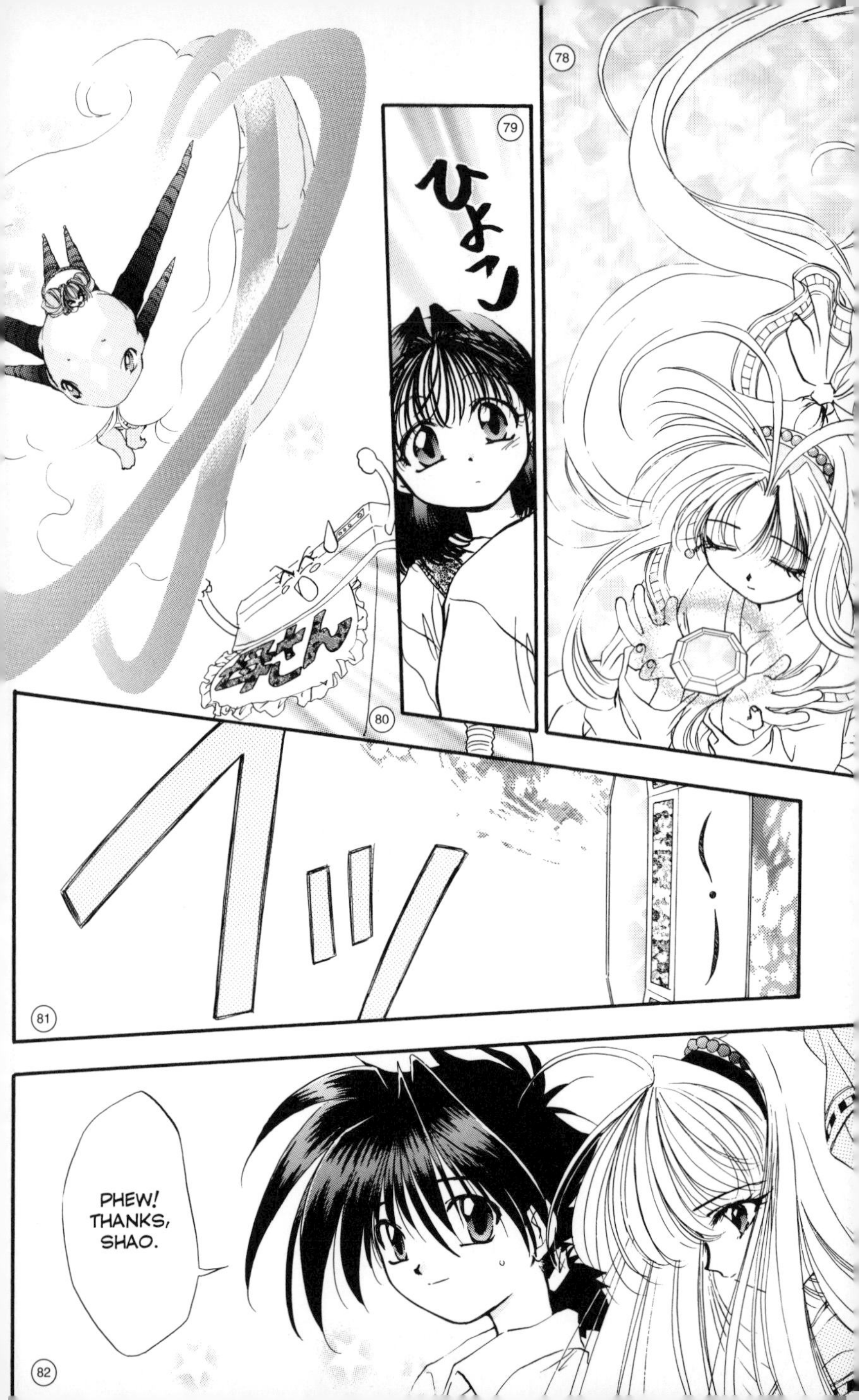
ハッ
PHEW! THANKS, SHAO.

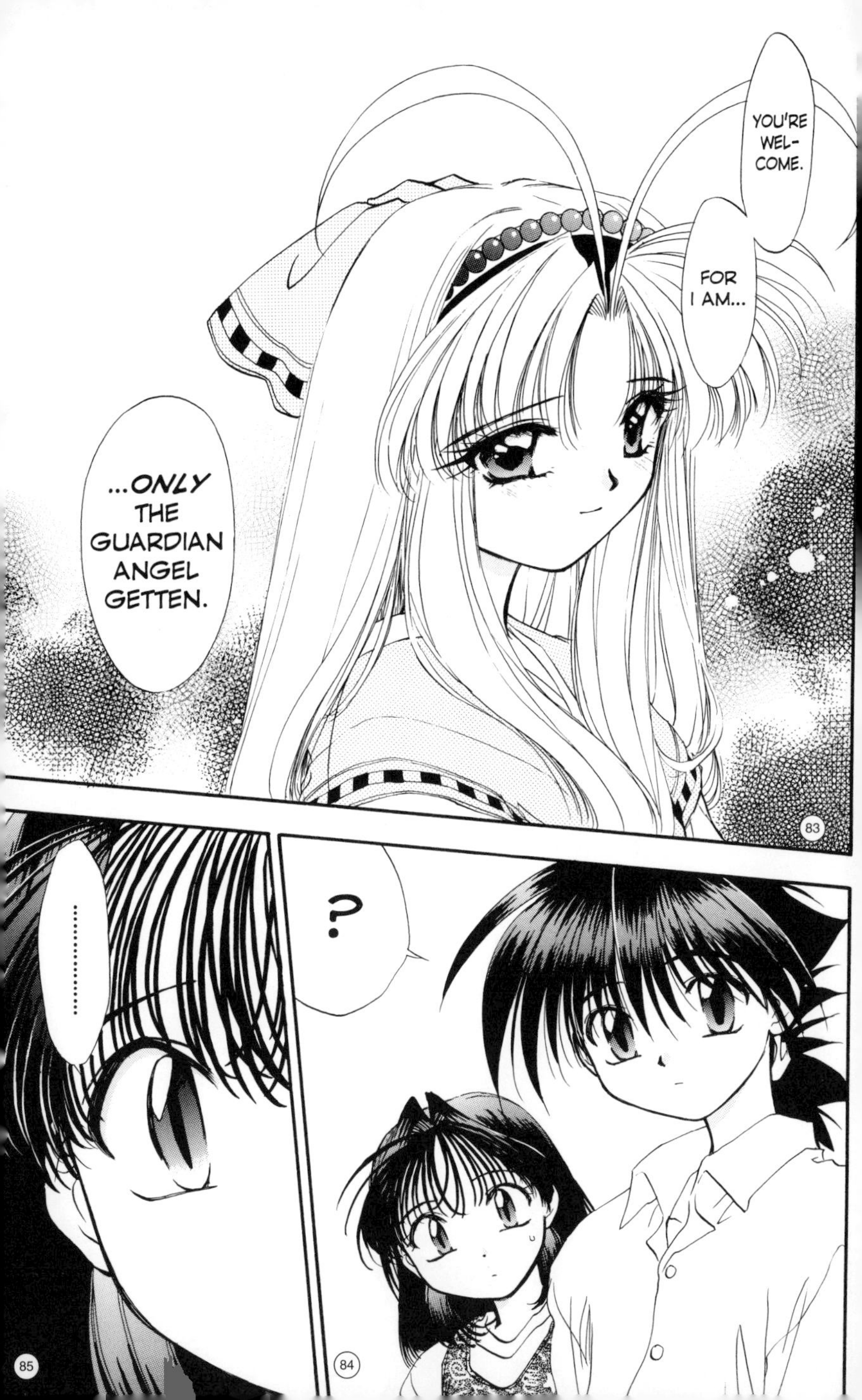
YOU'RE WEL- COME.
FOR I AM...
...ONLY THE GUARDIAN ANGEL GETTEN.
?
....

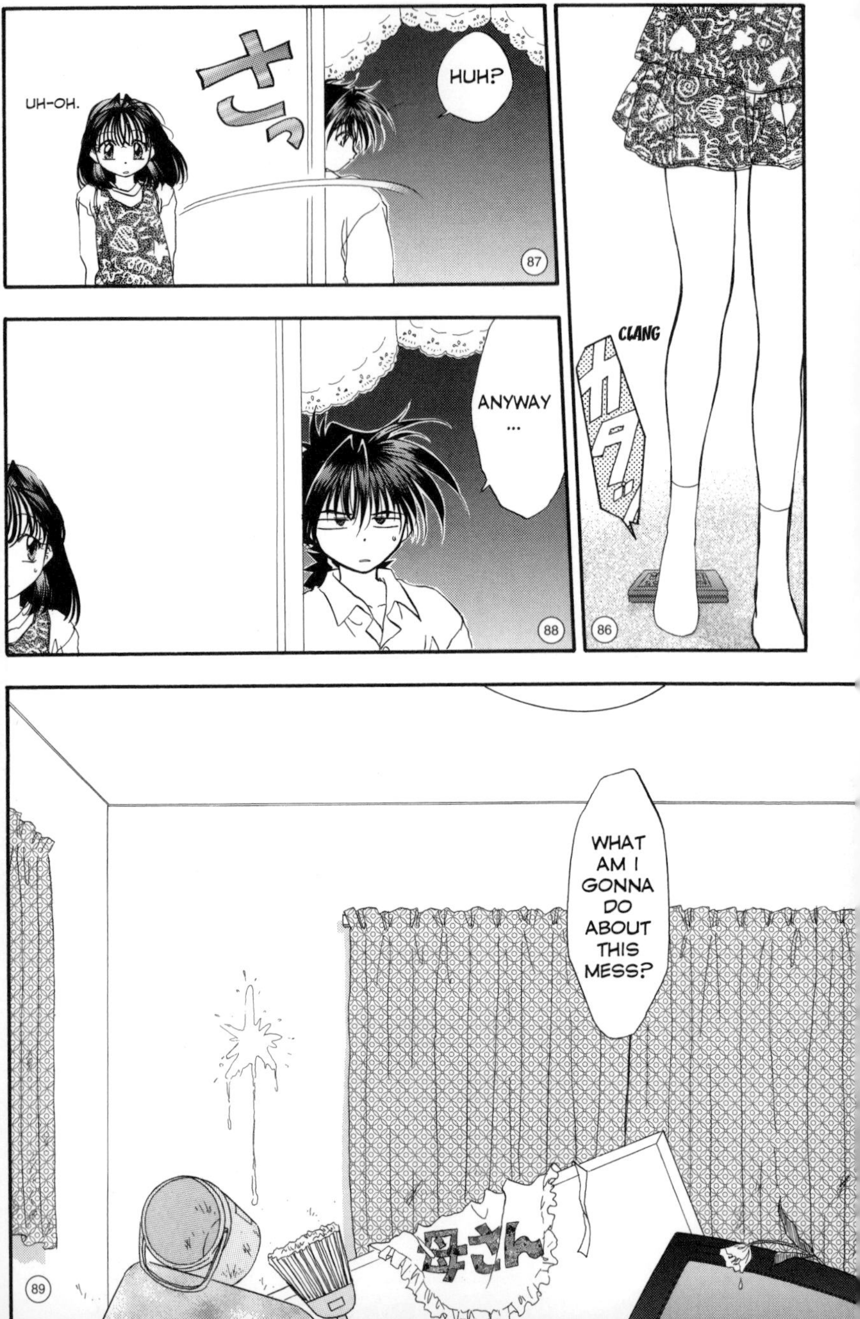
CLANG
HUH?
UH-OH.
ANYWAY ...
WHAT AM I GONNA DO ABOUT THIS MESS?

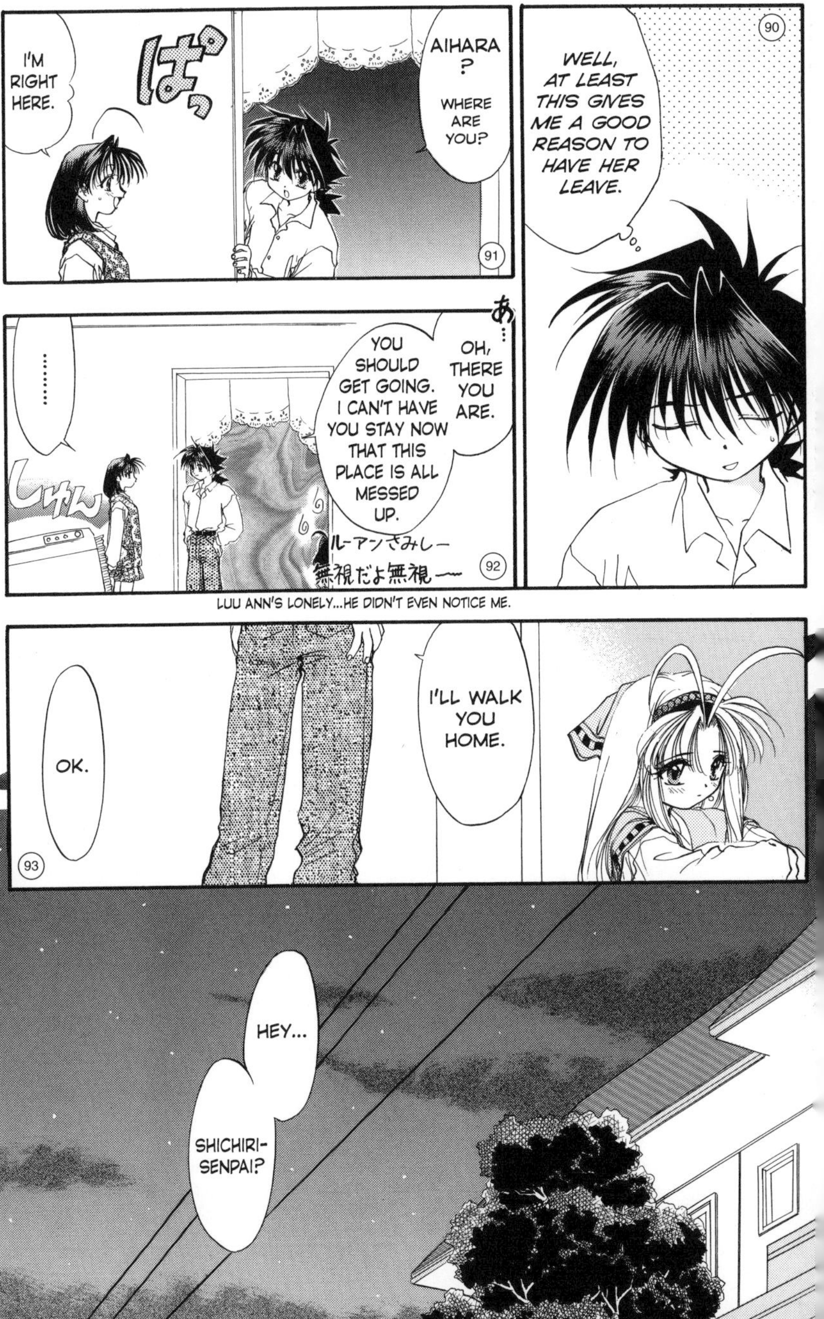
WELL, AT LEAST THIS GIVES ME A GOOD REASON TO HAVE HER LEAVE.
AIHARA? WHERE ARE YOU?
ぱっ
I'M RIGHT HERE.
あ…
OH, THERE YOU ARE.
YOU SHOULD GET GOING. I CAN'T HAVE YOU STAY NOW THAT THIS PLACE IS ALL MESSED UP.
ルーアンさみしー
無視だよ無視ー
しゅん
………
LUU ANN'S LONELY...HE DIDN'T EVEN NOTICE ME.
I'LL WALK YOU HOME.
OK.
HEY...
SHICHIRI-SENPAI?

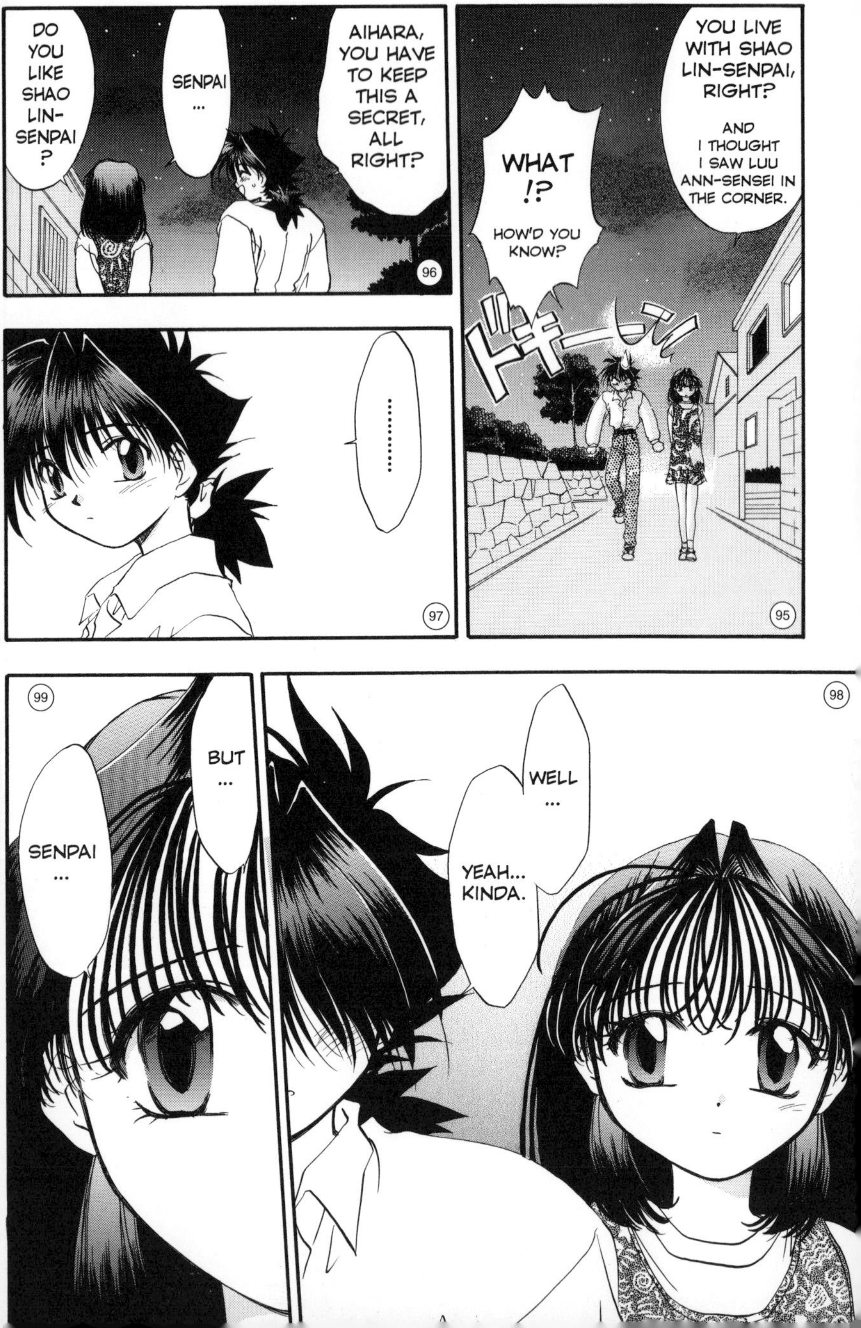
95
YOU LIVE WITH SHAO LIN-SENPAI, RIGHT?
AND I THOUGHT I SAW LUU ANN-SENSEI IN THE CORNER.
WHAT !?
HOW'D YOU KNOW?
96
AIHARA, YOU HAVE TO KEEP THIS A SECRET, ALL RIGHT?
SENPAI ...
DO YOU LIKE SHAO LIN-SENPAI ?
97
....
98
WELL ...
YEAH... KINDA.
99
BUT ...
SENPAI ...

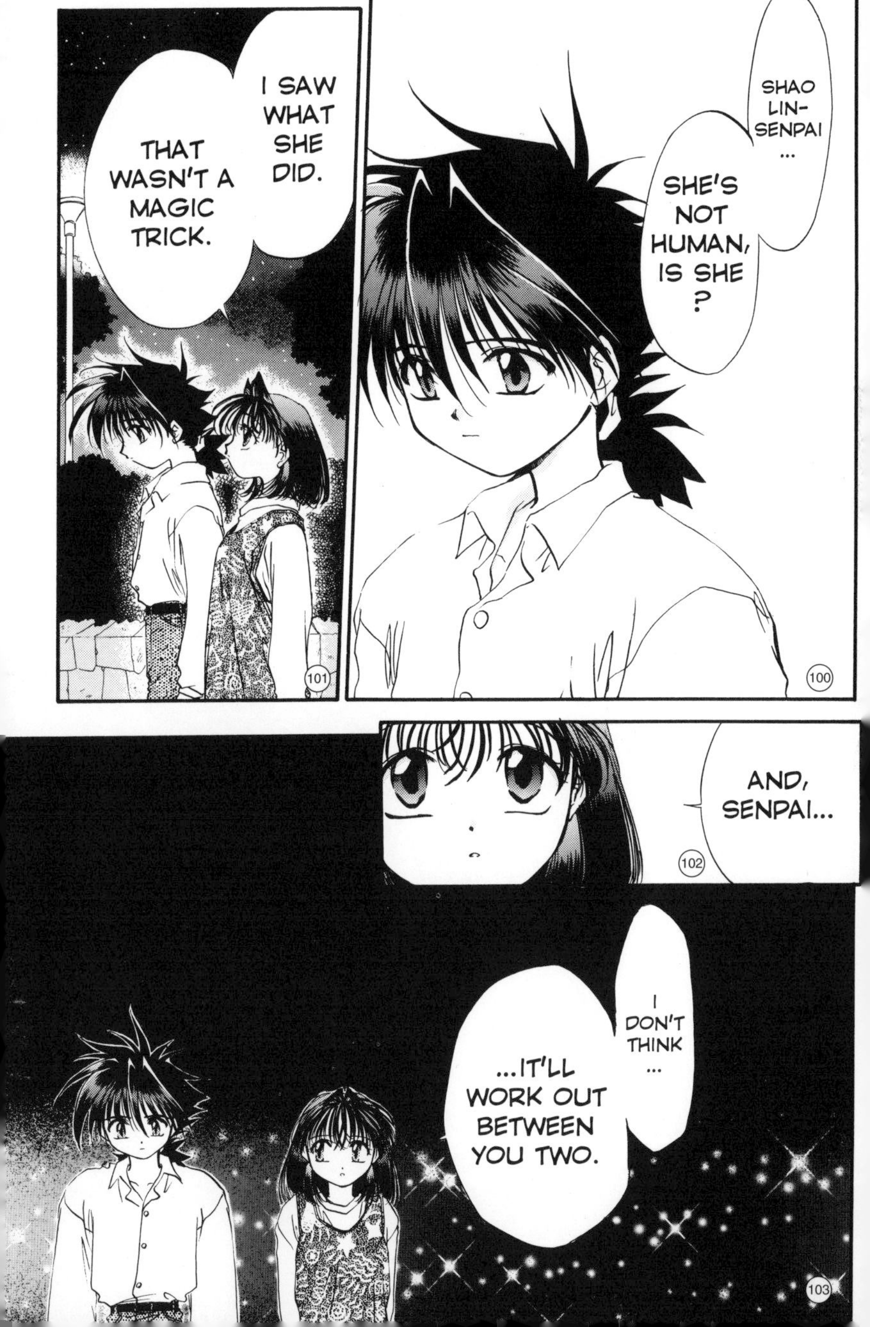

SHAO LIN-SENPAI ...
SHE'S NOT HUMAN, IS SHE ?
I SAW WHAT SHE DID.
THAT WASN'T A MAGIC TRICK.
AND, SENPAI...
I DON'T THINK ...
...IT'LL WORK OUT BETWEEN YOU TWO.

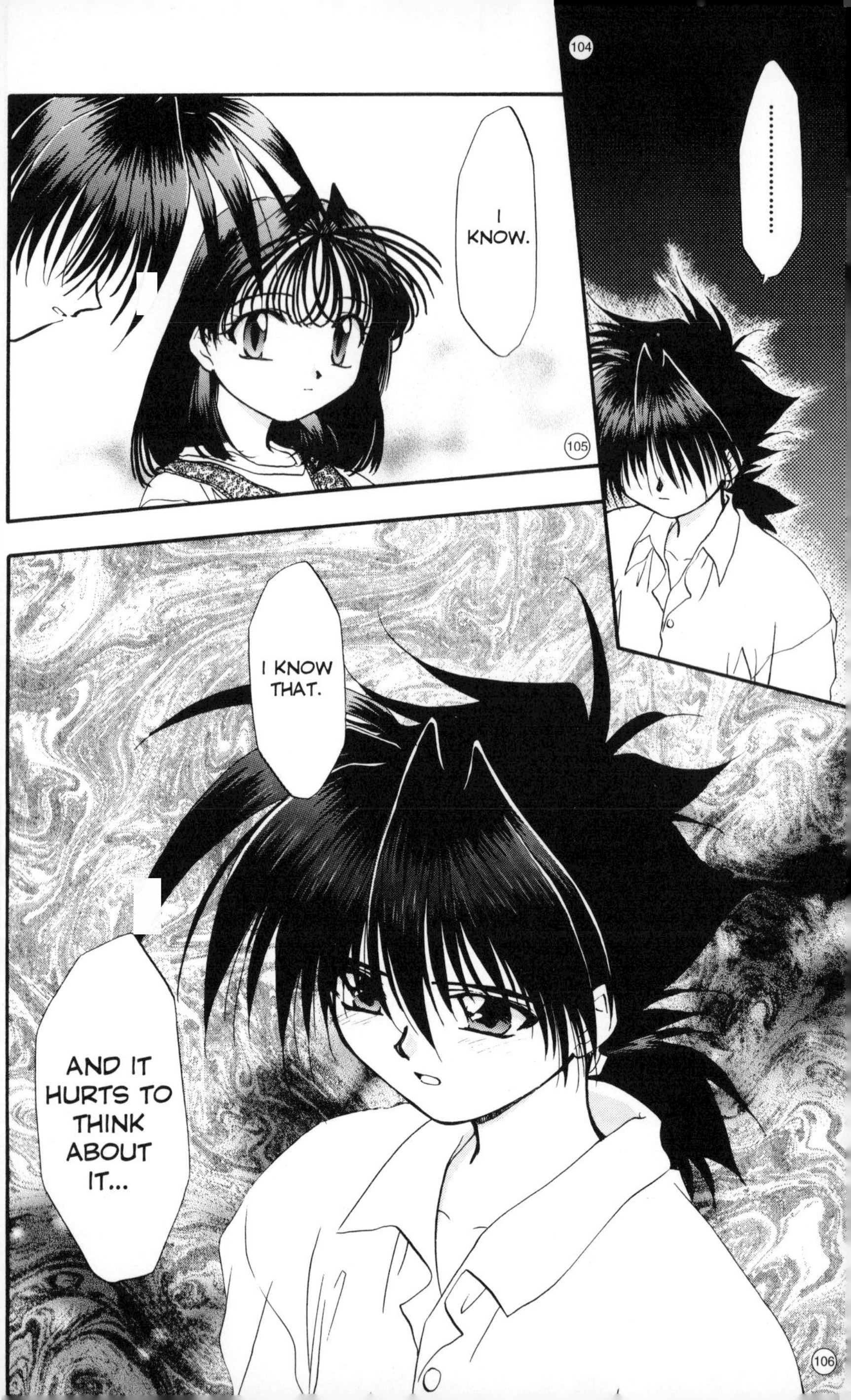
104
......
I KNOW.
105
I KNOW THAT.
AND IT HURTS TO THINK ABOUT IT...
106

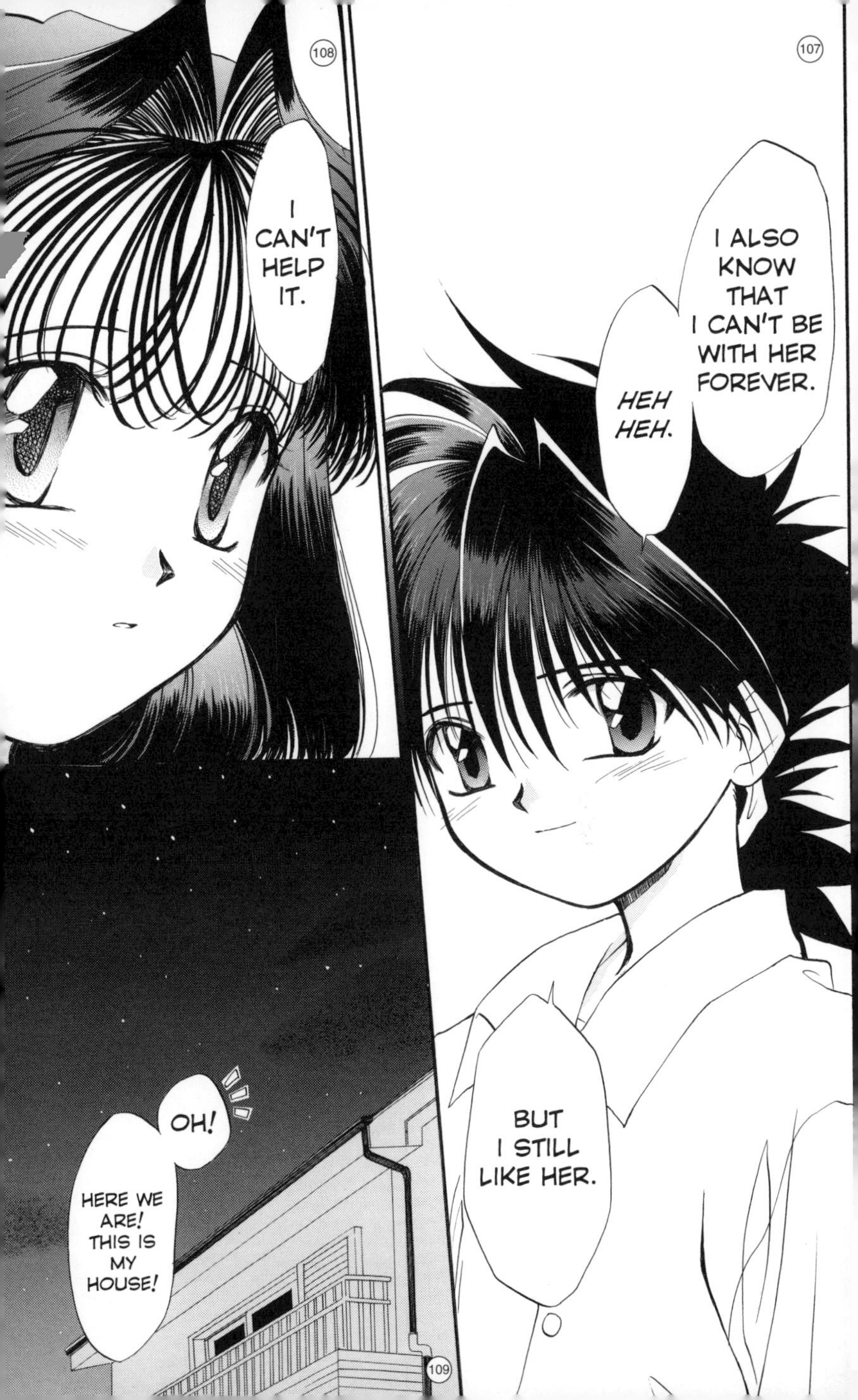
107
I ALSO KNOW THAT I CAN'T BE WITH HER FOREVER.
HEH HEH.
BUT I STILL LIKE HER.
108
I CAN'T HELP IT.
109
OH!
HERE WE ARE! THIS IS MY HOUSE!

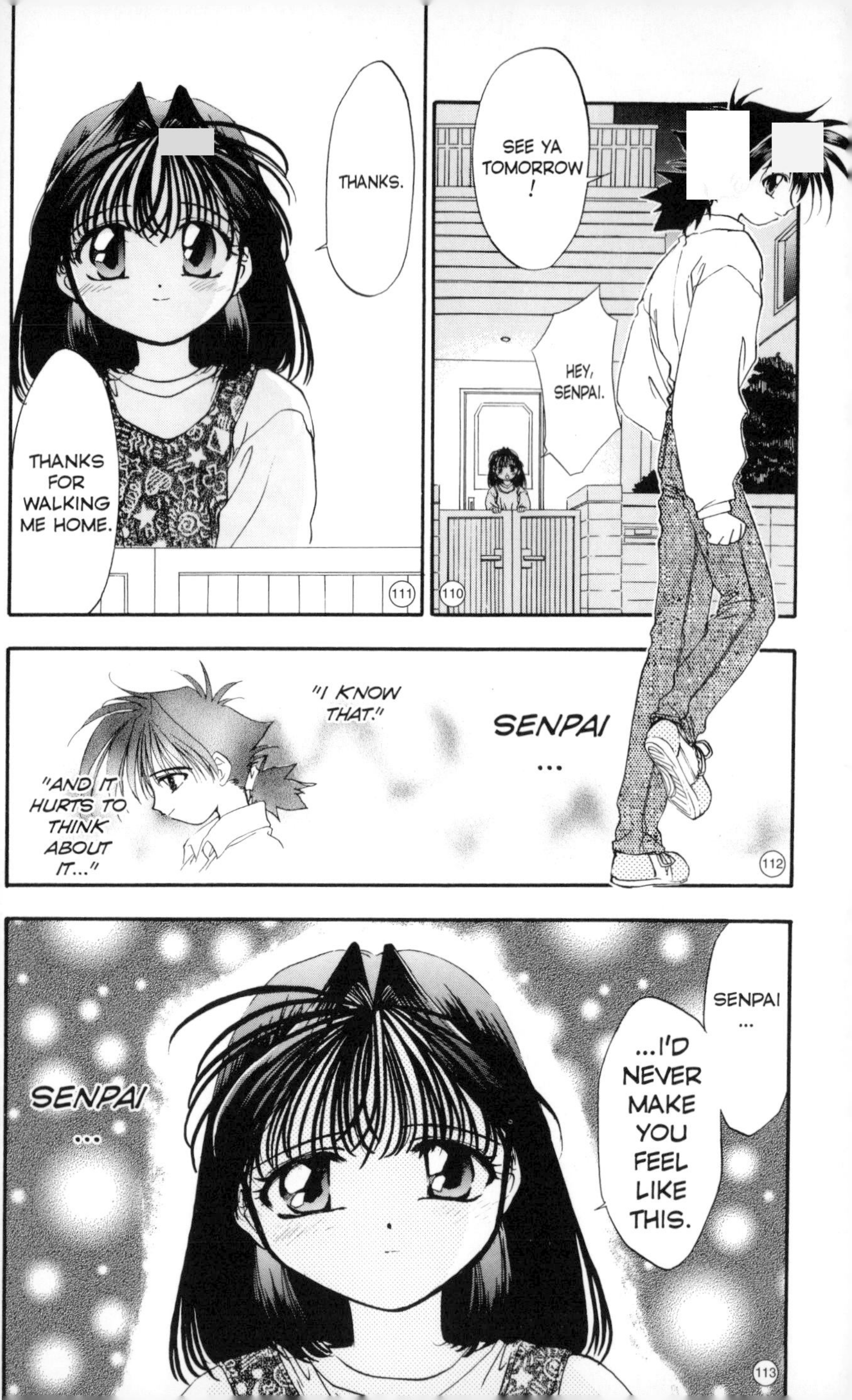
SEE YA TOMORROW!
HEY, SENPAI.
110
THANKS.
THANKS FOR WALKING ME HOME.
111
SENPAI ...
"I KNOW THAT."
"AND IT HURTS TO THINK ABOUT IT..."
112
SENPAI ...
...I'D NEVER MAKE YOU FEEL LIKE THIS.
SENPAI ...
113

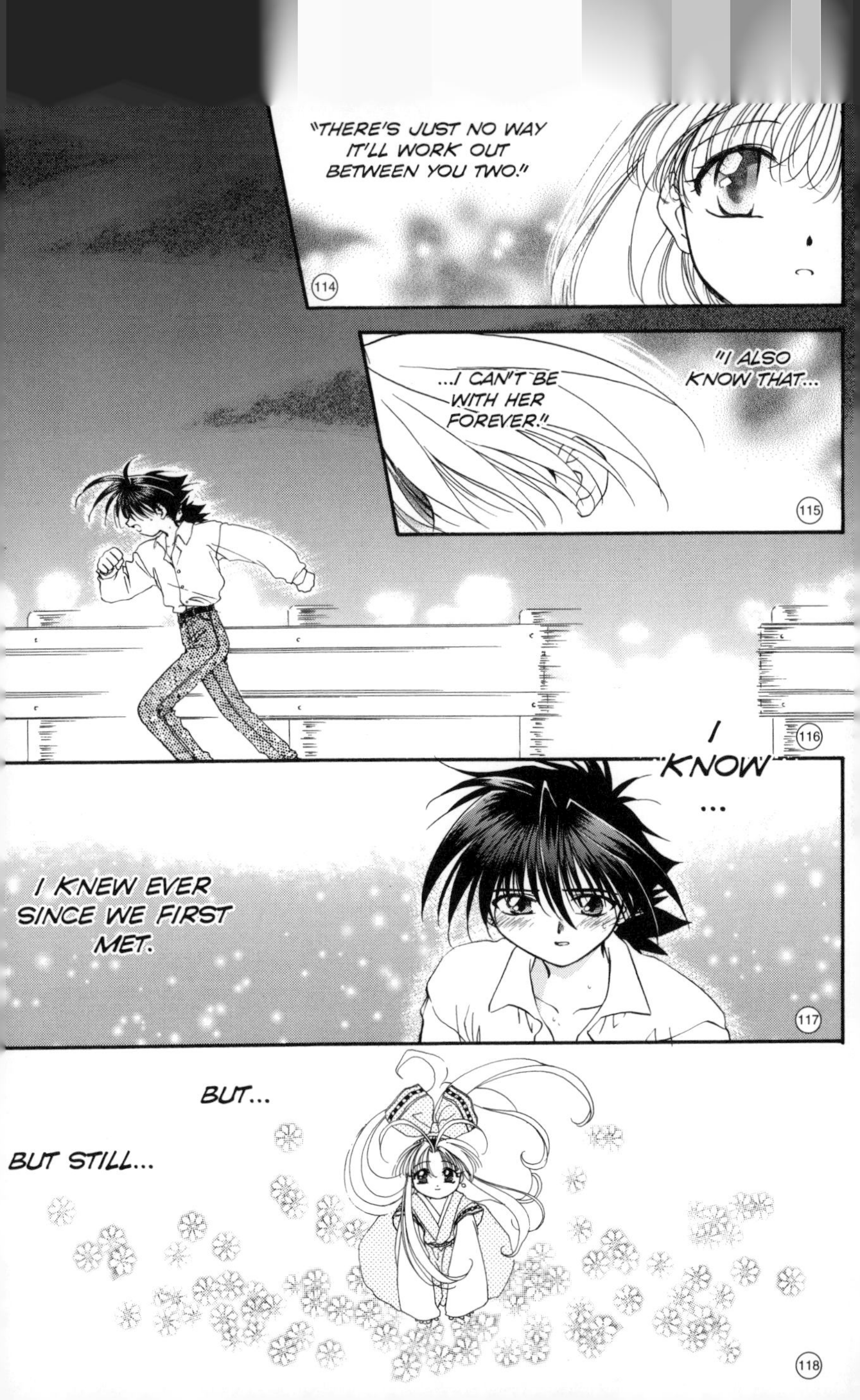
"THERE'S JUST NO WAY IT'LL WORK OUT BETWEEN YOU TWO."
114
"I ALSO KNOW THAT...
...I CAN'T BE WITH HER FOREVER."
115
116
I KNOW ...
I KNEW EVER SINCE WE FIRST MET.
117
BUT...
BUT STILL...
118

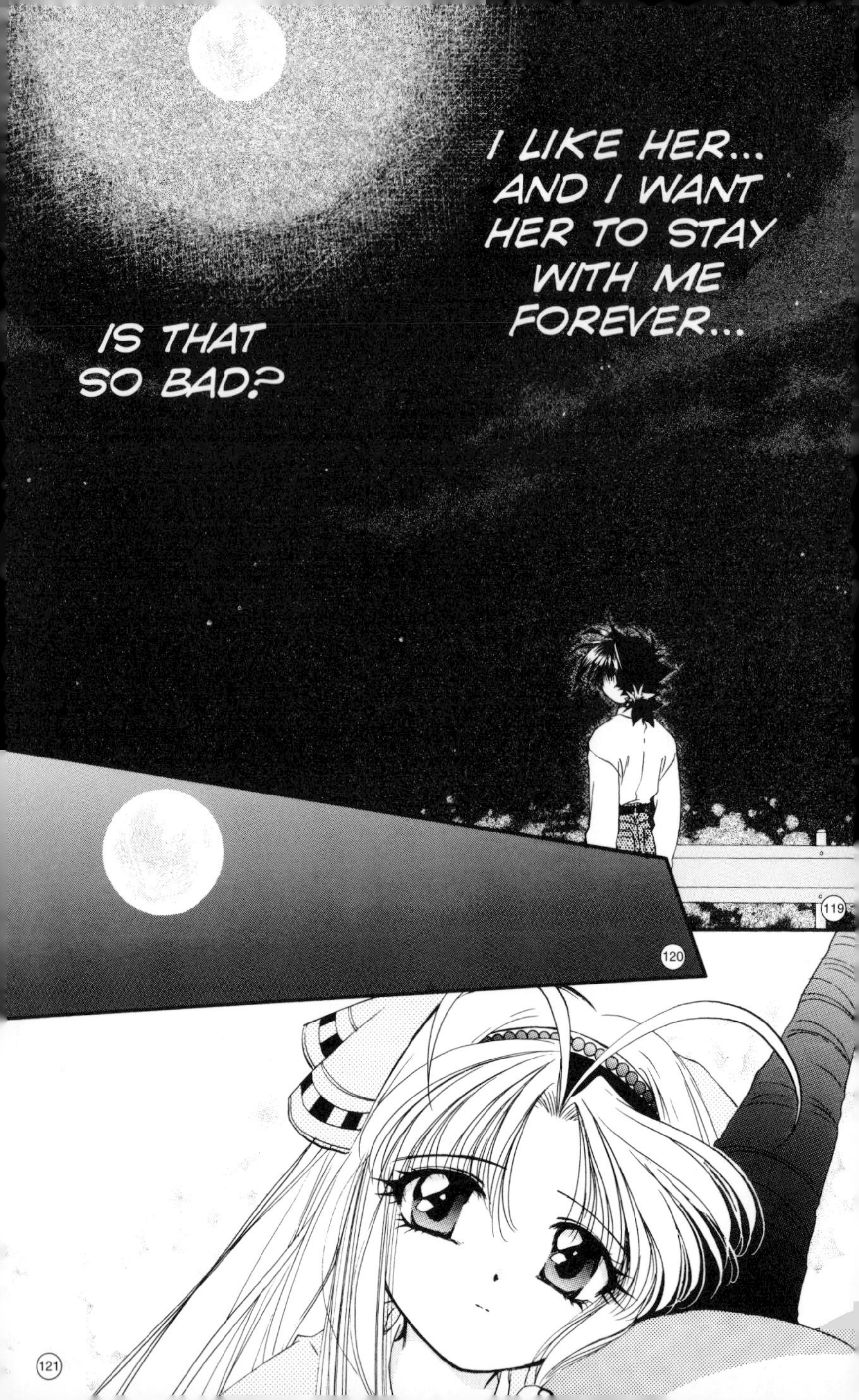
I LIKE HER... AND I WANT HER TO STAY WITH ME FOREVER...
IS THAT SO BAD?

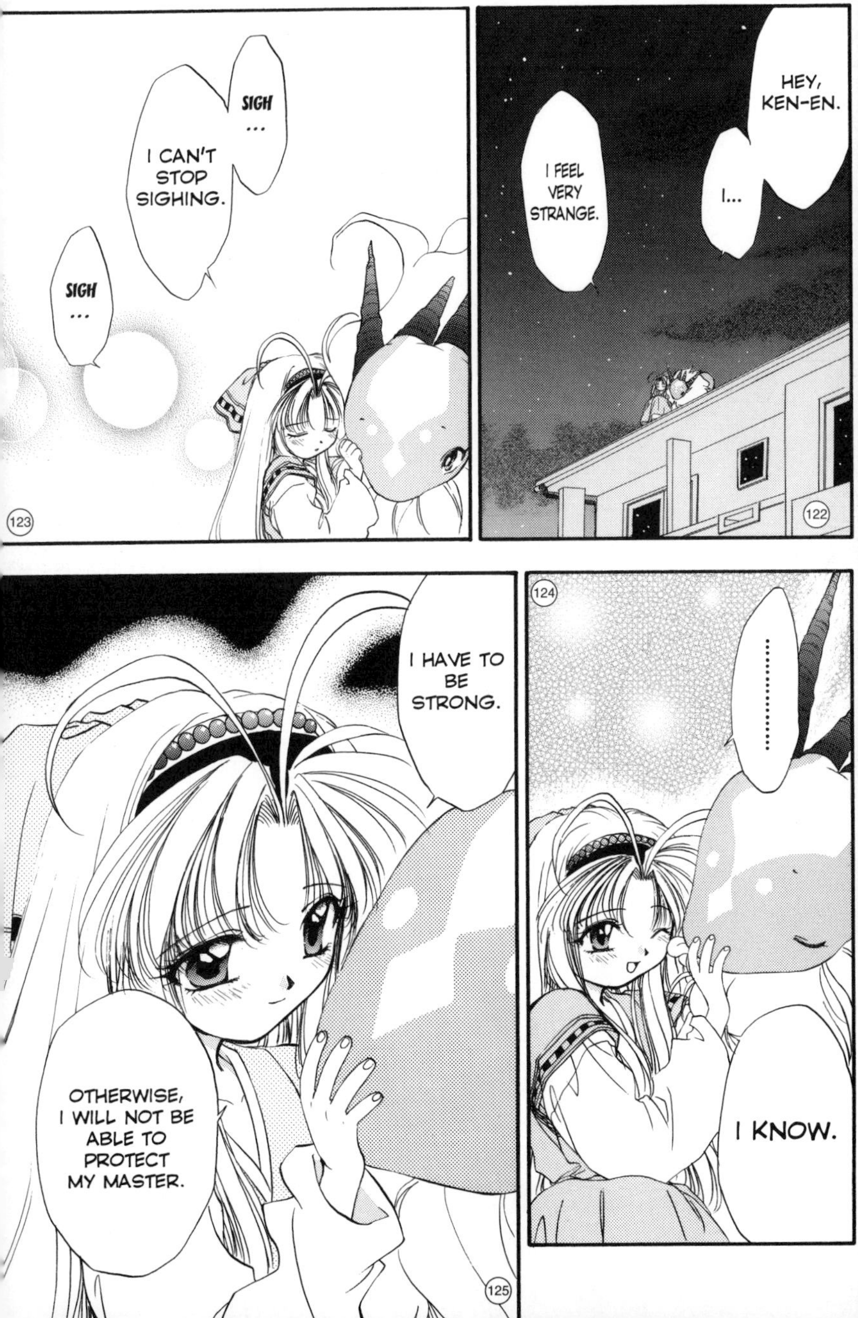
HEY, KEN-EN.
I...
I FEEL VERY STRANGE.
SIGH ...
I CAN'T STOP SIGHING.
SIGH ...
....
I KNOW.
I HAVE TO BE STRONG.
OTHERWISE, I WILL NOT BE ABLE TO PROTECT MY MASTER.

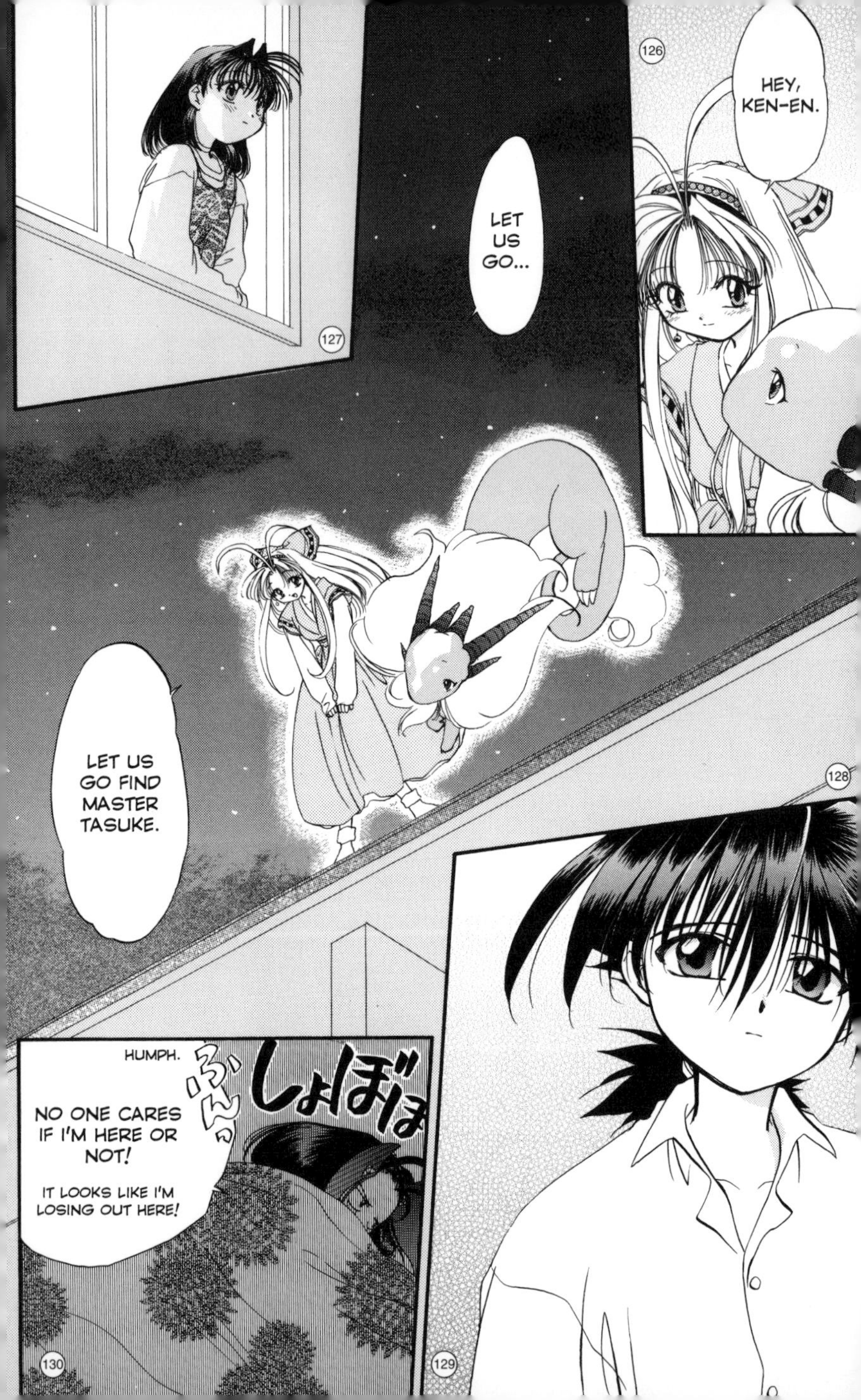
HEY, KEN-EN.
LET US GO...
LET US GO FIND MASTER TASUKE.
HUMPH.
ふん
しょぼぼ
NO ONE CARES IF I'M HERE OR NOT!
IT LOOKS LIKE I'M LOSING OUT HERE!

CHAPTER 24: MIXED EMOTIONS

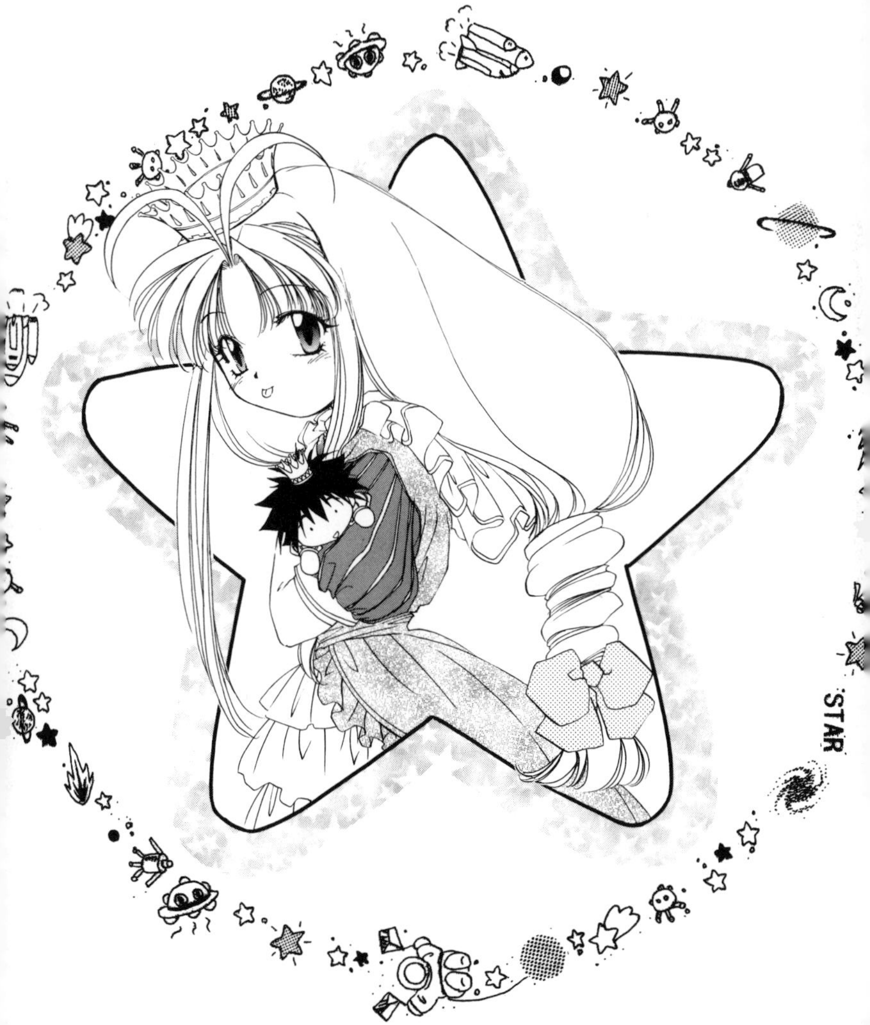
STAR

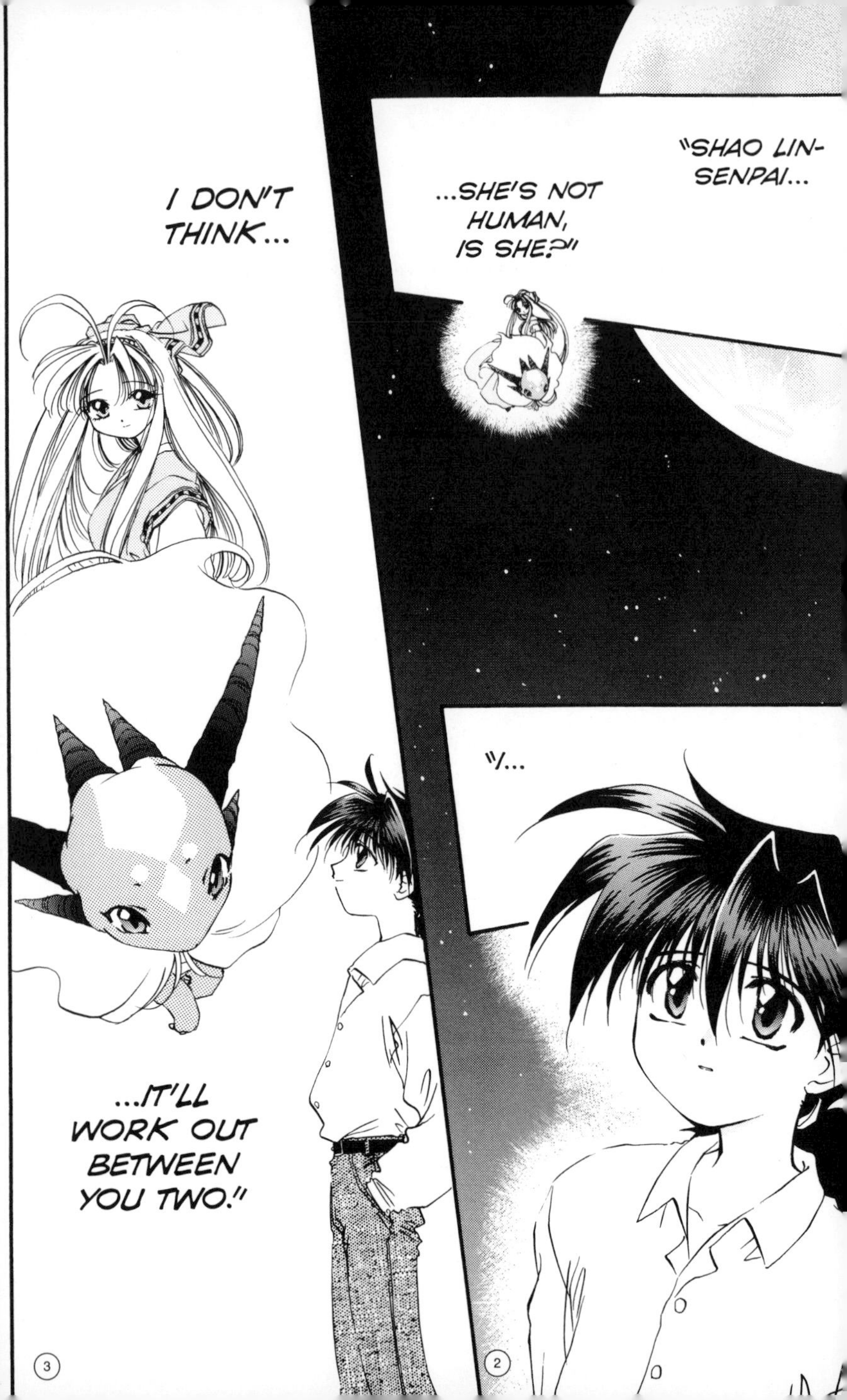
"SHAO LIN-SENPAI...
...SHE'S NOT HUMAN, IS SHE?"
"I...
I DON'T THINK...
...IT'LL WORK OUT BETWEEN YOU TWO."

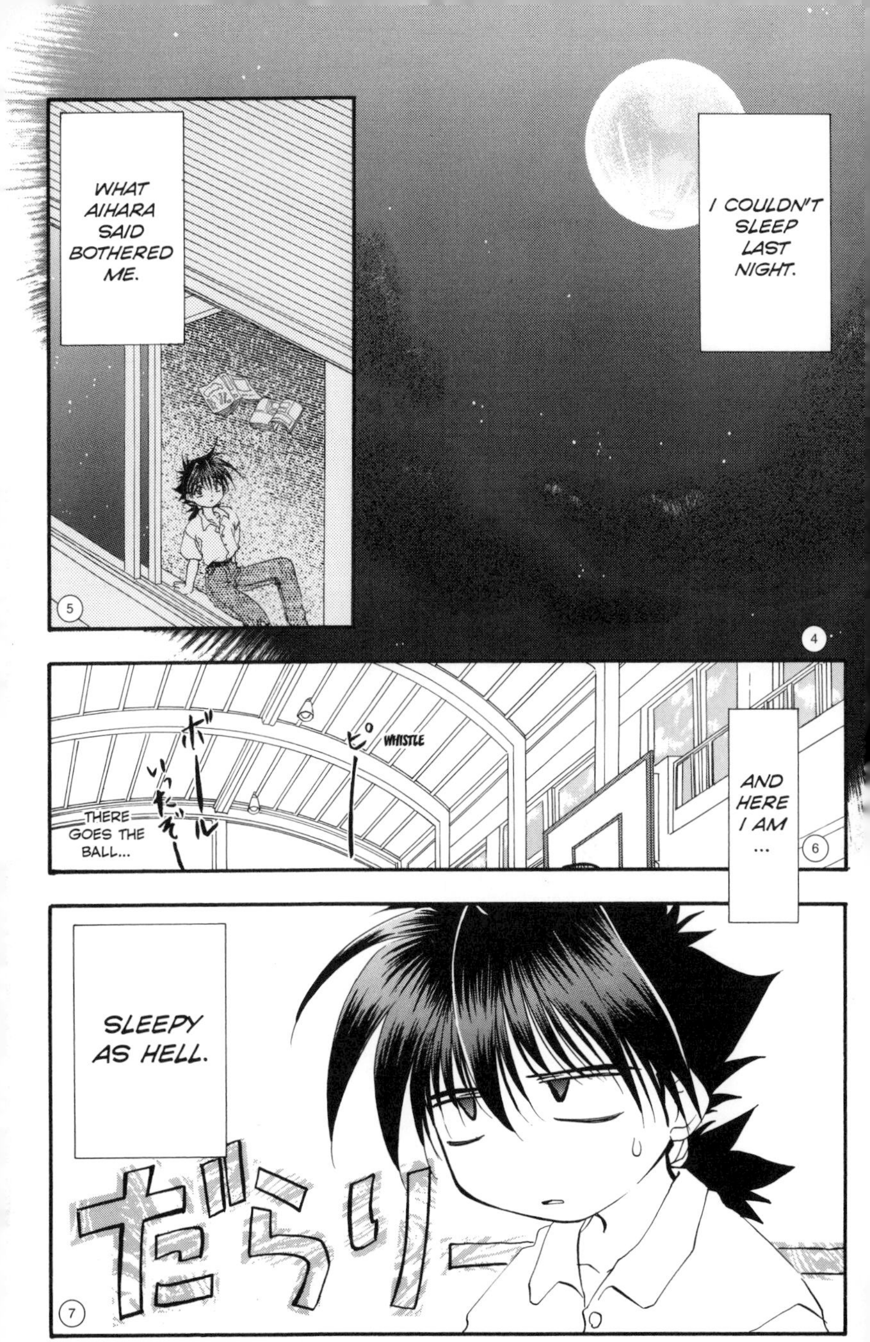
I COULDN'T SLEEP LAST NIGHT.
WHAT AIHARA SAID BOTHERED ME.
AND HERE I AM ...
ピー
WHISTLE
ボール いったぞー
THERE GOES THE BALL...
SLEEPY AS HELL.
だらりー

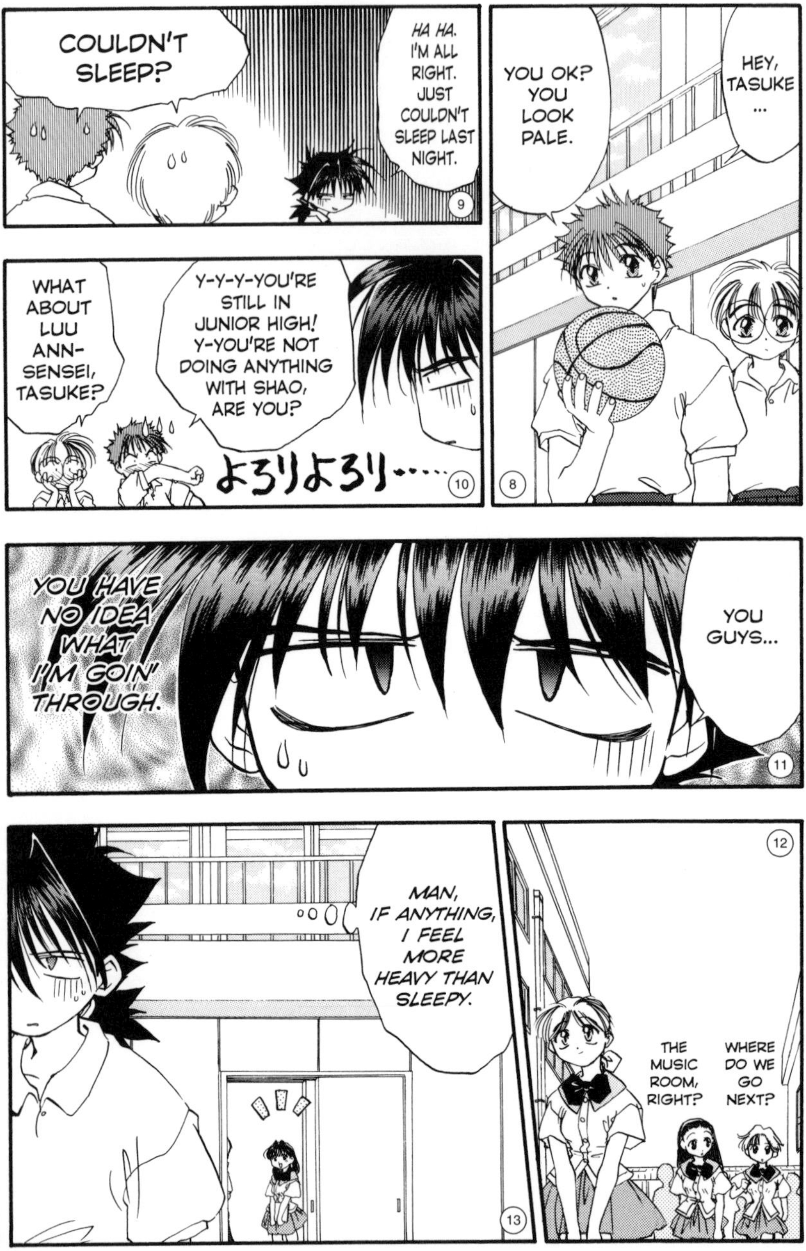
HEY, TASUKE ...
YOU OK? YOU LOOK PALE.
HA HA. I'M ALL RIGHT. JUST COULDN'T SLEEP LAST NIGHT.
COULDN'T SLEEP?
Y-Y-Y-YOU'RE STILL IN JUNIOR HIGH! Y-YOU'RE NOT DOING ANYTHING WITH SHAO, ARE YOU?
WHAT ABOUT LUU ANN-SENSEI, TASUKE?
よろりよろり……
YOU GUYS...
YOU HAVE NO IDEA WHAT I'M GOIN' THROUGH.
WHERE DO WE GO NEXT?
THE MUSIC ROOM, RIGHT?
MAN, IF ANYTHING, I FEEL MORE HEAVY THAN SLEEPY.

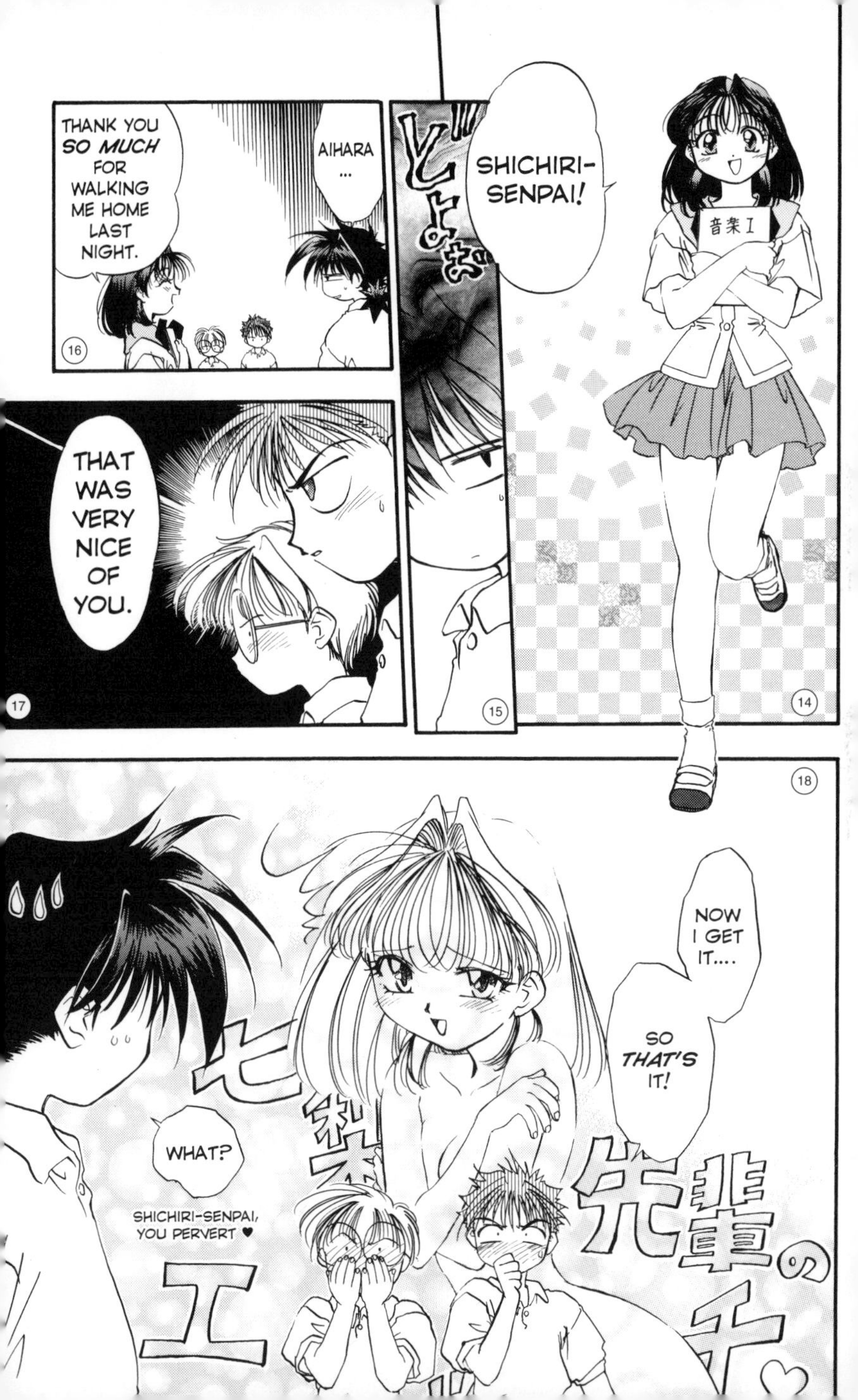
SHICHIRI-SENPAI!
音楽I
AIHARA ...
THANK YOU SO MUCH FOR WALKING ME HOME LAST NIGHT.
THAT WAS VERY NICE OF YOU.
NOW I GET IT....
SO THAT'S IT!
WHAT?
SHICHIRI-SENPAI, YOU PERVERT ♥
先輩の

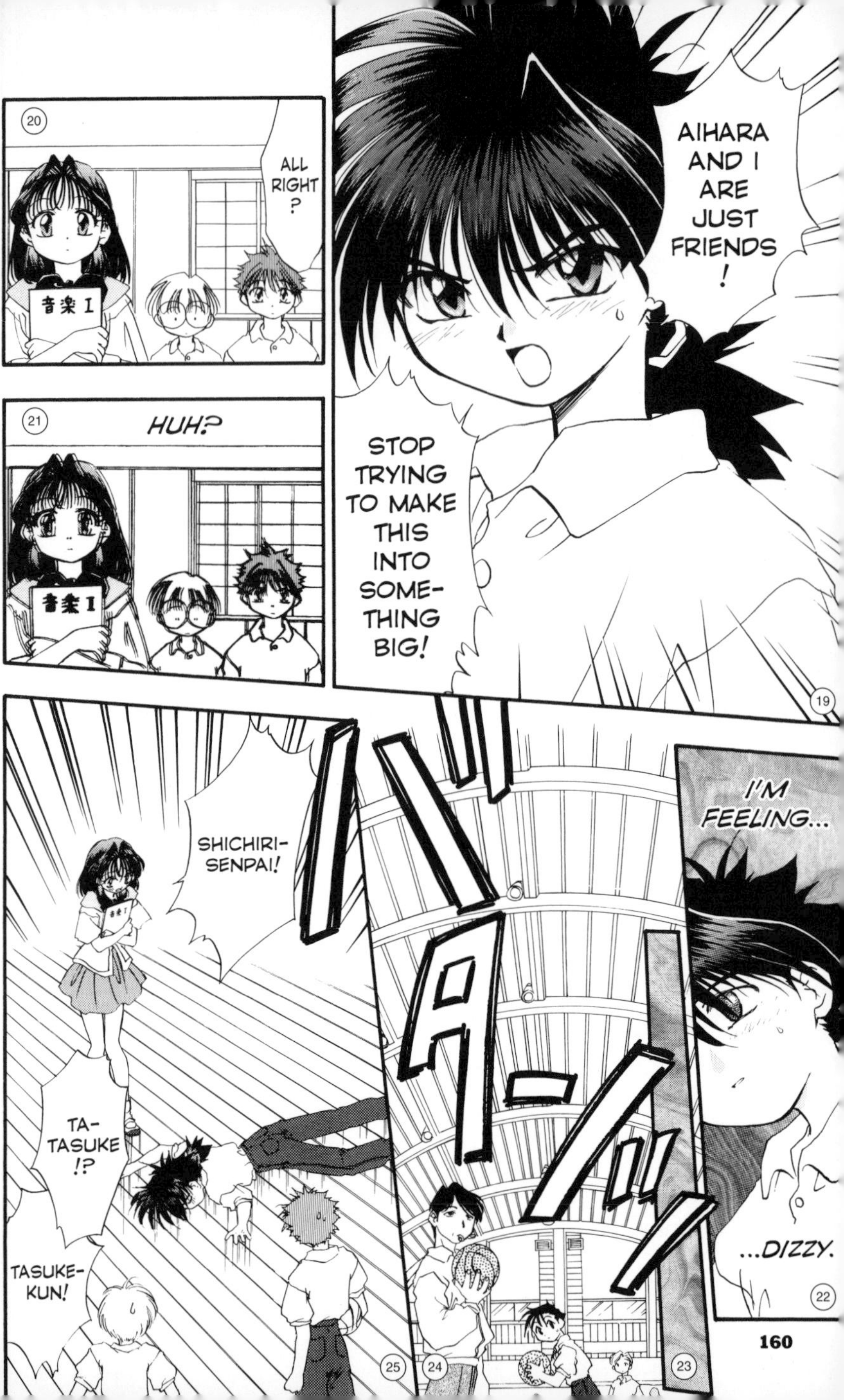
AIHARA AND I ARE JUST FRIENDS!
STOP TRYING TO MAKE THIS INTO SOME-THING BIG!
ALL RIGHT?
音楽 I
HUH?
音楽 I
I'M FEELING...
...DIZZY.
SHICHIRI-SENPAI!
TA-TASUKE!?
TASUKE-KUN!

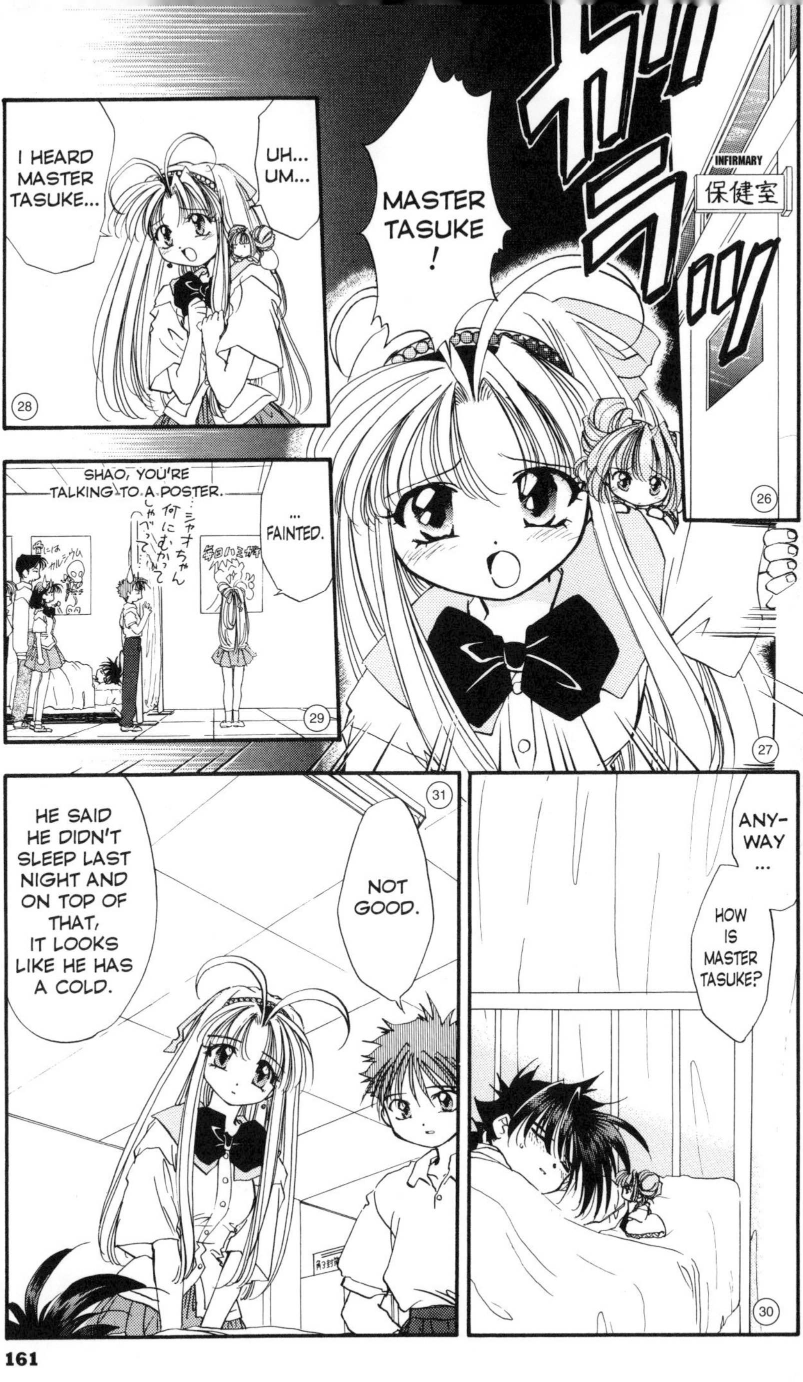
INFIRMARY
保健室
MASTER TASUKE!
UH... UM...
I HEARD MASTER TASUKE...
... FAINTED.
SHAO, YOU'RE TALKING TO A POSTER.
…シャオちゃん 何にむかって しゃべって…
骨にはカルシウム
毎日ハミガキ
ANY-WAY ...
HOW IS MASTER TASUKE?
NOT GOOD.
HE SAID HE DIDN'T SLEEP LAST NIGHT AND ON TOP OF THAT, IT LOOKS LIKE HE HAS A COLD.

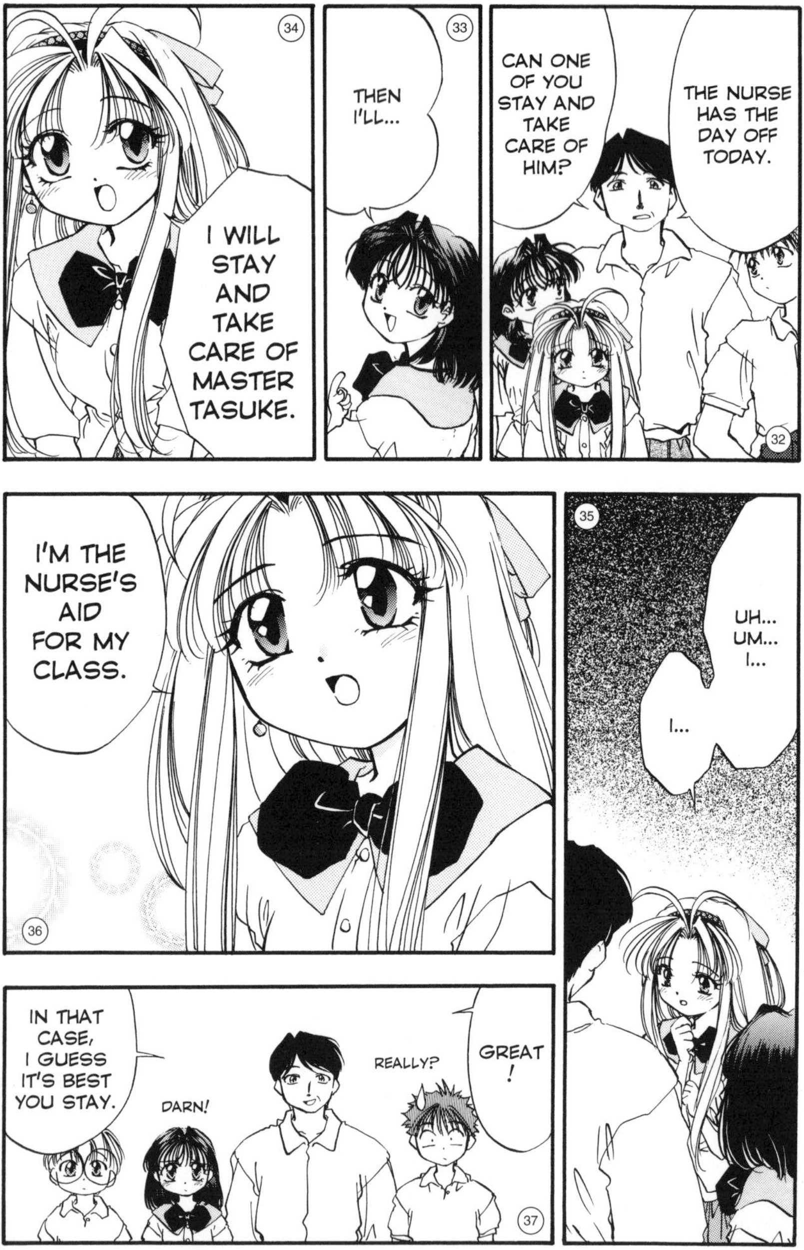
THE NURSE HAS THE DAY OFF TODAY.
CAN ONE OF YOU STAY AND TAKE CARE OF HIM?
THEN I'LL...
I WILL STAY AND TAKE CARE OF MASTER TASUKE.
UH... UM... I...
I...
I'M THE NURSE'S AID FOR MY CLASS.
GREAT!
REALLY?
DARN!
IN THAT CASE, I GUESS IT'S BEST YOU STAY.

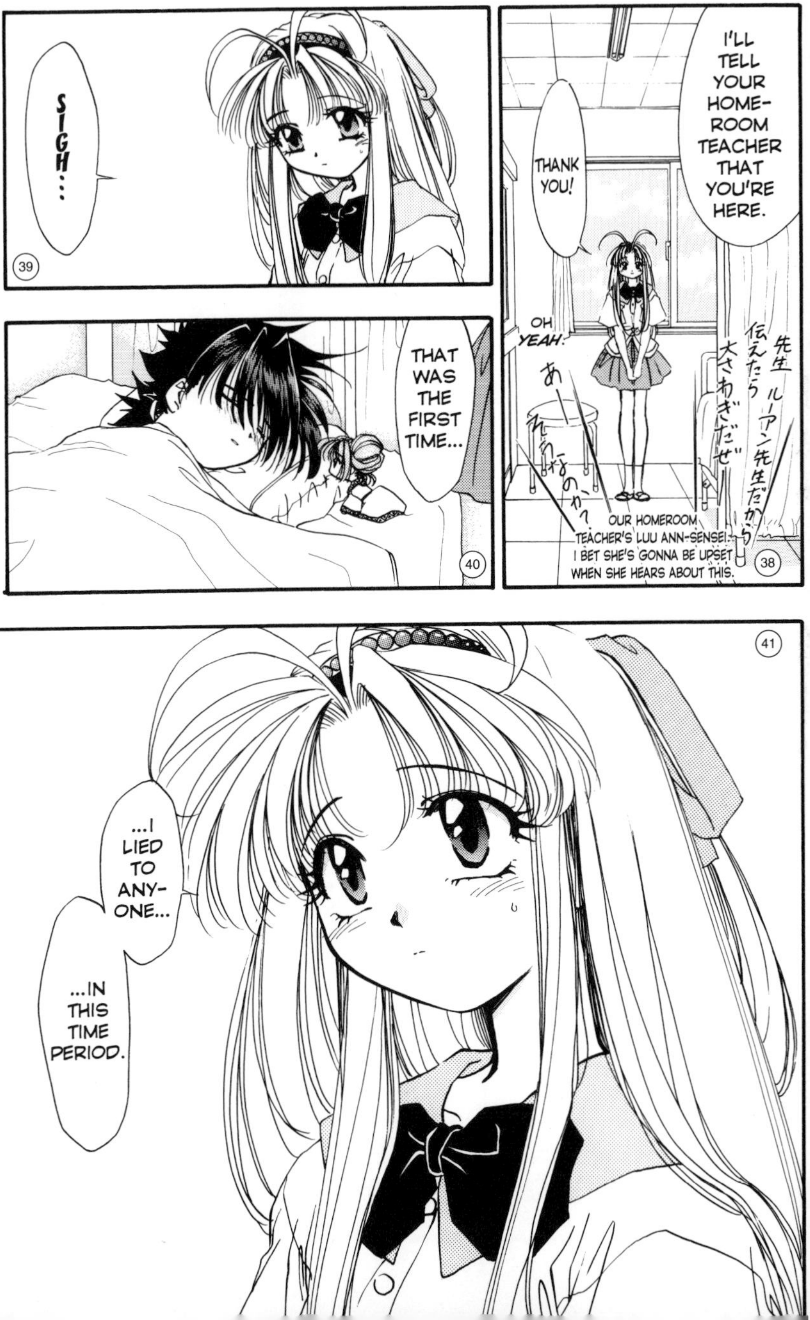
I'LL TELL YOUR HOME-ROOM TEACHER THAT YOU'RE HERE.
THANK YOU!
先生 ルーアン先生だから伝えたら大さわぎだぜ
OUR HOMEROOM TEACHER'S LUU ANN-SENSEI. I BET SHE'S GONNA BE UPSET WHEN SHE HEARS ABOUT THIS.
OH YEAH.
あー
38
SIGH...
39
THAT WAS THE FIRST TIME...
40
41
...I LIED TO ANYONE...
...IN THIS TIME PERIOD.

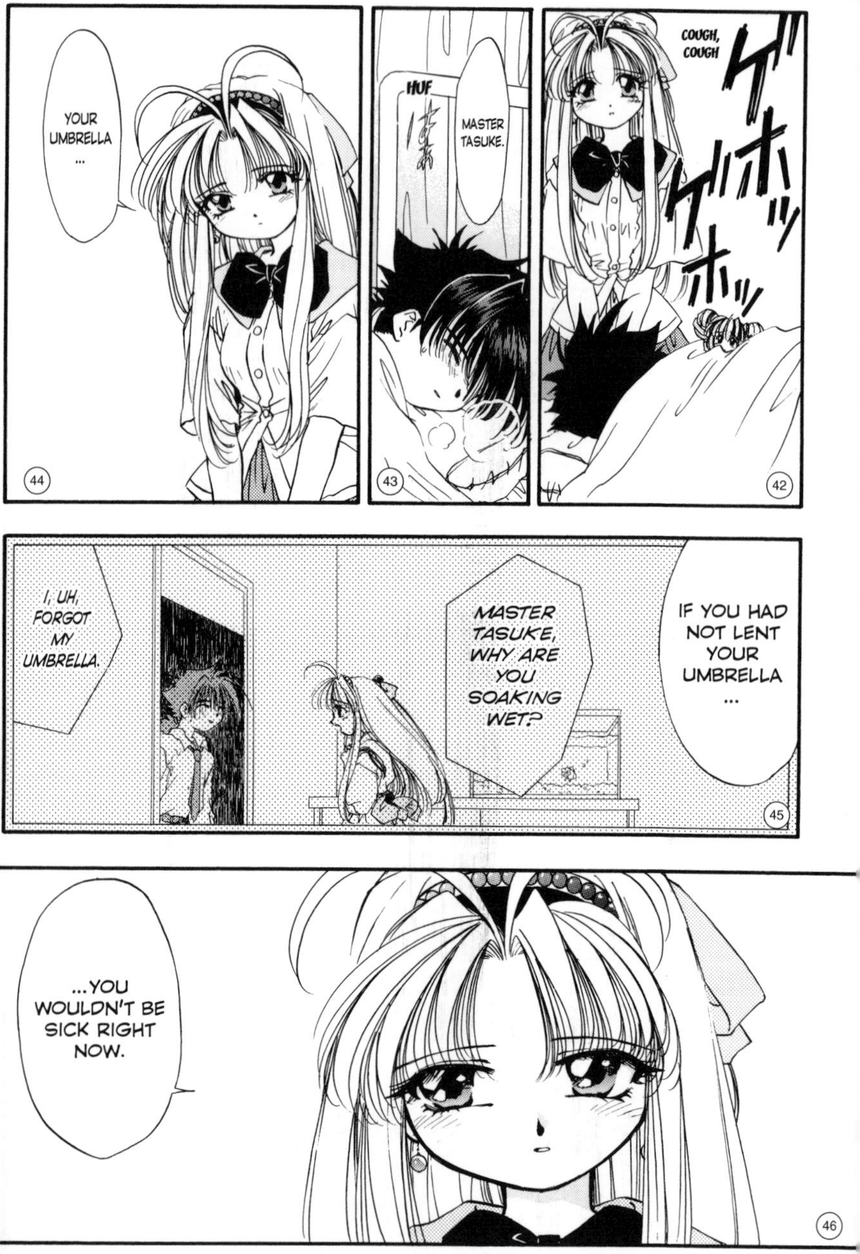
COUGH, COUGH
ゲホッ ゲホッ
HUF
MASTER TASUKE.
YOUR UMBRELLA ...
IF YOU HAD NOT LENT YOUR UMBRELLA ...
MASTER TASUKE, WHY ARE YOU SOAKING WET?
I, UH, FORGOT MY UMBRELLA.
...YOU WOULDN'T BE SICK RIGHT NOW.

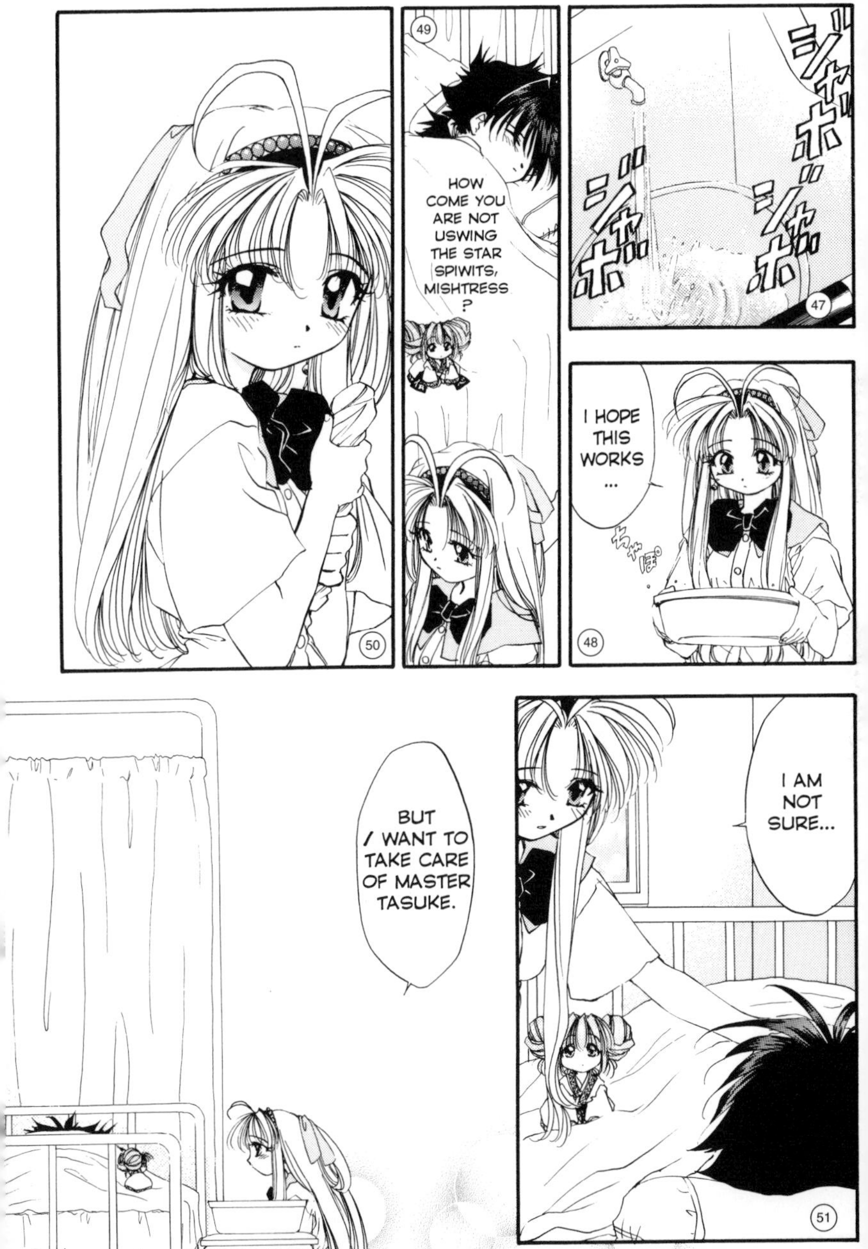
ジャボジャボ
ジャボジャボ
I HOPE THIS WORKS ...
ちゃぽ
HOW COME YOU ARE NOT USWING THE STAR SPIWITS, MISHTRESS ?
I AM NOT SURE...
BUT I WANT TO TAKE CARE OF MASTER TASUKE.

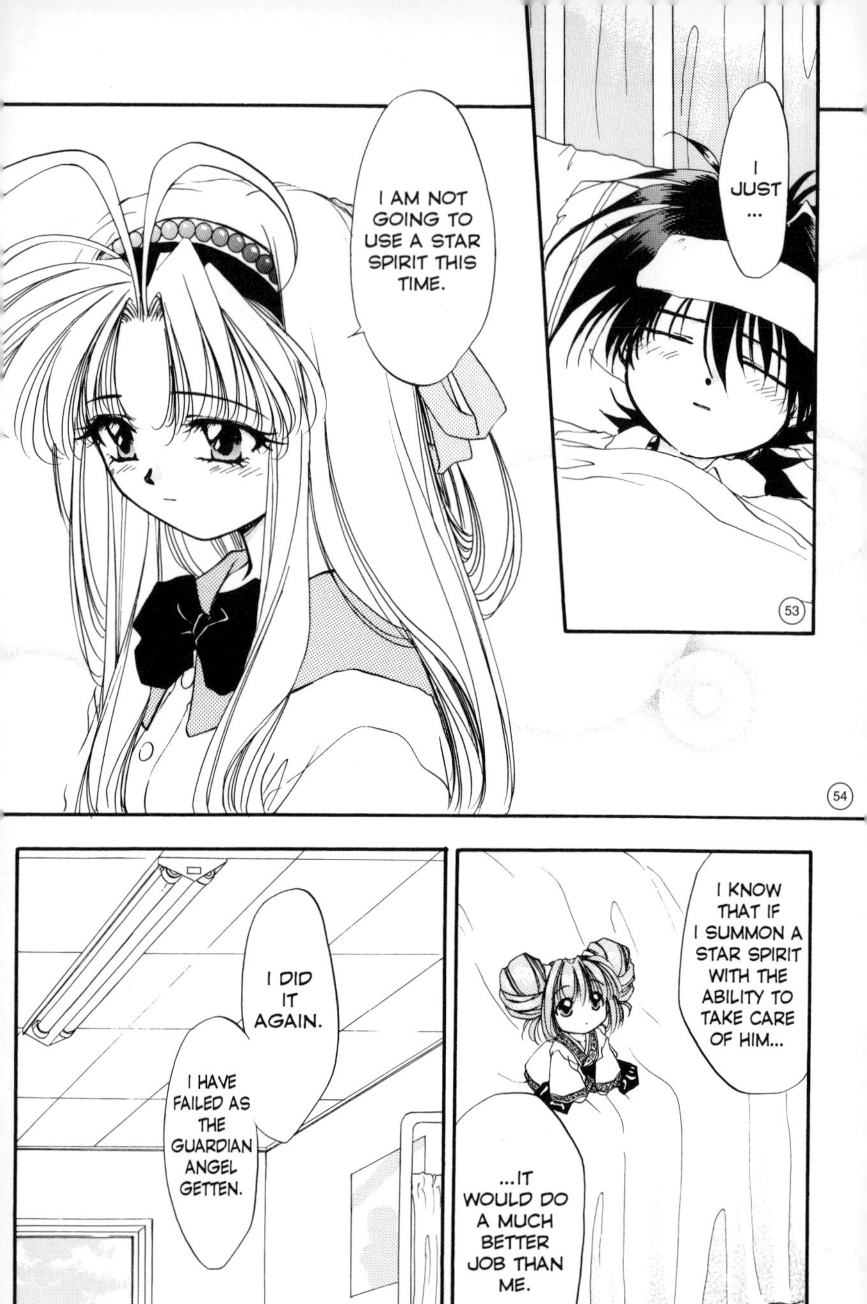
I JUST ...
I AM NOT GOING TO USE A STAR SPIRIT THIS TIME.
I KNOW THAT IF I SUMMON A STAR SPIRIT WITH THE ABILITY TO TAKE CARE OF HIM...
...IT WOULD DO A MUCH BETTER JOB THAN ME.
I DID IT AGAIN.
I HAVE FAILED AS THE GUARDIAN ANGEL GETTEN.

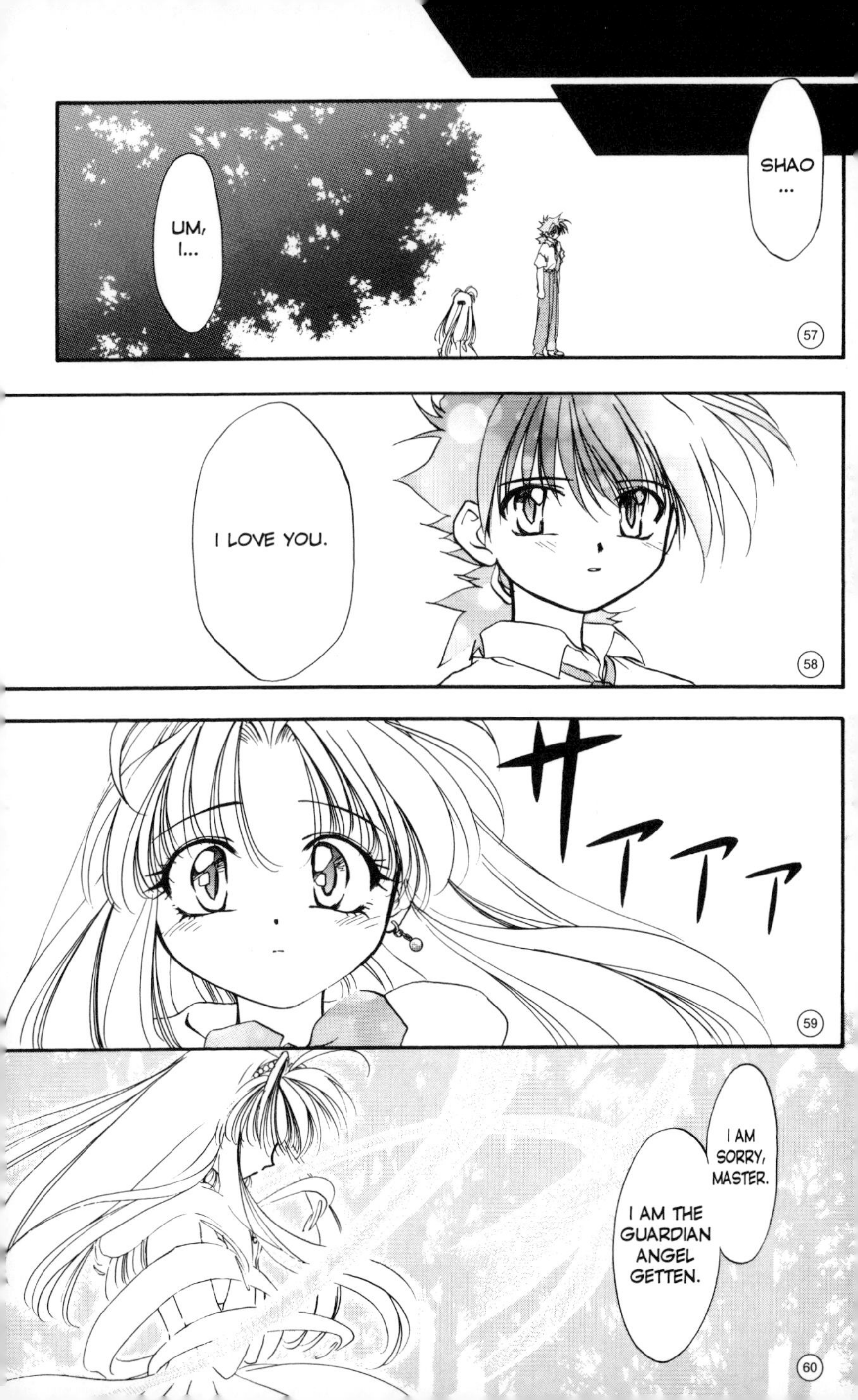
SHAO ...
UM, I...
57
I LOVE YOU.
58
サァァァ
59
I AM SORRY, MASTER.
I AM THE GUARDIAN ANGEL GETTEN.
60

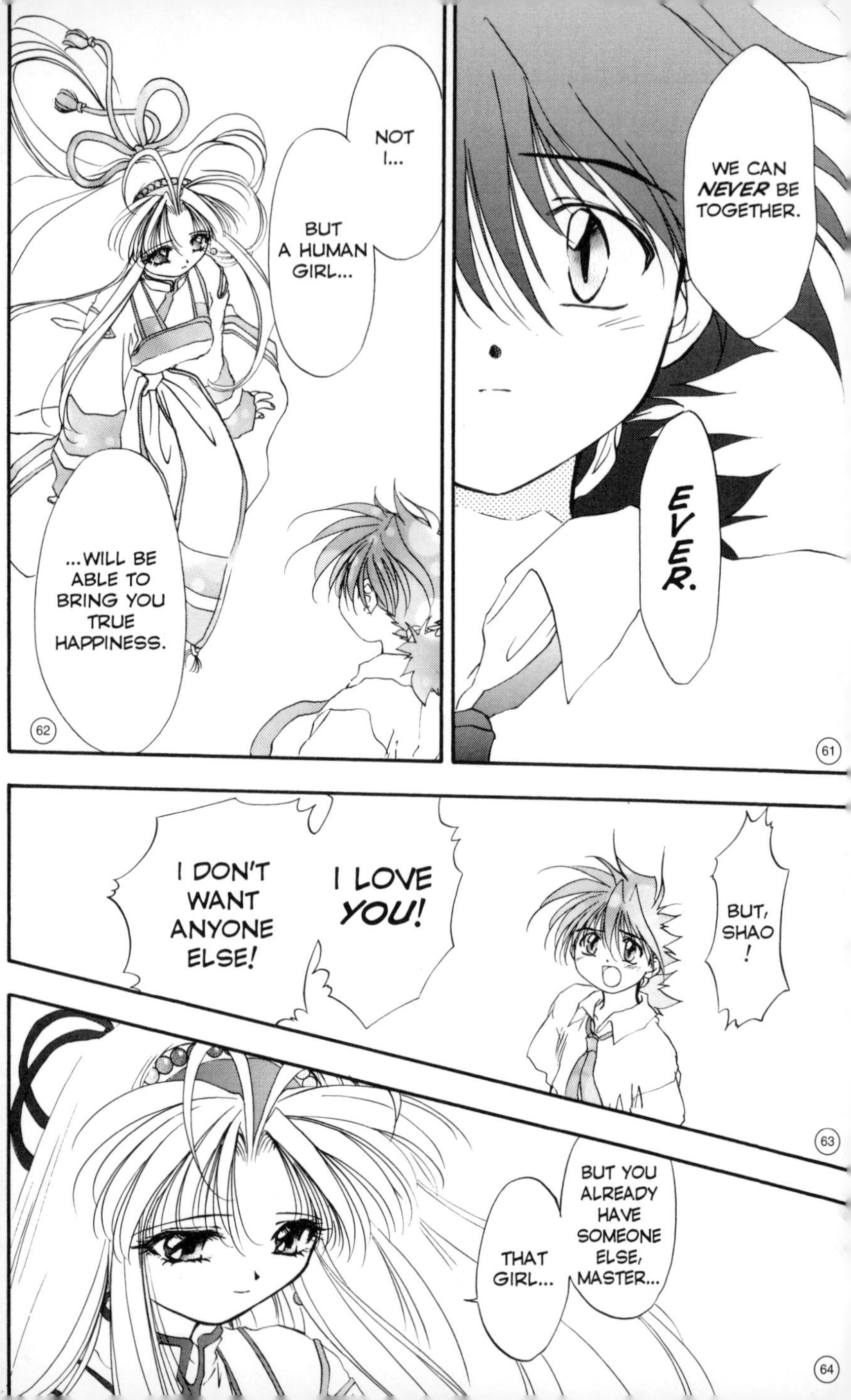
WE CAN NEVER BE TOGETHER.
EVER.
61
NOT I...
BUT A HUMAN GIRL...
...WILL BE ABLE TO BRING YOU TRUE HAPPINESS.
62
BUT, SHAO!
I LOVE YOU!
I DON'T WANT ANYONE ELSE!
63
BUT YOU ALREADY HAVE SOMEONE ELSE, MASTER...
THAT GIRL...
64

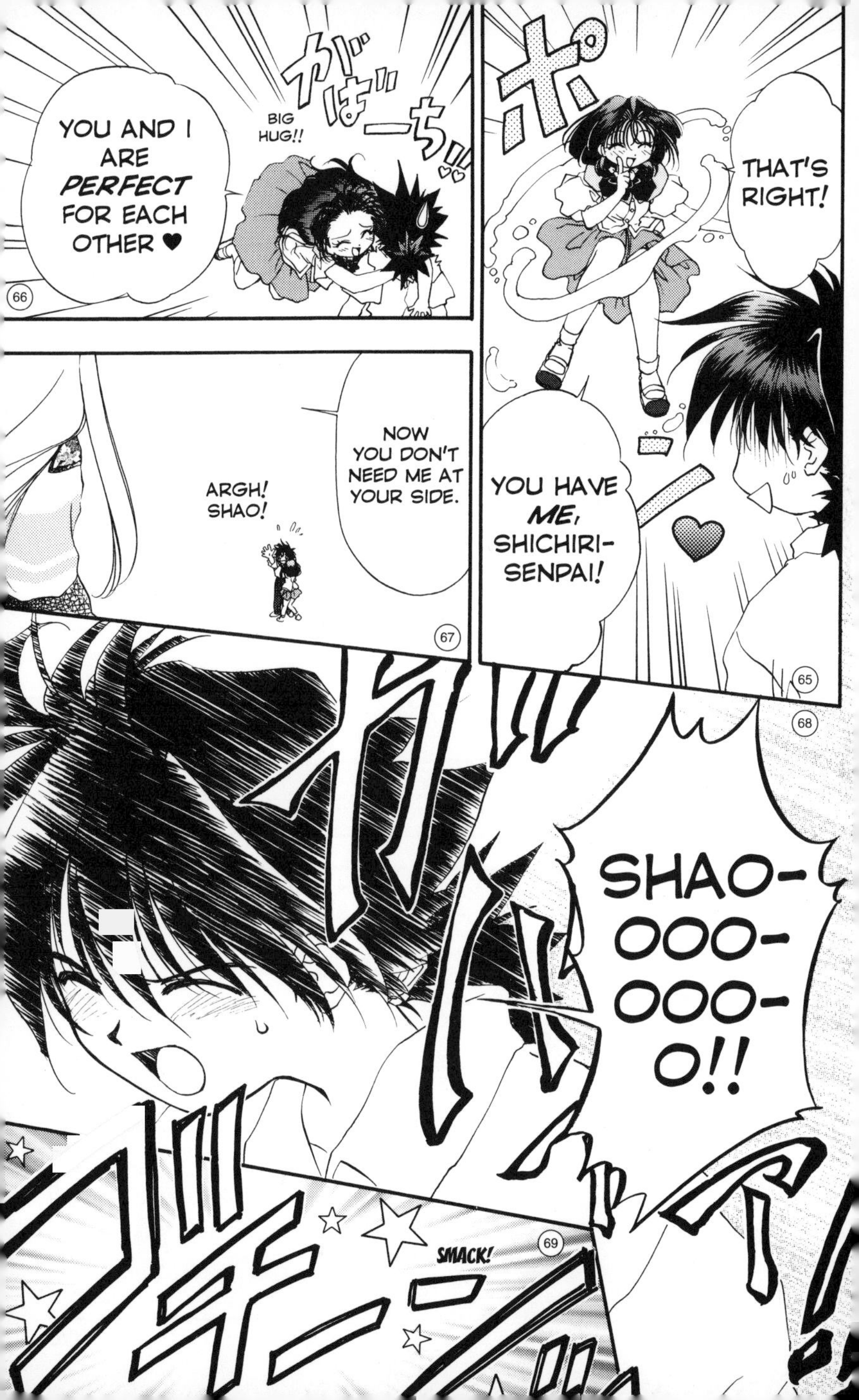

THAT'S RIGHT!
YOU HAVE ME, SHICHIRI-SENPAI!
YOU AND I ARE PERFECT FOR EACH OTHER ♥
BIG HUG!!
NOW YOU DON'T NEED ME AT YOUR SIDE.
ARGH! SHAO!
SHAO-OOO-OOO-O!!
SMACK!

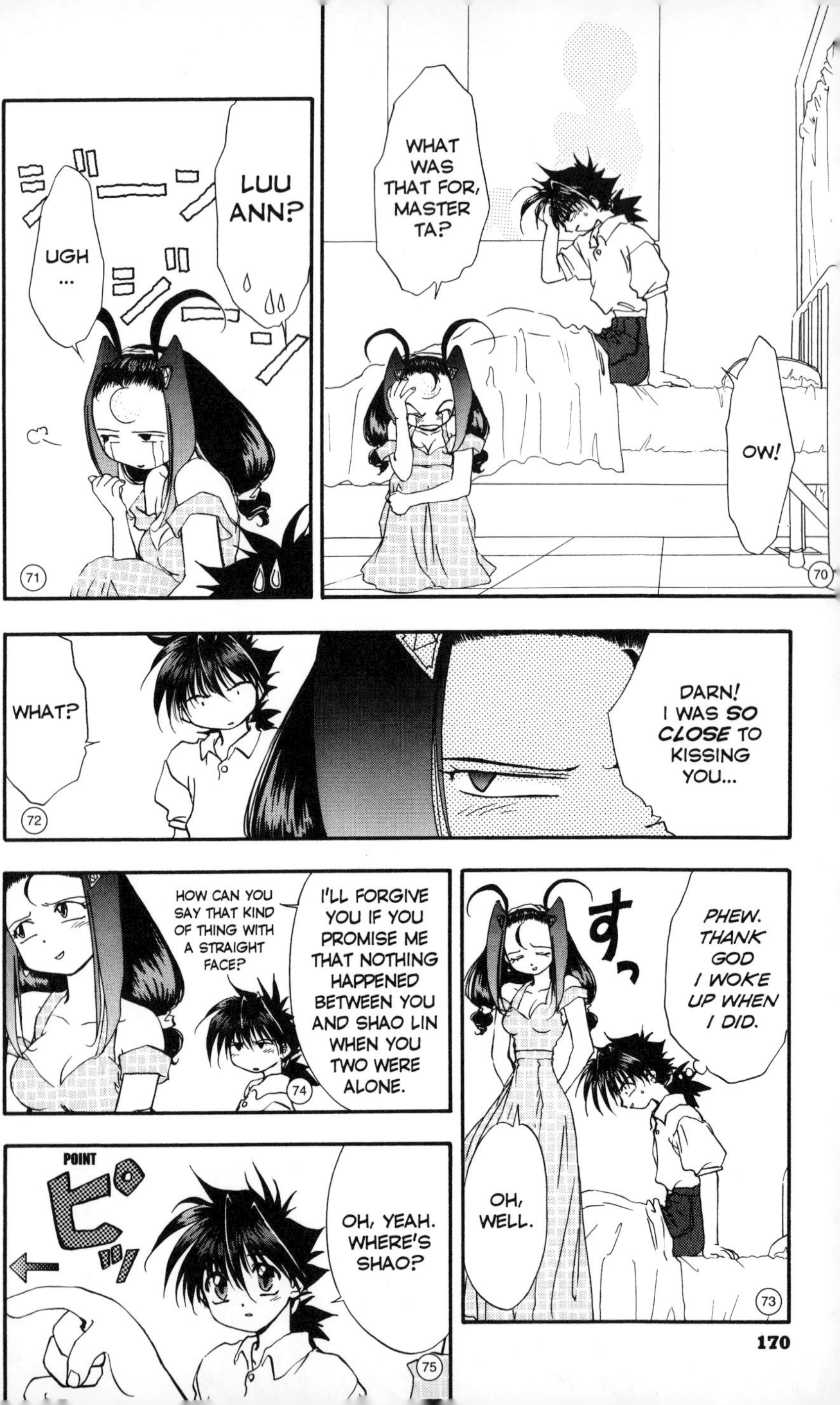
OW!
WHAT WAS THAT FOR, MASTER TA?
LUU ANN?
UGH ...
DARN! I WAS *SO CLOSE* TO KISSING YOU...
WHAT?
PHEW. THANK GOD I WOKE UP WHEN I DID.
すっ
OH, WELL.
I'LL FORGIVE YOU IF YOU PROMISE ME THAT NOTHING HAPPENED BETWEEN YOU AND SHAO LIN WHEN YOU TWO WERE ALONE.
HOW CAN YOU SAY THAT KIND OF THING WITH A STRAIGHT FACE?
OH, YEAH. WHERE'S SHAO?
POINT
ピッ

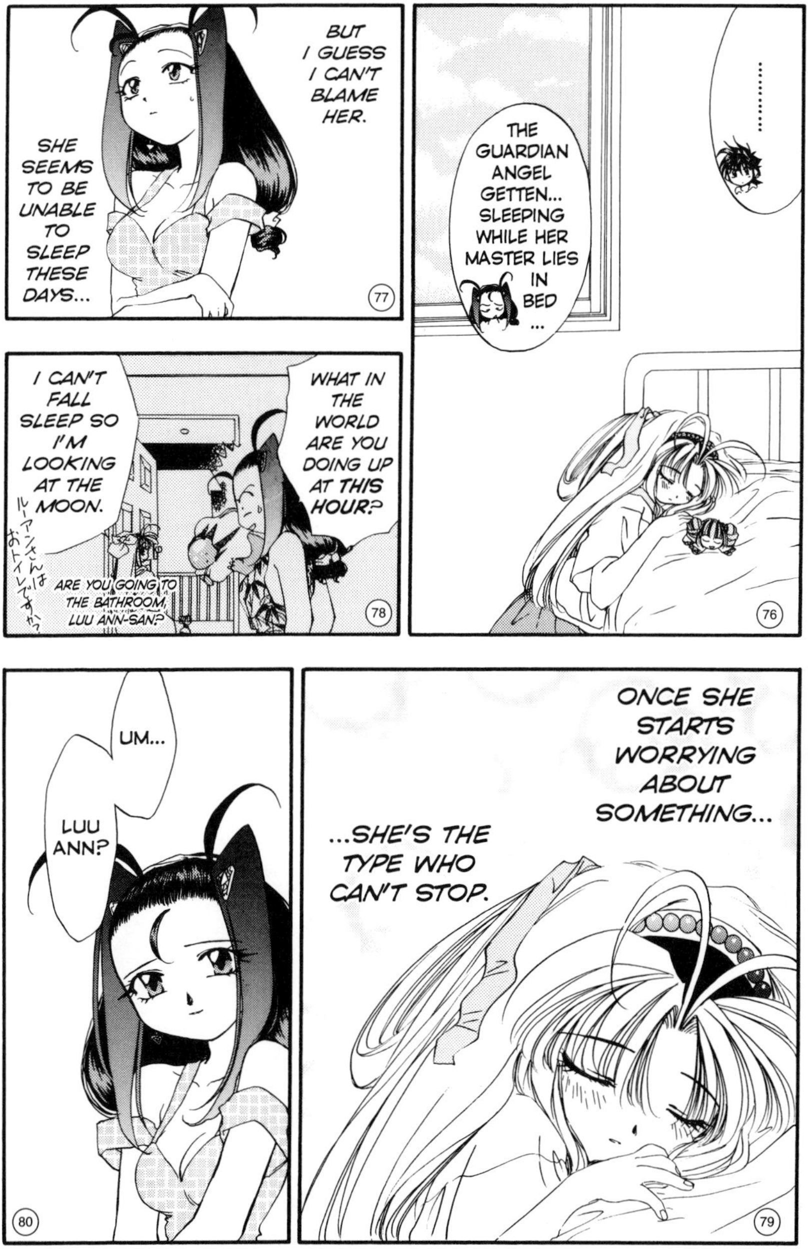
....
THE GUARDIAN ANGEL GETTEN... SLEEPING WHILE HER MASTER LIES IN BED ...
BUT I GUESS I CAN'T BLAME HER.
SHE SEEMS TO BE UNABLE TO SLEEP THESE DAYS...
WHAT IN THE WORLD ARE YOU DOING UP AT THIS HOUR?
I CAN'T FALL SLEEP SO I'M LOOKING AT THE MOON.
ルーアンさんはおトイレですか？
ARE YOU GOING TO THE BATHROOM, LUU ANN-SAN?
ONCE SHE STARTS WORRYING ABOUT SOMETHING...
...SHE'S THE TYPE WHO CAN'T STOP.
UM...
LUU ANN?

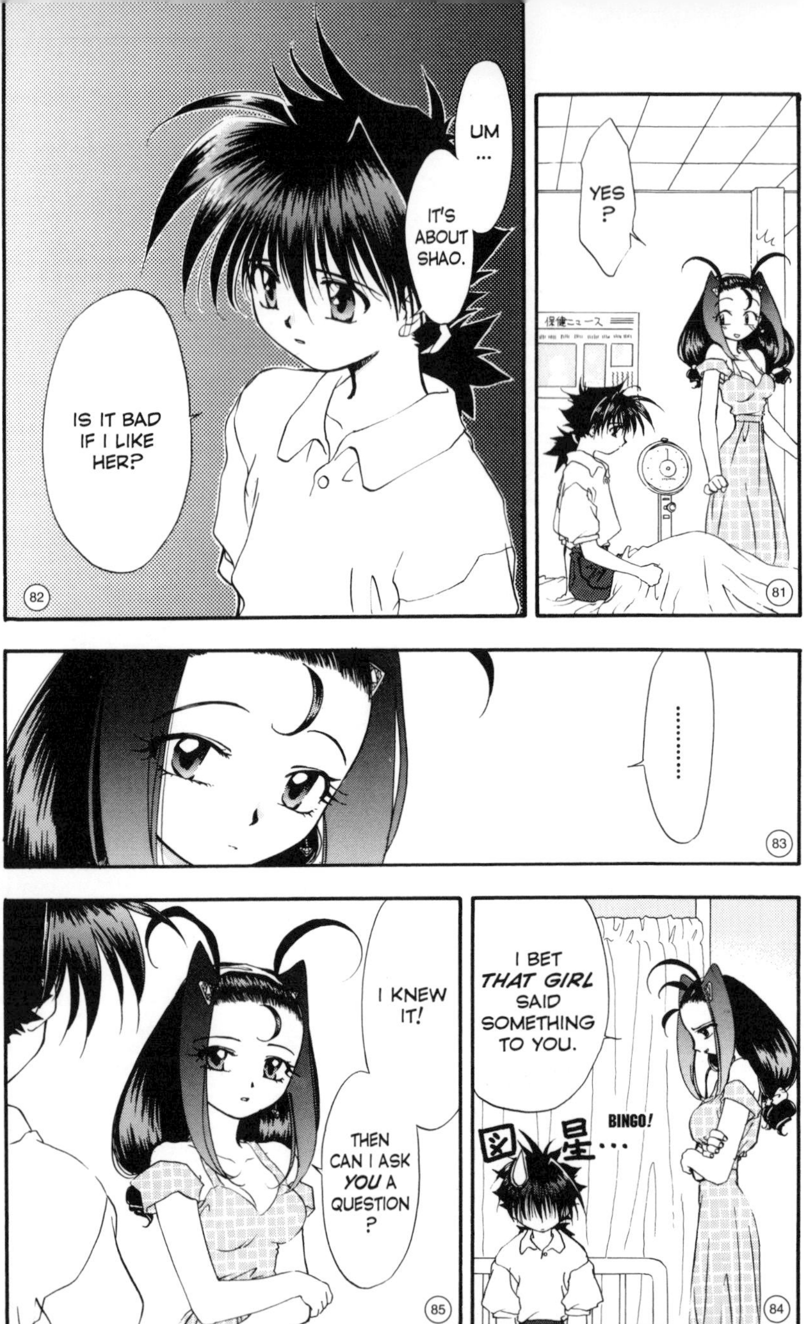
YES ?
保健ニュース
UM ...
IT'S ABOUT SHAO.
IS IT BAD IF I LIKE HER?
....
I BET *THAT GIRL* SAID SOMETHING TO YOU.
BINGO!
図星...
I KNEW IT!
THEN CAN I ASK *YOU* A QUESTION ?

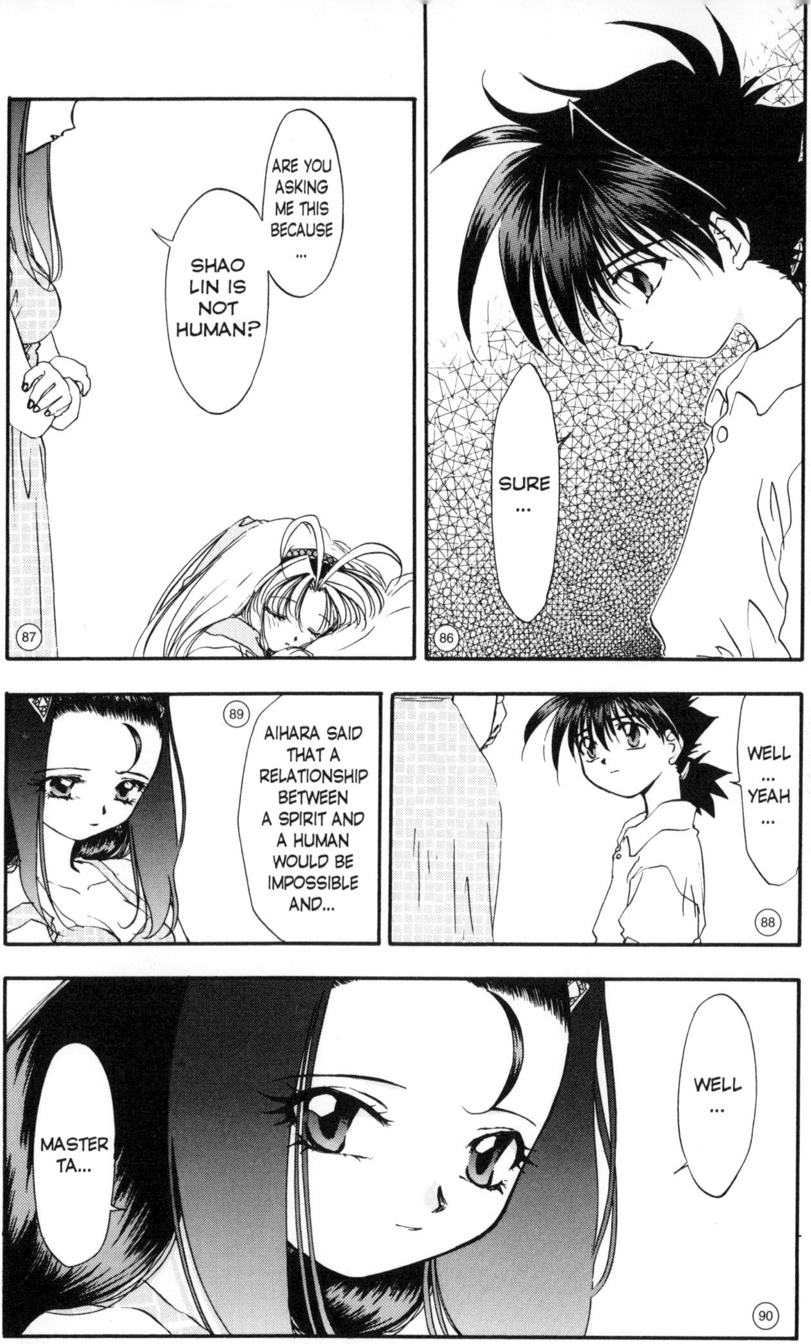
SURE ...
ARE YOU ASKING ME THIS BECAUSE ...
SHAO LIN IS NOT HUMAN?
WELL ... YEAH ...
AIHARA SAID THAT A RELATIONSHIP BETWEEN A SPIRIT AND A HUMAN WOULD BE IMPOSSIBLE AND...
WELL ...
MASTER TA...

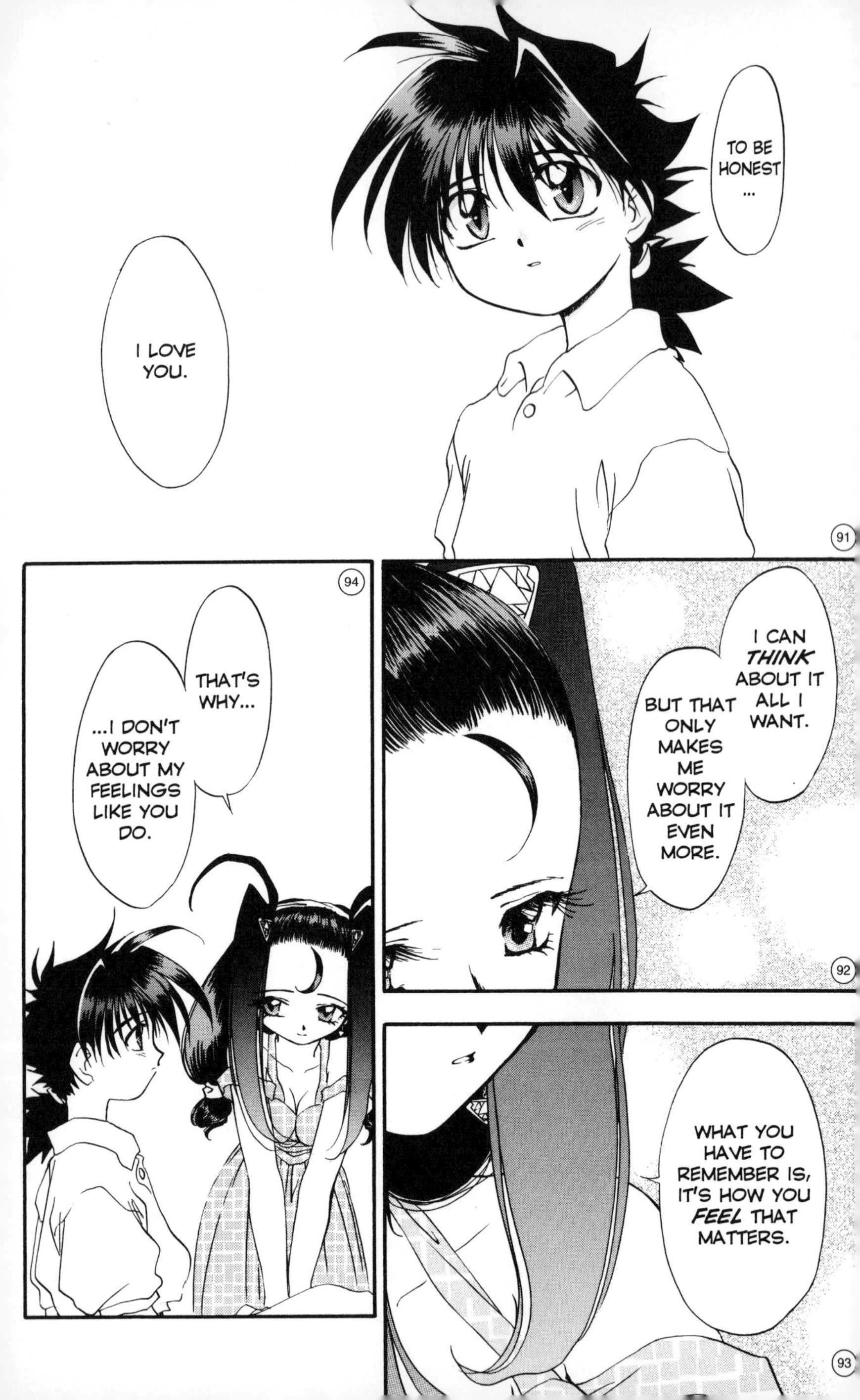
TO BE HONEST ...
I LOVE YOU.
91
I CAN *THINK* ABOUT IT ALL I WANT.
BUT THAT ONLY MAKES ME WORRY ABOUT IT EVEN MORE.
92
WHAT YOU HAVE TO REMEMBER IS, IT'S HOW YOU *FEEL* THAT MATTERS.
93
94
THAT'S WHY...
...I DON'T WORRY ABOUT MY FEELINGS LIKE YOU DO.

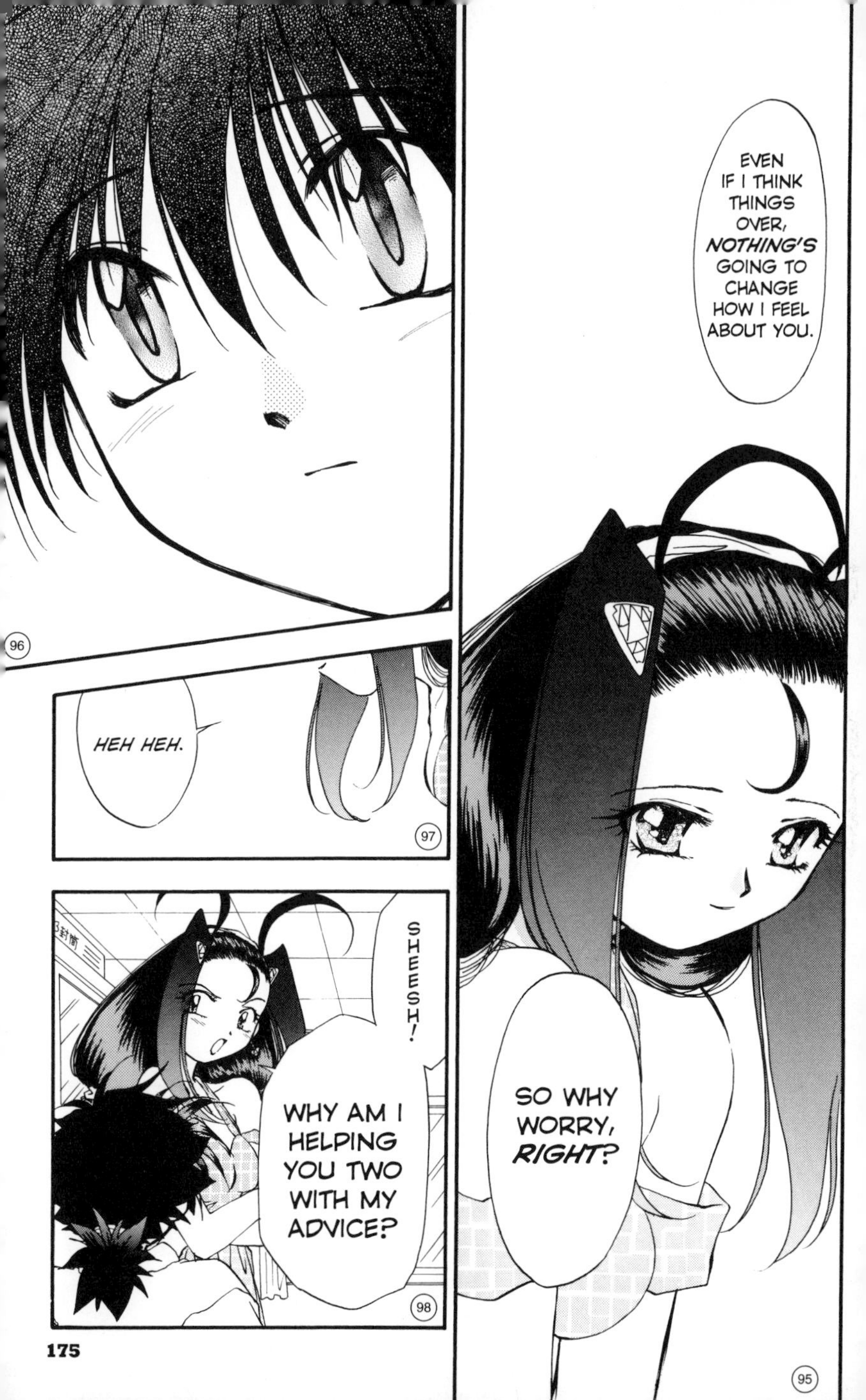
EVEN IF I THINK THINGS OVER, NOTHING'S GOING TO CHANGE HOW I FEEL ABOUT YOU.
SO WHY WORRY, RIGHT?
HEH HEH.
SHEESH!
WHY AM I HELPING YOU TWO WITH MY ADVICE?

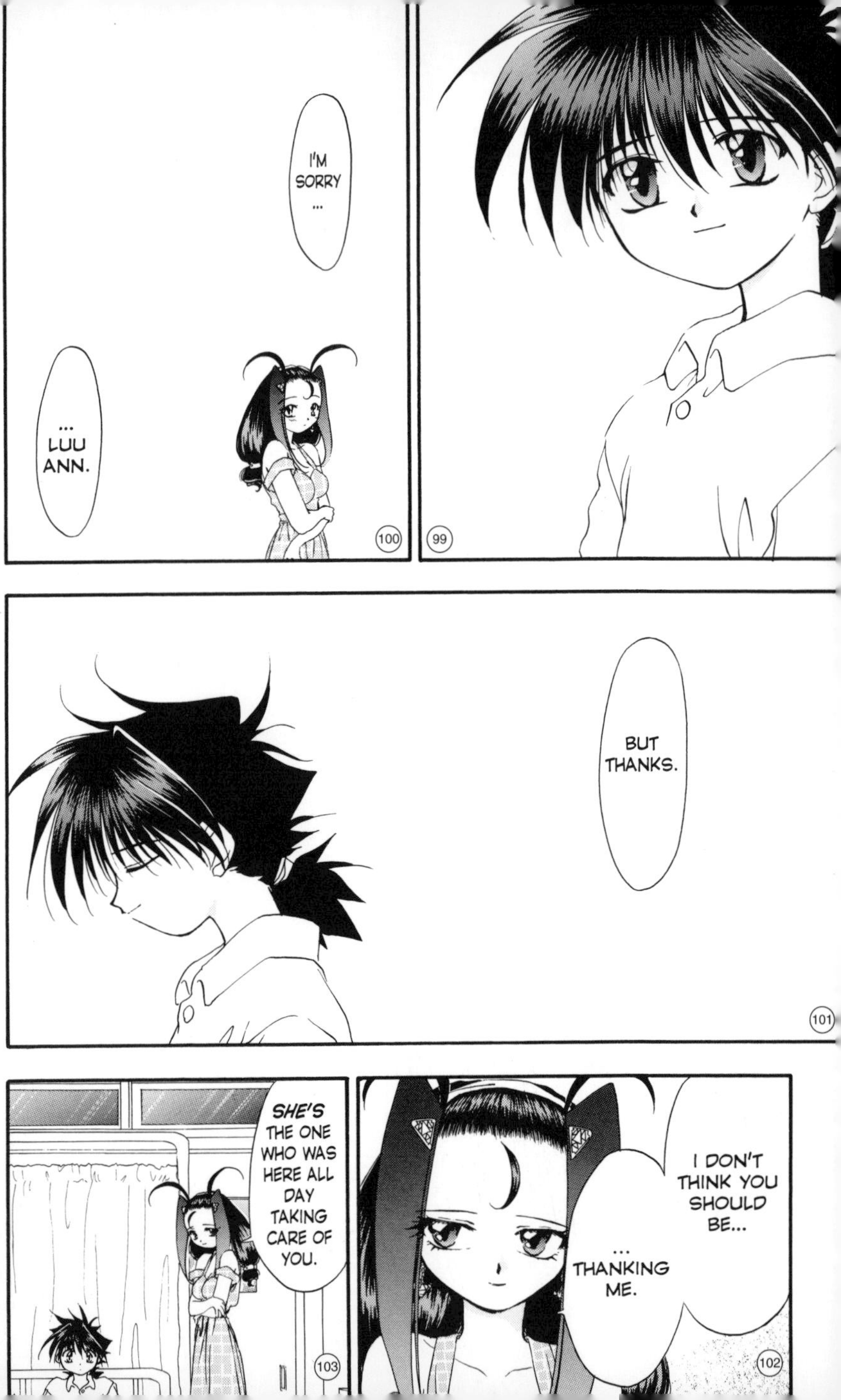
99
I'M SORRY ...
... LUU ANN.
100
BUT THANKS.
101
I DON'T THINK YOU SHOULD BE...
... THANKING ME.
102
SHE'S THE ONE WHO WAS HERE ALL DAY TAKING CARE OF YOU.
103

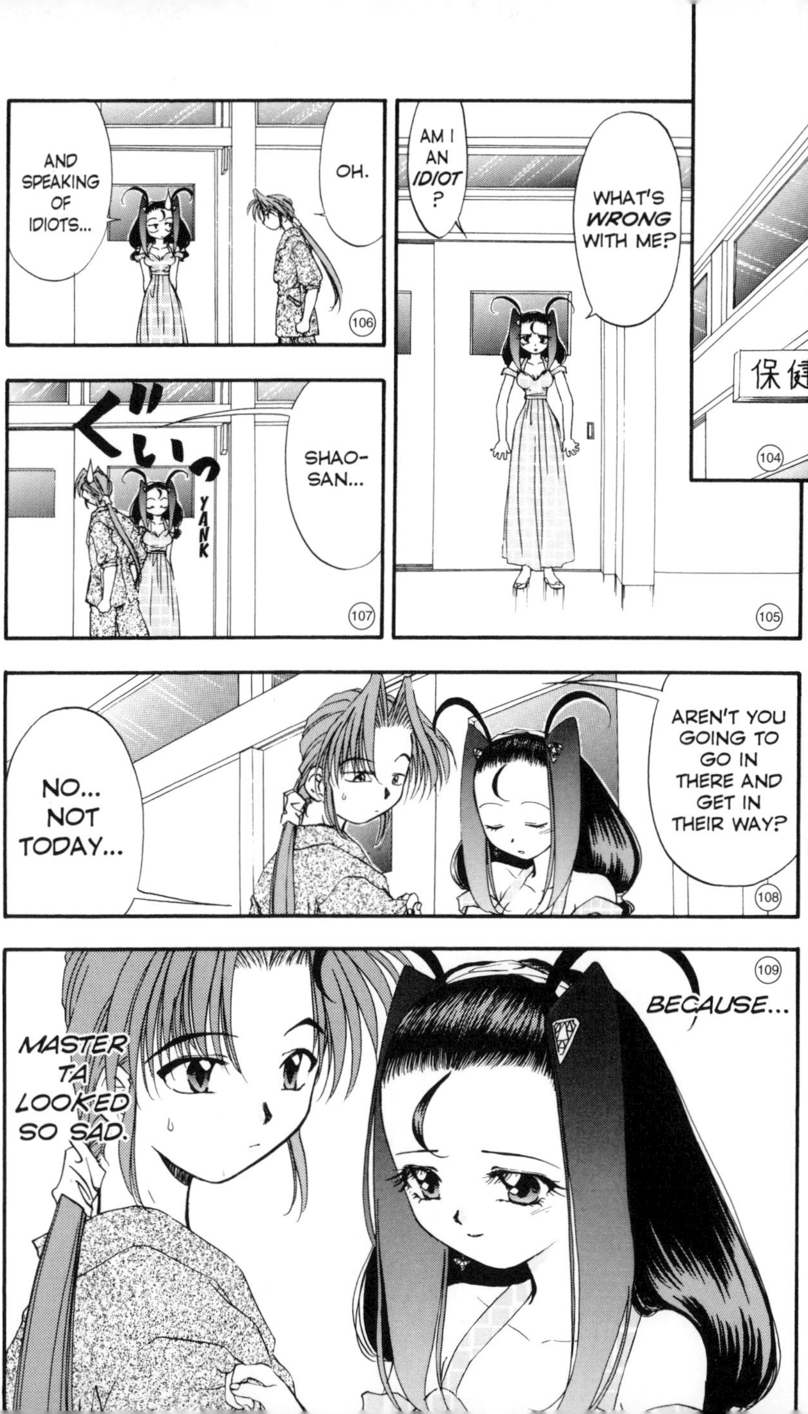
保健
WHAT'S WRONG WITH ME?
AM I AN IDIOT?
OH.
AND SPEAKING OF IDIOTS...
SHAO-SAN...
ぐいっ
YANK
AREN'T YOU GOING TO GO IN THERE AND GET IN THEIR WAY?
NO... NOT TODAY...
BECAUSE...
MASTER TA LOOKED SO SAD.

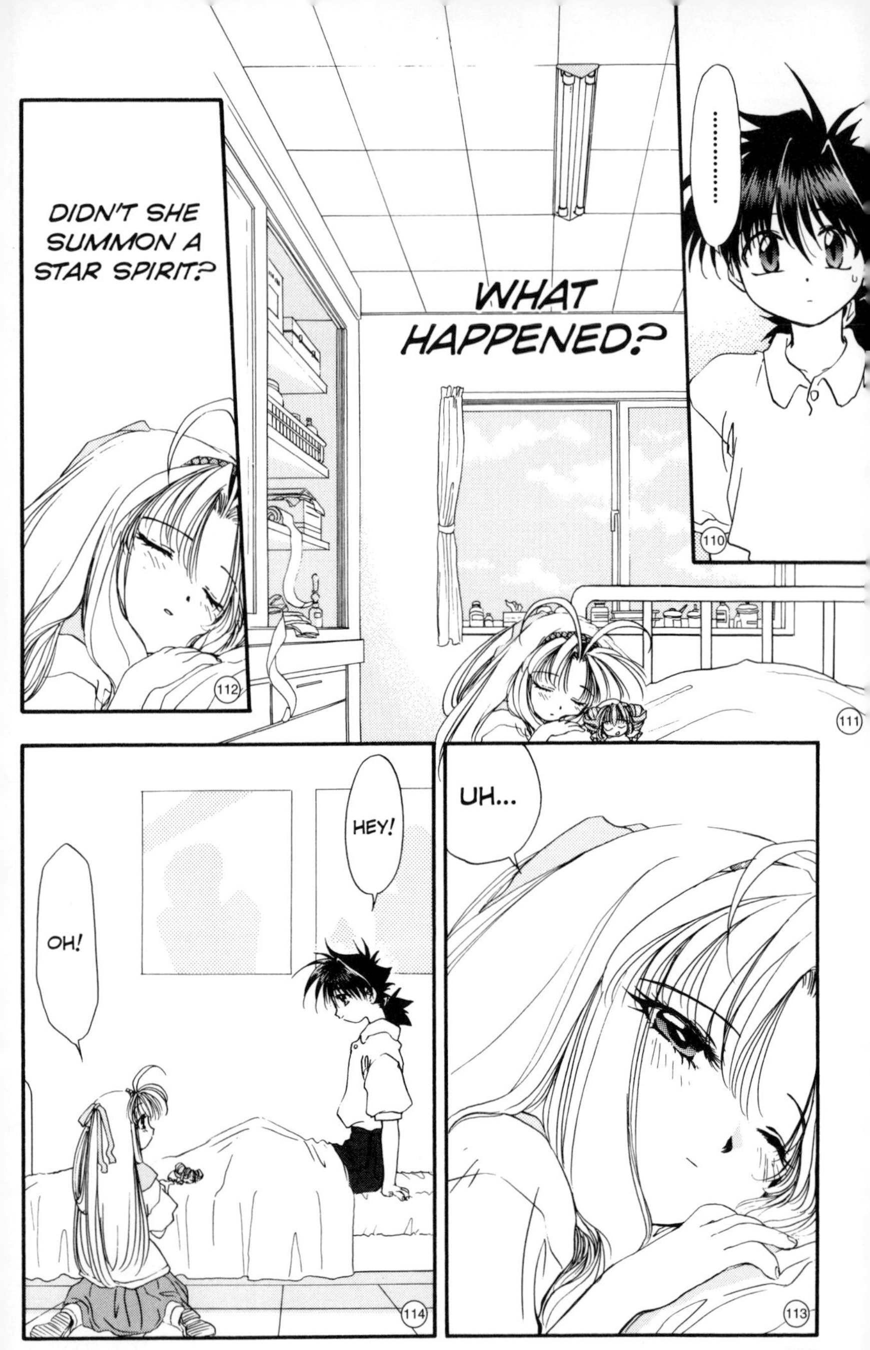
......
WHAT HAPPENED?
DIDN'T SHE SUMMON A STAR SPIRIT?
UH...
HEY!
OH!

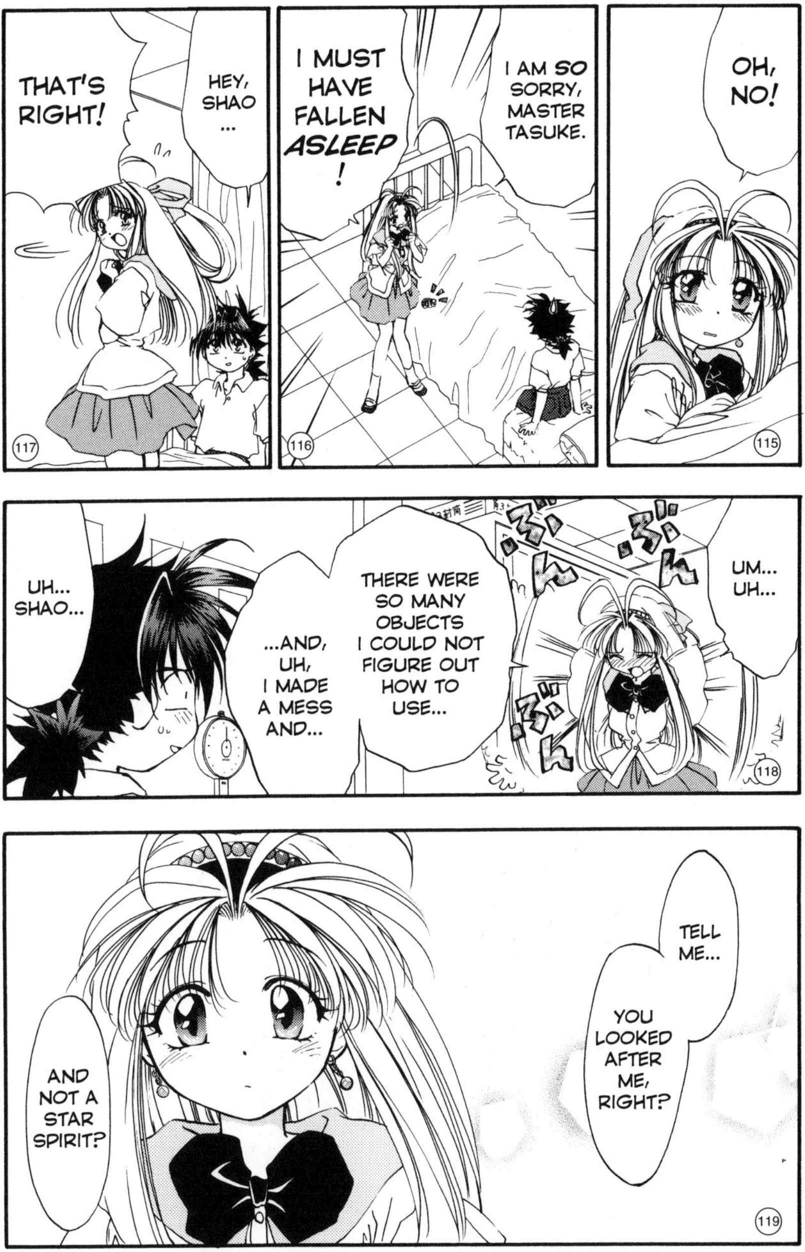
OH, NO!
115
I AM SO SORRY, MASTER TASUKE.
I MUST HAVE FALLEN ASLEEP!
116
HEY, SHAO...
THAT'S RIGHT!
117
UM... UH...
ぶん
ぶん
ぶん
THERE WERE SO MANY OBJECTS I COULD NOT FIGURE OUT HOW TO USE...
...AND, UH, I MADE A MESS AND...
UH... SHAO...
118
TELL ME...
YOU LOOKED AFTER ME, RIGHT?
AND NOT A STAR SPIRIT?
119

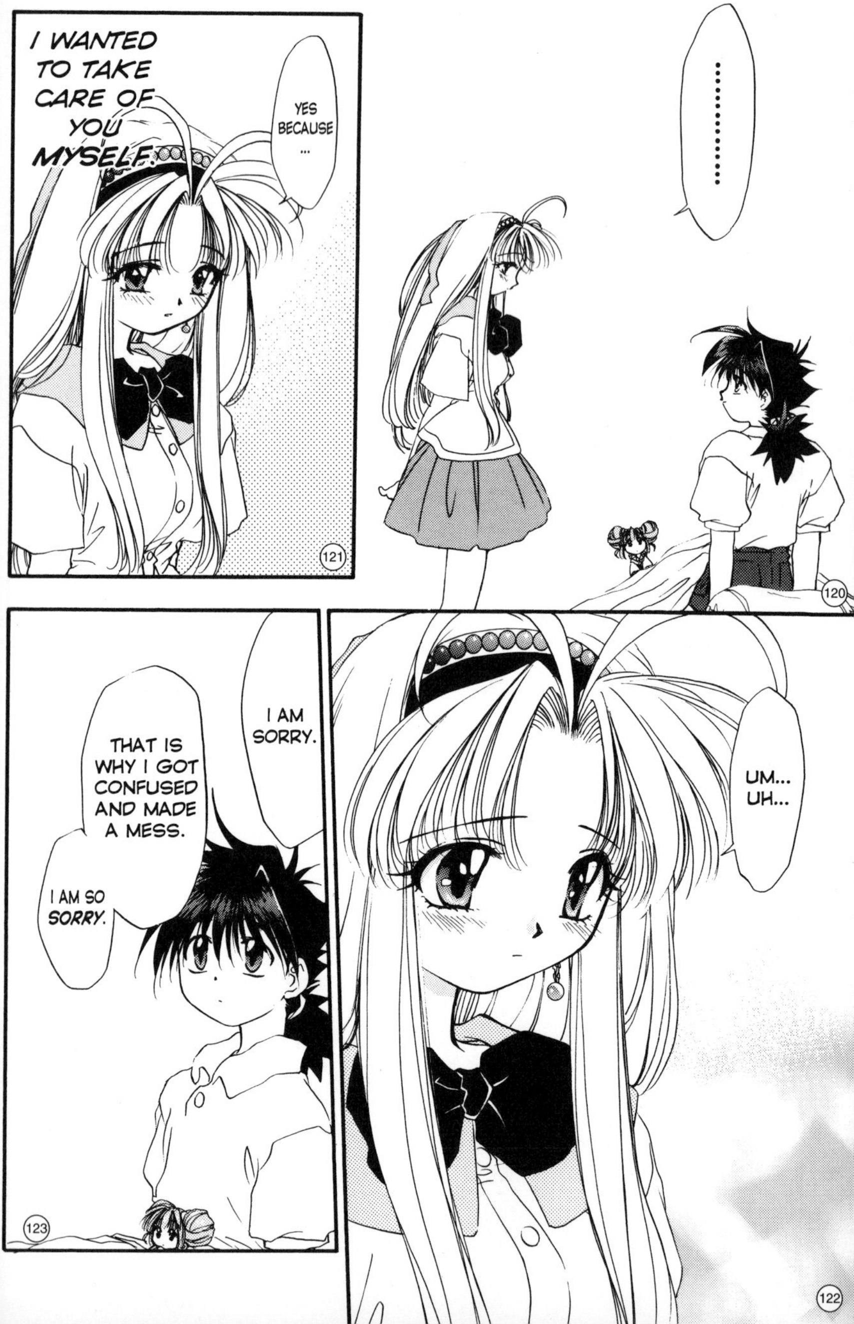

....
YES BECAUSE ...
I WANTED TO TAKE CARE OF YOU MYSELF.
UM... UH...
I AM SORRY.
THAT IS WHY I GOT CONFUSED AND MADE A MESS.
I AM SO SORRY.

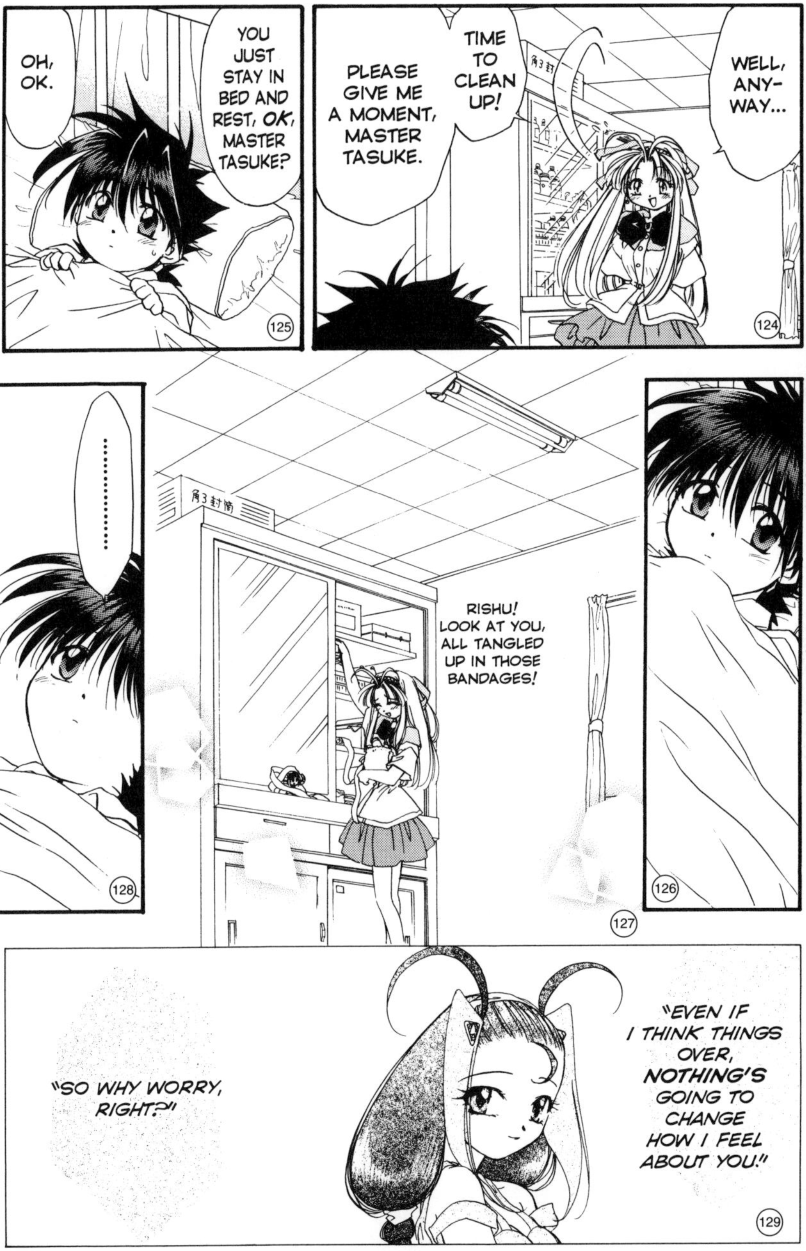
WELL, ANYWAY...
TIME TO CLEAN UP!
PLEASE GIVE ME A MOMENT, MASTER TASUKE.
YOU JUST STAY IN BED AND REST, OK, MASTER TASUKE?
OH, OK.
角3封筒
RISHU! LOOK AT YOU, ALL TANGLED UP IN THOSE BANDAGES!
....
"EVEN IF I THINK THINGS OVER, NOTHING'S GOING TO CHANGE HOW I FEEL ABOUT YOU!"
"SO WHY WORRY, RIGHT?"

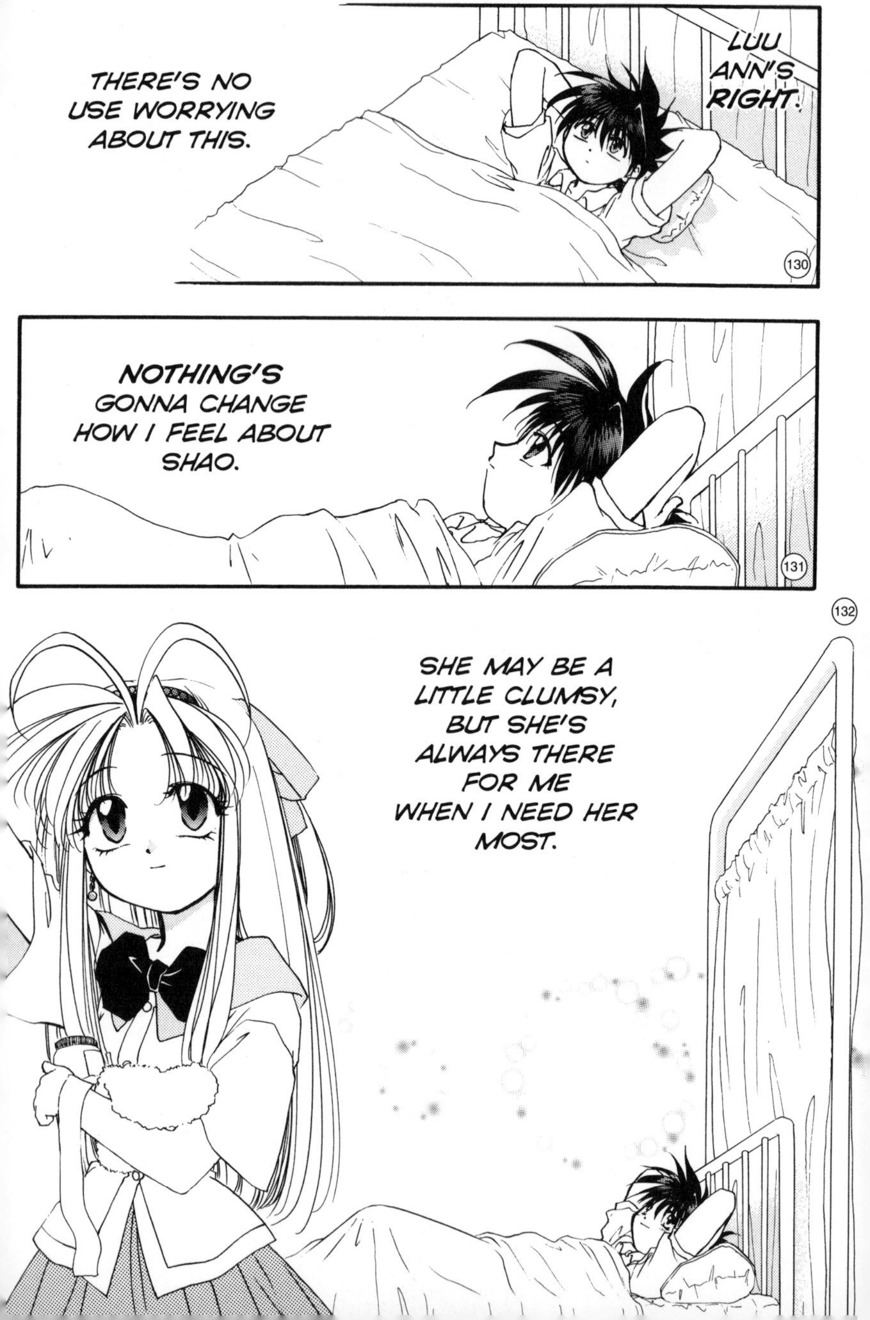
LUU ANN'S RIGHT.
THERE'S NO USE WORRYING ABOUT THIS.
130
NOTHING'S GONNA CHANGE HOW I FEEL ABOUT SHAO.
131
132
SHE MAY BE A LITTLE CLUMSY, BUT SHE'S ALWAYS THERE FOR ME WHEN I NEED HER MOST.

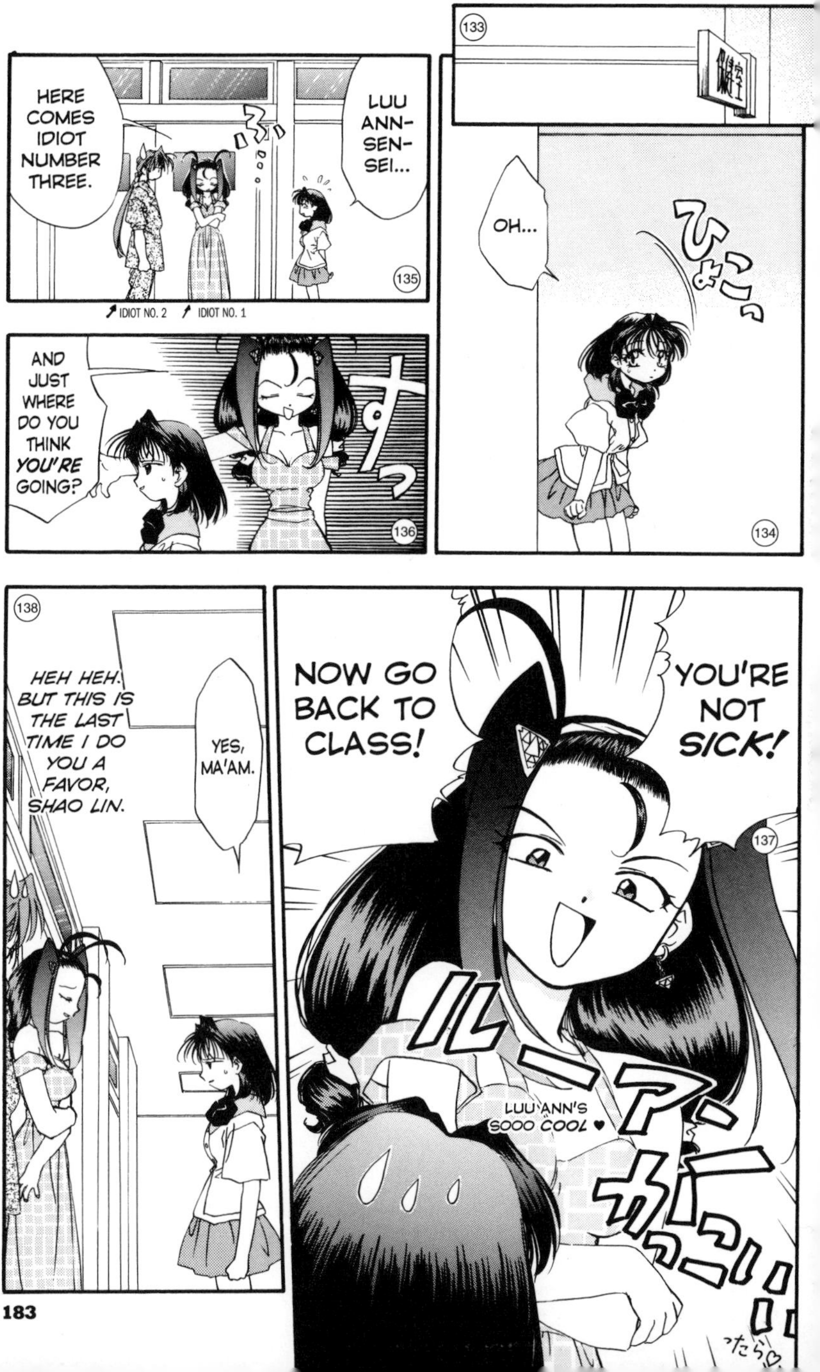
133
OH...
ひょこっ
134
LUU ANN-SEN-SEI...
HERE COMES IDIOT NUMBER THREE.
IDIOT NO. 2
IDIOT NO. 1
135
AND JUST WHERE DO YOU THINK *YOU'RE* GOING?
すっ
136
YOU'RE NOT *SICK!*
NOW GO BACK TO CLASS!
LUU ANN'S SOOO COOL ♥
137
138
YES, MA'AM.
HEH HEH. BUT THIS IS THE LAST TIME I DO YOU A FAVOR, SHAO LIN.

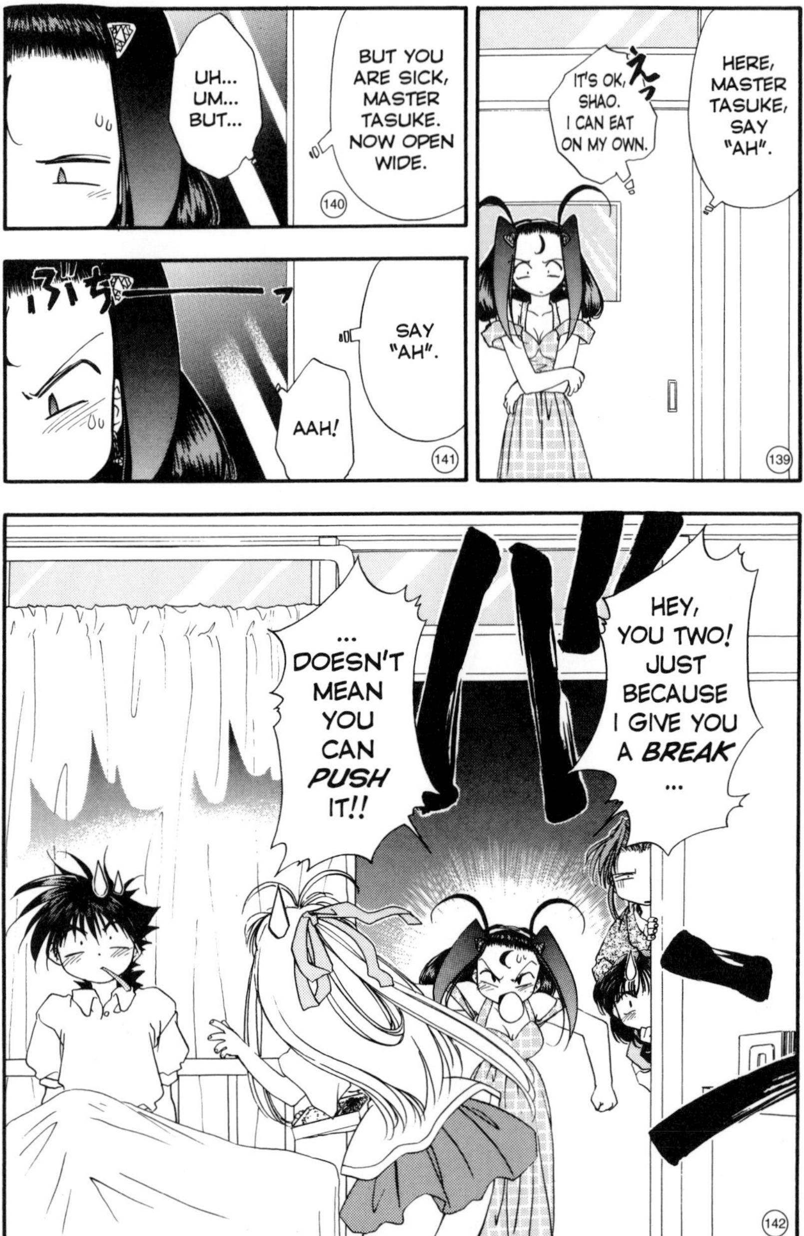
HERE, MASTER TASUKE, SAY "AH".
IT'S OK, SHAO. I CAN EAT ON MY OWN.
BUT YOU ARE SICK, MASTER TASUKE. NOW OPEN WIDE.
UH... UM... BUT...
SAY "AH".
AAH!
HEY, YOU TWO! JUST BECAUSE I GIVE YOU A *BREAK* ...
... DOESN'T MEAN YOU CAN *PUSH* IT!!

VOLUME 4 :END.

Guardian Angel
GETTEN
守護月天!
TM

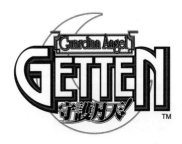

GUARDIAN ANGEL GETTEN, Vol.4

ART & STORY:
SAKURANO MINENE

Editorial Production: Coamix Inc.
Editor: Sam Kondo
Senior Editor: Jonathan Tarbox
Director of Sales: Yamamoto Hideki
Senior Manager,
GUTSOON!
ENTERTAINMENT: Michael Palmieri
General Manager: Kashimura Yukihiro
Editor-in-Chief: Negishi Tadashi
Publisher: Horie Nobuhiko

Art Direction: SPAZIO ARANCIA
Printing: Toppan Printing Co., (H.K.) Ltd.
Editorial Cooperation: C.P.U.GO
Sakurai Susumu

Published by GUTSOON! ENTERTAINMENT
P.O. Box 14148, Torrance, CA 90503

ISBN: 1-932454-28-4
First Printing, May 2004
10 9 8 7 6 5 4 3 2

Disclaimer: This publication may
contain graphic depictions of vio-
lence, sexual situations and/or language not suited to all readers. Par-
ental guidance is advised.